We Americans

. . . among democratic nations each new generation is a new people.

ALEXIS DE TOCQUEVILLE
Democracy in America

A TOPICAL HISTORY OF THE UNITED STATES

Consulting Editors

PAIGE ARTZT
Miami-Dade Junior College

G. PORTER EWING
Los Angeles City College

MYRON A. MARTY
Florissant Valley Community College

LEONARD PITT

California State University, Northridge

We Americans

VOLUME I   COLONIAL TIMES TO 1877

SCOTT, FORESMAN AND COMPANY   Glenview, Illinois

Dallas, Tex.   Oakland, N.J.   Palo Alto, Cal.   Tucker, Ga.   Brighton, England

Cover illustration: Tammany Society Celebrating the Fourth of July, 1812, by William P. Chappell, 1869. Courtesy, The New York Historical Society, New York City.

Dedicated to
the Tricentennial Generation.
May we Americans leave them
a cleaner environment,
a more just society, and
a world at peace.

Library of Congress Cataloging in Publication Data
Pitt, Leonard.
 We Americans.

 Includes bibliographies and indexes.
 CONTENTS: [1] From colonial times to 1877. — [2] From 1865 to the present.
 1. United States — History. I. Title.
E178.1.P55 1976b   973   75 – 35845
ISBN 0 – 673 – 15001 – 1 (v. 1)

2 3 4 5 6 – RRC – 80 79 78 77

Acknowledgments and Credits for maps, charts, and illustrations appear on pages 359 – 360.

Foreword

As the United States begins the third century of its national existence, Americans of all ages are looking back to the past in an effort to evaluate just where we as a people are today. Perhaps from this study of the past will come a firmer sense of purpose for the future. No one can deny that the rate and scope of change in all spheres of life have been remarkable. For example, the early English colony at Jamestown in Virginia was almost wiped out during an acute period of want, the so-called starving times. Yet today America is a land of vast wealth, and it recently became the first nation in history to reach an annual Gross National Product of $1 trillion.

The growth in the number of our inhabitants is also a striking development—from the 3.9 million Americans recorded in the census of 1790 to the 214 million citizens estimated in 1975. And the change in our pattern of living has been equally great. In 1790, for example, the vast majority of Americans were descendants of white immigrants from the British Isles. Their language, laws, and customs were derived from England, and they were overwhelmingly Protestant in religion. Today Americans are of different races, creeds, and cultural backgrounds. This book traces the contributions of all the groups who have met and interacted throughout our history: the descendants of the original colonists; the offspring of later immigrants from Europe; and our four large racial minorities—Indians, blacks, Chicanos, and Asian Americans.

We Americans offers a thematic, or topical, approach within a strong chronological organization. This format provides a clear, interesting, and fresh approach. It allows for a wide selection of topics including the role of women in American life in society at large as well as in the family, the search for an ideal community, the rise and growth of towns and cities, the shift from a rural to urban life style, and the ways whereby America's development has affected our natural environment. This is a sound and solid appreciation of the American past—one having an appeal both to instructors and students of the basic survey course.

Vincent P. De Santis
University of Notre Dame

Preface

On the eve of the American Revolution Patrick Henry told the Virginia Convention: "I know of no way of judging the future but by the past." An English contemporary, Sir Edmund Burke, wrote a few years later: "You can never plan the future by the past." These statements present a paradox to anyone who studies history. This paradox is especially confusing to young people, who sense that their nation's history is vitally important to an understanding of the times in which they live. But when events accelerate, as they now seem to be doing, history's pattern is blurred.

I hope that this book, by its thematic approach, will help link the past and present and eliminate some of the confusion. With the aid of my students I have identified eight important themes that have special contemporary meaning and can be traced back into the American past. These themes run like threads through the fabric of the book. They are Wealth, Power, War, Race, Nationality and Religion, Women and the Family, Community, and Environment.

In addition to its thematic, or topical, approach, the book offers a strong chronological framework. It is divided into five chronologically arranged parts that correspond to distinct periods of American history. Each of the five parts is introduced by two features: (1) a brief listing of important dates for the period; and (2) an overview that clearly ties together the events and developments relative to the eight topical chapters that follow. I believe that this organization will help clarify the pattern of history in the minds of students.

It is my expectation that both the students and instructors in the basic survey course will find the organization of *We Americans* more appealing than the more conventional organization of other texts. The emphasis on themes of enduring importance as well as on the role that all Americans have played in our national life is meant to personalize the story of the past and make it more interesting.

Instructors have many options in using *We Americans*, depending on the type of course they offer. Some will follow a strictly chronological approach, dealing with all chapters in Part I (Beginnings to 1789) before moving along to those in Part II (1789–1865). Others may want to assign all chapters on a given topic (Wealth, for example) before progressing to the next topic (perhaps, Power). Still other instructors can find their own variations by combining these two approaches. In any event, it will be found that the organization lends itself to greater flexibility.

To meet the needs of schools offering different types of courses, *We Americans* is offered in a single-volume clothbound version that covers American history from its beginnings to the present and in two paperbound volumes. Volume I covers from colonial times to 1877, and Volume II from 1865 to the present. An Instructor's Resource Book has been prepared by G. Porter Ewing, and a Study Guide by Robert Ellis and Tommie Jan Lowery. I am most appreciative of their work, which should enhance the use of the basic text.

It is impossible to write a book of this size and scope without incurring many debts. My gratitude and apologies, first of all, to the many unnamed scholars whose works I have consulted; limitations of space have prevented my citing more than a few of them by name. In particular, I am indebted to the editorial consultants for the work—Paige Artzt, G. Porter Ewing, and Myron A. Marty—whose thoughtful comments, suggestions, and advice helped and encouraged me through various stages of the manuscript. Vincent P. De Santis' detailed criticisms for Parts I, II, and III were most helpful. Then, too, I have benefitted from the advice and criticism of friends and colleagues. Those who have read sections of the work, made valuable suggestions, and saved me from careless errors include Ronald Schaffer, Rena Vasser, Ronald Davis, Gay Hayden, Paul Koistinen, Joseph Ernest, and Roy Merrens. Walter Smith and Kathryn Dabelow were also helpful. I am grateful as well to David Lash, an extremely resourceful research assistant. None of them is responsible for any of the faults that may remain in the book.

The Scott, Foresman editorial, design, and production staffs extended themselves greatly on the project. Most notably I want to thank Robert J. Cunningham for his patience and encouragement. The creative thinking and insight of David R. Ebbitt and Robert Anderson were equally valuable. I am grateful for the cooperation of Marilyn Reaves, Susan Houston, Mary Ann Lea, Barbara Frankel, Michael Werthman, Douglas C. Mitchell, Marnie Lynde, Robert Johnson, Robert Gruen, and Walter Dinteman.

I have also been helped by Norman Pitt, Sharon Smith, David Halfen, William A. Sommerfield, William Doyle, and the late George Vlach.

Members of the secretarial staff of my department at California State University, Northridge, who helped prepare or type the manuscript exhibited great forebearance. They are Mary Alvarez, Margaret Ball, Nancy Meadows, and Selma Rosenfeld.

Finally, I owe thanks also to my immediate family. My children, Marni, Adam, and Michael, put up with many inconveniences while their father was in the throes of "The Book." To my wife, Dale, who patiently researched, edited, typed, listened, and advised at every stage of this long project, I owe my very special love and gratitude.

Leonard Pitt
Los Angeles

Contents

Prints Div., The New York Public Library

OVERVIEW ■ **PART I: TO 1789**

Beginnings 2

Indian Civilizations Before Columbus 2
Explorers of North America 3
England in the New World 6
America as a Colony 8
The American Revolution 10
The Articles of Confederation and the Constitution
  14
The World in 1789 15

CHAPTER 1 ■ WEALTH

Off to a Good Start 18

Mercantilism 19
Mercantilism defined • Technology • Capitalism in the colonies • The poor

Workers: Free and Not So Free, Skilled and Not So Skilled 26
The economics of immigration • Skilled craftsmen

Farmers: Nine Tenths of the People 30
Acquiring land • Working the farms • Pioneer farming and commercial agriculture

Review / Questions 35

CHAPTER 2 ■ POWER

To Form a More Perfect Union 38

Ripening Discontent Under English Rule 39
Class structure in the colonies • Government in the thirteen colonies • Pre-Revolutionary uprisings

Revolution in the Making 44
The growing crisis • Philosophy and grievances • The Declaration of Independence • State governments under the Articles of Confederation

Pressure for a New Constitution 51
Problems for the young nation • Writing the Constitution • Power balanced among the three branches • Ratification and the Bill of Rights

An Aversion to Party Politics 55
Was colonial America democratic? • Forerunners of political parties

Review / Questions 57

CHAPTER 3 ■ WAR

The Shot Heard 'Round the World 60

Europe's New-World Frontier 61
Nation-states exploring trade routes • Dividing the colonial pie

Four General Wars 64
The wars of three monarchs • The French and Indian War

The American Revolution 71
The course of the war • The first "people's war" • Washington, the crucial leader • The Peace of Paris and its aftermath • War-making powers in the Constitution

Review / Questions 76

CHAPTER 4 ■ RACE

Red, White, and Black 80

The Indians: "Savagery" Versus "Civilization" 81
Indian cultures in the seventeenth century • Friendly contacts between Indians and early settlers • The shift to vicious fighting • The noble or barbarous savage? • Changes in Indian cultures • Indian ways that whites adopted • The gap between theory and practice

Blacks: Origins of Slavery 89
Racial slavery • Laws enforcing slavery • The slave trade • Varying conditions for slaves • The black role during the Revolution • A wave of abolitionism • The source of black culture in America

Review / Questions 97

CHAPTER 5 ■ NATIONALITY AND RELIGION

The New People 100

Immigrants and Native-Born: The "New Race" 101
Anglo dominance and the non-English settlers • Flaws in the melting pot

Protestants, Catholics, and Jews in a Protestant Nation 106
Calvinism and the Reformed tradition • The Great Awakening • Intolerance toward Catholics • Jews in the New World • The groundwork for religious freedom • Deism and the civil religion

Review / Questions 116

CHAPTER 6 ■ WOMEN AND THE FAMILY

All Men Are Created Equal 120

The Family, Nursery of All Society 121
The English family transported to America • Puritanism and the family • Getting married • Family structure and sexual morality • Birth and death rates • Growing up in the colonies • Black families

Women's Rights: An Era of Few Privileges 129
Early patterns • Work and refinements in the eighteenth century

Review / Questions 134

CHAPTER 7 ■ COMMUNITY

Citty upon a Hill 138

New Plantations and Holy Experiments 139
Opening up the new continent • The New England town • The open-country neighborhood • Plantations in the South

The City, Center of Colonial Society 146
The urban scene • The five major colonial cities • Urban government and culture • Smaller cities • The effect of the Revolution on cities • Community and the new nation

Review / Questions 153

CHAPTER 8 ■ ENVIRONMENT

The Howling Wilderness 156

Before the Europeans 157

A Virgin Land to Conquer 159
Christianity and nature • Cutting and clearing the forests • Wholesale destruction of game and fish • Some early controls

The Myth of Superabundance 163

Review / Questions 165

Selected Readings 166

Courtesy of the NY Historical Society

OVERVIEW ■ PART II: 1789–1865

A New Nation 170

Setting a New Government in Motion 170
Undeclared War with France 171
Political Factions and Jefferson's Election 172
The War of 1812 and Shifts in the Political Balance 173
The Westward Movement 174
The Jacksonian Era 175
Transportation and Urban Growth 176
American Expansionism 176
America Creates a Literature 177
Slavery: The Great Debate 179
Compromise and Crisis 180
Civil War 181

CHAPTER 9 ■ WEALTH

A Go-Getter Nation 184

The Economy of a New Nation 185
Questions of economic policy • Hamilton's system • A surge in economic growth • Boom and bust cycles

The Industrial Revolution 190
Steam power and labor-saving inventions • Education for an industrial society • Interdependent regions • The gospel of success • Industrialism and poverty • Life in the mills • The first unions

Farmers: Jefferson's Chosen People 199
The mixed blessings of farming • Distributing public land

Review / Questions 202

CHAPTER 10 ■ POWER

A Sovereign Nation 206

Power Blocs Before the Civil War 207
Aristocracy versus democracy • Strengthening the presidency and the Supreme Court • Regionalism: the Northeast • The West • The South • Rivalry over the economy and abolition • Compromises • Free or slave labor in the West? • The South secedes

Party Politics and the Rise of Democracy 218
The need for political parties • Federalists versus Republicans: the loyal opposition • President Jefferson, the loyal opponent • Decline of the Federalist and Republican parties • Democrats versus Whigs: the common man in politics • The machinery of party politics • Origins of the GOP

Review / Questions 226

CHAPTER 11 ■ WAR

In a "Century of Peace" 230

Trouble with England and France 231
Undeclared naval war with France • Causes of the War of 1812 • The U.S. war campaign • Wartime disunity and postwar nationalism

Stretching the U.S. Boundaries 234
The urge for more land • The Louisiana Purchase • Acquiring Florida • The Monroe Doctrine • Manifest Destiny • Polk adds Oregon and Texas

War with Mexico 238
Polk's aggression • Antiwar dissent • To the halls of Montezuma • Ending the war

The Civil War 242
A country divided • Organizing the war effort • Lincoln broadens the president's power • Generals and battles • The ruins of war • Lincoln's reconstruction plan

Review / Questions 251

CHAPTER 12 ■ RACE

America's Color Scheme 254

Indians Along the "Trail of Tears" 255
White greed for Indian land • Tecumseh's attempt to unite the Indians • The policy of Indian removal • The Creeks and the Cherokees • Pushing out the western tribes

Slaves in an Age of Democracy 262
Repercussions of a slave rebellion • Free blacks in the early years of the country • A black colony in Africa • Nineteenth-century slavery • Black resistance to slavery • Proslavery in the South, antiblack in the North • Activities of the abolitionists

Absorbing the Mexicans 270
The Spanish-Mexican stamp on the Southwest • Racial aftermath of the Mexican War • The rush for gold in California • The bandidos • Mexican heritage

Asian Americans: Trouble on Golden Mountain 273
Early American impressions of the Chinese • Hard times for Asian immigrants

Review / Questions 275

CHAPTER 13 ■ NATIONALITY AND RELIGION

For God and Country 278

The Frontier Melting Pot 279
The European emigration • Passage to the New World • The difficulties of making a new life • Nativism, a reaction against newcomers

The Kingdom of God in the New Republic   *284*
The Second Awakening • Spreading God's Word • The new sects • Growing numbers of Catholics • German Jews bring the Reform Movement • Religious attitudes and the Civil War

Review / Questions   *291*

CHAPTER 14 ■ WOMEN AND THE FAMILY

All Men <u>and</u> Women Are Created Equal   294

The Family Scene   *295*
Farm families and pioneers • Working-class families • Southern plantation families • Raising children • The nuclear family

The First Wave of Feminism   *299*
The cult of true womanhood • Legal and social handicaps • Mary Wollstonecraft, the founding mother • Pioneers in education for women • Abolitionism, training for feminism • Other training grounds • Three radical women • Changing the image and the reality

Review / Questions   *305*

CHAPTER 15 ■ COMMUNITY

Glimpses of a Better World   308

Utopias   *309*
Shaping the perfect community • The Shakers • Oneida Colony led by Noyes • Other religious communes • Owen's New Harmony, a secular commune • Fourier and Brook Farm

The City: What Price "Progress"?   *314*
New York City in the lead • Washington as a planned capital • A quieter pace in southern cities • The urban frontier • The perils of city living • Competition in the arts • Conflicting opinions on cities

Review / Questions   *321*

CHAPTER 16 ■ ENVIRONMENT

The Fairest Portion of the Earth   324

The Wilderness as Public Resource   *325*
Abundance belies Malthus' theory • The impact of the lumber industry • Fur companies and mountain men • Whale hunting and an early fuel crisis • Moving into the prairies and deserts • The landscape altered by the Industrial Revolution

The Wilderness Through Rose-Colored Glasses   *331*
Romanticizing nature • The earliest conservationists

Review / Questions   *335*

Selected Readings   *336*

EPILOG

Reconstruction 1865 – 1877   339

Presidential Plans for Reconstruction   *339*
Congressional Reconstruction   *340*
Impeachment of a President   *341*
Reconstruction Triumphant   *341*
Backlash in the South   *342*
The Compromise of 1877   *343*
The Reconstruction of Black Citizenship   *343*

Appendices 344

The Declaration of Independence   344
The Constitution   346
Presidents and Vice-Presidents   357
Population of the United States / 1800–1880   358

Credits and Acknowledgments 359

Index 361

Chronicles

EARLY EXPLORATION

. . . the first painters of the New World   82a

LIFE IN THE NEW NATION

. . . from the sketchbooks of Lewis Miller   210a

Biographical Profiles

Captain John Smith, A Labor Problem   27
Abigail Adams, A More Than Equal Woman   133
Alexander Hamilton, The Duel   220
Robert E. Lee, A Matter of Loyalties   246
Harriet Tubman, Underground Conductor   269

Maps

Discovering the New World   5
The Thirteen Colonies   9
Colonial Overseas Trade   21
North America in 1754   69
North America in 1763   69
Major Revolutionary Campaigns   72
Indians of North America   82
Geography of the Continental United States   160
Western Trails   174
Missouri Compromise, 1820   214
Compromise of 1850   215
Kansas-Nebraska Act, 1854   216

Election of 1860   225
Territorial Growth of the United States, 1783–1853   235
Mexican War   241
The United States on the Eve of Civil War   243
Tribal Lands Ceded to the Whites   259
Election of 1876   343

Charts

Parallel Wars in Europe and America, 1689 to the Present   65
Blacks and Whites in the Thirteen Colonies   90
National Origins of Americans in 1790   104
Congregations in 1775   107
Population of Major Cities in Early America   148
Exports from the U.S., 1790–1815   188
United States War Dead   250
The Increase in Cities, 1790–1860   314

t' Fort nieúw Amsterdam op de Manhat.

The fort of New Amsterdam, around 1626.

I

■ Part One   To 1789

Chronology

50,000–25,000 B.C.
Stone Age people cross land bridge to North America.

7000–2000 B.C.
Beginnings of Indian agriculture in Central America.

1200 B.C.–1532 A.D.
Olmec, Maya, Aztec, and Inca civilizations flourish.

1492
Columbus arrives in the New World.

1607
Jamestown, Virginia, founded by English expedition.

1640–1660
Black slavery emerges in English mainland colonies.

1754–1763
French and Indian War (Seven Years' War).

1775–1783
Revolutionary War.

1787
Constitution drafted at Philadelphia Convention.

1789
George Washington inaugurated president.

There we landed and discovered a little way: . . . we could find nothing . . . but fair meadows and goodly tall Trees; with such Fresh-waters running through the woods, as I was almost ravished at the first sight thereof.

GEORGE PERCY (1580–1631)
Author of two accounts of early Virginia

overview
Beginnings

Indian civilizations before Columbus

The earliest immigrants to North America arrived between 25,000 and 50,000 years ago. These first humans to inhabit the continent probably crossed from Siberia to Alaska during an ice age which exposed a natural land bridge that is now covered by the Bering Sea. These people were Stone Age hunters. For thousands of years they fanned out over the Americas. By the end of the last ice age—about ten thousand years ago—many of their larger prey were extinct. The hardy wanderers, who had spread from the Arctic to the tip of South America, now turned to hunting smaller animals and learned to grow crops. Their descendants are the many peoples known as American Indians.

Between 7000 and 2000 B.C. Indians began growing corn, beans, squash, and other foods in Central America (sometimes called Middle America or Mesoamerica). Farming provided a food supply they could depend on and eventually enabled them to begin creating settled communities. From as early as 1200 B.C. to about 400 A.D. the Olmec civilization grew and flourished in the lowlands of Mexico's Gulf coast. From 300 A.D. the Maya culture developed on the Yucatán peninsula, reaching its peak around 900 A.D. The Aztecs of the Mexican highlands built an empire that lasted from about 1300 until its destruction by the invading Spaniards in the early 1500s. In Peru the Incas ruled their empire for almost five centuries before they too fell before the conquistadors.

In many ways the American Indian civilizations rivaled those of Egypt, Mesopotamia, and China. They had great cities, gigantic stone temples, complex religions, and accurate calendars. These were feudal societies with priest-kings, warrior nobles, and a large peasant class. The glory of Indian civilization can be measured in the Aztec capital, Tenochtitlán (the site of present-day Mexico City). In 1521 Tenochtitlán had a population of eighty thousand—about twice that of the largest city in Spain. It was a political, religious, and trading center whose influence radiated over hundreds of miles.

Indians of Mexico and Central America influenced many of the tribes that lived to the north. Fifteen centuries before the coming of Columbus some of their skills had spread to North America. Yet there were tribes that kept their old ways until or even after the arrival of the Europeans. They did little if any farming and lived mainly by hunting, fishing, and gathering wild foods.

When the land area of what became the United States was populated only by Indians, there were about six hundred separate tribes. Some two thousand languages and dialects were spoken, many as different from one another as Chinese is from English. The Northeast was occupied by forest hunters and farmers. The most prominent of these were the Iroquois, a remarkably stable alliance of tribes centered in what is now upper New York State. In the Southeast lived an agricultural people, whom the Europeans called the Five Civilized Tribes—Cherokee, Creek, Chickasaw, Choctaw, and Seminole. They were noted for their flat-topped burial mounds and for the open plazas in their villages, both of which show influences from Mesoamerican Indian civilizations. Their arts included decorated pottery, flint beads, and copper ornaments. In the arid Southwest were the Hopi, Pueblo, and Zuñi Indians. Strongly influenced by the culture of the Mexican highlands, they built cleverly designed apartmentlike dwellings of stone and adobe (sun-dried brick), some high on the faces of steep cliffs, and they used irrigation to grow crops in that harsh, dry land.

It is not certain how many native Americans there were around 1492. Estimates range from 6 million to 60 million, with 1 to 8 million living north of Mexico. What is certain is that in 1900, when the whites had spread over the whole continent, there were only 237,000 Indians left in the United States.

Explorers of North America

The voyages of Columbus opened the New World to centuries of European exploration and settlement. But he was not the first outsider to make contact with the Indians. In 1003 Leif Ericson led a group of Vikings to Vinland (Newfoundland), where they clashed with people they called Skralings. Proof exists that the Vikings settled there for a while. Theories have been advanced that shipwrecked sailors or explorers from China, Japan, West Africa, Wales, Ireland, Greece, Palestine, and Egypt also touched the Americas long before Columbus. But even if such contacts were made, there is no evidence that they had any lasting impact.

During the fifteenth century, European traders were under pressure to find new routes to the Orient. Precious cargoes from India, China, and the Spice

Islands (the East Indies) had always reached western Europe through the Mediterranean and the Near East. But the powerful Ottoman Turkish Empire controlled the Near Eastern routes, and the practice of using Italian merchants as middlemen was becoming too costly. Cheaper, more reliable routes had to be found. The western Europeans, whose ships were the most advanced in the world, sought an all-water route. It was Columbus who tested the idea that such a route could be found by sailing west across the Atlantic.

Christopher Columbus (1451–1506), a sailor from Genoa, had a deep, almost overpowering sense of personal destiny and limitless faith in his own ideas. The Spanish rulers Ferdinand and Isabella sponsored his project and gave him the title Admiral of the Ocean Sea. On August 3, 1492, the newly named admiral sailed from Palos, Spain, with ninety men and three ships. They reached San Salvador (today's Watlings Island) in the Bahamas on October 12 and established a colony in Santo Domingo. Columbus returned to Spain fully convinced he had reached Asia by a new route. Three more trips, exploring the Caribbean and touching parts of Central America, failed to persuade him that he had discovered a whole new hemisphere.

The news of Columbus' discovery caused other explorers to set sail. John Cabot, a Genoese serving the English king, anchored off Newfoundland and New England in 1497 and may have sailed as far south as Delaware in 1498. Amerigo Vespucci, sailing first for Spain and a second time for Portugal, scouted the northeast coast of South America (1499–1500). His place in history is assured because the Americas were named after him. Pedro Cabral claimed Brazil for Portugal in 1500. In 1513 Vasco de Balboa crossed Panama and discovered the Pacific. The final proof that Columbus had actually found a New World was supplied by the Portuguese explorer Ferdinand Magellan, whose Spanish expedition sailed around the world between 1519 and 1522. France entered the hectic contest to claim parts of the New World with the voyages of Giovanni de Verrazano to New York Harbor (1524) and Jacques Cartier to Canada (1534 and 1535).

In a single generation Spanish conquistadors swept through the Caribbean and Central America. They subdued Santo Domingo, Puerto Rico, Jamaica, and Cuba and destroyed the Aztec empire in Mexico (1519–1521) and the Inca empire of Peru (1531–1533). The conquerors carried away unbelievable riches. Hoping to find even more wealth in the New World, the Spanish government sent explorers further north. Hernando de Soto led six hundred soldiers throughout the American Southeast and lower Mississippi Valley (1539–1543), and Francisco de Coronado explored the Southwest (1540–1542). During the next two centuries Spain established outposts and laid claim to land in what is now Florida, Texas, New Mexico, Arizona, and California, as well as other territory west of the Mississippi.

In the meantime, France sent adventurers into Canada, through the Great Lakes, and down the Ohio and Mississippi rivers. Samuel de Champlain sailed up the St. Lawrence River in 1603 on the first of eleven voyages. He explored the coast of Acadia (modern Nova Scotia) and founded Quebec, which became the capital of New France. French fur trappers and traders dealt widely with

Hudson 1610

Cabot 1497

Cartier 1534 and 1535

NORTH AMERICA

ENGLAND

FRANCE

EUROPE

ITALY

SPAIN

PORTUGAL

ATLANTIC OCEAN

Verrazano 1524

GULF OF
MEXICO

Columbus 1492

AFRICA

Vespucci 1499

Magellan 1519–1522

Cabral 1500

Balboa
1510

Drake 1577

SOUTH AMERICA

DISCOVERING THE NEW WORLD

5

the Indian tribes. In the seventeenth century the French empire in America included eastern Canada, the Great Lakes, and the Mississippi Valley, as well as Haiti and the Antilles in the Caribbean. Although the population of French colonists never became large enough to keep a firm grip on the vast territory and the vast wealth they claimed, the French were off to a fast start in America. The Dutch got a toehold in and around New York in the early seventeenth century, but in a matter of decades the English pushed them out.

The nations of western Europe had reached a stage of development which inspired overseas adventure, conquest, and colonization. During the Renaissance, from the fourteenth to the sixteenth centuries, Europe awoke from a long sleep. Science and technology developed better ships and more accurate navigation. In the towns a middle class of merchants and artisans emerged. Commerce revived, cities grew. Banking houses developed that supplied the funds needed to finance exploration and colonization. A small number of unified nations was created out of the multitude of small states which had characterized Europe in the Middle Ages. These new nation-states searched for overseas treasure and territories. The Indians of North and South America were the victims of that search.

European expansion was also stimulated by the sixteenth-century crisis of the Catholic church—the Reformation—which created groups of Protestant exiles anxious to seek religious freedom for themselves in the colonies. Some Catholics were also drawn to the new lands for religious reasons. They were eager to convert the Indians to the "true" Christianity. The Old World reached out to the New in many ways, sending its people, its ideas, and its skills. In return, America provided wealth and opportunities that bolstered the European nations and profoundly altered Western civilization.

England in the New World

During the expansion of Spanish holdings in America, England was a poor and disunited country. Because it came late to the colonial feast, it had to settle for what was then considered the crumbs: the Atlantic coast from Maine to Georgia. Queen Elizabeth I, who ruled from 1558 to 1603, supported overseas colonization as part of her effort to make England economically self-sufficient.

The first English colony was founded by Sir Walter Raleigh in 1585 on Roanoke Island, off what is now North Carolina. A few years later it mysteriously disappeared. The English made their first permanent settlement at Jamestown, Virginia, but only after overcoming great hardships. Colonists numbering 104 arrived in May 1607 after a five-month voyage. They were soon joined by 400 more. Yet by 1610, disease, famine, hostile Indians, and mismanagement had reduced the colony to a mere 60 people. In 1620 the *Mayflower* carried English Pilgrims to Plymouth, on the rocky New England shore. The Massachusetts Bay Colony, settled by Puritans in 1630, was a larger and more successful enterprise.

Most of the earliest English colonies were planned as business ventures under royal charters. Investors and government officials back in England made the rules for settlers, who had little or no say in how their colonies were run. This awkward system slowed economic growth and political development for a time. When greater flexibility was allowed, or when the colonists themselves got charters to settle new land, the colonies grew and prospered. A good example is the Massachusetts Bay Colony, which attracted more than ten thousand people between 1630 and 1640. It was largely self-governing because the original settlers had formed a joint-stock company (an early sort of corporation) and had brought with them a charter directly from the king. Their experience in organizing their own company and then in managing their own colony helped create an American tradition of self-determination.

Black Americans never shared in this tradition. The first black Africans were brought to Jamestown in 1619, one year before the *Mayflower* reached America. It appears that most of this party became bond servants, who had to work a certain number of years for their employer. Later arrivals from Africa came as slaves. As tobacco became a more popular export crop by the mid-seventeenth century, more slaves were brought here to work the fields. For the next two centuries the institution of slavery continued to grow in America. In 1789, when Washington (himself a slave owner) became president, many Americans defended slavery with the argument that the Africans were barbarians who needed to be civilized. Whites in Europe and America looked on blacks as inferior, even subhuman, and the fact that civilizations had flourished in black Africa for six centuries, or perhaps even longer, was unknown to them. Unfortunately, even if whites had understood African history, they probably would have behaved much the same toward blacks. Little effort was made to abolish slavery in the colonies because too many whites either benefited from slave labor or the slave trade or mistakenly believed that the institution would just disappear when it was no longer useful and profitable.

Because English colonization followed in the wake of the Protestant Reformation, it continued to be shaped by religious issues. Henry VIII, England's king from 1509 to 1547, had challenged the supremacy of the pope and created the Church of England (the Anglican church), which most of his subjects joined. But the establishment of a state church produced numerous splinter groups. The Pilgrims (known as Separatists in England) broke completely with the Anglican church because they felt it could never be reformed. They were persecuted and fled to America. The Puritans (or Nonconformists) tried to stay within the Church of England and purify it. But they too were hounded and many were forced into exile. They founded the Massachusetts Bay Colony as a model Puritan state and a place where they could practice their religion in peace.

The origins of Puritanism can be found in the writings of the French-born Swiss theologian, John Calvin (1509–1564). He preached that salvation was a completely personal matter, that God alone decided who would be saved and who would be damned eternally—neither priests nor popes nor kings could affect the decision. This belief threatened established state churches and the authority of monarchs who claimed they ruled by "divine right." In England Calvin's followers became increasingly important in the political and religious struggles with the Stuart king, Charles I (ruled 1625–1649). As a result of the English Civil War (1642–1649), monarchy by divine right and the Anglican church were temporarily overthrown. Oliver Cromwell and the Parliamentary army defeated the royalists, beheaded King Charles, and established a Puritan republic (the Commonwealth) in England.

Puritanism also played an important role in American history. Its rigid, authoritarian beliefs armed the colonists with a conviction that they were carrying out a divine mission. Also, the idea of personal salvation fostered a strong sense of individualism, and the insistence that churches should be governed by their congregations gave the members experience in running their own affairs and a desire for political self-determination. Although best known for their hard-nosed religious beliefs, the Puritans left some of their most lasting marks in nonreligious areas of American life. The Puritans emphasized reason and, therefore, literacy. They founded Harvard and other schools and introduced printing presses. The Puritan faith in the value of hard work (sometimes called the Puritan or Protestant Ethic) inspired many Americans to make the great effort needed to carve out a living in the harsh wilderness and to extend the frontier.

The closed world of the Puritans could not survive the pressures of a growing, changing society. Puritanism's spiritual power faded as science and prosperity undermined traditional beliefs. Religious faith was rekindled for a time in the early eighteenth century during the fiery revival movement known as the Great Awakening. But Puritanism continued to decline. Yet third- and fourth-generation New Englanders preserved much of the way of life and many of the social values of their Puritan ancestors. The frugal, prosperous Yankee traders and hard-working New England farmers mirrored their Puritan heritage.

America as a colony

The Puritan Commonwealth of England ended in 1660. The restored Stuart monarchy began to expand England's straggling outposts and struggling colonies and to organize them into a unified empire. After 1660 charters for *new* colonies were granted to proprietors rather than to joint-stock companies.

The economy of the British empire was based on the theory of mercantilism, a system that prevailed among many European nations in the seventeenth and eighteenth centuries. Mercantilism meant, among other things, strict government control over trade and manufacture and a reliance on colonies for resources to enrich the motherland. To these ends, the English Parliament passed a series of Navigation Acts (1651–1767) which required the colonies to supply those raw materials not produced in England. All manufactured goods had to come from England or, if from other countries, first had to go through English ports and pay duty there. All cargoes had to be carried by English or

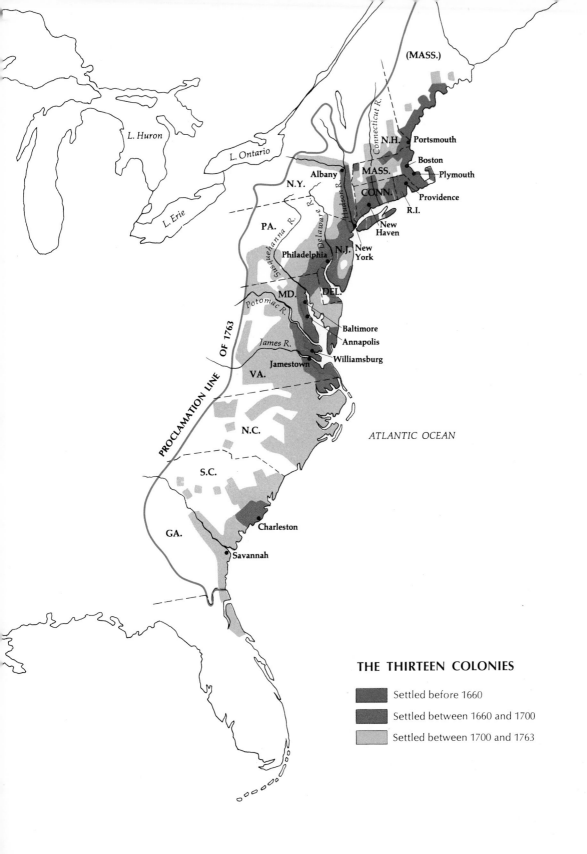

L. Huron

L. Ontario

L. Erie

Albany

Susquehanna R.

PA.

N.Y.

Delaware R.

Hudson R.

Connecticut R.

(MASS.)

N.H. •Portsmouth

•Boston
MASS. •Plymouth

CONN.
•Providence
R.I.

New
Haven

Philadelphia• N.J. New
York

PROCLAMATION LINE

OF 1763

Potomac R.

MD. DEL.

•Baltimore
•Annapolis

James R.

Jamestown• •Williamsburg

VA.

N.C.

ATLANTIC OCEAN

S.C.

GA.

•Charleston

•Savannah

THE THIRTEEN COLONIES

Settled before 1660

Settled between 1660 and 1700

Settled between 1700 and 1763

colonial ships so no foreign nations could profit from colonial trade. England in turn promised to provide military and naval protection for the colonies.

The targets of these mercantilist policies were the Dutch, French, and Spanish traders. The goal was to create a steady flow of raw materials and gold into England, all at the expense of other nations—most of which had their own mercantilist policies. By the mid-eighteenth century, the Dutch had been frozen out of North America, and England was a vastly wealthier country. The prosperity of the English colonies had also greatly increased, but the colonists were beginning to resent government controls on manufacture and trade. For the time being, though, they were managing to avoid the worst restrictions on trade and manufacture through smuggling and other dodges.

North America was both a battleground and a prize in a great game of empire in which the European powers competed for raw materials, land, and markets. In the 1600s and 1700s rivalry between England and France caused four major wars that were waged in Europe and India and on the high seas, as well as in North America. The struggle that decided the future of North America was the French and Indian War (1754–1763), which spread to Europe in 1756 and was called there the Seven Years' War. The conflict ended in almost total victory for England. The French lost nearly all their American colonies, including Canada. These gains, along with territory won elsewhere in the world, made Britain the leading imperial power of the day.

During the seventeen decades that passed between the founding of Jamestown and the Declaration of Independence, far-reaching changes took place in colonial America. Many new towns were founded, and villages grew into cities. By 1775 Philadelphia had become a busy world port with forty thousand residents. New York, Boston, Charleston, and Newport were also important cities. From a few settlers struggling to survive, the population swelled to perhaps 200,000 in 1690, nearly 1.6 million in 1760, about 2.8 million by the Revolution, and almost 4 million in 1790. Not only were there more people, they spread inland to settle an ever wider area of the continent. On the eve of the break with Britain, the majority of the colonists were English. But there were also 200,000 Germans in the colonies, along with many Scotch-Irish, a sprinkling of other European ethnic groups, and, of course, thousands of blacks. Although various forms of economic activity developed and many colonists became prosperous, there was discontent with British rule—a discontent that eventually grew into revolution.

The American Revolution

America's struggle for independence can be traced in part to Britain's stunning victory over France in 1763. Large war debts had to be repaid somehow, and the English thought the colonists should pay their share. After all, British troops had fought in America and protected the colonists from the French and their Indian allies, so why should the colonists not be taxed for administering the new empire? Thus Parliament tried to raise new revenues in the colonies, in two ways. 1) New taxes would be imposed. 2) Old taxes that had been avoided through bribery and smuggling would now be collected under strict enforcement of trade regulations. The plan was bound to anger many colonists.

Parliament passed the Revenue or Sugar Act (1764) and the Stamp Act (1765) at the urging of the Chancellor of the Exchequer, George Grenville. Grenville's policies enraged the colonists, especially the lawyers, editors, and merchants who would have to pay for the obnoxious stamps in order to conduct their businesses. It was not so much that they were challenging the right of Parliament to regulate trade; they were objecting to taxation without representation, which they believed violated their rights as British subjects. Colonial radicals called for a boycott of British goods and organized the Sons of Liberty to enforce it and to prevent the collection of the new taxes. Violence and the threat of violence forced many British officials to resign and made it impossible for the Stamp Act to work. The colonists' opposition led Britain to repeal the Stamp Act (1766), but Parliament still proclaimed the right to legislate for the colonies.

A new Chancellor of the Exchequer, Lord Townshend, tried to enforce new revenue measures. But many Americans claimed they could be taxed only by their colonial assemblies, where they were represented, and not by Parliament, in which they had no direct representation. Little wonder that the import duties under the Townshend Acts were as stiffly resisted as the Grenville tax measures had been. They brought little revenue to England and were repealed (1770) — all but the tax on tea.

There were other British policies that strained relations with the American colonies. Settlement of the area beyond the Allegheny Mountains was restricted by the Proclamation of 1763. The Currency Act of 1764 required that all debts be paid in hard currency instead of paper money issued by provincial assemblies. This angered merchants and plantation owners, most of whom owed large amounts to creditors in England. The Quartering Acts of 1765 and 1766 called for colonial governments to provide supplies and quarters for 10,000 British redcoats to be stationed in the colonies. A powerful undercurrent of resentment developed in America. Opposition became so strong that some colonial legislatures were dissolved. Active resistance began to take forms very close to outright rebellion.

In March 1770 there was a bloody encounter between redcoats and Bostonians. It began when a crowd of laborers taunted and threw rocks at British soldiers guarding the customs house. The soldiers finally opened fire. Five civilians were killed, including Crispus Attucks, a runaway slave. A dramatic trial followed, in which some of the soldiers were found guilty but were let off with light punishments. Sam Adams used the outrage caused by the Boston Massacre to spur radicals from other colonies to unite against British policies.

When Parliament imposed new taxes on tea, the colonials responded by dumping British tea into Boston Harbor (the Boston Tea Party of 1773). Parliament struck back hard in 1774 with what came to be known as the Intolerable

Acts. The port of Boston was closed; the colonial courts were shackled by a rule allowing soldiers and royal officials to be tried in Britain; and an even stronger Quartering Act permitted British troops to be housed in private homes.

These serious attacks on colonial rights provoked Americans to take strong countermeasures. They convened the First Continental Congress in Philadelphia in 1774. Its furious members urged the people to arm themselves. Detailed plans were drawn up to stop the importation and use of British goods and to end exports to the mother country. But it was not just events in Massachusetts that fired up colonial resistance. Parliament had made enemies throughout the colonies by passing the Quebec Act (1774). It recognized Roman Catholicism in Canada, which outraged the Protestant majority in the American colonies, and it added a huge tract of land west of the Allegheny Mountains to Quebec Province. This reduced the potential size and wealth of the American colonies and plucked valuable territory out of the reach of colonial land speculators.

Britain was determined to enforce the Intolerable Acts. General Thomas Gage replaced the civilian governor of Massachusetts in May 1774. During the following months sizable detachments of British troops were placed under his command in Boston. They tried to arrest the leaders of the Massachusetts rebellion and confiscate their arms early in 1775. On April 19, at Lexington and Concord, British redcoats and colonial Minutemen exchanged the first shots of the Revolutionary War.

The Second Continental Congress met in May 1775 to deal with the growing crisis. It voted to establish a Continental Army and appointed George Washington commander in chief. Meanwhile, the hostilities continued. Rebel forces besieging the British in Boston inflicted over a thousand casualties on the redcoats in the Battle of Bunker Hill (June 17). There was also fighting in the South and in Canada. Representatives at the Continental Congress made one last effort to restore peace and harmony between the colonies and Britain, but King George rejected their so-called Olive Branch Petition. He considered his American subjects to be in rebellion and hired German mercenaries to fight them. Publication of Thomas Paine's stirring tract, *Common Sense*, in January 1776 swayed public opinion in the colonies firmly in the direction of a total break with Britain. Congress drew closer to declaring complete independence, and by summer it was preparing for an all-out war.

The Declaration of Independence, written by Thomas Jefferson with the aid of Benjamin Franklin and John Adams, was issued on July 4, 1776. Many of the noble ideas in the Declaration can be traced back to the writings of the seventeenth-century English philosopher John Locke. Locke believed that society was created to protect people's natural rights and that a just society was based on a social compact between the people and their government. If a government violated those rights, the people had the right to overthrow that government. The Declaration of Independence was intended to unite the rebels and strengthen their cause by forcing people to take sides. It was also meant to gain foreign support, particularly from France, which was anxious to break the links holding together the British empire.

The Continental Congress faced serious difficulties in opposing the British army. Many of the colonists still could not bring themselves to renounce their loyalty to the crown. Because the colonists were beset by local fear, distrust, and jealousy, Congress was hard-pressed to finance the war, obtain supplies, and organize a reliable army. Colonial soldiers would not enlist for long periods of service because they knew they would be needed to care for their farms. And the rebels had few professional officers. Fortunately, Congress found a remarkably capable commander in the Virginia planter George Washington—the single most important figure in the Revolutionary War.

The British troops were well trained, highly disciplined, and well led, even though the top officers, General Sir William Howe and his brother Admiral Lord Richard Howe, seemed to have little enthusiasm for crushing the rebellion. The basic British strategy was to capture the colony of New York and thereby separate New England from the colonies to the south. But the plan backfired. At Saratoga, in October 1777, the embattled farmers of New York and New England forced "Gentleman Johnny" Burgoyne and his British army to surrender. This resounding victory convinced France that it should give the Americans substantial naval help.

From June 1778 until late in 1781 the war was in a stalemate, which worked to the advantage of the rebels. Washington went on the defensive and avoided fighting any conclusive battles with the redcoats. The British took the offensive, but their search-and-destroy missions never bagged very large forces, so most British victories meant little. Although the British regulars could win battles, they simply could not be everywhere at once or occupy enough ground to control the colonies and win the war. To prevent the British from gaining control of the colonies, Washington's forces had only to avoid an all-out defeat and keep the war going.

Washington's policy of patience and caution was rewarded. The British general Lord Cornwallis set a trap for himself by establishing his troops in a vulnerable position on the shore of the Yorktown peninsula, with their backs to the sea. While a combined army of Americans and French volunteers pressed down the peninsula, a squadron of French ships made it impossible for the British fleet to evacuate or reinforce Cornwallis' besieged army. The Battle of Yorktown ended on October 19, 1781, when the British laid down their arms.

When the Treaty of Paris took effect in 1783, after months of negotiations, the Americans had won a generous settlement. Britain recognized the rebels' independence and granted them title to land as far west as the Mississippi River. The Americans had liberated themselves not only from Britain but from the European social system—the new nation was a republic without kings or nobles. The birth of the American Republic was without doubt a great moment in the history of human freedom. The question now was whether the baby could survive infancy.

The Articles of Confederation and the Constitution

The Continental Congress ran the Revolutionary War, but it was not really a national government. At first the rebels operated under state constitutions, most of which were drafted during the Revolution. A national system of government, called the Articles of Confederation, was adopted in 1781. Since the aims of the Revolution included independence and the overthrow of Britain's centralized monarchy, it is understandable that the rebels wanted power divided among the various state governments. So under the Articles the national government was quite weak. There was no executive branch that might be turned into a new monarchy. National laws could be passed only if nine of the thirteen votes in Congress agreed; amendments to the Articles took all thirteen. Congress lacked the power to create an army, impose taxes, or regulate commerce. As a result, money and an army could be raised only by getting the states to agree to meet certain quotas.

The Articles of Confederation made sense for a people that had just gotten out from under a strong central government. It protected the authority of each state and placed local self-determination above all else. But it left the nation unable to deal with either domestic or foreign crises. Right after the Revolutionary War, the nation fell into an economic depression that resulted in part from Britain's refusal to grant the Americans shipping rights in the British empire. The decentralized national government under the Articles was unable to negotiate a settlement with the former motherland. Hard times caused the debtor farmers of western Massachusetts, led by Captain Daniel Shays, to rebel against legal punishments for nonpayment of debts. Shays' Rebellion scared many property owners. They, along with other people in various states, began to press for a new structure of national government that would be truly national but still protect individual rights.

The Congress of the Confederation responded to the pressure by arranging for a convention to revise the Articles of Confederation. At Philadelphia, in the sweltering summer of 1787, fifty-five delegates debated the reshaping of the American Republic. The discussions brought to light the intense conflicts between big states and small ones, northerners and southerners, slave owners and those who owned no slaves, farmers and merchants, westerners and easterners, debtors and creditors. But the delegates did not give up until they had forged a new constitution. It severely limited the powers of the states and elevated those of the central government. It provided for a two-house federal legislature, for a president chosen by a college of electors appointed by the states, and for separate executive, legislative, and judicial branches. It did not just revise the Articles of Confederation; it totally replaced them.

Ratification of the Constitution took place amid bitter debate in special state conventions. Resistance to the new document was greatest in the large states: Virginia, Massachusetts, Pennsylvania, and New York. Opponents of the Constitution feared that centralization of power would destroy the states and curtail personal liberty. Some undecided delegates to the ratifying conventions were finally won over when supporters of the Constitution promised that a Bill of Rights would be added to protect individual freedom. Those favoring the new system were called Federalists. Three of their leaders—Alexander Hamilton, James Madison, and John Jay—produced a series of penetrating essays favoring the new government, which were later collected and published as *The Federalist*. Federalist eloquence and the fact that more and more people were realizing the nation could never survive without a stronger central government finally brought about ratification. In June 1788 the Constitution of the United States of America became the law of the land.

The following February, in the first national election, General Washington received all sixty-nine electoral votes to become the first president. John Adams of Massachusetts was chosen vice-president. Washington was sworn in April 30, 1789, on the balcony of Federal Hall on Wall Street in lower Manhattan. New York City, with its Dutch gabled roofs and cobbled streets, became the first capital of the new United States.

The world in 1789

The world was radically different in 1789 from what it is today. The climate was colder and wetter. People were shorter, slighter, and far fewer in number. The vast majority of the world's population lived by farming, using age-old methods. Most Europeans were peasants who worked for big landowners. Few people anywhere could read, and most never traveled beyond their village boundaries. There were, of course, fewer cities than today, and they were much smaller. London, the largest, was probably the only city with a million people; Paris had only half that number. Most of the world was unexplored by Europeans. Blank spaces appeared on maps, with only some lines to mark the routes of the most daring explorers.

Distances appeared to be much greater then, because travel was so much slower. Land travel was mainly by foot, horseback, and ox-drawn or horse-drawn wagons and carriages. Water transportation was cheapest and fastest. London was very far from Boston, but it was easier to make that trip than to go overland from Boston to Lake Superior.

Most of the world's governments were autocratic, run by rulers whose powers were not limited by the will of the people. Europe had dominated the world in the three centuries following the voyage of Magellan. Still, large and important areas remained independent. The Chinese Empire under the Manchu (Ch'ing) Dynasty was then at the height of its splendor; most of Africa south of the Sahara and all of the Islamic world were outside European control. But the world of 1789 was one of kings and empires. Those outsiders who had heard of the birth of the United States were sure that the brash young republic would soon fall apart—it seemed impossible for a country to survive without a monarch. Yet a few short years later the American and French Revolutions were viewed as connecting links in a struggle for liberty that might in the long run destroy autocracy everywhere.

The Arch Street Ferry, Philadelphia.

Fetter not commerce! Let her
be as free as the air. She will
range the whole creation,
and return on the four
winds of heaven to bless the
land of plenty with plenty.

PATRICK HENRY (1736–1799)

1

1

Off to a Good Start

This country recently became the first nation in history with a Gross National Product of $1 trillion. (The GNP represents the total production of goods and services—or wealth—in a single year.) The United States took about two centuries to reach this production level. It may double this GNP in another ten or twenty years.

How did the United States become a "have" nation in a world of "have-nots"? How has wealth been created and distributed in the U.S.? The answers to these questions tell a great deal about America.

The human race has been fighting hunger throughout its existence. The invention of farming several thousand years ago helped ease the problem. But scarcity still rules much of the world, and population now seems to be outstripping food production. All the more wonder, then, that a handful of nations, among them the United States, got caught up in a whirlwind of technological change that made them well fed and wealthy.

Until recently the majority of Americans believed that more is better. But a growing number of citizens are now considering the *quality* and possible *limits* of growth. Our trillion-dollar economy is accompanied by vast problems: pollution of air, earth, and water, inflation, worker alienation, overcrowded cities, waste and crime, and inequality. If the country is to succeed in the future, it must come to grips with these issues. The political implications of economic growth—for example, the concentration of corporate power—will be dealt with in the chapters on Power. The ecological aspects will be the theme of the chapters on Environment.

The discussion of Wealth is divided into five chapters (1, 9, 17, 25, and 33), one in each of the book's five parts. Each chapter has three sections. The first section is a general study of economic growth and the distribution of the nation's wealth. It examines such factors as technology, human capital (labor), physical capital (the means of production), managerial skill, efficiency of business organization, income distribution, and the influence of the American Dream. The second section describes the role of workers, especially skilled workers and unions, in our economic development. The final section deals with farmers, who, for most of our history, were a majority of the population.

Mercantilism

Mercantilism defined

One reason why the nation is rich today is that it got off to a running start while still a colony of Great Britain. The birth of the United States was preceded by a century and a half of solid economic growth. Population had doubled every twenty or twenty-five years. New lands were constantly settled. Urban populations increased. Farm production, especially in rice, tobacco, and wheat, rose steadily over the years. Crude iron was manufactured. By 1760 the North American colonies ranked among the world's most important shipping regions. Colonial merchant vessels, most of which were built here, competed successfully in fishing, whaling, and cargo carrying. From 1700 to 1760 imports of finished goods from England increased more than sevenfold. Despite their bitter complaints against the English government in the 1760s and 1770s, the colonists had by then become a prosperous people. On the whole, middle-class families lived better here than in the mother country, because they had a better opportunity to own land.

No doubt England would claim the lion's share of credit for the prosperity of the colonies. In the seventeenth and eighteenth centuries the government of England, like those of other European states, followed the economic theory known as mercantilism. According to this theory, the world's wealth was limited and must be jealously collected and hoarded. Colonies were regarded as a source of raw materials to enrich the mother country and a place to sell its finished goods. To ensure an excess of exports over foreign imports, colonies were prevented from trading freely with other countries, and tariffs blocked foreign competition.

Beginning in the days of James I, England insisted that the American colonies produce mostly raw materials and let the motherland produce the finished goods. The colonists were offered bounties for producing certain raw materials, and English companies got special privileges and trading rights in the New World. In general, mercantilism meant strict government regulation of manufacture and trade.

England enforced its colonial policies through a series of Navigation Acts. The first Act (1651) provided that goods could enter the empire only in English ships. Later Navigation Acts (1660–1673) modified this rule but specified that certain exports like tobacco and sugar had to pass through England and pay duty there. Colonists were prohibited from exporting wool products (1699) and finished iron goods (1750). Some of the early regulations were intended to fight off competition from the Dutch, the world's most aggressive seagoing traders. The policy worked so well that England captured much of the world's sea traffic from Holland and competed successfully against the French, Spanish, and Portuguese. By the end of the

He that rules the sea, rules the commerce of the world and to him who rules the commerce of the world belongs the treasure of the world and indeed the world itself.

SIR WALTER RALEIGH (1552?–1618)

Seven Years' War in 1763, England overshadowed all rival nations in both commerce and military strength. After 1763 the colonists voiced strong complaints about certain restrictions on production and trade. But for long periods before then they had been left alone. And they continued to thrive despite the many restrictions of the Navigation Acts.

Technology

In the twentieth century, technological progress has been the mainstay of economic growth. By contrast, new technology was rather unimportant in the prosperity of the colonies. Most of the basic farming equipment had originated during the Middle Ages: the heavy-wheeled plow, the horse collar, the tandem harness, the iron horseshoe, and the windmill. The ancient waterwheel was a source of power for flour mills and sawmills, and the spinning wheel continued to produce yarn for cloth. Competition encouraged innovation in shipbuilding, but the tools of the mariner's trade did not change much.

Americans depended very little on the "sober reasoning of science" in their technology.* They worked at specific projects with limited objectives, rather than at ways of evolving general principles. The average craftsman used trial and error to improve on

the established techniques of his trade. This process later came to be called "Yankee ingenuity." But its practical effects were still limited, and the rate of technological change during the colonial period was slow.

Among the products of Yankee ingenuity were the Conestoga wagon and the Kentucky rifle. English wagons were too weak to haul heavy loads over trackless mountain routes. German wagonmakers of Conestoga Creek, Pennsylvania, designed a heavy-duty covered wagon with a deep, long bed that sagged in the middle to make the load shift to the center. It took a six-horse team to pull a Conestoga wagon. Similarly, European firearms were inaccurate and unreliable and took too long to load when Indians were shooting arrows from behind trees and rocks. Swiss-German gunsmiths at Lancaster, Pennsylvania, developed a weapon with a better sight and longer barrel for improved accuracy and with better balance for ease of handling. Most important, the ball was encased in a grease patch, which gave the bullet spin and prevented it from wobbling in flight. Pioneers carried these Kentucky rifles west with them.

Before the Revolution most tools were hand-operated. Human or animal muscle supplied the main mode of power. Relatively little use was made even of water power, except for grinding flour at the hundreds of flour mills that dotted the colonies. The first person to attempt to use steam power in North America was Christopher Colles, a Scotch-Irish millwright and engineer, who constructed a steam-driven water pump in 1771. The contraption collapsed after a few demonstration strokes but deeply impressed

---

*"Science and technology have different objectives," writes Brooke Hindle. "Science seeks basic understanding—ideas and concepts usually expressed in mathematical terms. Technology seeks means for making and doing things. It is a question of process, always expressible in terms of three-dimensional 'things.'"

the audience at the American Philosophical Society in Philadelphia. Colles tried to get New York City to use a steam pump in its water system, but the Revolutionary War broke out and the project was cancelled. Even so, the first steps had been taken toward a new source of mechanical power that would later bring a radical change in American life.

Capitalism in the colonies

For economic growth, physical capital in the form of machinery, land, and natural resources must be available. In America the most abundant of these was land, which attracted many investors. Slaves were another form of physical capital and another area for investment. (The labor of free workers is treated as a separate economic element. See pp. 26–30.)

Since there were no commercial banks until after the Revolution, American planters and merchants who wanted to invest in land, ships, or slaves had to borrow from English and Scottish merchants. America depended on outsiders for investment funds until the early twentieth century. In this sense, the colonies were in the same predicament as today's underdeveloped countries.

Colonial Americans had a knack for efficiency. It was not so much that individual businesses were especially well run, but that entire regions specialized in particular goods and markets. This lack of duplication of each other's efforts was a great economic boon. The South, the Middle Colonies, and the New England colonies each used their natural and human resources to greatest advantage. Regional specialization was the single most important factor underlying the economic growth of the country.

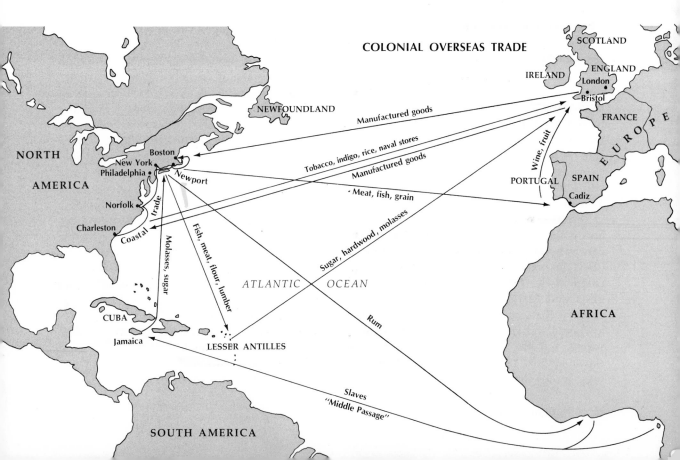

COLONIAL OVERSEAS TRADE

New England had a shallow, rocky soil, a short growing season, and a cold winter. These harsh conditions led many New England farmers to take to the sea as fishermen, whalers, and merchant seamen. By 1760 they were building their own ships at the rate of three hundred to four hundred a year. Ships loaded with dried cod, poultry, vegetables, salt beef and pork headed for the West Indies. There the merchants traded for gold and silver, which they then used to buy finished goods from England. Or they sailed the triangular trade route to Africa and the West Indies and home again. They carried rum and other goods from New England to Africa's Gold Coast and exchanged them for slaves. In the West Indies they sold their slaves and loaded their ships with sugar and molasses, which would be used to make more rum in the colonies. At each step they made a profit. Few seem to have worried about the moral implications of the slave trade.

The Middle Colonies—New York, New Jersey, Pennsylvania, and Delaware—concentrated on grain and livestock production. But because England had a surplus of these products, the Middle Colonists shipped much of their output to southern Europe and the West Indies. The rich soil and mild climate of these central states did not drive the settlers to seafaring. However, such inland cities as Philadelphia attracted oceangoing ships that sailed up the wide, deep rivers. As a result, they became busy ports.

The South was favored both by fertile soil and a long growing season. Here planters concentrated on tobacco, rice, and indigo (used to make a blue dye). Tobacco flourished in the Tidewater region (coastal Virginia and Maryland) and the Carolina hill country. Rice grew best in the South Carolina lowlands, indigo at higher levels. Labor was scarce, but the heavy work was done by slaves and by bonded white servants, who were under contract to work a certain num-

ber of years without wages (see p. 28).

Because crops produced in the South were in great demand in England, southern planters and merchants profited under Britain's mercantile policy. On the other hand, the rise and fall in tobacco prices badly hurt the Virginia and Maryland planters from time to time. Adding to the planters' financial troubles were their expensive tastes in household furnishings and their fondness for speculating in land. To pay the bills, they went heavily in debt to British moneylenders.

At the core of the thriving American economy were the merchants. The typical merchant kept many irons in the fire, since he could hardly make a living from any one specialty. From his countinghouse on the waterfront in a coastal city he sold real estate, made investments, lent money, underwrote insurance, distilled rum, peddled new and used ships, and sold finished goods, both wholesale and retail. Rarely traveling with his goods, he kept up a continuous correspondence with agents in other ports and relied on ships' captains for the latest market information. He was forever in debt to London and Bristol merchants and was constantly giving or refusing credit to local clients. His bookkeeping methods were sometimes quite primitive, but he inspired awe and respect among his contemporaries. Most businesses were family partnerships involving brothers, sons, and in-laws. One such successful firm was Robert Oliver and Brothers, located in Baltimore. Thomas and John Hancock were prominent Boston merchants, heavily engaged in smuggling at the time of the Revolution. Family fortunes that were made in maritime commerce were later invested in industry. In larger economic terms, the merchants kept up the flow of ocean trade, the lifeblood of the colonies. Their growing businesses attracted European capital, without which the colonial economy would have sagged.

Some southern planters displayed impressive skills in business management. Many built large fortunes, not only from the toil of their slaves but from business know-how and the diversity of their enterprises. In addition to being a planter, William Byrd of Virginia was also a wholesale exporter and importer, retail storekeeper, Indian trader, miller, and ore prospector. Land speculation was a major source of personal wealth.

The colonists were always short of cash. England hoarded gold and silver at home and at the same time discouraged the colonies from minting their own currency. And the wealthier southerners' love of expensive imported furniture enticed them to sign away their payment for tobacco and other goods before it ever reached their pockets. As a result, currency was scarce in America.

Mercantilist governments were wary of too much free enterprise. They preferred granting monopolies to select individuals or groups. To keep some control over the economy of the colonies, England paid bounties and subsidies and issued land grants, tax remissions, and prizes for quality goods. Corporations were almost unheard of in the colonies, but two were founded in the seventeenth century and four in the eighteenth. These were licensed by the crown for mining and land speculation. Without a license or official approval of some sort, it was hard to enter business. In addition, some local governments controlled wages, prices, and conditions of sale.

As the years passed, private enterprise and independent businessmen claimed a growing share of the total economy. But the mercantilist idea never died completely. Even though the colonists complained of the heavy hand of English paternalism after the French and Indian War (1754–1763), in their own assemblies they, too, set up mercantilist regulations when it suited their own needs. So it is often impossible to tell where free enterprise started and where government paternalism left off. The colonies operated

Merchants played a key role in the prosperity of the colonies by keeping up the flow of trade. By the middle of the seventeenth century the merchants, along with southern planters, had become the most powerful class in America.

DRIVE THY BUSINESS, LET NOT THAT DRIVE THEE. SLOTH MAKES ALL THINGS DIFFICULT, INDUSTRY ALL EASY.

EARLY TO BED AND EARLY TO RISE, MAKES A MAN HEALTHY, WEALTHY, AND WISE.

Poor Richard's Almanack *both reflected and helped perpetuate the work
ethic in the colonies. It also made its creator, Benjamin Franklin,
wealthy and famous.*

under a form of regulated capitalism—a mixture of government controls and free-market economy.

In the long run did England's mercantile policy, especially the Navigation Acts, benefit the motherland at the expense of the colonies? Did these regulations really inhibit the economic growth of America, as the rebels protested after 1763? Some historians point out that British merchants and bankers earned $2.5 million to $7 million more each year than they would have if there had been no Navigation Acts. On the other hand, the

Acts protected the colonies against foreign competition, especially from the Dutch traders. And in any case these regulations were weakly enforced. One British statesman noted that for the better part of a century Britain had treated the colonies with "salutary neglect." Even without legal restrictions most manufacturing would have been hampered by a lack of skilled labor and technology. It is significant that amid the feverish excitement of the Revolution, even the radical Sam Adams sometimes recalled the empire of the good old days before 1763. Certainly by the

1770s the rebels *believed* that the Acts hindered their welfare. And strongly held convictions are in themselves a historical force.

Another factor that contributed to America's economic growth was the work ethic (also called the Protestant Ethic, the Puritan Ethic, or—in Charles A. Reich's *The Greening of America*—Consciousness I). The German sociologist Max Weber, in his book *The Protestant Ethic and the Spirit of Capitalism* (1904–1905), contended that Calvinism accounted for much of the drive of prosperous people like the Americans. (According to the Calvinist doctrine, God rewarded the righteous and, therefore, material success was evidence of a virtuous life; material failure was evidence of a moral flaw.) Puritan New Englanders, Weber noticed, were far more aggressive capitalists than southerners, who were usually members of the Anglican church. He was much impressed by the popular sayings of Benjamin Franklin in praise of work, thrift, sobriety, and self-denial ("A stitch in time saves nine," "Waste not, want not"). Weber traced Franklin's proverbs back to the fountainhead of Puritanism, Calvin.

Undoubtedly the work ethic persuaded people to save their money, to work hard, and to do without at a time when these were useful virtues. Self-reliance and the courage to face hardship and danger in a new land were valuable assets in early America. Yet one can make too much of the Puritan Ethic as an economic stimulus. The world has seen prosperous nations which were neither Puritan nor capitalist and capitalists who were anything but Puritan. The work ethic cannot be altogether discounted; but it should be rated below the other growth factors.

The poor

In the New World land was abundant and easily obtained, and anyone who had land could make ends meet. While early Americans were not always well off, few people starved in New England and the Middle Colonies. Visitors to the southern frontier often complained of the shiftlessness, brawling, and drinking that went on among the poor white settlers. Many of them suffered from energy-sapping hookworm and malaria.

In America it was easier for the poor to make their way by honest work. In some parts of Europe, wrote Robert Morris in 1782, "nine-tenths of the people are exhausted by continual labor to procure bad clothing and worse food." In America "three days of labor produce sustenance for a week." Some commoners succeeded brilliantly in America. In his *Autobiography* the printer's apprentice Benjamin Franklin wrote about working his way up "from the poverty and obscurity in which I was born and bred to a state of affluence and some degree of reputation."

In the largest towns and cities the poor stood out more glaringly than in the country. In the city they had no way of growing their own food. The most desperate cases were the newly landed immigrants. A Philadelphian wrote in 1748, "It is remarkable what an increase of the number of Beggars there is about this town this winter." When winter came or when war cut off trade, some went hungry, some begged, and some even rioted. There were bread riots in Boston and Philadelphia in the 1720s when wartime scarcities made food unusually expensive.

Christianity defined charity to mean that the less fortunate would be cared for by their more fortunate "brothers." So the colonial towns took on responsibility for the poor. However, Christian charity often ran counter to the Puritan Ethic, which held that it was a sin to coddle a lazy person. Poverty was considered a personal problem, a fall from grace. By the same reasoning, it was assumed that any individual could rise up out of poverty by his own efforts. The American Quakers, who were among the most dedicated humanitarians, considered strong drink a major cause of poverty and publicly condemned it.

Charity was administered according to a variety of "poor laws" inherited from England but modified in the New World. The English maintained paupers and beggars in poorhouses and charity schools. They were given "poor relief" (direct handouts) from a special tax called the "poor rates." Sometimes they were put in private homes to work off the cost of room and board. Welfare was supervised by "overseers of the poor." Philadelphia, Boston, Newport, and other towns adopted variations of these English plans in the eighteenth century. Charleston allocated £900 for poor relief in 1743 and £6000 in 1759. In 1732 Quaker Philadelphia established the first public home for the poor to help needy immigrants.

Charity had its limits. When poor rates soared in Boston, the city pulled the welcome mat out from under penniless immigrants. Bostonians refused relief to many Scotch-Irish and to poverty-stricken war refugees from the interior. A public official in Boston, whose job it was to discourage strangers from settling in the city, turned away five hundred "undesirables" in the 1720s and 1730s. One Boston mob prevented an immigrant ship from unloading its passengers and reloading with grain for export, which they feared might raise the price of bread. Congregational ministers accused the wealthy of neglecting their Christian duty.

Although total destitution in America was relatively rare by European standards, the rich were steadily increasing their share of the pie. Their success accented the plight of the poor. Wealth was most evenly divided on the frontier or where there were many subsistence farmers. There the upper tenth of adult white males controlled about one third of the taxable wealth. By contrast, in commercial farming regions the upper tenth controlled over half the wealth. In Boston on the eve of the Revolution (1771), 15 percent of the white adult males held 66 percent of the taxable wealth, while 29 percent owned no taxable property at all. Since in some places ownership of property was required for voting, a number of men had no voice in government affairs. The declining opportunities of the younger generation to own land in the more settled communities may have contributed to colonial unrest at the time of the Revolution.

Workers: Free and Not So Free, Skilled and Not So Skilled

The economics of immigration

Labor was scarce and expensive in early America. There was far more work to be done—crops to plant, forests to cut, cities to build—than there were hands to do it. The scarcity of labor in America helps to explain why slavery was introduced, why wages were relatively high, why immigration was encouraged, and why Americans came to rely on machine technology.

Mark Twain once explained that he would rather have *employment* than *work*. So it was with many of the first English settlers. They prayed for "Spanish luck," whereby they could reach up and pluck gold from the trees and find rubies and diamonds to give to their children as toys. The straw boss of Jamestown, Captain John Smith, had nothing but contempt for the fortune seekers and

Captain John Smith (1580-1631)

THE PORTRAICTUER OF CAPTAYNE IOHN SMITH ADMIRALL OF NEW ENGLAND

A LABOR PROBLEM

"He that will not worke shall not eat except by sickness be he disabled." So declared Captain John Smith, president of the governing council of the struggling settlement at Jamestown in 1609. His was the first statement of the work ethic in America.

Smith had sailed from England in late 1606, one of seven councillors. The party, consisting of three ships and about one hundred colonists, arrived in Virgiania in May 1607. The expedition had been organized and sent by the Virginia Company of London, for Jamestown was less a colony than a business enterprise. Its main goal was to earn profits for investors back home, and the major undertaking was a search for gold. "Our gilded refiners with their golden promises," wrote Smith, "made all men their slaves in hope of recompense. There was no talke, no hope, no worke, but dig gold, wash gold, refine gold, load gold [onto] a drunken ship with so much gilded [mica-filled] durt."

The gold hunt left little time for building houses, digging wells, clearing land, raising crops, or dealing wisely with the neighboring Indians. Even if the colonists had left themselves time, most had neither the skills nor the incentives to establish a settlement. The colony was top-heavy with aristocrats—thirty-two present or future earls, four countesses, three viscounts, and nineteen barons—who considered such work beneath contempt. Smith insisted that they "never did know what a daye's work was."

Smith was a man involved in endless feuds and controversies. He had many adventures at Jamestown, including capture by the Indians. But the intervention of Indian Chief Powhatan's favorite daughter, Pocahontas, saved his life.

In the fall of 1608 Smith became the colony's sole councillor. To assure as many survivors as possible, he divided the colonists into several groups, each of which had to seek its own food supply. They received much help from the Indians during this "starving time." The following spring John Smith set out to force his companions to save their own lives by building a decent settlement, beginning to fish and farm in earnest, and laying in a supply of food to hold them over during the next "starving time." Still, by the time the next lot of colonists arrived in May 1609, only about one third of the original settlers were still alive. The arrival of the new contingent eroded the absolute power that Smith had held, and he returned to England in October 1609.

John Smith's outstanding leadership had not solved Jamestown's labor problem. Still, without him Jamestown went from bad to worse. The starving times continued until 1612 when John Rolfe, Pocahontas' future husband, introduced the cultivation of tobacco—a saleable crop. The Virginia Company then decided to sell land to serious farmers and planters. Adventurers and their servants needed a John Smith to drive them. Farmers and planters drove themselves.

dandies who first arrived there. "When you send again," he wrote to the authorities back home, "I entreat you rather send but thirty carpenters, husbandmen, gardners, fishermen, blacksmiths, masons and diggers up of trees' roots, well provided, than a thousand such as we have." In time, the illusion of sudden riches vanished, and the colonists settled for hard work.

Laborers were recruited from among England's poor, often by force. Sometimes they were sentenced, bribed, sold, or shanghaied into going to America. A motley crew of people crossed the Atlantic. The mayor of Bristol, England, described them as follows:

Some are husbands that have forsaken wives, others wives who have forsaken their husbands; some are children and apprentices run way from their parents and masters; often-times unwary and credulous persons have been tempted on board by men-stealers, and many . . . [who] have been pursued by hue-and-cry for robberies, burglaries, or breaking prison, do thereby escape the prosecution of law and justice.

Most English men and women migrated under some obligation to work in the New World. Judges sentenced many "rogues, vagabonds and sturdy beggars" to work off jail sentences in the colonies, usually for terms of seven years or longer. Few who wanted to go to America could afford the fare (about £10), so nearly three quarters of them came as bond servants. This meant they signed contracts promising to work from three to seven years without wages for employers who paid the price of their passage to the colonies. Those who signed such contracts on the European side of the water were called indentured servants (both copies of the contract were distinctively marked—or indented—for purposes of identification). Sea captains and merchants sold the contracts to American employers, who lined up to greet the ships and take away their servants as they came ashore. Slightly better off

were the redemptioners, or "free willers." They signed their work agreements in America and could bargain for slightly shorter terms of work. Some agreements required the employer to give the servant a plot of land and seed and tools enough to start a new farm when his term of labor ended. Thus most servants went on to become farmers or free wage-earners. The class of indentured servants lasted longer in the North than it did in the South, where slaves gradually replaced them.

The pay for wage workers was far higher here than in England—about 100 percent higher for skilled hands and 50 percent higher for unskilled. A Massachusetts carpenter could make from forty to seventy cents a day. A common laborer earned between eighteen and eighty cents. One farmer complained:

As to labour and labourers . . . You must give them what they ask: three shillings per day in common wages and five or six shillings in harvest. They must be at your table and feed . . . on the best you have. I have often seen Irishmen just landed, inconceivably hard to please and as greedy as wolves. . . . Our mechanics and tradesmen are very dear and sometimes great bunglers.

Skilled craftsmen

Skilled artisans were in special demand. A well-trained glassmaker, cabinetmaker, tailor, bootmaker, house carpenter, ship's carpenter, silversmith, or blacksmith could usually find steady work in any of the larger eighteenth-century towns. Skilled artisans who made goods for sale and employed journeymen or apprentices were called masters.

They often had small family businesses, attached directly to their homes. Their sons worked with tools, while their wives and daughters tended the shop. Some became exceptionally wealthy and influential. Benjamin Franklin, the printer, and Paul Revere, the engraver and silversmith, for example, became famous men in their own time.

The scarcity of labor undermined the standards of the skilled workmen. The traditional seven-year training period could not be maintained, since young apprentices kept drifting off. A Jerseyite complained, "Tradesmen . . . are permitted to follow their occupations, after having served a Master-Workman not above two or three Years, and sometimes not above a few months." The colonial governments lowered training requirements, but in time most of the regulations disappeared altogether.

In southern towns, skilled workers faced keen competition from slave artisans. Not only did wealthy planters have the annoying habit of buying finished goods in England, but they trained their slaves to become expert craftsmen. Many plantation owners had their own blacksmiths, carpenters, brickmakers, etc., and "rented" them to employers in Charleston and other southern cities. For this reason, white artisans feared and resented slavery and tended to move north.

In colonial times brainpower and musclepower were less sharply divided than they are now, and almost everyone could and did use hand tools. At some point in life nearly everyone, rich and poor alike, did some physical labor. Artisans made and repaired their own hand tools. (Those who made larger machine tools were known as "mechanics.") Colonial workshops were the trade schools for the coming Industrial Revolution.

Craftsmen took pride in their work. Silver-ware, cabinets, furniture, coaches, and fire-arms expressed the imagination as well as the skill of the makers—something that is virtually impossible with mass-produced goods. The final products were handsomely proportioned, finely executed, and in some cases exceedingly durable. Each craftsman had his own designs, although classical themes appeared in most works. Philadel-phia cabinetmakers were as good as those in England; Chippendale-style furniture pro-duced in eighteenth-century Philadelphia is to this day highly prized for its carving, de-sign, and solid construction.

Master workmen—silversmiths, coopers, wigmakers, etc.—formed guilds, which occa-sionally protected their interests by collective action. These associations helped maintain wages, prices, and conditions of apprentice training. The colonial governments opposed high pay for labor. In 1630 Massachusetts decreed that "carpenters, joyners, brick lay-ers, soyers, and thatchers shall not take above 2s. a day, nor any man shall give more, under paine" of heavy fines. The size, con-tent, quality, and price of bread was closely regulated. This was called the "assize" of bread. The first strike of master merchants in the colonies took place in 1741 when bakers stopped making bread in protest against government restrictions. But contests be-tween employees and employers did not arise until after the Revolution. The first genuine strike in the modern sense of the term—workers quitting to force their de-mands on their employers—occurred in Philadelphia in 1787 when printers struck for a six-dollar week.

Colonial artisans around the middle of the eighteenth century were often literate, inter-ested in science and in reason, and affected by the radical concepts of the European En-lightenment. The ideals of the Declaration of Independence appealed to them, and they took an active part in Revolutionary politics. They filled the ranks of the Sons of Liberty, which harassed the British, and joined the riotous mobs that sacked the governor's mansion or made life miserable for Stamp Tax collectors and customs agents. In Thomas Jefferson's thinking, the skilled workers, along with the farmers, would form the back-bone of the new republic.

Farmers: Nine Tenths of the People

Acquiring land

It is one thing to know how much wealth a society produces but quite another to know how evenly that wealth is divided among the people. It is the distribution of wealth that indicates a nation's welfare. Ownership or access to land was often the key to success in the preindustrial era, and nine tenths of the colonists made their living off the soil as farmers, planters, or farm laborers. The aver-age farm produced just enough to be self-supporting and contributed little to the over-all economic growth of the colonies. The family farm came to symbolize the nation's independence and pioneering spirit and to act as a profoundly important moral force in American politics.

If there was relative well-being among the mass of Americans, it was because many had enough land to scrape by on. Land was fairly easy to obtain. The poorest and most op-pressed white could normally acquire a patch on which to grow corn, hunt deer or rabbit, and thereby meet basic needs. There were various means of getting land. First, land was donated outright, especially to aristocrats or to friends of the officials who distributed the acreage. In the 1720s Virginia's Governor Spotswood gave numerous friends, who were also speculators, from ten thousand to forty thousand acres each merely on the promise of future payment. Second, the headright system allowed a settler fifty acres or more for each immigrant he brought over from the old country. Third, indentured servants usually ended up with some land from their masters at the end of their five- or seven-year contract. Fourth, squatting was a possibility. In many places new immigrants who were too poor to ante up the ten shillings or so required for a minimum purchase of land simply settled where they pleased. Pennsylvania had 100,000 squatters in 1726, and by midcentury the landowning class had no choice but to recognize their rights of possession. As the system of land tenure took shape, only blacks and Indians were permanently barred from becoming property owners.

Working the farms

There was always a frontier in the colonies, and farm families frequently set out on their own to pioneer new farms. Every step of pioneer farming required back-breaking labor. First the forest had to be cleared for planting. Some farmers preferred chopping down the trees, then stacking and burning them. Others adopted the Indian method of "girdling," or cutting away a ring of bark around the trunk and letting the tree die slowly. Once the trees had died, the farmer felled them, salvaged the lumber and firewood, burned away the stumps and underbrush, and used the ash as fertilizer. The average farmer felt lucky to prepare one stump-ridden acre a month.

The natural Strength and Fertility of the Soil we live upon, will, by Grazing and Tillage, always continue to us, the inexhaustible Source of a profuse Abundance.

WILLIAM SMITH (1728–1793)
New York jurist and historian

The plow, saw, hoe, spade, shovel, sickle, scythe, and fork were usually homemade and cumbersome. Besides planting and harvesting, farmers had to build dwellings, mend fences, chop firewood, and repair tools. Since crops would be scarce at first, they sometimes found it necessary to hunt game as well. In New England, even when the trees had been leveled, farmers still had to clear away boulders and rocks and nurse the thin soil. Only men and women with a stake in the land and a willingness to cope with adversity could make anything grow in these northern states. (Probably slaves would have been of little use.) Yet farmers could get by and live decently without cash or big investments in tools or seed. As one colonial declared:

My farm gave me and my whole family a good living on the products of it; and left me, one year with . . . one hundred and fifty silver dollars, for I never spent more than ten dollars a year, which for salt, nails and the like. Nothing to wear, eat or drink, was purchased, as my farm provided all. With this saving, I put money to interest, bought cattle, fatted and sold them, and made great profit.

Farmers had little trouble feeding themselves and their families. Their stock-in-trade was the versatile crop, corn: "the poor man's food, the pioneer's subsistence, the slave's usual handout, the feed of hogs, cattle, poultry and horses." Whites planted corn Indian style—in mounds prepared with fish

The vast majority of colonists made their living as farmers. In a pamphlet citing the advantages of immigrating to America, Benjamin Franklin reported that land was cheap, and a "hundred Acres of fertile Soil . . . may be obtained near the Frontiers. . . . hearty young Labouring Men, who understand the Husbandry of Corn and Cattle . . . may easily establish themselves there."

or other decaying matter. The corn crop ripened rapidly, needed little tending, gave high yields, and could be harvested at the farmer's convenience. It could be eaten as corn bread or as a hot dish that stuck to the ribs.

Other grains, and animals, also had a place in colonial agriculture. Wheat was a staple product in the Middle Colonies but was subject to disease in New England. Barley went for beer production. Oats were for horses—and for Scotch-Irish settlers who had the curious notion that humans could eat oatmeal. It was the very poor farmer indeed who did not have a horse to ride and oxen to pull the plow. Cattle supplied milk and meat. Sheep, a source of wool and meat, became increasingly common in New England.

Most farms were nearly self-sufficient. The French-born settler J. Hector St. John de Crèvecoeur observed: "The philosopher's stone of the American farmer is to do everything within his own family, to trouble his neighbors by borrowing as little as possible and to abstain from buying European commodities. He that follows that golden rule and has a good wife is almost sure of succeeding." Farm women and girls spun homegrown flax, hemp, wool, or cotton to make cloth and sewed the cloth into garments. Men and boys made furniture, wagons, tools, and other implements. This relative self-sufficiency distinguished the colonial farmer's life style from that of the mechanized and specialized farmer of our day. Absolute self-sufficiency was impossible, however. Guns

and powder, ax heads, kitchen pots, or a twist of tobacco had to be obtained from the country merchant or traveling peddler, in exchange for sacks of cornmeal, flour, or potash from burned trees.

Pioneer farming and commercial agriculture

The commercial farmer usually had it better than the pioneer farmer. His total acreage was probably larger (one hundred to two hundred acres) and the location closer to market. The family had cleared more land of stumps and invested more money in buildings and fences. The Middle Colonies, "the

bread basket of North America," had many commercial wheat farms. The "Pennsylvania Dutch" (Germans) of southeastern Pennsylvania set a high standard of excellence in agriculture. Many of their tidy plots and huge barns can still be seen today.

In general, agricultural efficiency improved very little in the colonial period. Farm technology changed so slowly that, as one historian expresses it, most farm tools "would have been familiar in ancient Babylonia." For the small farmer, modest improvements in life style came by abandoning worn-out land or selling an improved farm and moving on. But the increased distance from market and the difficulty of transporting goods might offset the advantages of moving. Though western land seemed endless, many factors—the crown, colonial proprietors, Indians, big landlords, speculators, tax laws, and the hardships of travel in the interior—reduced the amount of usable acreage. For decades angry tenant farmers of Pennsylvania, New York, and other colonies tried to acquire new land, while landlords and speculators schemed to keep it out of their hands. So, despite long hours of exhausting labor, the ordinary farmer's living standard rose very slightly, if at all.

Plantation agriculture was far more profitable than family farming. Larger acreage made planting more economical and allowed

The use of tobacco originated among Indians some time before Columbus' arrival in the New World. Tobacco from the West Indies was introduced in Spain in the mid-sixteenth century, and smoking quickly became popular in Europe as well as in the colonies. African slave labor was imported to America to cultivate and pick tobacco on the new plantations. Here slaves are shown housing, airing, and vending tobacco leaves.

a greater degree of crop specialization. The major export crop was tobacco. When King James I got his first whiff of a lighted pipe, he found it "loathesome to the eye and hateful to the Nose." But it had obvious recreational value and was touted by learned doctors as a cure-all for gout, hangover, and many other "grievous diseases wherewith we in England are so oftentimes afflicted." Exports of the "Jamestown weed" or the "stinking weed" quickly spiraled. In 1618 Virginia shipped 20,000 pounds of tobacco, and exports rose to 500,000 pounds in 1627 and 28 million pounds yearly by the 1680s. By then tobacco growing provided the foundation for an entire way of life in Tidewater Maryland and Virginia. An acid crop, tobacco drained the soil of valuable nitrogen. As a result; growers usually rated their second crop as the finest and their fourth as the last. After that they planted corn for a few seasons before moving west. Thus tobacco culture crept steadily inland.

For commercial farmers and planters, the availability of land and credit and the level of prices were matters of constant concern. Farmers who wanted to expand their operations often borrowed money to do so. Modest loans were sought from local storekeepers or already established farmers. But planters with big ambitions usually borrowed from the English merchants who bought their crops. If credit were to be "suspended for only ten years," Crèvecoeur said, "you would see a death of enterprise, a spirit of inaction, a general langour, diffuse itself throughout the continent. . . . The number of debts which one part of the country owes to the other would greatly astonish you."

Farmers and planters suffered from heavy taxes, high court costs, large debts, underrepresentation in government, poor roads, and lack of protection from Indians. Seventeenth-century planters repeatedly faced the problem of market instability. Tobacco planters realized that they were at the mercy of the

English merchants who bought their product, sold them goods, and loaned them money. Some wanted the government to limit the number of growers or to control prices or credit. They did not shrink from violence to make their grievances known and to demand government action. In the 1770s long-term indebtedness and shaky prices helped make revolutionaries out of the solid Tidewater planters, even the wealthy ones like George Washington.

As far as anyone could tell, the availability of land and the absence of industrialism would continue in America for some time to come. As Franklin wrote in 1760:

No man who can have a piece of land of his own, sufficient by his labor to subsist his family in plenty, is poor enough to be a manufacturer [industrial worker], and work for a master. Hence, while there is land enough in America for our people, there can never be manufactures to any amount of value.

Review

By the mid-eighteenth century the English colonies in North America had become an important world shipping center. Under a system known as mercantilism, raw materials were shipped to the mother country, and the finished goods were then sent back. The colonists often resented the control of their production and trade and English paternalism generally. But they also derived certain benefits under this system, and the controls were rather loosely enforced.

The most important reasons for the colonists' rapid economic growth were the abundance of land and resources, and their own developing business efficiency. They evolved a system of regional specialization and cooperation that led to a minimum of duplication.

Most Americans seemed to be hard working, thrifty, and ambitious—driven by the Protestant work ethic and inspired by the American Dream of success. Poverty, which was considered a personal failing, existed in the colonies, but it was much less a problem here than in Europe.

The demands of life in the New World created a constant labor shortage, and the lure of land and the freedom to move on caused the apprentice system to break down. These factors helped solidify the institution of slavery.

Although agricultural technology advanced very little before the Revolution, the availability of land boosted the colonies' wealth. Land ownership was widespread. But while the abundance of land gave Americans a feeling of confidence, the revolutionary spirit grew. Debts and wavering prices radicalized even the Tidewater planters.

Questions

1. Describe the way mercantilism worked. How did it benefit the mother country? Did it help the colonies in any way?
2. How did business efficiency develop in the colonies? What was the contribution of each region to the system?
3. What were some of the economic pressures that pushed the colonials to the brink of revolution?
4. Explain the attitude that colonists took toward the problem of the poor. How does their view contrast with current attitudes on poverty?
5. How was land distributed in the colonial era? How could people acquire it?

power

Congress Voting Independence, by Robert Edge Pine and Edward Savage.

This day the Continental Congress declared the United Colonies free and independent states.

From a notice in the Pennsylvania *Evening Post*, July 2, 1776

2

2

To Form a More Perfect Union

Watergate and its related scandals spotlighted the question of power—who has it and who wants it, who wields it and who abuses it. Is the presidency too strong? Is the legislative branch too weak? Do special interests control elections, Congress, and the administration? Confidence in government is at a low point. People feel cut off from government, powerless and apathetic.

"We are at a time in our national history when mistrust of the responsiveness of government to the popular will has reached a critical point—at which increasing numbers of Americans feel denied and even robbed of the power to influence public policy; a point at which the cry is 'return it to us.'" These are the words of former Nixon cabinet official Walter J. Hickel, in his book *Who Owns America?* (1971). Conservatives and liberals, young and old, whites and nonwhites, have all voiced the same frustration.

To understand power one must start with the Founding Fathers. No generation, not even our own, examined the question more searchingly than the men who wrote the Constitution. Basically they believed that power was a danger to liberty. It must be dispersed rather than concentrated, and all power must rest ultimately with the people. To what extent their ideals have been realized is one of the burning questions of our time.

Power—the way individuals or groups exercise control over others—is the overall theme of this chapter and four others in the book (10, 18, 26, and 34). In each chapter the first section deals with the relationship between authority and social and economic classes. The second section in each chapter describes the political system—how the electoral process works and how parties and politicians obtain power and hold on to it.

Ripening Discontent Under English Rule

Class structure in the colonies

The main sources of power in the colonial era were, first, the merchant and planter classes and, second, the English officials. There was no aristocracy of birth in early America, but there was an aristocracy of wealth. Power and authority gravitated to the rich.

When the first settlements at Jamestown, Plymouth, and Massachusetts Bay were under the threat of Indian attack, famine, and disease, the elite consisted of preachers and soldiers. Survival seemed to call for the leadership of men like Governor John Winthrop, the Reverend John Cotton, and Captain John Smith. But the clergy and military lost their supremacy as life became more secure, as labor became more specialized, and as surpluses grew. By the middle of the seventeenth century, merchants and big landlords had become the leading citizens in the North, and planters had taken the lead in the South. This elite would remain the most powerful class in America until industrialization brought profound change in the social and economic structure in the nineteenth century.

The wealthy colonial merchants and planters lived very well. They built handsome homes and filled them with elegant furniture. They stocked their libraries with leather-bound books, drank ale from silver mugs, and wore powdered wigs and frilled cuffs. Unlike the French, Russian, or English aristocracy, however, most of them worked full days at business affairs. These same men, who had made fortunes in shipping, trade, land speculation, slaves, or tobacco, controlled the colonial assemblies. They paid the taxes, lobbied for the laws, and held the best offices.

Closely allied to the planters and merchants were the lawyers, who had prestige, if not power. Next down the line were the artisans and mechanics. Farmers owned property and therefore could vote. Yet most of these groups were not represented in government. Below them were tenant farmers, day laborers and journeymen, stevedores and common seamen, bonded white servants, and free blacks. Lacking property, they could not vote or serve on juries. Neither could women, regardless of their social class. Slaves formed a separate racial caste at the bottom of the heap. Colonial social structure was anything but democratic.

The colonists generally accepted a social hierarchy as the norm. At an early date the Massachusetts legislature declared its "utter detestation and dislike that men and women of meane Condition should take upon themselves the garb of gentlemen, by wearing gold and silver, lace or buttons, points at their knees or to walk in bootes or women of the same rancke to weare silke." A man of upper rank who committed a minor crime could not be whipped for it, but he might lose the right to be called "Mister" or "Gentleman." In Maryland persons of "meane Condition" convicted of capital crimes could be hanged or drawn and quartered. But a "gentleman" was entitled to a proper and dignified beheading. Dress codes, legal codes, titles, and voting requirements drew a line between classes. In fact, social distinctions grew sharper as the decades worn on. In Massachusetts, religious qualifications for voting were replaced by property qualifications at the end of the seventeenth century. This move may have taken away the vote from about half the adult male population of that colony.

While classes were divided sharply, they never became rigid or permanent. A person

A person's stature in the colonies, as in Europe, was reflected in his or her manner of dress.

A NOBLE-MAN

A LADY

A GENTLE WOMAN

A GENTLE MAN

could move up—or down—on the social scale. Wealth could shift its owner up a class. Indentured servants could buy or earn their freedom, a landless laborer could become a farmer, an ordinary seaman could rise to captain or merchant, and an apprentice could open his own shop and become a master craftsman.

Government in the thirteen colonies

The control center of the British empire was located in London, thousands of miles from North America. The crown retained final responsibility for all that happened in America, although it shared authority with Parliament, which held the purse strings. The routine business relating to overseas colonies was handled by the King's Privy Council (an administrative agency) and the Board of Trade and Plantations.

On the American side of the Atlantic each colony had a governor who represented the king. The crown appointed him in the royal colonies, while the proprietors did so in the proprietary colonies (Pennsylvania, for example). In two colonies, Connecticut and Rhode Island, he was elected by property holders. The governor appointed judges, militia officers, and sheriffs. He called and dissolved the legislature and could veto its legislation. He worked with the councilors, who comprised the upper house of a two-house legislature. Normally they were appointed by the crown or the proprietors, although in Massachusetts and Connecticut they were elected. In most colonies the councilors acted as a supreme court. The elected assembly occupied a lower rung of government.

While representative government was an English tradition, it started in the colonies as a matter of administrative convenience rather than principle. The Virginia Company of London, the sponsoring corporation, felt that its struggling colony in Virginia would grow faster if the resident landowners became members of the corporation. So it asked the colonial governor to convene an advisory body, which in time became the first representative assembly in the colonies (1619). This House of Burgesses, as it was called, represented the entire propertied class. It later claimed the exclusive power to levy taxes. Similar bodies were authorized for later English colonies.

Considerable friction disrupted the administration of the colonies. Often newly rich and jealous of their rank, the members of the assemblies began to seize control over money matters and could twist the governor's arm by withholding his salary when he went against their wishes. By the 1760s they had wrested the greater share of power from the king's representative. Caught in the middle between the governor and the assembly were the British-born clerks and administrators, tariff collectors and soldiers, officers and maritime judges, who were stationed in the colonies to carry out the king's orders.

Pre-Revolutionary uprisings

The English considered themselves an orderly and law-abiding people, and so they were. But in America the class structure was flexible, and this led to instability. Social conflict was the rule. Small farmers and big planters, eastern gentlemen and western pioneers, old established families and newly emerging ones, debtors and creditors, landlords and tenants, masters and servants, recent immigrants and old settlers, and rich and poor tended to eye each other with suspicion. And, as we have seen, the assemblies squared off against the governors. The fact that England, the center of authority, was a long way off was another unsettling element.

Rebellion, sometimes violent, was not uncommon in the colonies. The greatest

A CITIZEN   A CITIZENS WIFE

A COUNTRY WOMAN   A COUNTRY-MAN

"They on th' Pillory stand in view: / A warning sirs to me and you!" Much of the crime in the colonies could be traced to the unstable social structure. Punishment was swift and, as illustrated in this Massachusetts broadside, public.

uprising prior to the Revolution was Bacon's Rebellion, which blazed across Tidewater Virginia in 1676. Nathaniel Bacon was a rich young planter from the backwoods who clashed with Sir William Berkeley, Virginia's iron-fisted governor for the past three decades. The disturbance was set off when the Indians rose up against the whites on the frontier and Berkeley refused to fight them vigorously. Earlier he had laid the groundwork for rebellion by refusing to allow westerners sufficient representation in the assembly. Infuriated by the governor's seeming lack of concern for their welfare, Bacon and a contingent of planters, servants, and slaves rode into Jamestown, demanding at gunpoint to be commissioned to fight the Indians. They burned the capital and took control over most of the inland part of the colony. Bacon had no intention of overthrowing the established order; he merely hoped for great-

er security and status within it. This first people's uprising in America ended when Bacon died suddenly of fever and Berkeley hanged thirty-seven of his followers. When Charles II heard of Berkeley's bloodbath, he exclaimed, "The old fool has taken more lives in that naked country, than I for the murder of my father." A century later Jefferson and other Virginians adopted Bacon as an early apostle of liberty in America.

When the Protestant rulers William and Mary succeeded to the throne of England and declared war against France (1689), two religious-political uprisings broke out in the colonies. The Protestant Association in Maryland, an anti-Catholic group of rebels in a Catholic colony, rose up and overthrew the government there. In New York, Jacob Leisler, a German trader, used the crowning of William and Mary as an excuse for a popular uprising against an autocratic government.

Leisler represented the small tradesmen and farmers who sought a voice in government and an end to the privileges held by wealthy merchants and landowners.

Three other uprisings are typical of the kind of organized violence that occurred before the Revolution. Culpeper's Rebellion (1677–1680) in Carolina overthrew the proprietary governor and set up a revolutionary government. Culpeper was tried for treason but acquitted. In 1741 small farmers and artisans of Massachusetts, hard-pressed by debt, demanded that the legislature establish banks to issue paper money backed only by land. But outraged merchants and creditors obtained a Parliamentary decree forbidding such a scheme. Between 1765 and 1771 the Regulator Movement gathered strength in Carolina. Complaining of lack of access to the courts, underrepresentation, and inadequate protection against Indians, a vigilante group of farmers calling themselves the "Regulators" seized the courthouse at Hillsborough. The governor ordered their arrest and classified them as traitors.

Street riots were also common in eighteenth-century cities. They were caused by artisans, laborers, sailors, and free blacks who, unlike the rebels mentioned above, had little or no stake in society. While they sniped at the rich and well-born, they rarely defied authority as such. In fact, their violence often *restored* order and corrected abuses when officials were unable or unwilling to do so. Rebel bands punished outlaws, secured land titles, corrected customs abuses, and prevented the navy from forcing men into service. In Virginia they destroyed tobacco crops in order to raise prices (1682). In Boston they stopped grain exports during a food shortage (1710) and closed down the houses of prostitution (1734 and 1737). Their actions forced a hospital in Marblehead, Massachusetts, to regulate a smallpox epidemic (1773–1774). And in New London, Connecticut, the rebels prevented one religious sect from interfering with the practices of another (1766).

Those in power often cursed the rebels but privately admitted that they were better behaved in America than in England. Here, at least, rioters avoided unnecessary bloodshed and carefully picked their targets. The authorities usually handled the rioters with a light touch and sometimes even silently approved popular rebellions. Riot laws were loosely framed and poorly enforced. The only sure cure for a riot, a standing army, was generally considered worse than the disease. Organizing the militia or sheriff's posses was almost useless, since the members were often friends and relatives of the rioters.

Rioters could often count on the sympathy of local officials. The king's agents—customs officials, tax collectors, surveyors, and redcoats—usually bore the brunt of the mob's anger. When royal surveyors tried to enforce the White Pines Acts of 1722 and 1729, which allocated special logs for use by the Royal Navy, a mob promptly "rescued" the timber and dunked the surveyors in a pond. Prominent local merchants, lumbermen, and magistrates stood by with folded arms. In November 1747, Boston's police hardly lifted a hand against rioters who prevented the Royal Navy from impressing (in effect, kidnapping) able-bodied seamen to serve with the royal fleet.

Harrassing customs officers was a favorite pastime in port cities. Rebels tarred and feathered many unlucky agents and often made off with goods that had been impounded at the customs office. Smuggling was fairly common in the port cities, and suspected smugglers were usually freed without penalty. Relatively few customs cases were tried in the colonies, because local juries rarely convicted for these offenses. Thus the tradition of challenging royal authority was well established before politics reached the boiling point in the 1760s and 1770s.

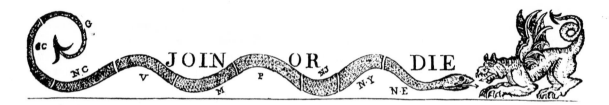

JOIN OR DIE

Revolution in the Making

The growing crisis

The revolution that began in the English colonies in 1763 was one of the great social upheavals of modern time. Like the French Revolution of 1789 and the Russian Revolution of 1917, the American Revolution changed the course of history.

The immediate cause of the American Revolution was England's attempt to make the colonies contribute money to running the empire. The war debt, created by the Seven Years' War, exceeded £133 million. To pay it off, Lords Grenville and Townshend asked Parliament to pass new revenue laws. These laws caused a furor in America from 1763 to 1765. The Sugar Act was the first attempt to tax the colonies in order to raise revenue rather than to regulate trade. Iron and hides were added to the list of goods that could be shipped only to England. The Currency Act prevented the colonies from issuing their own paper money, while the Stamp Act added a special tax to newspapers, legal documents, and even playing cards. Americans were forced to house and supply British redcoats under the Quartering Act. In addition, the Proclamation of 1763 was an attempt to slow the westward movement to the Ohio country.

The loudest outcry was against the Stamp Act. It touched the most vocal classes, especially the lawyers. Boston's James Otis argued eloquently for an end to taxation without representation. Patrick Henry claimed that the colonial assembly of Virginia had complete legislative authority. He denounced King George as a tyrant and in turn was accused of treason. "If this be treason, make the most of it," was his scoffing reply.

In retaliation, delegates from nine colonies to the Stamp Act Congress (1765) called for a boycott of British goods. This policy was effective enough to force Parliament to modify the Sugar Act and repeal the Stamp Act in the next year. Parliament issued a face-saving statement, reaffirming its right to make all laws for the colonies. The crisis was temporarily averted.

It is inseparably essential to the freedom of a people . . . that no taxes should be imposed on them, but with their own consent, given personally, or by their representatives.

DECLARATIONS OF THE
STAMP ACT CONGRESS, 1765

The Stamp Act resistance succeeded because of remarkable cooperation between the rich and the poor. The gulf between them was bridged by Sam Adams, a leader of the upper-class Caucus Club and a member of the Massachusetts legislature. He often visited the Green Dragon and other popular dives to conspire with unemployed laborers, leaders of street gangs, runaway slaves, and dispossessed artisans. Adams was the ablest organizer of rebellion—the ''grand incendiary'' of the people, to quote one English official. The Sons of Liberty formed under his direction in Boston, New York, and other port towns. They made life miserable for the merchants who imported English goods and for the stamp agents who enforced the law. Adams later became active in the Committees of Correspondence, which spread the rebellion throughout the colonies.

The crisis of authority flared up again in 1767 when the Chancellor of the Exchequer, Charles Townshend, took control of Parliament and issued new taxes. The Townshend Revenue Acts raised duties on colonial imports of lead, paint, glass, and tea. The Acts also gave the East India Company the right to bring tea into the colonies and sell it without paying duties. The outraged merchants of Massachusetts got the colonial assembly to condemn British taxing policies and to urge other colonies to resist, too.

Merchants again organized a boycott. When a ship belonging to the notorious smuggler John Hancock was seized, rioters forced the customs men to flee. Two regiments of redcoats were ordered to Boston in the fall of 1768 to bring the rebellious colonists into line. But the embargo spread. The House of Lords proposed that the Massachusetts rebels be tried for treason. The king agreed.

Stationing English troops in Boston escalated the struggle. The redcoats symbolized a standing army, a hated notion. The soldiers further angered local citizens by taking part-

A Massachusetts stamp master is stoned in effigy by the Sons of Liberty, while his mock funeral procession begins at left. In person, stamp masters were often not treated much more kindly.

The coffins in this account of the Boston Massacre represent the four victims: Samuel Gray, Samuel Maverick, James Caldwell, and Crispus Attucks. A fifth man was also wounded and later died.

time jobs during off-duty hours. On March 5, 1770, a crowd of workers cursed the "lobster-backs," as the British troops were called, and pelted them with snowballs packed with pieces of coal. Soldiers fired on the unarmed crowd, killing five people. A runaway slave, Crispus Attucks, who brashly dared the soldiers to open fire, was the first to die in what Sam Adams called "The Boston Massacre." Nine of the redcoats were tried for manslaughter, but most were acquitted through the efforts of their able defense attorney John Adams. Adams supported the Patriot cause but, unlike his cousin Sam, did not condone mob violence.

Weeks later, in response to a substantial drop in exports to the colonies, Parliament repealed the Townshend Acts (except the tax on tea). The rebels cheered their victory and dropped the embargo.

A year of relative calm followed, but the Tea Act of May 1773 revived the excitement. Through this new law Parliament hoped to save the mismanaged East India Company from bankruptcy. Parliament granted the company the right to export and sell tea directly in the colonies, bypassing the colonial middleman. In this way the company hoped to get rid of an inventory of 17 million pounds of tea. Angry colonial importers, smugglers, and the Sons of Liberty took to the streets to sabotage the law. On December 16, Sam Adams' rebels, disguised as Mohawk Indians, dumped 342 tea chests with $100,000 worth of tea into Boston Harbor. Other actions elsewhere prevented the importation, distribution, or sale of East India tea.

Parliament made up its mind to punish Boston for its Tea Party by passing a series of laws known in America as the Intolerable Acts. These regulations, issued in the spring of 1774, closed the port of Boston until the East India Company was paid for its losses. Parliament also moved the Massachusetts capital to Salem and reduced the authority of the colony's assembly. Smuggling violations were now to be tried in British courts in order to get around lenient American juries. And English troops were quartered in private houses. At the same time, Parliament stirred up the colonies by issuing the Quebec Act. The Act extended Canada's boundaries southward to the Ohio River, swallowing up land in the Ohio country that was claimed by Virginia and was eagerly wanted by Virginia land speculators. Nearly as irritating was the fact that it recognized Roman Catholicism in Quebec and gave Catholics civil rights there. To many New England Protestants this seemed a fiendish plot of the pope.

Philosophy and grievances

The First Continental Congress convened in Philadelphia in the fall of 1774 to deal with the Intolerable Acts. Fifty-five delegates gathered from all colonies except Georgia. They represented a wide range of political beliefs. Moderates like John Jay of New York and conservatives like Joseph Galloway of Pennsylvania took the lead. Until now the rebel argument turned on a narrow constitutional point: Parliament had no legal right to tax colonials who were not directly represented in Parliament. The popular slogan of the Stamp Act crisis was "No taxation without representation!" But gradually the rebellious colonists had become more radical. They wanted to change the form of government.

Most colonists admired the English system. But by the mid-1770s they felt that a headstrong king and a corrupt Parliament were twisting its principles. Actually the English government had undergone some reform in the preceding century. The monarchy had mellowed as the Civil War (1640–1649) and the Glorious Revolution (1688–1689) put an end to the absolute power of kings. Monarchs had to share authority with Parliament. Religious persecution had decreased. Thus George III was no all-powerful god-king like Louis XVI of France and the Russian czar.

To many English subjects the English government of 1689 appeared a nearly perfect instrument. Its strength lay in the balance of power among the king or queen, the nobility (the House of Lords), and the people (the House of Commons). Moreover, it protected certain liberties: trial by jury, habeas corpus, petition for redress of grievances, free assembly, due process of law, and freedom from taxation except by the vote of elected representatives. These rights of Englishmen were theoretically protected in the colonies as well as at home. What irked the colonial leaders was that all of these brilliant achievements in government seemed to be threatened by the recent actions of the king and Parliament.

The colonists were influenced by the eighteenth-century intellectual movement known as the Enlightenment. Leaders of the Enlightenment placed their faith in the scientific method and the use of reason. In the previous century the English philosopher John Locke suggested that a legitimate government represented a "social compact" or agreement between the governed and the rulers. Such a compact could be broken when the governed withdrew their consent. Americans were beginning to believe that they could preserve their rights as Englishmen only by breaking the old social compact and forming a new one based on a rational philosophy. In this sense the *means* of the Revolution were radical, while the *goals* were conservative.

Discontent in the colonies was widespread. Wealthy individuals had strong economic complaints as well as ideological arguments against England. They resented their growing dependence on British moneylenders for cash and credit. The Proclamation of 1763 that closed off entry to the West had narrowed their opportunities to speculate on land. Currency restrictions and the enforce-

In 1774 Congress called for a boycott of British goods to protest taxes and trade regulations imposed by Parliament. This English print shows Patriots forcing a Tory gentleman to sign a nonimportation document. The tar and feathers in the background were used to persuade the reluctant.

ment of trade regulations eroded their profits. Thus economics was one side of the coin, ideology the other.

The grievances of the poor, while less clearly expressed than those of the upper class, were also numerous. Any merchant seaman could be pressed into service in the Royal Navy for an indefinite tour of duty. Consumers had to pay inflated prices for imported goods, because British customs officials engaged in racketeering. Laborers resented having to compete with redcoats for part-time jobs. The Proclamation of 1763 angered pioneer farmers as well as wealthy land speculators. Being forced to quarter British soldiers in Boston and elsewhere could be a major expense for a small household. The small farmers of the South, who sold their rice or tobacco on consignment to big planters, took a sharp loss when Scottish merchants set up shop in the colonies. Thus both lower and upper classes had specific reasons to rebel.

How far the rebellion would go was still anybody's guess in 1774. Joseph Galloway, the gifted Pennsylvania lawyer, proposed that a new legislature, elected by the colonial assemblies, could share power with Parliament in America. His moderate plan called for a form of dominion government that would still recognize the English king as chief of state. The Continental Congress narrowly rejected Galloway's Plan of Union. (Canada later adopted a dominion government and remained in the British empire.)

At this point the radicals in the Continental Congress took command, led by Samuel and John Adams, Patrick Henry, Christopher Gadsden, and others. They pushed through the Declaration of Rights and Resolves, which rejected all parliamentary authority except in the area of external trade. At the same time, the Congress called for a new and widespread boycott against British goods. These rebels were called Whigs, after the party in England that favored popular rule.

Physical attacks on crown officials and their supporters increased. Massachusetts organized the Minutemen, a crack militia. In England, Parliament's efforts to restore harmony included a moving plea for moderation by Sir Edmund Burke. But such attempts failed to change the course of events.

Those colonists who opposed a break with England came to be known as Loyalists or Tories, after the conservative party in England. Few of them defended Parliament's bullheadedness, but they would not stomach independence as a solution. In their analysis Parliament was not attempting to be tyrannical but had fallen into a series of disconnected blunders. Most important, they respected the chain of sentiment, language, law, and religion that linked the colonies to the motherland. Snap that chain, and anarchy loomed, they felt.

In Virginia, Patrick Henry spoke of "liberty or death" and predicted war in Massachusetts. He was not far off. Parliament declared Massachusetts in a state of rebellion and ordered General Gage to seize the rebels' arms and to arrest their ringleaders. Pitched fighting broke out at Lexington and Concord (April 19, 1775), with nearly 355 casualties on both sides. The opening fire of this first battle of the American Revolution has come to be known as "the shot heard 'round the world."

The Declaration of Independence

In May 1775 the Second Continental Congress gathered in Philadelphia to manage the rebellion. It represented the radical transfer of power that occurs in all revolutions. In effect, this completely illegal body took upon itself the authority to rule the colonies, a right which had belonged to the king and Parliament. Radicals such as Sam Adams, John Adams, Benjamin Franklin, John Hancock, and Thomas Jefferson had the most

control over its affairs. By the time the Battle of Bunker Hill took place in June, Congress was dealing with a full-blown revolution. It named George Washington, a wealthy Virginia planter with a military background, as commander in chief of the army. Parliament had shut down practically all colonial trade and declared the Americans outlaws.

But oddly enough, as of January 1776 no one had thoroughly reviewed the possibilities of independence. Thomas Paine was the first to do so in his explosive pamphlet *Common Sense*. Paine had been fired from his government job in England for agitating for a

It is evident that they belong to different systems:
England to Europe — America to itself.

THOMAS PAINE (1737–1809)

strike of government workers. Benjamin Franklin had discovered him and urged him to go to America. Paine argued that it was not reasonable for the huge continent of America to stay tied to the apron strings of tiny England. He blasted the British system of government and went so far as to call the king an "ass" and a "Royal Brute." *Common Sense*, a forty-seven-page booklet which sold 120,000 copies in three months, was endlessly debated around army campfires, in taverns, and in government meeting halls. It still ranks as the country's most effective piece of political propaganda.

Fearing that talk of independence might infect bonded white servants, debtors, tenants, and even black slaves with dangerous ideas, the upper-class Whigs still shrank from cutting all ties with Britain. Yet in July

1776 the Continental Congress authorized Thomas Jefferson, Benjamin Franklin, John Adams, and two others to prepare a draft declaration of independence. They produced a brilliant document, mainly from the pen of Jefferson (1743–1826). To justify the Revolution, the Declaration of Independence listed a "long train of abuses" by the king. It spoke of "Life, Liberty, and the pursuit of Happiness" as fundamental rights and of government by the "consent of the governed." These phrases came from John Locke, although Jefferson deleted Locke's word "property" and substituted "the pursuit of Happiness," in order to give the document a softer, more "American" tone. The Declaration implied that the people had formed the British government of their own free will and were withdrawing on the same basis. Jefferson later explained that the Declaration was an "expression of the American mind" and that "I did not consider it as any part of my charge to invent new ideas." The document was proclaimed to assembled throngs and posted in town squares throughout the colonies to the accompaniment of cheers and drum rolls.

State governments under the
Articles of Confederation

Before a national government was organized, the states began forming experimental republican governments. The new state constitutions reflected a liberal spirit. They made the legislature nearly all-powerful and the governor almost powerless. Voting rights were extended, although not to the point of universal white manhood suffrage. Elections were made more frequent (semiannual in some states), property requirements for officeholders were lowered, and voting districts were arranged more evenly. Almost every state acquired a bill of rights. South Carolina had the most conservative constitu-

tion. In that state, only men who owned at least fifty acres of land were allowed to vote. To run for the senate, a person had to have an estate of £2000. And only Protestants were entitled to full civil rights. Democracy reached its high-water mark in the Pennsylvania constitution of 1776, which provided for a one-house legislature. (An upper chamber was believed to be an unnecessary hindrance to popular government.) It also eliminated the office of governor and threw out all property qualifications for voting or for holding office.

With the ink not quite dry on the Declaration of Independence, the Continental Congress created the Articles of Confederation as a constitution for the new nation. Fearful of centralized authority and confident of their own capacity to govern on the state level, the rebel Congress created the most decentralized government consistent with the idea of nationhood. The states remained sovereign, and the executive authority was put in the hands of a committee of the states. Each state had one vote in Congress. Money and military forces were to be raised from the states by quotas. Congress was specifically denied the power to raise an army. It was also forbidden to tax or to regulate commerce and had to share the money power with the states. Nine of thirteen votes were needed for Congress to pass any bill, and unanimous approval was needed for amendments to the Articles.

Owing to a deadlock over western land claims, it took five years for the Articles to be ratified. States with no claims in the West demanded that those that did have western holdings give up their claims. In the end, after Virginia gave up its western territory, all such lands became part of the nation's public domain. The Confederation went into effect in March 1781.

Pressure for a New Constitution

Problems for the young nation

The American Revolution was a power struggle that involved a contest over "home rule and who should rule at home." The home-rule battle was over by 1783, when England recognized the independence of the United States in the Peace of Paris. Whig merchants and planters, tenants and landlords, creditors and debtors, farmers and artisans, had all united in the war against Britain. But there comes a time in all revolutions when the feverish excitement wanes and the wounds begin to heal. The American Revolution sought a new status quo. The next phase of the struggle — deciding who would rule at home — took about five more years to resolve. During that time the Whig coalition showed signs of breaking up. The Whigs wanted further reforms that would make the new government powerful enough to prevent internal threats against law and order, protect the nation's trade against foreign competition, and generally broaden the avenues of economic opportunity.

Under the Articles of Confederation the new nation was facing depression, a dwindling national treasury, and stagnation in foreign trade. Both Britain and France closed their West Indies ports to American shipping. The depression in trade caused a decline in wholesale prices.

Hard-pressed debtors demanded that the states issue paper money. The uprising by debtors was most severe in western Massachusetts. Foreclosures on farm mortgages and the legislature's refusal to issue paper money or to stop legal action against debt-ridden farmers threatened ruin in the countryside. In 1786 backwoods farmers led by Captain Daniel Shays took up arms to protest state taxes, mortgage foreclosures, and jailing of debtors. Shays' Rebellion prevented the Massachusetts supreme court from meeting. The national government was powerless in such a situation. Finally the state militia tramped into the wintry backwoods and halted the rebellion. But the uprising had sent a chill down the spine of the propertied classes everywhere. Noah Webster announced in a widely reprinted newspaper article that he would "definitely prefer a limited monarchy" to a democracy. He would rather submit to the "caprice of one man than to the ignorance of a multitude."

Writing the Constitution

Shays' Rebellion lent urgency to proposals that the framework of government be revised. Congress limped along for weeks and months without a quorum as the delegates lost interest in the feeble government. A convention at Annapolis late in 1786 invited the congressional delegations to a meeting in Philadelphia to resolve the crisis. Some who wanted a more centralized government would have preferred a military take-over. These "nationalists" included Alexander Hamilton, Robert Morris, and Gouverneur Morris. In fact, they had tried to stage a take-over in March 1783 but had been blocked by General Washington. In 1787 the nationalists were pressing for a revision of the Articles of Confederation.

Fifty-five congressional leaders — merchants, moneylenders, landowners, slave owners, lawyers, and a handful of well-to-do farmers — met together in Philadelphia from May to September. Among them were George Washington, Benjamin Franklin, Alexander Hamilton, and James Madison. The prime movers at the meeting, led by

Madison of Virginia, made no bones about wanting a stronger national government, even if it meant scrapping the Articles of Confederation altogether.

Those who initiated the Constitutional Convention had clear-cut objectives. One was to provide greater protection for property owners against the rising tide of "have nots." They recognized that the country would be more sharply divided on the issue of property in the future. Another goal was to stem the democratic tendencies of the state constitutions, which gave the common people a greater voice in government. On the other hand, Madison and others greatly feared too great a concentration of power in anyone's hands, even the hands of the "rich and well-born" or of duly elected officials. Strong precautions were taken against such concentration.

The Founding Fathers were no fly-by-night rebels. They took their work seriously, poring over books on history, government, and philosophy to find the best models to follow. They concluded that each of the three basic types of government—monarchy, aristocracy, and democracy—had its own evils. A democracy, it appeared, always committed suicide by fomenting war between the rich and the poor. The inevitable result was the rule of a demagogue who became a tyrant.

The delegates disagreed strongly on many important points. The nationalists wanted to wipe out the states completely. Those who feared a strong central government wanted to preserve the Articles and the existing state governments as nearly as possible in their old form. One of them, Luther Martin of Maryland, seeing his colleagues' extreme eagerness to abolish the Articles, walked out of the convention. A moderate group, headed by Madison, wanted to keep the states but strip them of most of their powers.

Other splits developed: big states vied with little ones, northerners with southerners. By the end of June the delegates were deadlocked over plans for congressional representation and physically exhausted by the intense heat. Three states—Virginia, Pennsylvania, and Massachusetts—had by far the largest populations. They could easily dominate all branches of government if representation in Congress were to be based on numbers alone. And a walkout over this issue appeared likely. Franklin suggested hiring a preacher to invoke the Lord's help. But his proposal was killed by a tight budget and a fear that outside observers (the proceedings were held behind closed doors) might see the move as giving the last rites to a dying patient.

The Constitutional Convention came face to face with the issue of power. Power meant control and ultimately force. It implied centralization and suggested all the wrongs committed by the "Royal Brute" of England and his henchmen in Parliament. Power was a danger to liberty. According to James Madison, the chief architect of the emerging constitution, power rested on wealth and on the self-interest of organized groups. These could not and should not be stamped out, but they must be controlled. One answer, he felt, was to separate the legislative, executive, and judicial powers into three branches of government and have each one check and balance the others. "Ambition must be made to counteract ambition," Madison wrote. The balance-of-power idea was as old as Aristotle, but the nearest example of it was the

The great fabric to be raised would be more stable and durable, if it should rest on the solid foundation of the people themselves.

JAMES MADISON (1751–1836)

three-sided English system. There the crown, the House of Lords, and the House of Commons balanced off the interests of monarchy, aristocracy, and the common people.

Power balanced among the three branches

In the end the delegates showed an impressive willingness to compromise. Basically they were of the same mind on fundamental ideas of property and liberty and the powers of government. They agreed on a government with three independent branches—the executive, the legislative, and the judicial—and a federal system in which the states retained identity and influence but the central government looked after the national interests.

The argument between the big and little states over congressional representation caused great bitterness. But in the end the delegates settled on equal representation in the Senate and representation based on size of population in the House.

Northern and southern delegates compromised on matters of politics and economics—and particularly on slavery, which involved both. Some northerners were already violently opposed to slavery. Southerners demanded protection for the slave trade and guarantees for the return of runaway slaves. The Constitution, while it avoided mentioning the word slavery, allowed the slave trade to continue until 1808 and guaranteed the return of fugitive slaves who crossed state lines. For purposes of taxation and representation, all the whites of a given state would be counted, plus three fifths of the blacks. By not recognizing slaves as citizens, this compromise directly contradicted the idea of "the consent of the governed" in the Declaration of Independence. It would later torment the nation. Nevertheless, there would have been no United States of America without a basic North-South compromise on this issue.

East-West rivalries also had to be reconciled at Philadelphia. Pioneers were pushing the frontier steadily westward. Many easterners recoiled at the idea that wild-and-woolly frontiersmen might be allowed to form new states. A Pennsylvania delegate warned that "the encouragement of the Western Country was suicide on the part of the old States." On the other hand, shrewd southern delegates guessed that the West might help the South maintain its congressional strength against the North. They asked for the admission of new states as equals. Finally the matter was left to Congress, which admitted new states on a basis of equality but often after decades of waiting.

The Constitution also provided for an independent judiciary. All of English and colonial history pointed up the importance of such a branch. A federal court system was established, topped off by a Supreme Court. This body could review the decisions of lower courts. The Supreme Court eventually became equally powerful with the president and with Congress.

The longest debate concerned the question of the presidency. The nationalists wanted a new, separate branch of government—an executive with strong powers. Others feared that such powers might be abused. In the final draft, the president had considerable authority: to appoint top officials, to act as commander in chief of the armed services, to

The people should have as little to do as may be about the government. They want information, and are constantly liable to be misled.

ROGER SHERMAN (1721–1793)
American jurist and statesman

conduct diplomacy and sign treaties, to fight wars, and to pardon criminals. However, other branches of government would keep a check on his authority. In the last resort, a president who abused his power could be impeached. Treason, bribery, and "other high Crimes and Misdemeanors" against the state were grounds for impeachment. According to English tradition, this last would mean any act that undermined the Constitution. Some Founding Fathers believed the impeachment clause to be the most important feature of the basic framework of government. Madison considered it essential for "defending the Community against the incapacity, negligence, or perfidy of the chief Magistrate."

Ratification and the Bill of Rights

The Constitution still faced the hurdle of ratification. Since the delegates had been appointed by the state governments rather than elected by the voters, they could not claim a popular mandate. Even worse, by drawing up an entirely new document they had ignored Congress' instruction to *revise* the Articles of Confederation. There was a real danger that if they sent the infant Constitution back to Congress for ratification, opponents might kill it in its cradle.

To avoid this possibility, the delegates decided to seek ratification by special state conventions. Each state formed such a body by 1788. Those who favored ratification were aided by a series of brilliant newspaper articles written by Hamilton, Madison, and John Jay. These essays, which examine every facet of the Constitution, were later published as *The Federalist*. It still ranks as America's most important body of political writings.

Those who favored the old Articles of Confederation, such as Richard Henry Lee of Virginia and George Clinton of New York, called themselves Antifederalists. They tried to prevent the Constitution from coming to a vote. Sometimes they disappeared before a quorum call and had to be brought back by the scruffs of their necks. They failed to block the vote in any of the ratifying conventions, but they did force the backers of the Constitution to promise that Congress would add a Bill of Rights as amendments.

The Constitution was approved by a close vote. Voting patterns did not follow strict economic class lines but did have an economic bias. Regions dependent on external commerce or suffering a depression were inclined to accept the Constitution. City artisans, commercial farmers, merchants, and planters appear to have favored it. Areas involved in self-sufficient production, especially subsistence farming, tended to oppose it.

The Bill of Rights, as the first ten amendments to the Constitution are called, was originally suggested at the Virginia ratifying convention. Proposals for such a package had been turned down at Philadelphia by nationalists who wanted a stronger centralized government. The first ten amendments guaranteed individual freedom and restricted federal powers. The First Amendment guaranteed freedom of worship, speech, press, and assembly. Trial by jury was secured by the Sixth and Seventh Amendments. Other amendments protected the individual from unreasonable search and seizure, excessive bail and fines, and cruel and unusual punishment and guaranteed his right to bear arms in the interest of supporting a "well regulated Militia." The last two amendments reserved for the states and the people all rights and powers not specifically given to the national government by the Constitution.

Proposed by Congress in 1789, the Bill of Rights was ratified by the states within two years. Its ratification concluded the power struggle over "who shall rule at home." The struggle ended in a compromise that basically favored upper-class white men. Women, blacks, and people without property were excluded from any power in the new government. Yet the lower classes also had reason to hope for a better future in a free nation.

If I could not go to Heaven but with a party I would not go there at all.

THOMAS JEFFERSON   (1743–1826)

An Aversion to Party Politics

Was colonial America democratic?

Aside from the freedoms named in the Bill of Rights, Americans could make contracts and sell or buy property without restriction. Those who were not indentured servants or slaves could work for wages and move about freely. Property owners were assured that the government would not seize their land and would protect them from riotous mobs. They also expected that taxes would not eat into property and might actually help the economy. In other words, there was liberty in the marketplace. Widespread economic freedom in colonial America was reaffirmed by the American Revolution, especially in the new Constitution.

Most white adult males owned fifty acres or more and were therefore entitled to vote. But many other people were excluded from the decision making. The New England town meetings, for example, barred all "strangers"—Indians, blacks, Germans, Scotch-Irish, and Scottish settlers. They also excluded Catholics, Huguenots, Quakers, and members of other religious sects, as well as all dependents: women, servants, and tenants. Political minorities and dissenters were generally unwelcome.

Democracy in those days rested on a desire to maintain political and social order, rather than on a philosophical belief in the wisdom of the common people. The way to insure good order was for all families to be involved in village affairs. As one town charter said, there was a strong wish "to keepe . . . from us all such, as are contrarye minded." Peace and full agreement were the political objectives.

Forerunners of political parties

In most ways, colonial politics bore little resemblance to our own present political system. Professional politicians, platforms, and conventions did not exist in the eighteenth century. All developed after 1800.

Colonial government was run by gentlemen who donated their time as a community service. The rest of society was expected to accept their judgment without question. The effect could be seen on election day. The candidates came to the polls to pour out liquid refreshments and chat with the voters. Since there were no secret ballots, each voter told his preference to the clerk. The candidate thanked his voters, while his opponent made careful note of those who had snubbed him.

Mr Neilson's battle, with the Royalist Club

The colonists took an active part in local politics and often gathered at various men's clubs. This satirical sketch depicts politicking at the Royalist Club.

The Caucus club meets at certain times in the garret of Tom Dawes, the Adjutant of the Boston regiment. He has a large house, and he has a moveable partition in his garret which he takes down, and the whole club meets in one room. There they smoke tobacco till you cannot see from one end of the garret to the other. There they drink flip, I suppose, and they choose a moderator who puts questions to the vote regularly; and selectmen, assessors, collectors, firewards, and representatives are regularly chosen before they are chosen in the town.

Adams' father had politicked the same way in the men's professional and social clubs.

During the Revolutionary era politics took new forms. Boston's Committee of Correspondence was an offshoot of the Caucus Club, which was then led by Sam Adams. Twenty-one Bostonians were elected to the Committee, which spread rebel propaganda and preached resistance to new taxes. It soon won the official blessings of the Massachusetts assembly, and the idea spread to the other colonies.

Before the Revolution no one thought that the masses would take an active part in government. This changed during the Revolutionary War, and the state constitutions reflected a strong upsurge in popular participation. Between 1784 and 1786, citizens formed county conventions to air grievances over currency and other economic matters. These free-form political gatherings lasted several days but lacked permanent organization. They disappeared around the time of Shays' Rebellion.

Like those who love to fish but will not eat what they catch, the Founding Fathers were avid politicians but shied away from political parties. Permanent national parties reminded them of the English Civil War, in which the Parliamentary party fought the Royalist party tooth and claw. This political bloodletting in seventeenth-century England had forced many colonists into exile in America. Therefore, while colonists took *local* politics

However, there were aspects of local politics that still had a familiar ring. Every colonial capital had factions, cliques, and caucuses. Those who sought appointments to office, land grants, military commissions, or special privileges made political deals and compromises. In Philadelphia the Quakers and non-Quakers were locked in perpetual struggle. Anglicans and non-Anglicans opposed each other in New York.

John Adams' Journal of February 1763 provides a glimpse of city elections in colonial Boston:

for granted, they considered *national* politics a threat to constitutional government.

With the exception of Hamilton, few of the delegates at Philadelphia saw any positive value in national parties. Most, especially Madison, were dead set against them. They deliberately omitted any reference to political parties in the Constitution.

Under the awkward electoral college, citizens actually voted for electors, who then gathered to cast ballots for president. This complicated arrangement was meant to keep the masses from choosing a tyrant, but it was also designed to insure that all presidents would be elected on a nonpartisan ticket and would not be indebted to any one group. The electoral college worked this way during Washington's first election but not afterward. Still, many of the Founding Fathers would soon grow convinced that parties were a necessary evil to save the constitutional system from collapse.

Review

America was the first country born without a nobility or a peasantry. During the colonial era, power was wielded by the British crown and Parliament and by the local merchant and planter class. The problem of having the seat of power across the ocean caused friction. Colonists resented rule by the king's representatives and tried their best to thwart them. England imposed taxes on the colonies to help pay off war debts and added more restrictions to curb the growing spirit of rebellion. The Continental Congress of 1774 declared Britain a "foreign power" and polarized the thinking of Whigs and Tories. The Declaration of Independence, influenced by the Enlightenment, was an expression of American thinking and desires.

Revolutionary America was not democratic in any modern sense of the term. Initially, at least, no one felt that the mass of people could or should play a role in government, although the Revolution and state conventions began to change that view. The colonial social structure was based on definable classes, ranging from wealthy merchants and planters to indentured servants and slaves. About half the white males did not own property and so could not vote or exercise civil rights. But the social hierarchy was not as rigid as it was in Europe, and people moved from one class to another. The new state constitutions liberalized many laws and gave the people more say in government.

When the Articles of Confederation, which established decentralized government, proved unworkable, a new convention met in 1787. From this meeting emerged the Constitution of the United States, hammered out over months and built on compromise.

Questions

1. Describe the most important events, from 1763 on, leading to the Revolutionary War.
2. Describe the opposing positions held by the Whigs and Tories in the Continental Congress of 1774.
3. John Adams wrote, "Power must never be trusted without a check." What did he mean? Do you agree or disagree? Cite current examples to defend your position.
4. Read the Declaration of Independence carefully. Does any of it have meaning now, or is it simply a historical document?
5. Compare and contrast the Articles of Confederation and the Constitution. What positions did supporters and opponents take at the convention in 1787?

Paul Revere's engraving of the Boston Massacre helped turn the colonists against the British with its one-sided treatment of the incident.

3

59

3

The Shot Heard 'Round the World

In each of the chapters on War in this book (3, 11, 19, 27, and 35) the first topic is America and the world at large. This section reviews diplomatic relations as a background for studying specific military conflicts. The second section in each of these chapters deals with the nation at war — the way the country went to war, its tactics and battles, its war aims, manpower procurement, antiwar movements, militarism, and the domestic consequences. The present chapter concerns the colonial wars and the American Revolution.

War may be defined as organized conflict in which killing is not considered murder but is approved by society. Some naturalists and social scientists blame war on instinct or on human drives such as "the territorial imperative" (Robert Ardrey) or "man's natural belligerence" (Konrad Lorenz) or "the death wish" (Sigmund Freud). Yet these theories are open to debate. On the basis of the evidence it makes as much sense to say that warfare (which appears to have no *direct* parallel in the behavior of the lower animals) erupts because people have still not invented any way to prevent their aggressions from escalating into full-scale conflict. In any event, this book assumes that war is a *social invention* and that each instance of war can be traced to a *specific set of circumstances*.

According to a recent calculation, only 268 of the past 3426 years of recorded history have been free of war. In the past 300 years wars have flared up over commercial rivalry, dynastic conflict, religion, nationalism, the displacement of population, economic imperialism, and political ideology. While the United States has engaged in approximately 180 military actions of various kinds, Congress has declared war only five times.

America's cultural tradition has not been militaristic. The Founding Fathers strongly opposed a standing army. The Constitution put the military under civilian control, and, at least until 1945, the military establishment was not a major force in American life. The people have never fancied a military dictator and have preferred to believe that the aim of foreign relations is free commerce and peace. Organized antiwar sentiment dates back to the eighteenth century and has been expressed in every war since the French and Indian War in 1754.

This chapter concentrates on colonial expansion and imperialism and on the military aspects of the Revolutionary War. Preceding chapters have already touched on these themes. Chapter 1 dealt with the expansion of the British empire in economic terms. Chapter 2 discussed the problems Britain faced in running its empire after the Seven Years' War. The story here includes not only England but all the European nations that were engrossed in trading ventures, empire building, and dynastic contests. Many of the events occurred centuries before anybody thought of establishing the United States of America. Yet an understanding of this background is useful, if not crucial, to an understanding of America in world affairs today.

Europe's New-World Frontier

Nation-states exploring trade routes

Long before Columbus, Europeans had wandered to many distant corners of the globe. Vikings preceded the Genoese navigator to America by nearly five hundred years. Marco Polo made his famous round-trip voyage to China two centuries before Columbus set sail.

What was new in the fifteenth century was the involvement of European states in overseas adventures. Consolidated nation-states such as Spain and England had come into being in the fourteenth and fifteenth centuries. These kingdoms had suppressed internal fighting, taken over the territories ruled by independent princes, and set up stable governments. They were therefore free to expand overseas. By contrast, Germany remained a collection of minor states and warring fiefdoms. Until it was unified in the nineteenth century, it could take no part in the march of imperialism.

It was one of the greatest accidents of human history that made America part of Europe's frontier. In the fifteenth century China and India were the source of the most fabulous gems, spices, and tapestries. The best route to the Orient ran from Italy (Venice, Genoa, and Pisa) to Constantinople and the Levant (those countries bordering the Mediterranean Sea on the east). From there caravan trails crossed mountains and deserts and ended in China. But the Italians and Turks controlled this route, denying western Europeans access to the East. Hungry to share in the booty, the traders of western Europe began looking for new routes. Thus Columbus, backed by the Spanish monarchs Ferdinand and Isabella, set sail on a westward course to "Cathay" (China).

Sometimes the great movements of history seem to converge on particular individuals. Columbus was such a person. In the opening pages of his Journal he reveals why he undertook his voyage "by the route of the Occident"—that is, by a path "by which no one to this day knows for sure that anyone has gone." He hoped, he wrote, to enter the land of the Great Khan of the Indies and to make "a new chart of navigation." He also hoped to discover "the manner in which may be undertaken the conversion to our Holy Faith" of the inhabitants of that land, so that they could help Spain's holy war against Islam. Upon returning home, he looked forward to gaining personal recognition, so "that henceforth I might call myself by a noble title and be Admiral-In-Chief of the Ocean Sea and Viceroy and Perpetual Governor of all the islands and mainlands that I should discover . . . and that my eldest son should succeed me, and thus from rank to rank forever." Here in one paragraph, written by an artisan's son turned navigator, are the basic motives that inspired European explorers and colonists, not only in the fifteenth century but for centuries to come: adventure, religion, wealth, nationalism, rank, and power.

I discovered many islands, thickly peopled, of which I took possession without resistance in the name of our most illustrious monarch, by public proclamation and with unfurled banners.

CHRISTOPHER COLUMBUS (1451–1506)

For about four centuries after Columbus' discovery, America remained essentially an arm of western Europe. The Europeans considered the New World an important arena, if not *the* most important, in their contest for wealth and power. The gold and silver plundered from Montezuma's palace, the lumber and fur extracted from the northeastern forests, and the tobacco and sugar grown by slaves in the New World made up the purse of the game of empire and dynasty building played by Europe's monarchs. The colonials were pawns in the game. When a war broke out in Europe, they were expected to fight in the colonies. When a peace was signed in Europe, they were expected to put down their arms. True, those who lived in Albany or Boston or Williamsburg had their own war aims. But if these aims conflicted with the ones discussed by the diplomats at Paris, London, or Madrid, then so much the worse for the colonials.

Dividing the colonial pie

New World diplomacy started immediately after Columbus' first voyage, when Spain and Portugal at the pope's urging divided the new territory between themselves. Under the Treaty of Tordesillas (1494) they drew a north-south line on the globe 370 leagues west of the Cape Verde Islands. The treaty line cut through the eastern bulge of South America and gave Brazil to Portugal. The rest of the New World lands went to Spain. But this arrangement was short-lived. Once the other European powers could muster the ships and men for overseas adventure, the exclusive rights to America were broken.

Beginning in the seventeenth century, control over North America was contested by Spain, France, and England and, to a lesser extent, by the Netherlands, Sweden, and Russia. In what would become the United States, Spain, the strongest European power until about 1660, occupied a borderland that stretched from Florida to Texas to New Mexico and finally to California. St. Augustine, Florida, was founded in 1565 as a military fort, and Spanish missions were established there and in California. Spain continued to expand in America until the eighteenth century. Although no longer at the height of its powers, it was a thorn in the side of France and England in such areas as Florida and the lower Mississippi Valley. The Netherlands had a valuable trading post at New Amsterdam (New York) until England captured it in 1664. The czars of Russia claimed fur-rich Alaska and even sent agents as far south as California. The Swedes briefly had a colony on the Delaware River.

While England at one time or another clashed with all of its American rivals, only the contest with France took on monumental proportions. France had established colonies in Quebec and the Caribbean and sent explorers and fur traders into the Mississippi and Ohio valleys. Under Louis XIV it developed a grand strategy of controlling the heart of the continent from the Great Lakes to New Orleans. France's objective was to buy furs from the Indians and at the same time to limit England's expansion from the east and Spain's expansion from the west.

For a brief moment in 1686 the kings of France and England became more interested in European cooperation than in fighting over fur and land in America. In the Treaty of Whitehall they declared neutrality, agreeing that even if they fought a war in Europe, they would keep the peace in America. In practice the opposite occurred. The two powers could not resist plundering each other's merchant ships and Caribbean plantations. They came to blows in the Ohio-Mississippi region. Instead of remaining neutral they observed a policy of "no peace beyond the line." This meant that despite any mutual cooperation between them in Europe, in the far reaches of the Atlantic, the Caribbean, and the Pacific, all bets were off; all friendship treaties were null and void. So the two empires became embroiled in a series of four dynastic and commercial wars, beginning in 1689. Each war in Europe had a counterpart in America (see chart, p. 65). In 1763 England drove the French out of America and became the world's dominant colonial power.

Indians figured importantly in the imperialistic struggle (see also Chapter 4 on Race). In the competition for the fur trade, the Iroquois joined Britain, while the rival Algonquins sided with France. In the South the Cherokee were friendly to Britain until the mid-eighteenth century. The Creek nation was unfriendly toward the Florida tribes and so allied itself with Spain, as did the Yamasees after unsuccessfully rising against the English in 1715.

Even as colonials, Americans felt they were destined to expand to limitless horizons. By the time of independence the trade routes of American merchants ran to the Caribbean, South America, Africa, and Europe. Their eyes also turned to the western frontier, to the region beyond the Appalachian Mountains. It is not far-fetched to say that "freedom of the seas" and "open-door diplomacy" had their origins in the prenational period.

While Americans remained very much the pawns of England, they liked to think of themselves as not only physically separated from the Old World but also detached from its diplomacy, its intrigues, and its wars. Americans considered themselves morally superior to their Old World brothers. Tom Paine's *Common Sense* (1776) appealed to their sense of separatism by observing:

Any submission to, or dependence on, Great Britain, tends directly to involve this Continent in European wars and quarrels, and set us at variance with nations who would otherwise seek our friendship, and against whom we have neither anger nor complaint. As Europe is our market for trade, we ought to form no partial connection with any part of it. *It is the true interest of America to steer clear of European contentions*, which she never can do, while, by her dependence on Britain, she is made the makeweight in the scale of British politics.

Four General Wars

The wars of three monarchs

Of the roughly 175 years of colonial and Revolutionary history, 42 were spent at war, not including the additional years spent fighting Indians who were allied with France or Spain in the fur trade. A number of skirmishes between English and French and between English and Spanish took place on the fringes of the mainland colonies before 1688. But the fighting was scattered and failed to settle anything.

Americans have been involved in all of the nine general wars fought by western nations in the past three centuries. Five of the conflicts occurred before the U.S. Constitution was written: King William's War (1689–1697), Queen Anne's War (1702–1713), King George's War (1744–1748), the French and Indian War (1754–1763), and the Revolutionary War (1775–1783). (See chart, opposite.)

The colonial picture changed at the outset of King William's War, when Britain invaded France to maintain the balance of power on the continent. The long-festering rivalry between the French and Algonquins on one side and the English and Iroquois on the other resulted in several massacres in Canada and New York. During a blizzard in February 1690, a party of Indian warriors and French *coureurs de bois* (trappers) attacked the English fort at Schenectady. It was innocently guarded by two snowmen and nothing more, and the raiders fell upon men, women, and children as they slept in their homes. Sixty were killed and as many were taken prisoner, while some escaped toward Albany. Similar attacks were carried out on the Maine-New Hampshire border and at Portland, Maine. In swift retaliation Sir William Phips led an expedition of fourteen hundred men from Massachusetts to Acadia, Nova Scotia. There they seized Port Royal, looted the shops, and stole the communion plate from the church (Puritan soldiers justified this on religous grounds). The men returned to Boston in triumph. Phips later tried to capture Quebec but failed. This abortive attack was the first joint military action by several English colonies: Massachusetts, Connecticut, and New York. Much to the colonists' chagrin, King William's War settled nothing, for the treaty left Acadia in French hands.

In many ways Queen Anne's War and King George's War were replays. In Queen Anne's War the same rivalry over the fur trade stirred up the borderland. The French and Indians attacked Deerfield, Massachusetts, in 1704. The British recaptured Acadia, but a force of fifteen warships, forty-six transports, and many armed colonists failed to conquer Quebec. In 1745, during King George's War, the New England colonists cooperated with the British fleet and seized Louisbourg on Cape Breton Island. But to their annoyance, they had to return it to the French when the war ended. Schenectady, Acadia, Deerfield, and Louisbourg were legendary battlefields by the time of Lexington and Concord.

The raids and skirmishes on land were accompanied by piracy and privateering on the high seas. Protestant pirates loved pillaging the Spanish Main, as Spain's possessions in the Caribbean were called. Privateers (merchant captains commissioned by colonial governments to capture enemy merchant ships) chased their victims with great gusto and frequently with enormous rewards. Given the mercantilist theory that a proper national goal was acquisition of the largest possible share of the world's limited supply of wealth (see Chapter 1), pirates and privateers were valued agents of economic policy.

Not only was the Atlantic coastline threatened by raiders, but the inland valleys were assaulted by Indian warriors and foreign soldiers. In addition, merchant seamen were impressed into the Royal Navy. Officially declared wars also disrupted commerce, sometimes with serious consequences. Because the French laid waste to several British possessions in the West Indies during Queen Anne's War, the port of Philadelphia, which traded actively with the British island colonies, suffered serious economic losses. Pennsylvania wheat, flour, and bread backed up on the Philadelphia wharves, immigration declined, and real estate sales fell.

The militia was the main source of military manpower in those days. Practically every adult white male from sixteen to sixty years of age was considered a member of the militia—except in Pennsylvania, where Quaker pacifism held sway. As such, he could be called up for duty at any time and was subject to regular drill with his own weapons. On short notice he might have to help construct a fort, or stand watch, or trudge off into the woods to seek out the enemy. Sometimes men volunteered or were drafted as part of an expedition to capture French territory. Colonial assemblies did everything in their power to retain direct command of the militia—in other words, to preserve civilian control. A militia controlled by the governor, the king's representative, meant a standing army—a hated institution.

In spite of the frequent wars during the colonial period, pacifism was not unheard of. The Quakers were the most openly pacifist group. In 1689 the Quaker intellectual and proprietor of the Pennsylvania colony, William Penn, wrote a remarkable proposal for settling international wars. In founding Pennsylvania, he instructed his colonists to stay on friendly terms with the Indians, which they did with good results.

Oddly enough, warfare was becoming less brutal in Europe in the eighteenth century, although it retained an edge of savagery in America. Between the end of Queen Anne's War and the beginning of the French Revolution, generals fought for limited objectives only. Civilian and military casualties were relatively light. The intellectual community of Europe began to believe that war, like earthquakes, torrential rains, and accidental fires, was an unpredictable hazard but not a major disaster.

Attacking from ambush and fighting hand-to-hand, the woodland Indians were more than a match for the early settlers. Massachusetts placed a few top-notch militiamen

---

PARALLEL WARS IN EUROPE AND AMERICA, 1689 TO THE PRESENT

In Europe	In America
War of the League of Augsburg, 1688–1697	King William's War, 1689–1697
War of the Spanish Succession, 1701–1713	Queen Anne's War, 1702–1713
War of the Austrian Succession, 1740–1748	King George's War, 1744–1748
Seven Years' War, 1756–1763	French and Indian War, 1754–1763
The American Revolution, 1778–1783	American Revolution, 1775–1783
Wars of the French Revolution, 1793–1802	Undeclared French War, 1798–1800
Napoleonic Wars, 1803–1815	War of 1812, 1812–1815
World War I, 1914–1918	World War I, 1917–1918
World War II, 1939–1945	World War II, 1941–1945

SOURCE: Thomas A. Bailey, *A Diplomatic History of the American People*, 4th ed., p. 6.

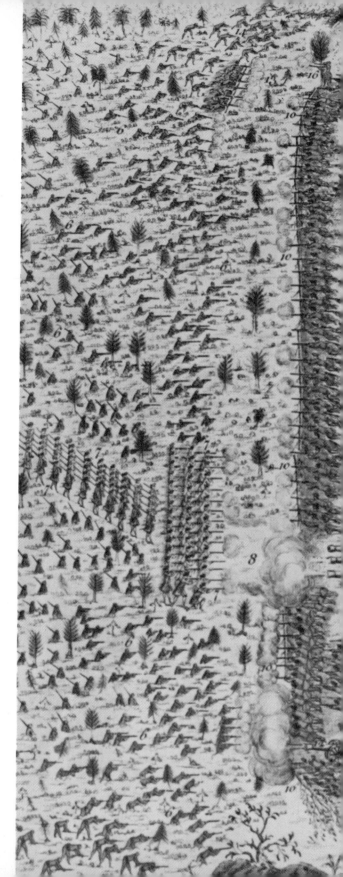

A French artist's view of an Iroquois warrior (above). French soldiers and Algonquin warriors attack the British and their Iroquois allies at Fort William Henry, on the shores of Lake George, in 1775 (right).

on half-hour call—they were the early model for the Minutemen of the Revolutionary War. The buckskin-clad militiamen sometimes carried Kentucky rifles, the first weapons that matched the Indian bow and arrow for accuracy and deadliness. On home ground, defending their own land and families, the farmer-soldiers fought exceptionally well. But when they fought in another colony, or against French or Spanish regulars, or had to go on extended duty and therefore miss the planting or harvesting season, their performance fell off.

The French and Indian War

Anglo-French rivalry reached a peak during the French and Indian War (1754–1763), called in Europe the Seven Years' War (1756–1763). Unlike previous contests, this one began in America and spread to Europe. It resulted from the deliberate effort by the English colonists to stop France's inroads into the Ohio Valley and the Nova Scotia

The British colonies bordering on the French are properly frontiers of the British empire; and the frontiers of an empire are properly defended at the joint expense of the body of the people in such empire.

BENJAMIN FRANKLIN (1706–1790)

peninsula. French settlers numbered only about sixty thousand compared to a million English colonists, but they had forged a powerful alliance with the Huron and Algonquin Indians and had a special talent for wilderness diplomacy and trade.

The strongest resistance to the French came from Virginia, whose royal charter gave it an enormous claim in the West. As Colonel Thomas Lee wrote expansively to the Board of Trade in 1750, "Virginia is Bounded by the Great Atlantic Ocean to the East, by North Carolina to the South, by Maryland and Pennsylvania to the North, and by the South Sea [Pacific Ocean] to the West, including California." This magnificent if theoretical domain of some 360,000 square miles was three times the size of the British Isles.

At the end of King George's War in 1748, the Ohio Company of Virginia, a large land syndicate interested in developing the trans-Appalachian West, sent a party to investigate its grant on the upper Ohio River. The French, anticipating trouble, strengthened their defenses at forts such as Niagara, Detroit, and Duquesne. In July 1754 Colonel George Washington, under official orders of the Virginia governor, tried to dislodge the French at Fort Duquesne (at the present site of Pittsburgh) but was forced to retreat. England then sent General Edward Braddock with a force of about two thousand redcoats and militiamen to the scene. His lack of familiarity with the forest cost him not only the Battle of the Wilderness (July 1755) but his very life.

This disaster brought about a major political crisis in Pennsylvania. For over half a century, since William Penn had founded the colony, Pennsylvanians had enjoyed friendly relations with the Indians. But as part of their tactics in the war, the French stirred up the Indians against the frontier settlements, which demanded protection from the colonial government. As a matter of conscience, the Quaker-dominated legislature in Philadelphia opposed all war and refused to vote any money for defense. But most Pennsylvanians were non-Quakers who wanted to undercut the authority of the Friends (Quakers). Scotch-Irish pioneers demanded western border defenses. When they did not get their way, they massacred a party of peaceful Delaware and Shawnee Indians who had lived harmoniously with whites for half a century. Their action forced a declaration of war in the assembly. Cash bounties were offered for the scalps of Indian men, women, and children. The Quaker radical John Woolman urged the Friends in the government to resign and disavow any responsibility for these warlike and inhumane acts. A large number did so. Some refused to resign, however. Of these, many compromised their principles by voting for arms. In any event, Quaker rule in Pennsylvania was at an end, as was Penn's experiment in brotherly love.

The Indian question prompted the colonies to cooperate on some solutions. In each of the four wars the colonists moved closer together on politics and military matters.

Their best effort came in 1754 when representatives of several endangered colonies met at Albany to discuss Indian relations. Here, Benjamin Franklin presented his Albany Plan of Union, which proposed a council of delegates from the colonies to draft laws, levy taxes, raise armies, and handle Indian affairs. It also called for a special executive, appointed by the king, to deal with the Indians. Even though the plan was rejected, it signified a growing awareness of the special problems relating to Indians and was a forerunner to the Articles of Confederation a generation later.

When the colonial conflict spread to Europe in 1756, Britain forged an alliance with Prussia, while Spain entered on the side of France. The major powers fought not only in Europe and North America but in the Caribbean, the Pacific, Africa, and Asia. The war went badly for Britain until William Pitt became prime minister and pursued the fighting with greater vigor. The tide of battle turned in Britain's favor in 1758.

The Seven Years' War reached a climax in one of the most important battles in American history. The Battle of Quebec broke the power of the French in North America. In 1759 a young British general, James Wolfe, daringly sent a detachment to climb the steep cliffs that guard the approaches to Quebec. Then, on the Plains of Abraham, the English soundly defeated a French army led by General Montcalm. Both generals died in the battle. After several more years of inconclusive fighting, France surrendered. At the Treaty of Paris in 1763 France handed over to Britain an incredible prize: all of Canada and all French-held territory east of the Mississippi except for the city of New Orleans. Britain also acquired East and West Florida. Many Englishmen felt Britain's glory was now greater than that of ancient Greece and Rome combined. Church bells in England rang out the victory until the bell ropes frayed.

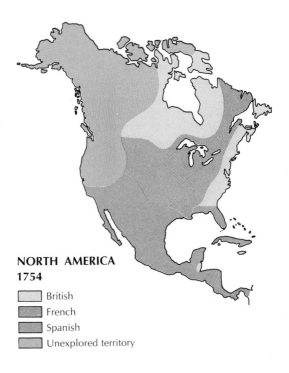

NORTH AMERICA 1754

- British
- French
- Spanish
- Unexplored territory

NORTH AMERICA 1763

- British
- Spanish
- Unexplored territory

New Yorkers topple a statue of George III in 1776. King George III was the
target of American protest that resulted in a total break with Britain and led
to the Revolutionary War.

The American Revolution

The course of the war

In modern times revolution often follows in the wake of war. The French Revolution of 1789 was preceded by a long series of wars that virtually bankrupted the country. Similarly, World War I spawned the Russian Revolution of 1917, and World War II helped bring about the Communist take-over of China in 1949. So from a historical standpoint it is not surprising that the Seven Years' War led to the Revolutionary War from 1775 to 1783. Britain's efforts to finance its newly won empire (described in Chapter 2) kindled a colonial rebellion a decade later.

What is surprising is that the American rebels *won* the Revolutionary War. Even Washington was amazed:

It will not be believed that such a force as Great Britain has employed for eight years in this Country could be baffled in their plan of Subjugating it by numbers infinitely less, composed of Men sometimes half starved; always in Rags, without pay, and experiencing, at times, every species of distress which human nature is capable of undergoing.

George III and his ministers felt the same bewilderment. How could a "disorganized rabble of peasants," lacking trained soldiers, defeat the well-drilled redcoats, led by first-rate officers and backed by the world's greatest navy? The redcoats had won nearly all of the major battles. Then why did Britain lose the war?

Certainly the British did not lack for a strong overall strategy. They planned to slice the colonies in two by driving a wedge of redcoats through the Hudson River Valley of New York. Then they would cut the two parts into even smaller pieces. But a major snag developed in putting this plan into action. In the summer of 1777 General John Burgoyne began to move southward from Canada. He should have been aided by Sir William Howe, who had over thirty thousand soldiers and hundreds of ships in New York City. But instead of going north, Lord Howe was diverted into attacking Philadelphia. He captured this target but opened the way for Burgoyne's defeat. Without having to worry about Howe coming from behind, the American armies, led by Generals Benedict Arnold and Horatio Gates, were able to surround Burgoyne at Saratoga, New York. The defeat and surrender of Burgoyne in October 1777 was a great military coup for the Americans—perhaps the most crucial victory in the entire war. It convinced France of the seriousness of the rebel effort.

Tyranny, like hell, is not easily conquered; yet we have this consolation with us that, the harder the conflict, the more glorious the triumph.

THOMAS PAINE (1737–1809)

France soon allied itself with the rebellious colonists. Eager to get back at Britain for the loss of Canada in 1763, the French king gave secret financial aid in 1776 and promised military support later on. Eventually the French sent ammunition, ships, men, and money, which greatly eased the cause of independence. The diplomatic alliance with France was a major factor in the rebel victory.

As General Washington took up winter quarters at Valley Forge, Pennsylvania, in 1777–1778, some of his cold and hungry soldiers went home, while others deserted to

**MAJOR REVOLUTIONARY
CAMPAIGNS**

the British. But the ones who endured that bleak season provided an inspiration to the Patriot cause. Dogged resistance would play a large role in the American victory.

Late in 1778 the British mounted a new offensive, this time in the South. It was led by the aggressive Lord Cornwallis, who punched through rebel defenses in South Carolina and drove north. Nathanael Greene's Patriot army inflicted heavy losses on the redcoats in North Carolina, however. Although Cornwallis did not lose any decisive battles there or in Virginia, he concluded that he was making little progress in the South and decided to pull his troops out of the Yorktown peninsula.

He never quite made it. Cornwallis had expected the Royal Navy to evacuate his troops, but a French fleet prevented the English ships from entering Chesapeake Bay. With Washington and about eight thousand men pushing southward along the Yorktown peninsula, Cornwallis was trapped. The Battle of Yorktown on October 19, 1781, marked the last major clash in the Revolutionary War. As the redcoats stacked their guns and surrendered, the band played "The World Turned Upside Down."

At this moment England faced the dilemma of greatly expanding its war effort or stopping it altogether. From a military point of view Britain could easily have pursued the war further, but its leaders grew convinced that the economic cost would not be worth the effort. On March 4, 1782, the House of Commons voted to end the war in America on the assumption that the costs of renewed battle would outweigh the potential gains.

The first "people's war"

The American Patriots won out against poor odds because they democratized the war and made the Revolution the first "people's war" of modern times. The financial and human burdens of war were spread over a broad popular base. The rebels fought what would be known today as guerrilla warfare, along with conventional battles. Washington's strategy was to fight in small units, stand and give battle only when victory was reasonably certain, flee when defeat was at hand, make surprise attacks, and live off the land. Of course, the Patriots were forced to fight many pitched battles with bayonets and muskets. But they much preferred the new style of fighting they had learned from the Indians and which was well adapted to the American terrain. The farmers in arms who lurked behind stone walls, trees, and hedges and fired their rifles with deadly accuracy made poor targets for the redcoats.

Manpower recruitment proved a great headache to the Americans. The army was made up largely of farmboys, since the colonies had no professional soldiers. A draft law was passed, but it had little effect in rounding up an army. Draftees could be exempted if they were married, paid a fee, or found a substitute to fight for them. As a result, the draft was more like a tax system than a means to recruit soldiers. Enlistees signed up for a matter of months rather than for years or for the duration of the war. Most of them expected to return home in time to plant or harvest their crops.

The citizen army fought on a shoestring budget. Congress had only limited war-making powers and could not enforce the draft, levy taxes for sustaining an army, or draw from a pool of professional officers. As Washington complained, "Almost the whole of the difficulties and distress of the Army have their origin" in the "want of powers in Congress." Congress insisted on doling out to General Washington just enough military aid for him to continue the war. More, they felt, might empower him to become a tyrant and topple the civilian government. The

An English artist satirizes both the British victory at Bunker Hill in 1775, which resulted in two British casualties for every one American, and the outlandish hairstyles of the time.

British redcoats in hand-to-hand combat with rebel forces at Bunker Hill. British soldiers were trained to advance in formation and hold their lines. While the Patriots also fought conventional battles, they preferred using "guerrilla tactics," which they had learned from the Indians.

states used printing presses to crank out money, which inflated the dollar value of goods. This democratized the financing of the war: the entire citizenry paid for it.

For all their hardships, the Patriot armies proved an important point after two or three years of fighting. While British forces could land wherever they pleased, they could not occupy the entire countryside at once. All territory not occupied by redcoats could be controlled by the Patriots. Moreover, whenever the British moved about, they were extremely vulnerable to attack. Yet their troops had to move to force the fighting, while the Patriots could play for time and merely hold

their own. This was Washington's strategy for survival.

The king's troops faced other problems. They had to pacify a vast area, yet there were few large metropolitan centers to capture. It was no easy matter to supply and equip an army over three thousand miles from home. The rebels lured them inland, and this cut them off from their main sources of supply and naval strength.

Britain's army and navy worked at cross-purposes for invasion and occupation. The high command made little effort to enlist Loyalists and incorporate them into their strategy. The few who did sign up proved

Naked and starving as they are, we cannot enough admire the patience and fidelity of the soldiery.

GEORGE WASHINGTON (1732–1799)

unreliable in the heat of battle. Hessian mercenary soldiers, hired by Britain, antagonized the public wherever they went. British officers also had a snobbish attitude that stiffened popular resistance.

Washington, the crucial leader

Looking back on the Revolutionary War, one cannot say enough about Washington's leadership. While his military skill proved less than brilliant and he and his generals lost many battles, George Washington was the single most important figure of the colonial war effort. His original appointment was partly political, for the rebellion that had started in Massachusetts needed a commander from the South to give geographic balance to the cause. The choice fell to Washington, a wealthy and respectable Virginia planter with military experience dating back to the French and Indian War. He had been denied a commission in the English army and had never forgiven the English for the insult. During the war he shared the physical suffering of his men, rarely wavered on important questions, and always used his officers to good advantage. His correspondence with Congress to ask for sorely needed supplies was tireless and forceful. He recruited several new armies in a row, as short-term enlistments gave out.

At a critical moment in the spring of 1783 Washington prevented a military coup. At the army encampment at Newburgh, New York, many officers complained about Congress' failure to provide back pay, pensions, food, and clothing allotments. Backed by General Gates and by Gouverneur Morris and other civilians who hoped to centralize the national government, the disgruntled officers prepared to send Congress an ultimatum: if Congress refused to meet their demands, they would take over the government. Washington personally urged the officers to reject the "infamous propositions" put before them. They accepted his advice, and so ended the first and only attempt at a military coup in American history.

The Peace of Paris and its aftermath

At the Peace of Paris in 1783 the American commissioners—John Jay, John Adams, and Benjamin Franklin—skillfully won a favorable settlement. They held out for the Mississippi River as the boundary on the west, cleverly outmaneuvering France, which was trying to sell its American allies short. Britain recognized the independence of the United States with generous physical boundaries, though several fringe areas were to be held jointly with Britain and Spain. The United States received fishing rights off Newfoundland and Nova Scotia. Slaves captured by the British were to be returned to their owners. Congress was supposed to "earnestly recommend" that the states restore land seized from the Loyalists, but the states failed to cooperate, and most land was not returned. The worst blow to the U.S. was Britain's flat refusal to grant the Americans trading rights in the British empire, including the West Indies. Since commerce was the lifeblood of the infant country, this was a grave handicap. For some years to come the search for profitable sea trade would be a major concern in the new United States.

Lucky is the revolution that avoids a reign of terror—and the American Revolution was

Americaner Soldat.

such a rebellion. Revolutionaries often try to unnerve the enemy through mass imprisonments, kangaroo courts, assassinations, firing-squad executions, destruction of public records, arson, gagging of the press, and general disruption of law and order. The American rebels did relatively little of this; most harrassment of Loyalists was confined to New England. Nor did the Loyalists resort to terror. Instead, the Tories fled to Canada or England, leaving their property behind. Many later returned and were granted amnesty.

War-making powers in the Constitution

The Founding Fathers' experience in the Revolution influenced their decisions on military affairs when they drafted the Constitution and the Bill of Rights. So as to "provide for the common defense" they placed the army under the command of the newly created chief executive. But by the same token they tried not to create the monster known as a standing army, a permanent band of paid soldiers. This, they felt, could destroy civilian government altogether. So they placed a two-year limit on congressional appropriations for the army. This policy did not apply to the navy, since, as Madison explained, the navy posed no threat to the people's liberty.

As veterans of "a bloody war against a bloody Tyrant," the authors of the Constitution were careful how they allocated the war-making power. They feared that a tyrant masquerading as a president could easily stir up a war to satisfy his own ambition and then justify it in the name of the people. They therefore provided that only Congress could declare war. Once war was declared, the president would take charge as commander in chief of the armed forces. By dividing the war powers, they clearly intended for Congress to check the president's authority and thereby prevent military adventurism. In later years the practice has not always coincided with the theory.

Review

North America was a prize European powers competed for in the seventeenth and eighteenth centuries. England and France became the major combatants and fought a series of wars. The French and Indian War finally assured Britain's supremacy on this continent. Although Americans liked to think themselves above European conflicts, they were actually a part of them. Up through the Revolutionary period they fought five wars that involved Europe. King William's War (1689–1697) against France witnessed the first joint military operation by several colonies, but it settled nothing. Queen Anne's

War (1702–1713) and King George's War (1744–1748) also ended with conditions much the same as they had been before the hostilities. The French and Indian War (1754–1763) was different in that it began in America and spread to Europe. The Battle of Quebec broke the back of the French in America. The American Revolution (1775–1783) drastically reduced Britain's hold on the continent.

Britain won most of the battles in the Revolution but lost the war. While the British fought a conventional war, the rebellious colonists, on home ground, fought what today could be called a guerrilla war, with a broad-based citizen army. Washington proved a great leader who shared the hardships of his troops, acted decisively, and stood as a symbol to his countrymen.

The Revolution avoided a bloody aftermath. For the most part, the rebels did not terrorize the Loyalists, and the Loyalists departed without launching a guerrilla counteroffensive of their own. At the Peace of Paris in 1783 Britain recognized American claims to a vast area but refused them trading rights in the British empire—a serious blow to the new nation.

Questions

1. List some of the motivations that gave rise to the age of exploration.
2. Which European countries maintained colonies in the New World in the sixteenth and seventeenth centuries? What areas did these nations control?
3. In today's world, do you think the U.S. should have a draft army or a professional army? Why?
4. If Great Britain was so much more powerful than its colony, why did it lose the war? Describe the circumstances that led to this surprising outcome. What different strategies did the two armies employ?
5. How does the Constitution deal with military affairs and war-making powers?

race

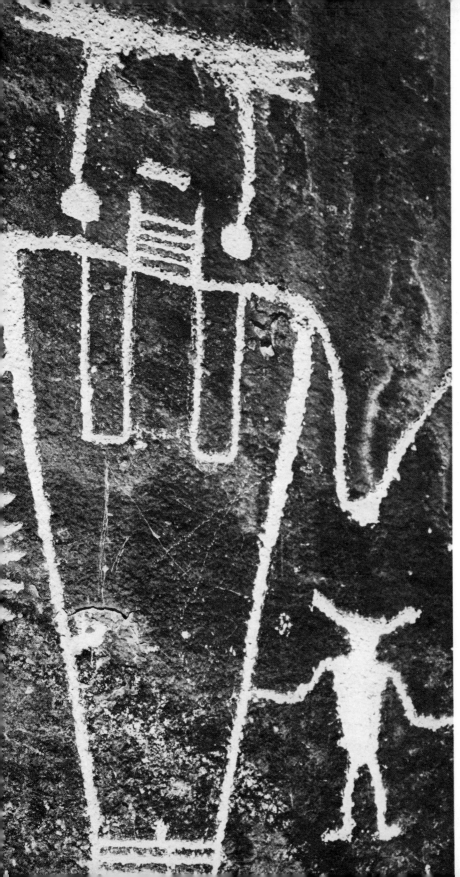

Petroglyphs, or rock carvings, provide some of the oldest evidence of Indians in America. These figures are from Little Rainbow Park in Dinosaur National Monument, Utah.

4

4

Red, White, and Black

The prejudice that separates "us" from "them" on the basis of skin color can be found among many peoples. Racism may occur whenever two or more peoples meet who look different enough to be classified by their physical features. White racism has been painfully apparent since the time of Vasco da Gama, when Europeans began to range over the globe conquering, colonizing, and sometimes enslaving "colored" peoples.

Typically, racial collisions occur in four distinct ways, each of which has appeared in the pages of American history. *Involuntary migration* took place when Africans were brought as slaves to America. *Military conquest* happened when the U.S. seized parts of Mexico in 1848 and took control of the Philippines in 1898. *Gradual frontier expansion* occurred in the West, where white settlers pushed the Indians aside. And *voluntary migration* has taken place when Mexicans, Cubans, Puerto Ricans, and Asians have entered the country.

The chapters on Race (4, 12, 20, 28, and 36) deal with the relations between whites and four racial minorities in American history: Indians, blacks, Chicanos, and Asians. (Discussions of Mexican Americans and Asian Americans begin in Part Two.) These chapters describe the contributions of minorities to the dominant culture, their efforts to achieve social justice, and the myths and stereotypes that have held them back. Related aspects of ethnic history are covered in the chapters on Nationality and Religion.

Earlier chapters have already touched on racial conflict in America. The South's economic dependence on slavery, the endorsement of slavery in the Constitution, and certain aspects of Indian warfare have all been described. The shift from early friendly contacts to hostility and fighting between Indians and white colonists and the origins and spread of slavery as a social institution will be explained in this chapter.

The Indians: "Savagery" Versus "Civilization"

Indian cultures in the seventeenth century

Many older books about American history group all Indians together and portray them as having had an unchanging existence until the coming of whites. Like trees, deer, and other elements of the landscape, they seemed to have no history of their own. Actually, Indian culture varied enormously from tribe to tribe, and while change was slower than among Europeans, it was constant.

When the English came to North America in the seventeenth century, there were nearly six hundred separate tribes north of Mexico. Each had developed in its own way and at its own pace. There were six main regional groupings. The *Northeastern Woodland Indians* lived in distinct communities and hunted in the forests along the Atlantic seaboard. They were the descendants of an advanced culture (the Hopewell culture) in the Ohio Valley. Among them the Iroquois of New York were the most impressive group. Further inland and less exposed to the English were the *Plains* and *Mississippi Woodland Indians.* These tribes of small-game hunters had settled down to farm about 1000 A.D. The group reached its cultural peak after it acquired horses from the Spaniards in the seventeenth century. The *Southeastern Indians,* whom the Europeans called the Five Civilized Tribes, were the Cherokees, Creeks, Chickasaws, Choctaws, and Seminoles. They built giant flat-topped burial mounds and lived in thatched huts grouped together on open plazas, a town design reminiscent of the Indians of Middle America. They made elaborately decorated pottery, flint beads, and copper ornaments.

The *Southwestern Indians* lived in remarkable apartmentlike complexes built of stone and adobe. Strongly influenced by the culture of the Mexican highlands, these Hopi, Pueblo, and Zuñi Indians irrigated their fields and produced fine pottery, stone carvings, and etched shells. The *California Indians* thrived on fish, small game, and an abundance of nuts and berries. They lived in tiny but very stable settlements for about five thousand years before the coming of the Spaniards. Finally, there were the *Northwestern Indians,* who were influenced by Siberian and Eskimo cultures, rather than those of Mexico or Middle America. Fish and small game were the staples in their diet. They were noted for extraordinary craftsmanship in stone and wood sculpture.

Friendly contacts between Indians and early settlers

For a few years after the settlement of Jamestown, contacts between the Indians of the Atlantic seaboard and the English colonists were friendly by and large. The early Europeans were more interested in trade than in land, and for trade they needed the help of

We found the people most gentle, loving, and faithful, void of all guile and treason, and such as live after the manner of the golden age.

ARTHUR BARLOWE (1550?–?1620)
English navigator under Sir Walter Raleigh

the Indians. In Virginia the Indians considered the whites too few and too weak to bother attacking. They even hoped to enlist the whites in their constant fights with the tribes of the Piedmont region to the west. Europeans' horses, muskets, powder, armor,

Ingalik
Tanana
Kutchin

Hare

NORTHERN

Kaska

CANADIAN

Slave

Tlingit

Haida

Beaver

NORTHWESTERN

Cree

Chinook
Yakima

PLATEAU

Assiniboin

Algonquin

Ottawa

Nez
Percé

Crow

Mohawk
Oneida
Iroquois

Wampanoag

Ute

Sioux

Winnabago

Onondaga
Cayuga
Seneca

Pequot

Mattole
Maidu

Shoshone

Comanche

PLAINS

Sauk

Potawatomi

Kickapoo

Pomo

GREAT BASIN

Pawnee

Miami

Delaware

Miwok

Illinois

NORTHEASTERN
WOODLAND

CALIFORNIA

Paiute

Ute

Arapaho
Cheyenne

Powhatan

Salinan
Chumash

Navaho
Hopi

Osage

Shawnee

Mohave

Zuñi

Pueblo

Creek

Cherokee

Yuma
Papago

SOUTHWESTERN

Chickasaw

Creek

Cochimi

Apache

SOUTHEASTERN

Choctaw

Opata

Concho

Seminole

MEXICAN

Coahuiltec

Huichol

INDIANS OF NORTH AMERICA

Tarascan

Toltec

CENTRAL

Maya

Aztec

AMERICAN

Mixtec   Zapotec   Maya

CHRONICLE: EARLY EXPLORATION
. . . the first painters of the New World

Teeming with a variety of strange animals, abundant with previously unknown vegetation, peopled by a curious race with unusual customs, the "new found land" of North America was a fascinating place for the early explorers. Many of them brought painters along to record the extraordinary sights in the New World for the people in the Old. Among the first were Jacques Le Moyne, who accompanied a French expedition to Florida in 1564, and John White, who made several voyages with British explorers in the 1580s. Engravings made from their paintings were published in Europe in 1590 and 1591.

Two hundred years later much of the New World was still unexplored. One of the first to make a scientific study of plant and animal life was William Bartram, a Philadelphia naturalist, who traveled through the Southeast during the 1760s and '70s. Bartram's carefully detailed drawings, his catalogs of species known and unknown, and his journal (published as his Travels *in 1791) won the praise of naturalists in America and in Europe.*

The Manner of Their Fishing, by John White

They have different kinds of fish, many of them never found in our waters, and all of an excellent taste.

William Bartram

John White

John White

William Bartram

The French Reach Port Royal, by Jacques Le Moyne (engraving by Thomas de Bry)

William Bartram

Prom. Lupi.

John White

William Bartram

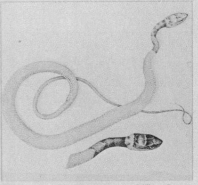

William Bartram

William Bartram

John White

This world, . . . is furnished with an infinite variety of animated scenes, inexpressibly beautiful and pleasing, equally free to the inspection and enjoyment of all. . . .

William Bartram, *Travels*, 1791

A Woman of Florida, by John White

The Conjurer, by John White

These people live happily together without envy or greed. They hold their feasts at night, when they make large fires to light them and to show their joy.

Their rype corne

Their greene corn

Corne newly sprong

Their sitting at meate

The place of solemne prayer

The house wherin the Tombe of their Herounds standeth.

SECOTON

A Ceremony in their prayer strange iestures and songes dans abowt posts carued on the to lyke mens faces.

The Village of Secoton, by John White

The Cliff Palace of Mesa Verde, in what is now Colorado, was continually expanded during its two-century occupation. The people of Mesa Verde were skilled potters and farmers, as well as architects. They had complex religious practices and traded with tribes as distant as California and Mexico. Up to four hundred people may have occupied the Cliff Palace at one time before its abandonment, for unknown reasons, in the fourteenth century.

and sailing vessels aroused the Indians' curiosity but not their fear.

At first Indians and whites found it easy to share the same farm lands. There was plenty of land for everyone. They visited each other's villages, gossiped, exchanged gifts, and attended each other's feasts. In at least one famous instance they were joined together in matrimony. Chief Powhatan's daughter Pocahontas married John Rolfe of Jamestown. Members of the two races occasionally fought, but the contests did not disrupt the generally peaceful relations between whites and Indians.

Once the English had survived their "starving time" and shifted in the 1620s from trading for furs with the Indians to planting crops on their own land, relations grew rapidly worse. Land-hungry colonists began making deep and permanent inroads into Indian farming and hunting areas. Here lay the fundamental conflict that would wrack Indian and white societies from the 1620s on.

The European concept of private land ownership was hard for Indians to comprehend. To them the land was Mother Earth—a universal, mystical life force. If land was property at all, it was communal property. They never understood how it could be chopped into small parcels or how people could own the land any more than they could own the air. The Indians finally traded away their land by bits and pieces, but this was forced on them in two ways. First, they came to depend increasingly on European goods, and, second, the whites began demanding more and more territory and would take it from them if they refused to trade.

The shift to vicious fighting

In Virginia the war between "civilization" and "savagery" dates from the uprising of the Powhatan Confederacy in 1622. For years Chief Powhatan had tried to appease the whites' appetite for new land until a point was reached where he believed there was no stopping them. The Powhatans then rose up in a carefully planned all-out war on the Virginia settlements, killing 347 white settlers. Retaliation was swift and relentless. One colonial leader declared, "Now we have just cause to destroy them by all means possible." The whites attacked the Indians, laying waste their fields and destroying their homes and canoes. The defeated had to pay tribute in the form of food, fur, and other goods. Each tribe of the Confederacy was forced to sign a separate treaty and was placed on a reservation—only to be evicted by the next wave of white settlers. Powhatan's son attempted another uprising in 1644, but with even less success.

The Indians of New England suffered a similar fate. The years of peace ended when the Puritans began to demand more and more land. The turning point came in 1637, when without warning or provocation whites descended on an Indian village beside the Mystic River in Connecticut. In what came to be known as the Pequot War, they set fire to the village, burning some six hundred Indians alive in their homes. "It was a fearful sight to see them frying in the fire," wrote the Plymouth governor, " . . . and horrible was the stink and stench therefor. But the victory seemed a sweet sacrifice and they gave praise thereof to God."

After about 1660 the Puritans had the Wampanoags of Massachusetts completely under their power. For the next fourteen years the young chief Philip (Metacom) secretly tried to unify the New England tribes for a counterattack. King Philip's War (1675–1676) broke out when the warriors at-

Settlers lived under the constant threat of Indian attack, inspired in large part by the colonists' demand for more and more land and by their mistreatment of the Indians. Tales of Indian savagery were often used to justify further mistreatment.

tacked over half of the ninety white settlements in New England, destroying about a dozen of them and killing hundreds of whites. The Puritans, who slaughtered Indian women and children with gusto, denounced Philip as a "hellhound, fiend, serpent, caitiff and dog." Betrayed by Indian allies, Philip was shot and killed, and his family was enslaved. His corpse was quartered and his head displayed on a pole in Plymouth for twenty-five years.

After winning the French and Indian War in 1763, the British decided they could cut off most gifts to the Indians. This enraged the Algonquin tribes of the Ohio Valley, who were traditional enemies of the British. Indian resentment was further heightened by powerful religious leaders who advised their people to resist the spread of white culture. The Ottawa chief Pontiac, a former ally of the French, forged a coalition of eighteen tribes to resist British authority in the Ohio Valley. What the whites called Pontiac's Conspiracy ("War for Indian Independence" would have been just as appropriate) started in 1763. It brought havoc to numerous wilderness fortresses and settlements, most importantly Fort Detroit. During the fighting, British General Jeffrey Amherst advised his officers: "You will do well to try to inoculate the Indians by means of blankets, as well as to try every other method that can serve to extirpate this execrable race. I should be very glad if your scheme for hunting them down by dogs could take effect." In his view, Indians were "the vilest race of beings that ever infested the earth." Pontiac beseiged Detroit for almost a year, and his rebellion continued until 1766.

The 1770s marked an important turning point for the Iroquois. At the time of the Revolutionary War the Iroquois Confederacy held the balance of power in the Appalachian backland. While they generally favored Britain for its attempts to restrain the westward movement of white settlements, most of the tribes of the Confederacy decided to remain neutral and sit out the family quarrel of the whites. Only the Mohawks, led by Chief Joseph Brant, took definite sides. They joined General Burgoyne's campaign in New York. Indian warriors made devastating sweeps against the towns of the Mohawk Valley in 1778. These attacks were soon avenged by the American General John Sullivan. In Pennsylvania and New York he wiped out some of the most advanced Indian settlements in North America. The five thousand Patriots who severely defeated a combined force of English and Iroquois at Newtown, New York, in 1779 broke the Iroquois' strength. Sullivan's officers toasted "civilization or death to all American savages!" Most of the Mohawks retreated into Canada, leaving the Iroquois nation permanently split and shorn of much of its power.

At no time did the English seek to destroy all Indian nations. Quite the contrary, they always considered the fur trade one of the mainstays of the empire. Without Indian cooperation the fur trade would have perished. The French were stiff competitors. To keep beaver and other pelts flowing to Britain instead of France, the English established several trading companies. The most notable of these was the Hudson's Bay Company. Britain's greatest success in the eighteenth century was its ability to woo the Iroquois over to the English side. The Five Nations of the Iroquois Confederacy—Mohawk, Seneca, Onondaga, Oneida, and Cayuga—served as the middlemen between the tribes of the West, who did the actual trapping and hunting, and the fur trading posts of the East. In exchange for furs the English gave the Indians weapons, blankets, various metal items, and, of course, rum and whiskey.

Whites also tried to enslave Indians. Of the thousands of Indians who were taken prisoner in the seventeenth-century wars, some were sold as slaves to West Indies planters. This practice conformed to an ancient but dying European tradition of enslaving "heathens" captured in a "just war." In general, however, the whites failed in trying to make slaves of their Indian captives — partly because the Indians were highly susceptible to diseases carried by whites. Many more Indians died from diseases like smallpox, measles, typhoid, tuberculosis, and syphilis — for which they had no immunity — than died in warfare. Furthermore, Indian slaves could readily disappear into the forest and find their way back to their own villages. When the white slave traders began to import blacks in large numbers, the futile efforts to enslave Indians were given up for the most part.

Savages we call them, because their manners differ from ours.

BENJAMIN FRANKLIN (1706–1790)

The noble or barbarous savage?

The American colonists had a split image of the Indians. On the one side was the picture of the noble savage. The French philosopher Jean-Jacques Rousseau popularized the idea of the noble savage, and Benjamin Franklin and others took it up in America. Indians were seen as innocents living in a state of nature, untroubled by the corrupting influences of property, greed, and pettiness. They lived in rhythm with nature, which produced a poetic and philosophic turn of mind. Above all, they cherished their freedom. This view was especially fashionable among intellectuals and city people, who had never lived on the frontier. In contrast to such romantic theorizing, some missionaries, fur traders, and government officials who knew the Indians at first hand had developed a deep respect and admiration for their culture.

The image of the barbarous savage was much more widespread in America. The pioneer farmers, looking at Indians through their gun sights, did not see innocence or nobility. The Indians, most whites believed, were by nature brutal and warlike. Thus the Declaration of Independence complained bitterly that the king was stirring up "the merciless Indian Savage, whose known rule of warfare, is an undistinguished destruction of all ages, sexes and conditions." Further-

more, whites believed that the Indians lacked proper concepts of God, progress, property, and orderly government. For at least two centuries, presidents and common folk, northerners and southerners, soldiers and farmers, historians and missionaries, children and adults viewed the Indians in this negative light.

Many Indians were indeed ruthless to their enemies. But the stereotype of the barbarous savage illustrates what Sigmund Freud called "projection" — attributing one's own bad characteristics to others. Pioneers enjoyed few refinements in their lives and suffered from monotony, illness, and backbreaking work. They believed themselves to be tainted with original sin and tempted by Satan. Many were *drawn* to the "primitivism" of the Indians (and blacks). But at the same time, they feared the loss of civilization on the frontier — feared their *own* barbarous actions. To seize Indian land they often killed innocent men, women, and children. This was easier to do if they pictured Indians as inhuman.

Did the English treat the Indian better than other European colonists did? They certainly considered themselves far more humane than the Spaniards, their mortal enemies in the great ideological contest between Catholics and Protestants. They accepted as gospel truth their own propaganda line, the "black legend of Spanish cruelty to the Indians." Yet while the Spaniards did in fact kill vast numbers of Indians, it is also true that they regarded Indians as children of God, with souls, and protected them by law. They were willing to marry Indian women and acknowledge their offspring and to grant equal social status to Christianized Indians. The Spanish were more interested in exploiting Indian labor than in robbing them of their land. Of all the major European colonizers, the French had the best overall relationship with the Indians. They had no interest in exploiting their labor or pushing them off the land.

Changes in Indian cultures

From the earliest times, Indian cultures had been constantly changing. The more dynamic eastern tribes had accepted or rejected the cultural gifts of neighboring peoples for centuries. But with the arrival of the colonists the process was speeded up, and the changes became more profound. Muskets and knives improved the Indians' capacity to hunt and triumph over their enemies. Iron kettles outlasted clay pots and woven baskets. Metal hooks simplified fishing. The Europeans' sheep provided mutton, a pleasant change in diet, as well as wool for warmth. The horse, which strayed or was stolen from the Spaniards in New Mexico in the 1680s, was traded away successively to other tribes until it galloped into the Great Plains area in the early eighteenth century.

These exotic four-legged creatures revolutionized the life style of the Plains and Rocky Mountain Indians like the Sioux and the Nez Percé. Instead of tending small vegetable gardens and hunting locally, the Sioux were now able to follow the buffalo for hundreds of miles, to haul heavier camping gear, and to fight enemies more effectively. Everything, from the size of their tepees to the intensity of their religion, changed. Eventually, some Plains peoples could not conceive of life without horses. The Navajo say, "If there were no horses, there would be no Navajos."

Like all cultures, Indian tribes could absorb certain changes into their way of life without destroying it. But they acquired one product—whiskey—that brought nothing but ruin. Along with disease, it was the single most destructive element introduced by the whites.

Compared with the French and Spaniards, the English made only hit-or-miss efforts to convert Indians to Christianity. As worshipers of many gods, the Indians could accept Jesus as long as they did not have to abandon their own Spirits. Protestants were less tolerant of this attitude than Catholics. Some Indians adopted Christianity and lived under white protection. The peaceful Delaware Indians, for example, enjoyed fifty years of good relations with the whites at Conestoga and Lancaster in Pennsylvania.

While most Protestant ministers supported the wars against the Indians, a few took a different approach. In New England the Puritan John Eliot translated the Bible into an Indian language and converted some two thousand "praying Indians" by the time of King Philip's War. Roger Williams, who believed that Indians had full rights to the land and deserved equal consideration as human beings, converted many Indians by preaching in an easygoing and intimate manner. Still, Protestantism was a white "gift" which Indians did not take to with great enthusiasm, partly because whites rejected intermarriage. This was a point some whites understood. William Byrd of Westover, Virginia, observed that "a sprightly Lover is the most prevailing Missionary that can be sent amongst these, or any other Infidels."

Indian ways that whites adopted

Indians contributed much to American culture. At the top of the list perhaps is a host of foods—maize or corn, beans, squash, and pumpkins. That vital export item, tobacco, was originally a sacred Indian plant. Herbal remedies, some of them far more effective than European medicine, were slowly adopted by white doctors. The Indians' knowledge of woodcraft was unexcelled, and the Europeans were eager to learn their skills. Snowshoes, buckskin clothes, and canoes were also copied by the colonists. Many words in American English—caucus, papoose, and powwow, for example—were borrowed or adapted from Indian languages. Unfortunately, the colonists rejected the Indians' reverence for the land, although it is far better appreciated today.

Indirectly Indians also added to American political thought. The framers of the Constitution looked into Indian confederations and forms of tribal democracy. Benjamin Franklin scolded his fellow delegates to the Albany Conference of 1754 for failing to take up the Indian methods of peaceful cooperation. Influenced by the Enlightenment, Jefferson and others cited Indian tribal democracy as a form of social contract. In other words, the idea of the consent of the governed in the Declaration of Independence was distantly related to Indian practices, especially those of the Iroquois.

Maize, or corn

The gap between theory and practice

In theory the English, and later the Americans, presumed that the Indian tribes were independent nations with rights to their territories. Thus England's Proclamation of 1763 declared that no land could be issued to whites who deprived Indians of their rights to ownership. Furthermore, colonists could acquire land titles only by legally buying the land from the Indians.

While the Americans did not include the Indian tribes in their new social compact—the Constitution—they did agree to let them keep their own territory on the fringes of white settlement and live freely according to their own ways. The policy of dealing with Indians as sovereign nations was built into the Constitution, which granted Congress the power to regulate Indian trade.

On paper, then, nothing seemed to prevent a decent and humane relationship between whites and Indians. The Northwest Ordinance of 1787 was full of promise:

The utmost good faith shall always be observed towards the Indians, their lands and property shall never be taken from them without their consent; and in their property, rights and liberty, they shall never be invaded or disturbed unless in just and lawful wars authorized by congress; that laws formed in justice and humanity shall from time to time be made, for preventing wrongs being done to them, and for preserving peace and friendship with them.

Unhappily, the hopes expressed in this document did not materialize.

Blacks: Origins of Slavery

Racial slavery

"About the last of August [1619] came in a dutch man of warre that sold us twenty Negars." With these words John Rolfe reported the first arrival of Africans in British North America, one year before the coming of the *Mayflower*. Most of this party of blacks appear to have become bond servants who served for a limited period of time, more or less on a par with white indentured servants. Later shipments of blacks were less fortunate. By slow stages the term of bondage for blacks was lengthened, and their personal rights were restricted. Most important, their children and all succeeding generations were made slaves for life. By the end of the century nearly all Negroes on American soil were slaves.

It is impossible to overstate the importance of "the peculiar institution," as slavery was once called, in American history. Without the labor of black men and women brought in chains from Africa, the economic progress of the United States (and other New World countries) would have been far slower. Slaves created vast wealth directly through their labor, chiefly in agriculture. Since the slave trade provided an important incentive to rum manufacture, ship building, and overseas commerce, it also boosted the economy indirectly. The slavery that began so early in colonial times remained basically unchanged for the next two hundred years and eventually resulted in a bloody civil war. And more than a century after emancipation the scars of slavery were visible in the lower social status of blacks. The distinctive Afro-American culture was born of the blacks' need to adjust to the realities of slavery and at the same time to band together against it.

Did slavery cause racial prejudice, or did racial prejudice grow out of slavery? The continuing debate over this question may never be settled. It appears, though, that the English were already racially biased in Elizabethan times and exported their prejudices to the New World. The English language was filled with terms that favored whiteness over blackness. The devil, for example, was known as "the black prince." Shakespeare's Othello symbolized the Elizabethans' fascination for African "primitivism." According to the Elizabethan belief, blacks got their skin color from "Ham's Curse," which God leveled on Noah's son as a punishment. Seventeenth-century African travel accounts classified blacks not only as different but as inferior: blacks went about shamelessly naked and engaged in immoral sexual practices; they were superstitious; they were descended from wild animals with whom they cavorted; and they had no family life.

Elaborate racial myths grew up to justify slavery. Americans believed that the "barbarians from the Dark Continent" were physically strong but stupid. They concluded that blacks were fit for the sweaty work of growing tobacco and rice. Whites, by contrast, were thought to be smarter but not well suited for physical labor. Thus the intelligent masters would control the strong but dull slaves. Whites would tame the blacks' "barbarous nature," civilize them, and offer them the blessing of Christianity.

Laws enforcing slavery

Slavery began to take shape between 1640 and 1660. During these years white masters tried to solve the labor shortage by making their black bond servants into permanent slaves. But there were obstacles to this scheme. Slavery, a dying institution in England, had no basis in early colonial law. Even the old practice of enslaving "heathens" captured in "just wars" was no longer legal.

Servants were inclined to aid and abet runaways. To counter this trend, slave owners offered cash for the return of runaways. Floggings and fines awaited those who helped escapees. White servants who were found guilty of abetting runaways of either race were punished by having their period of indenture lengthened by several years. Black servants who did the same might be sentenced to permanent servitude — in effect, to slavery.

Life servitude for blacks was first legally recognized by a Virginia court in 1660–1661. About the same time, the Virginia assembly declared that henceforth *non-Christian* servants imported into the colony would be slaves for life. By 1682 it decreed the same fate for imported *Christian* servants. Also, the children of slave mothers became slaves at birth. In the Virginia assembly of 1705 all slaves were described in legal terms as real estate.

The slave trade

The slave trade reached its peak in the eighteenth century. At first, the Royal African Company of England had a monopoly on importing slaves, and shipments were irregular. At the end of the seventeenth century the field was thrown open to all competitors. As a result, the population of blacks in the colonies soared. By the 1760s slavers were carrying nearly 100,000 Africans to the New World each year, many of them to England's colonies. The slavers realized from 30 to 100 percent profit on their investment, and many of the fortunes of Boston, Salem, Providence, and Newport were built in part on the slave trade.

Whites set up forts along Africa's Slave Coast, near the mouth of the Niger River. They dealt with the black chieftains of the Western Sudan, who did the actual hunting and capturing. A mild form of slavery was common in West Africa as an offshoot of tribal warfare. Once whites began to offer rum, iron bars, cotton goods, and cowrie shells in exchange for slaves, the chieftains started to wage wars in order to take prisoners. "Slavery," says the black poet Lerone Bennet, "was a black man who stepped out of his hut [in Africa] for a breath of fresh air and ended up ten months later in Georgia with bruises on his back and a brand on his chest."

The voyage from Africa, called the "middle passage," lasted from sixty to ninety days. Conditions on the slave vessels resembled those in a cattle pen. Each black had a space below deck approximately sixteen inches wide, five feet long, and as many feet high. Olaudah Equiano, an African who made the voyage and lived to write about it (in an autobiography published in 1791), describes what he saw and felt:

When I looked round the ship too and saw a large furnace of copper boiling, and a multitude of black people of every description chained together, every one of their countenances expressing dejection and sorrow, I no longer doubted of my fate; and, quite overpowered with horror and anguish, I fell motionless to the deck and fainted.

. . . I was soon put down under the decks, and there I received such a salutation in my nostrils as I had never experienced in my life: so that with the loathsomeness of the stench and crying together, I became so sick and low that I was not able to eat, nor had I the least desire to taste anything.

BLACKS AND WHITES IN THE THIRTEEN COLONIES

	BLACKS	WHITES	TOTAL
1760	300,000	1,300,000	1,600,000
1770	500,000	1,600,000	2,100,000
1780	600,000	2,200,000	2,800,000
1790	756,300	3,172,400	3,928,800

SOURCE: Adapted from Donald B. Cole, *Handbook of American History*, p. 50.

To prevent uprisings, slave traders generally kept the slaves shackled below decks, where the heat and stench were incredible. Dr. Alexander Falconbridge, a ship's surgeon, reported that on one voyage at least six hundred Africans were taken on board. "By purchasing so great a number, the slaves were so crowded that they were obliged to lie one upon another. This caused such a mortality among them that . . . nearly one half of them died before the ship arrived in the West Indies."

The human cargo was exercised only during good weather and was fed cooked beans or cereal spooned from a common bucket. Escape attempts, mutinies, and suicides by drowning were common. Rebels were flogged. Those who fell sick of dysentery or smallpox (including white crewmen) were sometimes dumped into the ocean. The average mortality rate on slave vessels ran to about 16 percent, but it was not uncommon for a ship to lose as much as half or two thirds of its human freight. Slaves were usually taken first to the West Indies for several months of "seasoning." They were then transferred to the mainland colonies. The total time from captivity in Africa to final location on an American plantation ran from six months to a year.

The Tidewater region received the greatest number of slaves during the colonial era. Virginia had 23 black servants in 1624–1625 and 300 in 1648 (when there were 15,000 white inhabitants). By 1671 there were 2,000 blacks in a total population of 48,000, and in 1700 the number of blacks had risen to 16,000. By the time of the founding of the Republic more than half a million blacks lived in the colonies.

Varying conditions for slaves

Slaves were used in the northern colonies, though to a far lesser extent than in the South. In Pennsylvania, New York, and New Jersey, they sometimes worked at crafts in competition with white artisans. Most of

New England's slaves were domestics, although in Rhode Island they worked on large dairy and tobacco farms. Many Newport merchants were involved in the slave trade, and in 1749 blacks constituted 11 percent of the population of Rhode Island. Some Puritan communities considered slaves as legal persons who could own property, sue in court, and seek legal remedies against brutal masters. While few blacks actually sued, their right to do so opened the way to the abolition of slavery by court decrees in the 1780s.

The life of a slave hinged on a host of economic, geographic, and cultural factors. Treatment of slaves varied from fatherly care to vicious exploitation. The Tidewater aristocracy had a reputation for leniency, but the rice and indigo plantation owners of South Carolina were considered much tougher. The size and type of plantation greatly affected the conditions for slaves. A big Carolina rice planter who used three hundred or four hundred hands on a single estate usually lived in Charleston and left his field operations in the hands of overseers. These bosses were notoriously tough and often cruel. On tobacco farms of the hilly uplands west of Chesapeake Bay, where less than ten hands might be enough, slaves usually had an easier time. Where blacks worked alongside their masters in the fields or in homes as skilled craftsmen, the relationship with whites veered more toward paternalism. Personal servants generally fared best of all. They ate better food and often grew their own vegetables and sold them locally. When they were sick, they got medical attention. Slaves rented for work in the cities could sometimes even earn their own wages.

Only in rare and extreme cases were slaves educated. South Carolina passed a law in 1740 absolutely forbidding the education of slaves. One who profited from a kind owner was Phyllis Wheatley. Born in Africa and brought to America as a girl, she was the personal maid of Mrs. Susannah Wheatley of Boston, who taught her history, astronomy, geography, and Latin classics. In 1773 she was freed and sent to England for her health. There she published a book of poems, including "On the Death of Reverend George Whitefield" and "His Excellency George Washington." Surprisingly, none of her work concerned the plight of blacks.

As the number of slaves increased, so too did the threat of rebellion and the owners' need for protection. Where blacks outnumbered whites, as in the Carolina lowlands, every white man carried a gun at all times. Over fifty slave revolts broke out in the colonies before 1761. In the spring of 1712 a group of New York slaves killed nine people as part of a plot to murder their masters and escape. When caught, six committed suicide and twenty-one were executed: "Some were burnt, others hanged, one broke on the wheele, and one hung live in chains." In 1741, on the mere rumor of a second plot in the same city, eleven Negroes were burned at the stake, eighteen hanged, and fifty deported to the West Indies.

By the eighteenth century all the colonies had slave codes. These codes, which varied from colony to colony, limited the right of blacks to own property, to testify and sue in court, to serve in the government, to manumit themselves (buy their freedom), to marry, to serve in the militia, or to bear arms for self-protection. All punishment of slaves was left up to the masters. The courts had no authority in this matter, as they did in Brazil and Spanish America. Segregation as such played no part in the system, since the races lived and worked side by side and even attended some churches together. Free blacks usually possessed the barest minimum of rights and privileges, for the master class considered them a dangerous influence on slaves.

Sexual relations between whites and nonwhites were officially prohibited but oc-

Slaves "seasoned" in the West Indies were sold to colonial planters in exchange for lumber, livestock, grain, and rum. Purchasers carefully examined them for any problems of health or age that would make them incapable of hard labor. Since slaves were considered nothing more than property, little thought was given to preserving their families.

curred frequently anyway. The number of mulattoes in the colonies was evidence of the constant violation of this taboo. Sometimes cohabitation was by mutual consent. More often, white males forced themselves on black women at will, which increased the tension between the white male owner and the displaced black male slave. Cohabitation between whites and Indians (who were not slaves) was usually by mutual consent and not so emotionally charged.

Conditions of slavery in Brazil, Spanish America, and the Anglo-French Caribbean were less harsh than in America. There the laws and customs governing slavery were more lenient. It was easier for slaves to become free, and slave families were given more protection. Slaves were granted certain personal liberties, and they had the right of self-protection. The free black enjoyed more civil rights there than in the English colonies. American white society feared both the black person and the slave; white colonists in Brazil feared only the slave. In Brazil slavery was removed by slow stages until finally in 1888 "the golden law" was passed. This act abolished the institution altogether and freed all slaves in the country.

The black role during the Revolution

Slavery clearly contradicted the spirit of equality of the American Revolution, and many whites were painfully aware of this. "I wish most sincerely there was not a slave in the province," wrote Abigail Adams to John Adams in September 1774, when a threatened slave uprising was uncovered in Boston. "It always appeared a most iniquitous scheme to me to fight ourselves for what we are daily robbing and plundering from those who have as good a right to freedom as we have." Her husband shared her views in the matter, as did other Whigs.

But Thomas Jefferson's position was typical of many southern Revolutionary leaders. He owned slaves. And he probably fathered several children by a mulatto woman, though he never acknowledged his mulatto family.

A newspaper ad for a runaway slave belonging to Thomas Jefferson, author of the Declaration of Independence.

RUN away from the subscriber in *Albemarle*, a Mulatto slave called *Sandy*, about 35 years of age, his stature is rather low, inclining to corpulence, and his complexion light; he is a shoemaker by trade, in which he uses his left hand principally, can do coarse carpenters work, and is something of a horse jockey; he is greatly addicted to drink, and when drunk is insolent and disorderly, in his conversation he swears much, and in his behaviour is artful and knavish. He took with him a white horse, much scarred with traces, of which it is expected he will endeavour to dispose; he also carried his shoemakers tools, and will probably endeavour to get employment that way. Whoever conveys the said slave to me, in *Albemarle*, shall have 40 s. reward, if taken up within the county, 4 l. if elsewhere within the colony, and 10 l. if in any other colony, from
THOMAS JEFFERSON.

He doubted that blacks were the intellectual equals of whites, or even of Indians. Yet he considered slavery not only unjust to blacks but a vicious moral influence on whites: the children of white masters, he felt, were coddled under this system and often became tyrannical. In the Declaration of Independence Jefferson intended to denounce the slave trade. An early draft of the document attacked George III for waging "cruel war against human nature itself, violating its most sacred rites of life and liberty in the persons of distant people, who never offended him, captivating and carrying them into slavery in another hemisphere, or to incur miserable death in their transportation thither." But other southerners insisted on removing these bitter words from the Declaration. As president, Jefferson appointed the free black Benjamin Banneker, an accomplished mathematician and inventor, to serve on the Capitol Planning Commission.

Blacks participated actively in the Revolutionary War, hoping to gain their freedom when the fighting ended. The runaway slave Crispus Attucks, who died during the Boston Massacre, was the first martyr to the cause. The black militiaman Peter Salem fired the shot that killed British Major Pitcairn at Bunker Hill. Another black, Salem Poor, was honored for bravery in the same battle. Most colonies forbade blacks to join militias because a black man armed with a gun or mounted on horseback raised the spectre of slave rebellion. Yet in the crush of battle, black volunteers were usually welcomed on the firing line. They had fought in the wars against the French and Indians, and when they volunteered in the Revolutionary War, they were not turned away. This was despite the fact that in 1775 Congress specifically barred blacks from the armed services, an order that General Washington repeated a few months later.

In 1775 Virginia's royal governor, Lord Dunmore, offered freedom to slaves who left the plantations of rebel planters and joined the English cause. Hundreds of blacks took up his offer, stealing away on penalty of death to serve Dunmore as river pilots, foragers, scouts, and foot soldiers. Some died on the field of battle for the Tory cause, and when the war ended, many sailed away to Canada. By December of 1775 Washington reversed his previous order and allowed the enlistment of free Negroes. A black regiment was raised, and eventually over five thousand blacks, slave and free, served in the American army and navy, most of them in integrated units. Blacks fought in many battles, including Lexington and Concord, Ticonderoga, Trenton, Princeton, and Yorktown. In the Battle of Rhode Island some four hundred blacks successfully held off fifteen hundred British regulars.

A wave of abolitionism

An abolitionist gound swell swept across the colonies in the Revolutionary era, touching even the southern colonies. The first antislavery society was formed in Philadelphia in 1775 with Benjamin Franklin as president. A year later the Society of Friends decreed that Quakers must free their slaves. In New England, antislavery societies agitated for the end of the slave trade and slavery. North Carolina tried to discourage slave imports by placing a tax of £15 on each Negro brought into the colony. South Carolina had a similar law for a time. The number of private emancipations grew rapidly; most of them set terms for gradual freedom. The Massachusetts courts ruled in 1783 that the state constitution, by recognizing the equality and freedom of all men, had in fact abolished slavery there. Other states followed suit. By 1790 three quarters of New England's thirteen thousand blacks were free. In the Middle Colonies one quarter of the fourteen thousand Negroes had been released from slavery.

These are the people by whose labor the other inhabitants are in great measure supported. . . . These are the people who have made no agreement to serve us, and who have not forfeited their liberty that we know of.

JOHN WOOLMAN (1720–1772)
Quaker leader and abolitionist

In 1775 the Continental Congress promised to put an end to the slave trade. During the next few years Delaware, Virginia, Maryland, South Carolina, North Carolina, and Georgia outlawed it. Practical considerations also influenced the thinking of slave owners and traders. Planters in South Carolina, who were outnumbered by blacks, feared that an unlimited importation of Africans would create a strong probability of rebellion. (This appeared to be true in the West Indies.) The white slavers were also afraid that bringing in more blacks would depress local prices.

Despite the abolitionist ferment, America was not quite ready to scrap the "peculiar institution" altogether. A crucial moment in the history of slavery was the Philadelphia Convention of 1787. When Virginia's George Mason proposed that the Constitution should outlaw slavery completely, a Connecticut delegate replied: "Let us not intermeddle. As population increases poor laborers will be so plenty as to render slaves useless. Slavery in time will not be a speck in our Country." For many, the belief that slave labor would gradually become obsolete was reason enough not to outlaw it. However, a provision was made for ending the slave trade by 1808.

The source of black culture in America

How much of their African culture did blacks bring with them to America? This question

Although the slaves in this painting are dressed in colonial attire, their instruments are believed by some to be of African origin. The stringed instrument resembles a molo and the drum a Yoruba instrument called a gudugudu. The dance may also be of Yoruba origin. The purpose of the scarves and stick is not known. Because black family and community ties were broken by the slave trade, very little African culture survived in America.

has been widely debated in the twentieth century. That a rich and varied civilization flourished in their native land is no longer in dispute. Anthropologists and other scholars have dismantled the myth of the "Dark Continent" and African "barbarism." The question is how much African culture was kept intact by the slaves in America and survived. Anthropologist Melville J. Herskovits argued that while numerous Africanisms blended into the humor, dialect, vocabulary, dance, music, diet, and folk medicine of the blacks, the infusions were very faint. The fact is that Africans came here by ones and twos, without family or village friends. They lost touch with their native languages, religions, and customs. Their new culture came mainly from their masters. Thus the Afro-American culture of the United States results from the experiences of blacks in this country, not in Africa. As August Meier and Elliott Rudwick have written:

The major forces shaping Negro life in the United States, from the first use of black men on the tobacco farms of Virginia to the civil rights revolution spawned in the modern cities, lay in the American environment. It is mainly to the plantation and to the ghetto that we shall have to turn if we are to understand Negro history and Negro life in America.

Review

Numerous Indian cultures existed in North America at the time of European settlement, ranging from the simple to the very complex. The earliest encounters between Indians and European colonists were friendly. Indians helped the Europeans survive, and the Europeans engaged the Indians in trade and employed their talent for trapping. At first the two groups shared the land. But as the colonists began to expand their agriculture, they encroached on Indian farming and hunting territory. Whites' demand for more and more land set off a chain of conflict. Still, Indians remained important to the colonists, who enlisted them to help fight their wars.

Colonists viewed Indians with dual vision: one eye saw a noble savage, the other eye looked upon a barbarous beast. The Indians held Mother Earth to be sacred and could not understand the idea of private land ownership. Yet the Indians and whites borrowed from each other's cultures. Among other things, the colonists adopted many Indian foods, while the introduction of the horse dramatically changed the Plains Indians' way of life. But the Europeans also brought whiskey and disease to the Indians.

At first the colonists recognized Indian land rights and treated the Indians as free people. As late as 1787 the Northwest Land Ordinance still gave some hope that whites and Indians would find a way to live together peacefully.

The first Africans were brought to the colonies one year before the *Mayflower* arrived, and they appear to have become bond servants. By the end of the century nearly all Negroes in the colonies were slaves. The colonies' economic progress would have been much slower without the labor of the men, women, and children who came in chains. As the system of slavery was institutionalized, a philosophy arose to justify its existence. The slave trade flourished, and many New Englanders built their wealth on it.

A wave of antislavery sentiment swept the colonies in the Revolutionary era. But in order to avoid what they feared might be a fatal division at the Constitutional Convention, the delegates did not try to abolish slavery. Slavery uprooted hundreds of thousands of Africans, made possible a profitable plantation system of agriculture, and created a sectional conflict that led to the Civil War. Even today we are not yet rid of its consequences.

Questions

1. Describe the initial contacts between Indians and whites. What went wrong?
2. The British, the French, and the Spanish all dealt with the Indians. How did their attitudes differ?
3. What did the Indians and Europeans learn from each other that was new? What cultural acquisitions caused the most change in their lives?
4. How did black servitude evolve into slavery? Include a description of the slave codes.
5. Many of the Founding Fathers, including Thomas Jefferson and Benjamin Franklin, believed in the abolition of slavery. Why wasn't this belief written into either the Declaration of Independence or the U.S. Constitution?

nationality and religion

Quaker meetings, open to all, involved sitting and waiting for the Spirit of God to make itself known to some member of the congregation. That member would then lead the meeting in discussion and prayer. The Spirit of God, as the Quakers perceived it, often led them to take active roles in social reform movements.

5

5
The New People

Modern America, beset by so many problems, has managed to avoid both religious strife and conflicts of nationality. Unlike India, the Middle East, and Northern Ireland, to name but a few trouble spots, the United States can take comfort in the fact that here questions of religion and nationality do not now lead to violence or the threat of anarchy. Racial injustice may produce violence, but there is no need for a Presidential Commission on Religious or Ethnic Freedom. To be sure, ethnic bigotry exists. Issues like prayer in the public schools and federal aid to parochial schools remain unresolved. But America's tradition of church-state separation and religious liberty still holds up today.

Throughout this book Nationality and Religion are bracketed under one heading. The chapters with this title take up the ethnic and religious history of white America. Theology and ethnic identity are considered in close conjunction. Parts One and Two, covering the years up through 1865, deal with a period of relative quiet. Parts Three and Four—from the end of the Civil War until the end of the First World War—treat a much more troubled period in ethnic and religious history. The last Part focuses on the peoples of eastern and southern European background— the "white ethnics," as they have recently come to be known—and their place in American politics and culture.

The basic theme of this chapter (as well as Chapters 13, 21, 29, and 37) is the ethnic identity of white America. The contributions of various European nationalities to American culture are mentioned, but most stress is laid on the serious problems of adjustment that European immigrants faced after arriving in the New World. Many of their problems sprang from their religious beliefs and national backgrounds.

Three main theories have been proposed to explain how ethnic and religious groups are absorbed into American society. According to the *melting-pot theory*, all the immigrants blend together into a new, uniquely American "stew." This theory enjoyed great popularity for a century or so. But obvious "cracks" have appeared in the melting-pot concept. A second model, *cultural pluralism*, assumes that groups of different national origin may retain their separate identities for generations. America, according to this theory, could be a nation of separate but equal groups. The third theory, *Anglo conformity*, is that the Anglo-Saxon heritage prevails, with immigrants conforming to the Anglo-Saxon model. Each viewpoint will be dealt with in the chapters on Nationality and Religion.

Immigrants and Native-Born: The "New Race"

Anglo dominance and the non-English settlers

To some, the new American environment seemed a perfect melting pot of nationalities. One of the earliest attempts to define American identity makes this point. In his book *Letters from an American Farmer* (1782) the French settler J. Hector St. John de Crèvecoeur asks, "What . . . is the American, this new man?" His answer is:

He is an American, who leaving behind him all his ancient prejudices and manners, receives new ones from the new mode of life he has embraced, the new government he obeys, and the new rank he holds. He becomes an American by being received in the broad lap of our great Alma Mater. Here individuals of all nations are melted into a new race of men, whose labours and posterity will one day cause great changes in the world.

Crèvecoeur defines the American as a "mixture of English, Scotch, Irish, Dutch, Germans and Swedes." He omits blacks and Indians in his description of the American melting pot.

But Crèvecoeur fails to take into account the overwhelming influence of the British in America. The settlers of Protestant British background established numerical and cultural dominance in the colonial period. Despite some conflict among themselves and despite the mixture of other European nationalities through immigration or intermarriage, the Protestant British remained secure in their language and customs, government and laws, and religious institutions. This is the source of "Anglo dominance."

The U.S. census of 1790 (the first reliable ethnic breakdown) reflects the strength of the Protestant element in the late colonial period. Nearly half of the 3.1 million whites in the U.S. in 1790 were of English origin, and an additional 12 percent were Scotch-Irish and Scots. (A century earlier the percentage of English was considerably higher.) The next largest group of whites were the Germans with 7 percent. (See chart, p. 104.) Also scattered throughout the colonies were Irish Catholics, Dutch, French, Swedes, Spaniards, Portuguese, Finns, Norwegians, Danes, Italians, Bohemians, Poles, and Jews of various nationalities. But the language, laws, customs, and religious practices were predominantly English. So, too, was the entire colonial establishment, with the possible exception of some French Huguenots.

Although Georgia was founded as a haven for the poor of Europe, it soon became, like many of the other colonies, a refuge for those fleeing religious persecution as well. This 1732 engraving depicts a group of German Lutherans setting out from Salzburg for Georgia with their pastor.

The Scotch-Irish, who immigrated in great numbers after about 1716, hailed from the Ulster area in Northern Ireland. Their Scottish forebears had settled in Ulster early in the seventeenth century, hoping to develop a potentially rich land. As Presbyterians, the Scotch-Irish detested both the Catholic Irish and the Anglican English. The English had long restricted the Scots' religion and hampered their woolen industry, and in 1715 they raised their rents and tithes (taxes paid to the Anglican church). This caused many Scotch-Irish to set sail for the colonies.

Settlers from Ulster often came in organized groups led by clergymen. Preferring to steer clear of the English, they headed into the frontier regions of Pennsylvania and then into the back country of the southern colonies. There they focused their fierce hatred on the unlucky Indians. Notorious squatters, the Scotch-Irish took over whatever "empty" land they found, regardless of who owned it. They thumbed their noses at the colonial establishment of Quaker merchants in Pennsylvania and Tidewater planters in Virginia. Yet many of these antiestablishment types took an active part in colonial affairs. Patrick Henry, for example, came from a backwoods Scotch-Irish clan. Their disdain for authority was a spur to the Revolution, and most became staunch Patriots. By 1775 the Scotch-Irish (along with a much smaller group of native Scots) numbered some 250,000.

The Germans began arriving in considerable numbers in the 1680s, and about 100,000 came in the first three quarters of the eighteenth century. The majority were Protestants from the Palatinate in southwest Germany. They had fled the region to avoid the onslaught of French Catholics during the religious wars of the seventeenth century. Some who spent time in Britain as refugees were invited by William Penn to settle in Pennsylvania. He promised that the Quakers would let them live according to their convictions of religious liberty and pacifism. The first party arrived at Germantown near Philadelphia in 1683, where they were nicknamed the "Pennsylvania Dutch" (from the German word *Deutsch*, which means "German"). Between 1720 and 1740 many ultimately settled in Virginia, Carolina, and Georgia, as well as in Pennsylvania. Sometimes they received subsidies or other direct aid from colonial proprietors or assemblies. By 1775 one third of the population of Pennsylvania was German.

Groups of German Pietists often migrated as organized communities under the command of a respected pastor. The Pietists were Lutheran sects—Moravians, Mennonites, Schwenckfelders, and Inspirationalists— who wanted to bring about greater religious devotion in the German Lutheran church. They held on to their Old World religious beliefs, language, and customs. Some Penn-

The Moravians, a sect originating in the fifteenth century, led a life based on Christian teachings as revealed in the Bible. They were fervent missionaries; in the colonies they converted many blacks and Indians, as well as whites.

sylvania Dutch communities were short-lived, but the Old Amish Order of Mennonites, also known as the "Plain People," took root. To this day the Amish maintain "closed" communities. They live primarily by farming and handcrafts, shun the use of electricity, dress in somber clothes, maintain their own school system, and speak mainly Pennsylvania Dutch, a dialect of German. They are one of the oldest and most successful examples of cultural pluralism in America.

The real Dutch immigrants from Holland became part of Anglo-America in 1664 when Britain took possession of the Dutch settlements that stretched from Manhattan up the Hudson River to Albany. The transition to English rule in New Netherland was smooth and peaceful. In Crèvecoeur's time, when eighteen different languages were spoken in

I could point out to you a man whose grandfather was an Englishman, whose wife was Dutch, whose son married a Frenchwoman, and whose present four sons have now four wives of different nations.

J. HECTOR ST. JOHN DE CRÈVECOEUR (1735–1813)

New York, intermarriage between the Dutch and English was common. The English also absorbed a tiny Swedish colony along the Delaware River without resistance.

The persecuted French Calvinists known as Huguenots began entering the English colonies in the seventeenth century and became renowned for their industrious habits, aggressive business practices, and elegant living. They were invited to settle almost everywhere from Massachusetts to South Carolina in the hope that they would introduce silk manufacture, wine making, and other enterprises for which they were famous. The noted engraver and silversmith Paul Revere came from a Huguenot family. About 55,000 Huguenots were identified in the 1790 census.

The non-English settlers carved distinctive marks on colonial culture. Swedish settlers in the Delaware Valley introduced the log cabin to America. Germans of Conestoga Creek, Pennsylvania, made the first Conestoga wagons. Other Pennsylvania Dutch devised the Kentucky or "long" rifle used by Daniel Boone and other "long hunters" of the colonial frontier. Huguenot craftsmen fashioned much of the pewter tableware for which the colonial era is famous. The old Dutch settlers of New York added to the English language place names like Harlem and the Bronx and such words as cruller, cookie, boss, stoop (meaning "porch"), and spook.

Flaws in the melting pot

It is tempting to accept Crèvecoeur's vision of the melting pot. There was a good deal of intermarriage and cross-cultural exchange among the English, Scotch-Irish, Germans, French Huguenots, Dutch, and Swedish settlers. All were Protestants and western and northern Europeans. The dominant English in America prided themselves on providing a haven for victims of absolutism and religious tyranny. The British government had from time to time stopped the free influx of newcomers to the colonies, and this was a source of complaint that was mentioned in the Declaration of Independence.

But the English colonists harbored a hostility to "foreigners" that surfaced in times of stress. During the French-English conflict from 1689 to 1713 the Huguenots were harassed almost everywhere. The Pennsylvania official James Logan in 1727 characterized the

NATIONAL ORIGINS OF AMERICANS IN 1790

	PERCENTAGE OF TOTAL
English	49%
African	19
Scottish (including Scotch-Irish)	12
German	7
Irish	3
Dutch	3
French	2
Spanish	1
Swedish	1
Other	4
Total number of whites	3,172,444
Total number of blacks	756,329
Total population	**3,928,773**

Scotch-Irish as being "bold and indigent strangers" who squatted on private property and attacked the Indians at the drop of a hat. "It is strange . . . that they crowd in where they are not wanted," he wrote. Franklin complained in 1753 that the German immigrants were "the most stupid of their nation." They were clannish, slavishy obedient to Old World customs and authority, and woefully ignorant of the English language. And they were a threat to the English colonials, who were at the helm of American politics. It irked Franklin to see interpreters at work everywhere: "I suppose in a few years it will also be necessary in the Assembly to tell one-half of our legislators what the other half say." In Pennsylvania the pacifist Germans were totally indifferent to the outcome of the French and Indian War. For this, the colonial assemblies cut off all public subsidies to German immigrants.

In New England the Puritans at first welcomed the Scotch-Irish Calvinists. They thought these new immigrants would ease the labor problem and settle western Massachusetts as a buffer against the French and Indians. But when it became apparent not only that the Scotch-Irish were poor but that they would not support *both* the Presbyterian and the Congregationalist church, their welcome was short-lived.

Jefferson spoke plainly about the dangers that might arise from immigration. Of course, he insisted, immigrants are entitled to "all the rights of citizenship." But he added that every precaution must be taken to

New Amsterdam (later renamed New York), with its gabled roofs and canal, was very similar to Dutch towns in the Old World. Even after the British took possession, the Dutch influence persisted.

see that the newcomers from the absolute monarchies of Europe do not corrupt America's free institutions.

Crèvecoeur's melting-pot theory applied to a limited extent in colonial America, where a fair amount of intermarriage occurred between various nationalities. But the English element prevailed. By far the largest number of settlers came from England. Their language became the language of the United States, and their religion and laws were the foundations of the new country. It is the image of the Anglo-Saxon American that stands out most clearly in 1789.

Protestants, Catholics, and Jews in a Protestant Nation

Calvinism and the Reformed tradition

To understand the grip that religion had on the colonists, we must recall that for centuries Christians had interpreted life in this world in terms of salvation and life after death. For Christians, life on earth was only a way station to eternity. Most believed in the divine origins of the Scriptures and in revelation—that is, that God could reveal His truth to people. Reason and science offered fewer satisfactory answers to big questions than did religion. In the New World it was not uncommon for colonists to be swept away in floods, drowned at sea, lost in snow storms, trapped by forest fires, and slain in Indian attacks. Babies often died of mysterious diseases, and healthy adults were stricken by sudden catastrophes. Such tragedies were best understood as an expression of God's will.

Early America was a Protestant community with a decidedly Calvinist flavor. All but a tiny handful of the five thousand religious congregations in the English colonies on the eve of the Revolution were Protestant (see chart, opposite). Only about one percent of the congregations were Catholic, and three twentieths of one percent were Jewish.

The Calvinist or Reformed tradition originated with the French theologian John Calvin (1509–1564). In England it took the form of Puritanism and in Scotland, of Presbyterianism. Calvin's book *Institutes of the Christian Religion* (1536) taught that the Bible, not the pope, was the truest source of knowledge and belief. He stressed predestination: owing to Adam's fall, people were totally depraved and could attain salvation only by the grace of God, not through any action of their own. God's will was absolute, and humans had no free will. Some would be saved, but not all. To avoid God's anger people had to acknowledge His supremacy by leading holy lives. Faith, not good works, was the road to salvation.

Calvin's Protestantism was associated with the rise of the middle class in England, France, and Holland. Merchants, artisans, and others who lived in towns or cities or owned property in the country were most attracted to his doctrines.

The English who wished to purify the Church of England (also called the Anglican church or, in the U.S., the Episcopal church) of practices not sanctioned in the Bible were known as Puritans. The Pilgrims of Plymouth, the Congregationalists of Massachusetts, the Quakers of Pennsylvania, and the Presbyterians of the Middle Colonies were all theological cousins, descended from a common spiritual grandfather, Calvin.

In Britain the Church of England was an established church (one which collects its own taxes or is supported by public funds). But it had a difficult time in America. Under the rule of the Bishop of London, the Anglican churches in the colonies were constantly short of ministers. The mother church sent out missionaries, but both ministers and missionaries regularly complained of the uphill work of maintaining their parishes. Virginia was the main center of Anglican strength in America, and everyone living there was presumed to be a member of that church. However, in the middle and northern colonies both the Congregationalists and the Presbyterians outnumbered the Anglicans.

The first Reformed congregation to arrive in America were the Pilgrims or Separatists. Despairing that the Church of England would ever really purify itself, they cut themselves off entirely from the mother church, left England, and sought refuge abroad. In Leyden, Holland, the Pilgrims gained religious freedom but had to endure poverty and loss of status. They resolved to move again, this time to the New World. Backed by a group of traders who wanted to establish them in the Virginia colony, they crossed the ocean in 1620 on the *Mayflower*. A navigational error brought them to Cape Cod in New England, outside the bounds of their charter. Fearing a possible rebellion by the non-Separatist majority on shipboard, they drafted an agreement known as the Mayflower Compact (see p. 141) and went ashore. They established Plymouth as an independent colony. It lasted until 1692, when it became part of the Massachusetts Bay Colony.

Puritans who had not separated themselves from the Church of England were the next to migrate to America. They had not originally intended to leave England, but the Anglican Bishop Laud was making life there miserable for them. In America they hoped to prove that the Bible could provide the basis for a decent life on earth. These Puritans arrived in the New World in 1630 and founded Massachusetts Bay Colony. This was the beginning of the Great Migration (1630–1640), a period during which twenty thousand Puritans sailed to the shores of America.

In the New World the Puritans founded a congregational government which made the local church members—all adults who could prove a religious conversion—the final authority in the church. These congregational churches practiced self-government. The "Saints," or the "Elect," as the church members were called, hoped to realize their goals by "conversion, legislation and, most of all, endurance." They believed they were carrying out God's will. Allowing for original sin and the snares set by the devil, they sought nothing less than perfection in all worldly matters.

CONGREGATIONS IN 1775

DENOMINATION	NO. OF CONGREGATIONS
Congregational	668
Presbyterian	588
Anglican	495
Baptist	494
Quaker	310
German Reformed	159
Lutheran	150
Dutch Reformed	120
Methodist	65
Roman Catholic	56
Moravian	31
Congregational Separatist	27
Dunker	24
Mennonite	16
Jewish	5
Other	16
Total	5,124

SOURCE: Winthrop S. Hudson, *American Protestantism*, p. 4.

Keeping their communities free from sin was a serious task of colonial Puritans. Believing that God had appointed them to build a New-World Zion, they sought perfection on earth.

The move to the New World presented a chance for a fresh start in religion. If history was predetermined, then the discovery and settlement of the New World was God's way of offering humanity a new beginning, a new way to be saved. Thus a "mood of eager expectancy" characterized religious life in New England.

The Puritans rejected both the wanton life of the king's followers at the royal court and the chaste life of monks. They believed that the good life must be filled with *both* useful work and the steady contemplation of God. Simplicity and holiness were the foundations of their daily lives. Whether riding a horse, dipping candles, keeping an account book, enjoying the marriage bed, plowing a field, or darning a sock, good Puritans were expected to meditate on God and the destiny of their own souls.

Work, which was referred to as one's "calling," was particularly important in the Puritan scheme of things. Each person had to have a calling and had to rest content with it, even if it was as humble as pushing a wheelbarrow. A man without a calling was "*impious* towards God . . . *Unrighteous* towards his *Family,* towards his *Neighborhood,* towards the *Commonwealth.*" But Puritan ideology had much broader objectives than just work, thrift, and sobriety. The early Puritans addressed themselves to the whole person—to the spirit as well as the flesh—and to the demands of the entire community as well as to those of the individual. The Puritan Ethic was combined with what has been called the "Puritan passion to reform the world."

Quakers, or the Society of Friends, were another English Protestant sect that placed a distinctive mark on the colonies. The founder of the sect, George Fox (1624–1691), believed that Christ existed within every person and that He often made Himself known in a sudden flash. Quakers also held that all members were priests of the religion. In their early years, the Friends had the Protestant passion for reform. They pursued their own beliefs about civil authority with great zeal, refusing to pay taxes, swear oaths, fight wars, or even remove their hats as a show of obedience to nonchurch officials. For a time they filled the jails of England. George Fox and William Penn spent years in prison.

The early Quaker missionaries to the colonies held meetings in every colony from New Hampshire to South Carolina, with or without permission. Their strongest bases were in Rhode Island, Pennsylvania, and West Jersey. Although the Friends and Puritans shared the common goal of purifying religion and bringing people closer to God, the Massachusetts Puritans persecuted the Quakers. They put them in wooden pillories, whipped them, and even banished them from the colony. They executed four Quakers prior to 1661. The Puritans simply refused to tolerate the Quakers' belief in the "Christ within" and the "priesthood of all believers."

In 1681 William Penn established Pennsylvania as a Quaker colony. It was a "holy experiment" where Quakers and others could live in peace, love, and prosperity. Owing to conflicts between the Penn family and the settlers, the "holy experiment" failed. But the colony itself prospered. The Quakers of the second and third generations adopted quieter forms of activism, turning their energies to commerce, finance, crafts, and farming. John Woolman (1720–1772), an early abolitionist, was typical of the new activism, which was humanitarian but less abrasive. The Quakers were to dominate Pennsylvania politics for the next three quarters of a century.

Not all the colonists, especially those in the eighteenth century, took such a serious view of life. This series of drawings accompanied a letter Ben Franklin sent to a friend in which he attempted to prove that "God—since He gave man elbows—intended him to drink."

The Great Awakening

All religions pass through periods when fervor declines. So it was with Protestantism in the colonies in the eighteenth century.

The God that holds you over the pit of hell, much as one holds a spider,
or some loathsome insect over the fire, abhors you, and is dreadfully provoked;
his wrath towards you burns like fire; he looks upon you as worthy
of nothing else, but to be cast into the fire.

JONATHAN EDWARDS (1703–1758)

Worldliness and materialism were on the increase. Having chased out some of the "agents of the Devil" (the Indians), the colonists had a more secure life. Many merchants, farmers, sea captains, artisans, and lawyers had become prosperous. They built large, comfortable houses, filled them with fine furnishings, and commissioned painters to do family portraits. Some Puritans had given up worrying about hellfire and damnation. Some wondered whether it was God or their own hard work—their own free will— that had brought them such success.

Another problem was the continued presence of "strangers"—heretics and others— who neglected worship and threatened community morality. At no time did a majority of colonial settlers attend church regularly. While New England villages were built around their churches, parishes in the South often spread out over miles of thinly populated plantation country. On the frontier it might be impossible to cross swollen rivers or hike through snow drifts to attend services. Even in the older, more settled communities most people were not churchgoers. Puritan church officials complained that as the population grew, the size of the congregations shrank.

Moreover, there was the question of what to do with the younger generation who had never experienced a religious conversion. Were they to be denied church membership simply because they had not been tested by God? Was it their fault that Indian wars, famines, epidemics, drownings, and other punishments from God occurred less often? Congregationalist ministers hit upon the Half-Way Covenant as a compromise. It allowed the children of the Elect, who had not themselves experienced conversion, to have their own children baptized. This, in turn, permitted the third generation to take part in some of the church sacraments, although full church membership was withheld until they underwent a real conversion.

External events also affected the Puritan churches. When James II, a Catholic, came to the English throne in 1685, he set up the Dominion of New England, which included all the New England colonies. The new royal governor clamped down on the independence enjoyed by the churches in the Puritan colonies. And he allowed Anglicans to share space in Congregational churches. The Massachusetts Saints fell into a mood of despair. Not even the Glorious Revolution of 1688–1689 that brought the Protestant monarchs William and Mary to the throne of England helped them. Under Massachusetts' new royal charter (1691) other churches were allowed to coexist with the Congregationalists. An Anglican church began to meet regularly in Boston, the heart of American Calvinism.

The loss of their religious monopoly rattled the older Massachusetts Saints. Some of them imagined that witches had brewed their trouble. In Salem in 1692 they participated actively in the witch trials (see p. 142). By the time the trials ended, popular respect for Massachusetts' religious leadership had reached a low ebb.

During these years a few ministers complained that religion was becoming intellectualized and the fear of hell was disappearing. They were critical of sermons that were little more than lectures on natural law and God's goodness.

From the 1720s to the 1740s there occurred a revival of religious fervor known as the Great Awakening. This movement in America paralleled religious revivals in Europe. In Germany, Holland, Switzerland, and France the movement was called Pietism. In England it was known as Methodism and for the most part remained within the Anglican church. Wherever it appeared, its objective was the same: to restore emotional, intuitive religion, so that people would meet God directly and fall before His blinding glory.

Among the first clergymen to lead the way was Jonathan Edwards, a powerful Congregationalist preacher of Northampton, Massachusetts. An intense young man, Edwards was well read in both natural science and theology. At the age of thirteen he wrote a scholarly paper on spiders. At seventeen he graduated from Yale. The "loose morals" of Northampton's young people angered him. He wrote:

Many of them [were] very much addicted to night walking, and frequenting the tavern, and lewd practices. . . . It was their manner very frequently to get together in conventions of both sexes for mirth and jollity, which they called frollics, and they would often spend the greater part of the night in them.

Edwards also criticized them for displaying "indecent" behavior at church meetings. He resolved to preach five sermons to convert these sinners. His sermon "Sinners in the Hands of an Angry God" opened with a frank warning of his intention to frighten the audience. When he preached in the quiet rural churches of the Connecticut Valley, adults and children shrieked and rolled in the aisles. They crowded up to the pulpit begging him to stop. He stressed a religion based on intuition or mystical experience, and painted a despotic and supreme God. Yet he did not reject reason. Both faith and reason were important. By quoting the Bible,

he tried to show why God had good reason for His anger toward people. If God were as kindly as some believed, He would not cause children to suffer and die.

The Great Awakening was spread through the colonies by George Whitefield, a dynamic young Church of England minister. Whitefield, who had read Edwards' sermons and was impressed by them, made a speaking tour of America in 1739 and 1740. Traveling eight hundred miles in less than three months, he preached 130 sermons. He preached out of doors, on courthouse steps, and from any pulpit. Audiences converged by the thousands. Benjamin Franklin was one of ten thousand people who crammed into a Philadelphia prayer meeting. While the young Franklin was not among Whitefield's many converts, he was affected by the clergyman and put a contribution in the offering box.

George Whitefield preaching a sermon. A listener once wrote, "When I saw Mr. Whitefield come upon the scaffold, he looked almost angelical. . . . My hearing him preach gave me a heart wound."

The Great Awakening was an evangelical movement, calling for a spontaneous conversion to Christ or a revival of devotion to Him. Revivals have come and gone since that time but never with such a jarring effect. The Awakening cut across class, geographic, and denominational lines, leaving few people untouched by the excitement of revival. Practically every Protestant denomination split. The "Old Lights" denounced the excessive emotionalism of the revivalists and the ignorance of some of their ministers. They also questioned the permanence of the conversions. In the opposing camp the "New Lights" praised the evangelists' ability to direct lost souls onto the path of righteousness. Ministers argued furiously in public over the pros and cons of the movement.

The tiny Baptist sect made the biggest gains during the Great Awakening. The Baptists believed that baptizing babies violated the Scriptures and that adult immersion was needed for salvation. Only those who freely chose to be baptized could be saved completely. During the Awakening the New Light Congregationalists swung over to this idea. Over 130 new Baptist churches sprang up in New England alone. By the Revolutionary War, as we have seen, the Congregational and Presbyterian churches boasted the most members. Baptists and Anglicans were about equal in size, and the Quakers ranked fifth.

There were many side effects from the Great Awakening. Several religious colleges were founded to train the Awakened. Since Harvard and Yale resisted the revivals, the New Lights formed Princeton, Brown, Queens (Rutgers), and Dartmouth. New charities were set up; new missionaries were sent to the Indians and blacks; new Bible study groups were formed. Many of these organizations cut across denominational lines. Since the revival movement emphasized that all people were equal in the eyes of God, the Great Awakening had a democratizing effect that would show itself in the Revolutionary era.

Intolerance toward Catholics

Catholics were the most despised and persecuted religious group in colonial America, more so even than the Jews. The hatred of "papists" went back to the reign of Henry VIII (1509–1547) during the struggle to establish a state church in England. It had nationalist as well as religious overtones, for the English feared that France or Spain would invade their island to restore Catholicism and, after the Glorious Revolution of 1688–1689, royal absolutism. During King William's War, (1689–1697) Puritan New England's fear of the French Catholics and their Indian allies reached a level of hysteria. To a lesser extent colonists also feared that Spanish Catholics would attack the southern colonies.

Roman Catholicism entered English North America via Maryland. The colony's Catholic proprietor, Lord Baltimore, offered a haven for Catholics who were being persecuted in Anglican England. He did not intend Maryland to be just Catholic, but a place where Catholics could live on equal footing with Protestants. In fact, Lord Baltimore deliberately invited Puritans to settle there in order to have a religious balance in the colony. In 1649 the Maryland assembly passed an Act of Toleration which provided that "no persons professing to believe in Jesus Christ should be molested in respect of their religion, or in the free exercise thereof, or be compelled to the belief or exercise of any other religion against their consent." Efforts to build an American refuge for Catholics in Maryland ended in 1688 when the Protestant monarchs William and Mary succeeded to the throne of England. Anglicans then gained control in Maryland and made the Church of England the established church. Later, in 1789, Baltimore became the seat of the first Roman Catholic bishop in the United States, John Carroll, whose cousin, Charles Carroll, was a signer of the Declaration of Independence.

> *There shall be liberty of conscience allowed, in the worship of God, to all Christians (except Papists).*
>
> ROYAL CHARTER OF MASSACHUSETTS, 1691

Catholics faced various forms of legal discrimination in nearly all the colonies. Jesuits living in Massachusetts could be executed. In New York they could be imprisoned for life. Virginia Catholics could not serve in the militia, and during the French and Indian War they were disarmed. In several colonies, including Pennsylvania, they had to pay special taxes. In Georgia all officeholders had to swear an oath of nonbelief in the Catholic doctrine of transubstantiation (the transformation of sacramental bread and wine into the body and blood of Christ). New Englanders played a fireside game called "Break the Pope's Neck" and celebrated Pope's Day on November 5, which ended with burning a figure of the pope. Only in Rhode Island did Catholics enjoy full civil rights.

The alliance with France during the Revolutionary War dampened anti-Catholic feeling. Protestants could see that the Catholic French soldiers, including the heroic Lafayette, did not have horns or cloven hooves. In 1775 Washington denounced Pope's Day as ridiculous and childish, and after that it was no longer celebrated in America.

Jews in the New World

Jews, like Catholics, first came to the New World on the *Niña*, *Pinta*, and *Santa Maria*. Several of Columbus' crew were Jews, including Luis de Torres, who was the first to set foot on land. In 1658 a party of twenty-three Jews arrived in New Amsterdam and established the first Jewish community. This small group came from Recife, a Dutch colony in eastern Brazil. They were *Sephardim*, Jews of Iberian descent, who after their expulsion from Spain in 1492 had sought refuge in many countries, most comfortably in Holland. (The east European Jews, the *Ashkenazim*, did not begin migrating to the U.S. until the latter part of the nineteenth century.)

Although Holland was noted for its religious tolerance, Governor Stuyvesant of New Amsterdam (New York) considered the Jews "blasphemers of the name of Christ." With the backing of the Dutch Reformed church, he tried to expel them. However, the directors of the Dutch West India Company, who ran the colony, took a milder approach and allowed them to stay. When Stuyvesant refused to permit Jews to join the army, one of their number, Asser Levi, insisted on his right as a resident of the colony to be a public watchman. Stuyvesant again objected, and the Company again overruled him. Jews won the right to worship publicly by about 1695 and formed Congregation Shearith Israel (Remnant of Israel), which still exists. Between 1741 and 1748 twenty-four Jews received full citizenship in New York.

Small groups of Jews, most of whom were merchants or traders, settled in various towns along the Atlantic coast. In the 1660s a party of Spanish Jews arrived in Newport, Rhode Island, where they found shelter under the colony's umbrella of religious protection. In 1763 they dedicated Touro Synagogue, which remains a splendid example of colonial architecture and of the material wealth of Newport. Jews trickled in from various parts of western Europe. Most were merchants like Aaron Lopez of Newport, who was active in the West Indies trade.

Many settled in Charleston, but after 1750 Philadelphia had the largest and most active Jewish community.

All of the Jewish communities were small. Even by the time of the Revolution there were fewer than two thousand Jews in the colonies. This number did not include a single rabbi. Religious life was not really hampered, however, since any ten adult male Jews can establish a synagogue.

Like all colonials, Jews were divided on the Revolution. Some supported the Tory cause, but Jewish awareness of the importance of freedom placed the large majority on the Whig side. They served the Patriot cause in a number of ways. Some joined the Sons of Liberty in support of the boycotts. Others entered militias and the Continental Army. David Emanuel of Georgia, a noted Revolutionary fighter, was eventually elected governor in 1801. Still other Jews supported the cause financially.

The Jews in the colonies were a cultural oddity, particularly in the Bible commonwealths of New England. Popular opinion labelled them "Christ killers," but they were also the civilization of the Old Testament, which the Calvinists hoped to reconstruct. Thus the colonial view of Jews was two-sided.

The groundwork for religious freedom

Most early seekers came here to worship God according to their own lights, not to help foster religious freedom for everyone. But this attitude led eventually to a broader concept that involved everyone's religious rights. Toleration was necessary for encouraging international trade and immigration and for opening new land and acquiring new hands to do "God's work in America." As the Lords of Trade once instructed the Virginia council, "A free exercise of religion . . . is essential to enriching and improving a trading nation; it should be ever held sacred in His Majesty's colonies."

After the Glorious Revolution, Parliament passed the Toleration Act of 1689, which brought religious peace to the mother country. This helped pave the way for toleration in the colonies, which increased as the European religious wars of the seventeenth century faded into the past. The French philosopher Voltaire noticed, "Were there but one religion in England its despotism would be fearful; were there but two, they would cut each other's throats; but there are thirty, and they live in peace and happiness."

The two most important figures in the struggle for toleration were Roger Williams of Rhode Island and William Penn, who opened the door to religious freedom in Pennsylvania. In Williams' eyes, "forced worship stinks in God's nostrils," for it creates a community of hypocrites. Better that church attendance should be voluntary and each worshiper seek God in a private and personal way. He also held that church and state must be separated for the benefit of both. As a corollary, Williams believed that there should be universal manhood suffrage for the proper governance of church and state.

On the eve of the Revolution religious liberty was complete in Rhode Island, Pennsylvania, Delaware, and New Jersey. The struggle continued in New York, Maryland, the Carolinas, and Georgia. In these colonies the Anglican church was the established church, but there was religious freedom for most citi-

When I signed the Declaration of Independence I had in view not only our independence from England but the toleration of all sects.

CHARLES CARROLL (1737–1832)

zens. In Virginia, where the Anglican church was also dominant, Baptist preachers could still be jailed. In Puritan Massachusetts and Connecticut the Congregationalists' church was the established church, supported by taxes from all the citizens. Quakers, however, no longer had to fear for their lives in Massachusetts.

During the pre-Revolutionary era the Church of England made the mistake of trying to establish a resident bishop in America. But in the colonies the Anglican church, like the other churches, was largely regulated by local officials, including laymen. Religion had become a private affair beyond the control of the church hierarchy in England. Dovetailing with other controversies like the Stamp Act, the proposal for a resident bishop touched off the "Bishop's War" (1767–1768). Radical pamphleteers charged that an Anglican bishopric would be as bad as the worst form of monarchy and papacy. America must have no national religion, they cried. Each Christian denomination was as pure as the next, and all were as pure as Anglicanism. Rather, let there be the "distribution of power" which comes from a number of churches. (Here the radicals anticipated Madison's argument in 1787 concerning constitutional checks and balances.)

Religious liberty was imbedded in the federal Constitution and in most state constitutions. The trend started in Virginia, where Jefferson and Madison were the key spokesmen for this principle. In 1784–1785 Patrick Henry introduced a bill into the Virginia assembly to tax all citizens to pay teachers of Christianity. Rejecting this move to strengthen an established religion in Virginia, Jefferson argued for free worship as a natural right: "Our civil rights have no dependence on our religious opinions, any more than our opinions in physics or geometry . . . truth is great and will prevail if left to herself." Virginia approved Jefferson's concept and did away with established religion altogether.

Other states did the same, until only Massachusetts and Connecticut still had established churches, which continued until the nineteenth century. Jefferson ranked his Bill for Religious Freedom along with the Declaration of Independence and the founding of the University of Virginia as his proudest achievements.

James Madison wanted the Constitution to erect a "solid wall" between church and state. Thus the First Amendment reads, "Congress shall make no law respecting an establishment of religion, or prohibiting the free exercise thereof." His original draft of this amendment showed that he wanted this concept to apply to the states as well as to the federal government. But at that point it was not so interpreted. A century later the Supreme Court held that the First Amendment was also binding on the states. Yet Madison was satisfied that the crucial point was firmly stated. Church and state were absolutely separate, and the government could not aid religion or interfere with it in any way.

Deism and the civil religion

While all the Founding Fathers were born Christians, during the Revolutionary era they tended to embrace Deism. This was a nonsectarian religion based on reason and natural law.

Deism emerged from the European Enlightenment (also called the Age of Reason). This was a period of rapid scientific advance. The British physicist Isaac Newton (1642–1727) reported finding "universal laws of nature" which proved the existence of a rational deity. God, it seemed to those who accepted Newton's theory, was not a terrible Jehovah who brought down plagues to demonstrate His supreme powers or made people kneel to beg forgiveness and seek redemption in Christ. He was more like a kindly gentleman (English, no doubt) who made clocks and other wondrous machines, wound them up, and sat back to watch them tick. Instead of joining actively in human affairs, He went into semiretirement. The Deists believed that God existed and should be worshiped. They believed that people should lead virtuous lives and help each other. But they also believed that Christ had no special significance, nor did redemption, the Bible, or supernatural revelations. In his *Autobiography* Franklin confesses to Deism when he says:

I never was without some religious principles. I never doubted, for instance, the existence of the Deity; that he made the world and govern'd it by his Providence; that the most acceptable service of God was the doing of good to men; that our souls are immortal; and that all crime will be punished, and virtue rewarded either here or hereafter.

The Founding Fathers focused on public morality and law and order more than they did on salvation or love of Christ. Washington in his Inaugural Address referred to "that Almighty Being who rules over the universe." Without taking sides with any church, he proclaimed November 26 to be "a day of public thanksgiving and prayer." Jefferson, who advocated Deism so strongly that his enemies called him an atheist, referred in his writings to a "Creator" (all men "are endowed by their Creator with certain inalienable Rights"). He also called America a promised land, like the "Israel of old." Other leaders referred to a "higher law" than any human law. This viewpoint amounts to a form of "civil" or "republican" religion. Every president down to our own time has publicly supported it, regardless of his private religious beliefs.

Colonial America left behind a complex religious heritage. This heritage included a work ethic and an emphasis on self-reliance and individualism. It involved a diversity of sects and numerous institutions of higher learning. It favored congregational self-government, which was a forerunner of secular democracy. It saw the beginnings of fundamentalism and of civil religion. And most important of all, from our perspective, it eventually produced a tradition of religious liberty which has held up well over the years despite instances of serious abuse.

Review

The English were by far the dominant ethnic group in seventeenth-century America. But as the eighteenth century wore on they began to lose some ground, at least in numbers. Scotch-Irish and Germans poured into the colonies. Groups from other countries also immigrated, often as religious communities seeking to preserve their old ways in the New World. Non-English-speaking settlers brought new customs and values to the colonies. Even with all the newcomers, however, the English remained the largest and most influential group in the country at the close of the century.

For various reasons, including the hardships and uncertainties of life in the wilderness, religion played a very big part in the lives of the first colonists. The settlers were Protestants of various sects related to Calvinism, all seeking new beginnings in America. The Puritans were the most zealous and intolerant, but their fervor faded as they became caught up in their own material success. The Great Awakening of the eighteenth century revived their original fervor as well as the fervor of all the other Protestant denominations. Catholics, for both religious and political reasons, were the most despised group in colonial days. Jews, a tiny minority in the colonies, still numbered only some two thousand by the time of the Revolution.

In the colonial period America experienced a shift from religious intolerance, to tolerance, to a belief in religious liberty. Some people wanted religious toleration as a matter of principle, others simply because it made good business sense and would help build a prosperous nation. After the Revolution the right to free religious expression was written into the federal Constitution and most of the state constitutions. But barriers still existed for Catholics. The Founding Fathers, many of whom were Deists, incorporated their desire for separation of church and state into the First Amendment. This endowed America with a heritage of religious liberty that has lasted to the present.

Questions

1. Do you think the melting-pot theory, cultural pluralism, or Anglo conformity best describes colonial society? Which theory best describes America today?
2. Americans often use the word "Puritan." What did it mean originally, and what does it mean today?
3. What circumstances led to the cooling off of Puritanism and the coming of the Great Awakening?
4. Discuss the growth of religious liberty in Pennsylvania and Maryland.
5. Explain Deism. How did it affect the thinking of the Founding Fathers?

The First, Second, and Last Scene of Mother

Prudence Punderson.

Sober Puritan attitudes toward death, and hence toward life, were reflected in couplets from the New England Primer: "While youth do chear / Death may be near" or "Time cuts down all / Both great and small." They were reflected in needlework pictures as well. Prudence Punderson saw herself, c. 1775, first as a baby being rocked in a cradle, then as a young woman crafting her needlework, finally as the "P.P." occupying the coffin. She titled this work "The First, Second, and Last Scene of Mortality."

6

6

All Men Are Created Equal

The distinguished American historian, Arthur M. Schlesinger, Sr., wrote in 1922, "From reading history textbooks one would think half our population made only a negligible contribution to history." He predicted that the situation would soon improve. Over fifty years later the rebirth of feminism is finally beginning to place the role of women in proper historical perspective. In this book the chapters on Women and the Family (6, 14, 22, 30, and 38) deal with this vital and much neglected topic. The first section in each of these chapters discusses the economic and social function of the family and related themes such as marriage customs, child rearing, and education of the young. The second section in these chapters centers on women's rights—the legal and social conditions of women, their educational status, and their role in the job market generally. The activities of feminist organizations are also recorded.

The fact that the first part of these chapters places women in the context of the family is not intended to deny the role of women in society at large. Had women not been so confined by tradition and prejudice to the home—had they been welcomed into politics and professions—there would undoubtedly have been Founding Mothers along with the Founding Fathers. The pairing of women and family merely points up the fact that throughout much of American history the accepted and most important sphere for women was the family: feeding and clothing the family, nursing the sick, educating and rearing children, caring for the home, working alongside their husbands on farms and in family businesses, and settling new communities. Indeed, the family, the most basic of all human institutions, is another much neglected topic in most history books; it has never received the attention it deserves.

The present chapter focuses on the colonial family structure, Puritan morality, and child rearing in early America. Because historians know much more about the way ordinary people lived in the New England colonies than in the South, the emphasis here is on Puritan family life. This chapter also covers women's rights during the Revolutionary era. When the Founding Fathers wrote in the Declaration of Independence that "all men are created equal," they meant no offense to women. But they certainly had no intention of sharing political power with them by letting them vote, much less hold office. Nevertheless, in an age of rationalism like the eighteenth century, the subject of the rights of women was inevitably broached, if only by a tiny group, as part of the general discussion of the rights of people.

The Family, Nursery of All Society

The English family transported to America

The type of family institution that the British transplanted to the New World was in some respects greatly affected by the rise of the middle class and the rapid growth of towns and cities. The middle-class family of the seventeenth century can be described as nuclear and inward-turning—that is, it consisted basically of parents and their children living under one roof, apart from in-laws, married siblings, or distant relatives. The ideal was to live in a single-family house in a stable neighborhood away from the "lower class." Families sought more privacy, so that interior doors were put up and used more often. The individual family was considered a vital social unit.

In seventeenth-century England, women were pushed out of skilled trades and guild organizations in which they had been active. As women's outside options narrowed, the focus on housekeeping increased. Domesticity emerged as a virtue. The wife's job was to maintain a thrifty and orderly household. When her husband traveled on business, she managed his affairs and took care of his property. Together they nurtured and educated their children.

Those who organized English colonies valued the family for its stability. Attempts to establish colonies with single men had failed. It was widely believed that their downfall could be traced to the absence of family life. Settlements that included women and children took permanent root. As one early Virginia governor remarked, colonies needed to be filled with "honest labourers burdened with children." The Virginia House of Burgesses once debated whether a man or a woman was more important in establishing a new plantation and finally ruled it a draw. To encourage females to settle Virginia, the Burgesses granted fifty acres of land to each married woman in the colony. Also, the Virginia Company shipped a boatload of ninety maidens—"agreeable persons, young and incorrupt . . . [and] sold them with their own consent to settlers as wives at the cost of their transportation," or 150 pounds of tobacco.

Puritanism and the family

For Puritans, the family had strong moral and religious underpinnings. Calvin disapproved of the monk's life. He considered marriage not only a good way for adults to

Puritans who violated the strict sexual codes could be sentenced to the ducking stool. The basis of Puritan punishment was humiliation.

channel lust but the best way for them to multiply and make God's earth bountiful.

Early colonists viewed the village, the church, and the commonwealth in terms of families, not individuals. Cotton Mather considered the family the "nursery of all society." To protect this nursery the Puritans enacted a set of laws intended to make the family structure secure. Adultery was punishable by death. Unmarried people who had sexual relations could be sentenced to imprisonment, whipping, dunking, or other public humiliations. Single women had to live with licensed families, who would guide their morals. Bachelors paid a special tax for their freedom. Husbands whose wives were in Europe could be fined or exiled if they failed to bring them over within a reasonable period of time. Couples who bickered or separated were called on the carpet by a local official and ordered to make a go of their marriage or be jailed or fined.

The Puritans hoped their laws would cre-

ate an ideal society. But the harshness of these laws was softened by the Puritan sense of reality—the ordinances were often not strictly enforced.

Getting married

Too much wealth and status were at stake in a marriage to let young people choose their own mates. Parents did the picking and negotiated the dowry with or without their children's consent. Certain families struck it rich in marriage. The "marrying Carters," the Burwells, the Harrisons, the Pages, the Fitzhughs, and other "first families" of Virginia made their names by selecting wealthy mates. Willful young people who refused to accept their parents' choices had the option of staying single.

Parents permitted some leeway in courtship. Seventeenth-century New Englanders encouraged the curiously innocent custom of bundling. In the dead of winter fully clothed young couples were allowed to curl up under the covers to get to know one another better in a sinless way. (A wooden board often separated them.) The custom seems to have lasted until the time of the French and Indian War, when British soldiers who were quartered in colonial homes interpreted the rules of the game too liberally.

In some respects Puritan morals were surprisingly relaxed. As Freud and others have pointed out, all societies restrain sexual activities so that energy can be channeled toward community needs. Otherwise people will "make love, not war" and perhaps little else. Sexual repression is often the rule in societies where scarcity exists and hard work is demanded. However, by a custom known as "publishing the banns," the Puritans and Anglicans took care of the problem of premarital sex. Couples who intended to marry signed a formal premarriage contract. This legal document linked their properties and relieved them from some of the stricter moral laws that applied to single people. Those who engaged in premarital sex could shake off any guilt feelings by simply rising in church to confess their sin. Many did so.

Puritans were expected to avoid the madness of romantic love, which might interfere with the love of God. In fact, all emotions were tightly reined for that same reason. But warm and loving relationships did exist, as the letters of Anne Bradstreet "To my Dear and loving Husband" make clear. But Michael Wigglesworth's letter to the widow Mrs. Avery asking her hand in marriage was more typically Puritan in its formality and restraint. He cited ten practical reasons for the union and assured her "that I have . . . been led hereunto by . . . sound reason and judgment, Principally Loving and desiring you for those gifts and graces God hath bestowed upon you, and Propounding Glory of God, the adorning and furtherance of the Gospel."

To the Puritans marriage was not a religious ceremony, since the Bible made no mention of the bond between husband and wife as a sacred one. Marriage was a civil contract, and the ceremony was performed either by a public official or a minister acting in a civil capacity. Quakers carried the matter to its logical extreme. The couple stood up in the meeting house and simply declared themselves married. In most colonies, decades passed before the clergy was called on to marry couples (1692 in Massachusetts). The usual colonial New England wedding was a simple affair. No one played a wedding march or gave a benediction; the bride had no special wedding gown or flower bouquet; the couple did not cut a wedding cake or ride off on a honeymoon. Instead, bride and groom held hands, exchanged vows, and signed a paper.

Early marriages were not discouraged. For example, William Byrd's sister died in childbirth at age sixteen. However, since a man was expected to be entirely self-supporting before taking a wife, most young people had to wait longer. In seventeenth-century Ply-

Couples were encouraged to build large families.

Since he is thy Husband God has made him thy head and set him above thee and made it thy duty to love and reverence him.

BENJAMIN WADSWORTH
The Well-Ordered Family, 1712

mouth the average bride was between twenty and twenty-two and the average groom between twenty-five and twenty-seven.

If a spouse was unfaithful or a marriage absolutely unworkable, Puritan law permitted annulment or divorce. However, few couples ever resorted to this. Some divorces were allowed in Congregational New England, but none was granted in Anglican New York during the entire colonial period.

Family structure and sexual morality

The Puritan family was patriarchal. Husbands and fathers were the undisputed heads of families. In the elegant phrase of the English Puritan poet John Milton, it was "he for God only, she for God in him." Martin Luther, the original Protestant, had advised women to "remain at home, sit still, keep house, and bear and bring up children." But Puritans also believed that a woman had to make her own covenant with God. For this she had to read the Bible and be able to think for herself. In practice many Puritan women were of an independent turn of mind.

Contrary to myth, the early American family was not basically an extended family where several generations lived under one roof. This had not been the custom anywhere in western Europe for several centuries. The typical colonial household was a nuclear family, made up of the married couple and their children, plus any servants they could afford. When parents or in-laws became too old or infirm to live alone, they often moved in with married children, but otherwise they lived apart. The nuclear structure of the American family has really changed very little in the past 250 years.

In seventeenth-century New England, married life generally began in a tiny one-room house of stone or wood and thatch. A hearth was used both for cooking and heating, and a partially finished loft at one end of the house provided some extra space. The cottage usually had no inner partitions or walls.

How two adults, six or seven children, plus one or two servants managed to keep their sanity in a cottage of this sort remains a mystery to our generation. Winters were especially difficult, for the family was kept indoors much of the time. In March 1631 Thomas Dudley of Boston wrote to a friend in England, apologizing for his cramped writing style because he had "no table, nor other room to write in, than by the fireside upon my knee, in this sharp winter; to which my family must have leave to resorte, though they break good manners, and make mee many times forget what I would say, and say what I would not." If the members of the Puritan family managed to survive these tight quarters, it may be because they took out their frustrations on their neighbors. The court records of early Plymouth show that neighbors were constantly bickering and suing one another for slander and filing complaints about property lines and other irritating problems.

The strict code of sexual morality in the colonies was undermined in several ways. Males, both married and single, frequently had relations with the household's female white bond servant or black slave. White servant women were normally expected to remain single throughout their indenture, for if they married and had children they might devote less time to their master's household. By the same token they were expected to have no sexual relations while single, and certainly not to give birth out of wedlock. Prosecution of servant women for bastardy was one of the most common cases at law in the colonial courts. They were constantly being hauled into court and accused of having illegitimate babies or abandoning or killing them.

Another threat to the family ideal was the overall loosening of sexual morality that spread from Europe to America in the eighteenth century. In the cities and larger towns along the eastern seaboard, young men openly visited prostitutes and kept mistresses. Wealthy men could even arrange illicit love affairs with young women of upstanding families. In his *Autobiography* Benjamin Franklin is quite candid about his mistresses. Prostitutes, mostly poor immigrant women, were available in inns and taverns. Some of these places soon became bawdy houses. From time to time irate wives, backed by equally irate preachers, tried to close them down, but their efforts rarely had a lasting effect.

John Durand's oil painting Children in a Garden *illustrates the adult style of clothing which even young children wore. These two were obviously the children of a wealthy family.*

Birth and death rates

In preindustrial societies the children's work helps the family to prosper. Since infant mortality is generally high, the pattern is to have many children. In the late seventeenth and eighteenth century the population of colonial America doubled every twenty-five years or less. Some of the increase was due to immigration, but most of it came from natural growth. America was relatively free of the epidemic diseases that ravaged Europe. Between 1730 and 1750 the population grew from 629,000 to 1,170,000. Twenty years later it reached 2,148,000.

Sometimes, owing to the remarriage of widows and widowers, the number of offspring in a family reached heroic proportions. Sir William Phipps had 25 brothers and sisters. Benjamin Franklin was one of 17 children. One patriarch, who died in 1771, left 108 children, grandchildren, and great-grandchildren. Another left 157 living descendants. A New England woman went to her grave in 1742 leaving begind 5 children, 61 grandchildren, 182 great-grandchildren, and 12 great-great-grandchildren.

The mortality rate for persons under twenty-one was approximately 25 percent. The death of infants and children and of women in childbirth was an accepted fact of life. Of Cotton Mather's fifteen offspring, only two survived him. But people who lived to be twenty-one had longer life-spans than we

A monument to the four sons of Appleton and Lydia Holmes, who died, probably from some infectious disease, within two months of each other. They ranged in age from seven to twelve. Fifty percent of all deaths in the late eighteenth century were of children under ten.

would expect. In Plymouth the life expectancy for an adult was sixty-nine years for a man and sixty-two for a woman. Those are amazing ages for any preindustrial community.

Growing up in the colonies

The life cycle was divided differently in the seventeenth century. An offspring was considered an infant until it reached six or seven years of age. These boys and girls wore tiny bows on their cloaks to signify infancy. For the first year or so they were nursed by their mothers or wet nurses, bundled close to the fire in winter, and kept within earshot of adults at all times. Older infants enjoyed considerable freedom to play and run about. They did not have to work but were sometimes subjected to rugged physical conditioning. Josiah Quincy recalled that from three and a half years on he was snatched from his warm bed each morning, even in the middle of winter, and dunked three times into icy water.

When children reached the age of six or seven, the infants' bows were snipped off to mark the end of childhood and the beginning of adulthood. In New England they then began to participate in adult work and play. Boys started with simple jobs such as fence mending, and girls were given domestic chores such as candle dipping. The child of ten or so was often "bound out" for several years. He or she was placed in the home of a relative or stranger to learn a trade or do menial work and to be properly disciplined — parents always feared they were too indulgent. Even wealthy families apprenticed their youngsters. Adult responsibilities unfolded steadily, so that by his early teens a boy might be paying taxes, drilling in the militia, or executing his father's will (John Winthrop, Jr., did so at the age of fourteen). He might even be sued for slander at that early age. This was less true of girls, most of whom were considered legal minors and dependents of a father or eldest brother so long as they remained single.

Child-rearing advice that is given by pediatricians and psychologists today was in those days supplied by the clergy. Because children often died, it seemed urgent to correct their natural laziness at the earliest age. Even an "infant" could go to Hell and suffer for its sins. One clergyman had this to say about combatting stubbornness in children: "Children should not know, if it could be kept from them, that they have a will in their own . . . neither should these words be heard from them, save by way of consent, 'I will' or 'I will not.'" According to some theories of child psychology, there was enough repression of hostility, withholding of affection, and stunting of individuality to create generations of neurotics and psychotics.

Among the earliest colonists most education took place at home. Children learned skills by watching their parents work in the home and around the farm, or by the apprentice system. Older children as well as fathers and mothers taught young children to read, write, and "figure." In order to assure literate congregations, Massachusetts Bay Colony required its towns to have elementary schools from 1642 — six years after it had established Harvard College to supply an educated clergy. Long before the Revolution, schooling was traditional everywhere in New England.

The Fifth Commandment — "Honor thy father and thy mother" — had special meaning to the seventeenth-century colonists. In one Puritan community it was translated into law as follows:

If any child or children above 16 yrs. old of competent understanding, shall curse or smite their natural father or mother, he or they shall be put to death, unless it can be sufficiently testified that the parents have been unchristianly negligent of the education of such children.

There is no record that anyone ever received the maximum penalty. Seventeenth-century children were supposed to bow and curtsy to their parents and use the formal address "Honored Madam" and "Honored Father." But parents also had certain obligations to their children. Numerous laws required parents to support and educate their children and to protect them from physical harm. Furthermore, parents could be punished for abusing their children without good cause. Besides, there was also considerable love and affection between parents and children.

Strange as it may seem today, adolescence—that stage of development from the onset of puberty to adulthood that is now taken so much for granted—was simply not marked off in the consciousness of the time. Teen-agers were not supposed to experience a period of stormy emotions or awkwardness, and coming of age was not celebrated by confirmation in church or by any other rite. Adult responsibilities that began at six or seven continued to unfold beyond twenty-one years of age, so that the attainment of majority status was not sharply defined. A young man became a freeman and gained full voting powers in the affairs of the community sometime between twenty-five and forty years of age, depending on which community he lived in.

In spite of the repression that children faced in early America, growing up was in many ways easier, more gradual, and less shadowed by self-doubt and uncertainty than it is today. Male and female roles were clear-cut, and adult models were stronger. Since there were fewer careers open, youngsters agonized less over the search for "a proper calling." What evidence there is shows that young people were far more self-reliant and did not suffer from "identity crises."

Black families

The character of the black slave family was determined first and foremost by the needs and wishes of the slave master. If the master permitted his slaves to marry, it was often as a means of breeding more slaves. The marriage was only as permanent as he wished to make it. Since slaves could be sold from one owner to another, they could not depend on permanent and exclusive relationships. Children over the age of ten could be, and often were, separated from their parents at a moment's notice. Amid the perils of the slave market, the bond between mother and child, especially the young child, was the most enduring family tie.

The slave mother was the focal point of all family life. The slave system made the black man important as a biological father, but it placed no value on him as a parent. He had much less influence on his children's upbringing than did their mother. The black woman, although she might be exploited or humiliated by her white owner, remained the head of her own cabin. As such she never submitted fully to black male authority. The black mistress of a white planter could expect certain favors of him. Similarly, the "mammy" or wet nurse of the white babies had a high status among slaves. These social benefits contributed to black matriarchy.

Free blacks enjoyed greater liberties than slaves, which carried over to their family life. They were able to marry legally and raise children very much on the order of a white family—if they were permitted to earn enough.

. . . until death or distance do you part.

From a marriage ceremony of two slaves performed by a planter

Women's Rights: An Era of Few Privileges

Early patterns

Today's concern for women's liberation had little precedent in colonial America, which was very much dominated by men. Women were expected to stay home, bear children, and care for their families. But in the seventeenth century, work spheres were still the same for men and women. Husbands also stayed home and labored on the family farm or in a workshop attached to the house. Marriage then had a functional economic and social unity that it later lost.

The pioneer colonial woman lived a rugged existence. The 101 passengers on the *Mayflower* included 18 married women and 11 girls. Three of the married women gave birth on shipboard, one woman drowned while coming ashore, and 11 died of sickness during the first winter. The surviving females raised crops, cooked food, nursed the sick, acted as midwives, wove and spun fabric, sewed clothes, made soap, shoes, and candles, and sometimes even hunted game to supplement the diet. And, of course, the wives gave birth and nurtured their children.

The Virginia planter William Byrd, while on an expedition to the Carolina backwoods in the eighteenth century, encountered "a very civil woman . . . [who] shews nothing of ruggedness or immodesty in her carriage, yett she will carry a gun in the woods and kill dear, turkeys, &c. shoot down wild cattle, catch and tye hoggs, knock down beeves with an ax and perform the most manfull Exercises as well as most men in those parts." Pioneer women of this sort were typical in the American West for the next two centuries.

For the first few generations a completely independent colonial woman was a rare figure. Anne Bradstreet (1612–1672), who arrived in New England with her husband in 1630, had difficulty in gaining acceptance as a poet. She described the problem in *The Tenth Muse Lately Sprung Up In America* (London, 1650):

I am obnoxious to each carping tongue,
Who sayes, my hand a needle better fits,
A Poets Pen, all scorne, I should thus wrong;
For such despight they cast on female wits:
If what I doe prove well, it wo'nt advance,
They'l say its stolne, or else, it was by chance.

Bradstreet was the first advocate of feminine equality on record in American history.

Although the Puritans believed that women as well as men should be literate so that they could read the Bible, the intellectual life was considered to be appropriate only for men. John Winthrop's Journal includes a notation about the Connecticut governor's wife, who went insane, "giving of herself wholly to reading and writing." Instead, she should have "attended her household affairs, and such things as belong to women, and not gone out of her way and calling to meddle in such things as are proper for men, whose minds are stronger."

Anne Hutchinson, a contemporary of Bradstreet's, competed with men in an area they regarded as their own special prov-

If any men are so wicked . . .
as to deny your being rational creatures,
the best means to confute them will be
proving yourselves religious ones.

COTTON MATHER (1663–1728)
Puritan clergyman and author

ince—religious affairs. This produced fateful results. She arrived with her husband and children in the Massachusetts Bay Colony in 1634 at the age of forty-three and took issue with what she considered the coldly rational religious condition of the colony. She also condemned certain religious practices that emphasized salvation through good works rather than through God's grace. At first she had the protection of Governor Henry Vane and the Reverend John Cotton. But the governor was recalled to England and the preacher reversed his stand, leaving her without support. A special meeting of twenty-five ministers declared her guilty of heresy. When she refused to confess the "error" of her beliefs, she was excommunicated, tried, and convicted. She fled with her husband to Rhode Island, the colony of a fellow radical, Roger Williams. Thirty-five families followed her, and they established the town of Portsmouth. She eventually moved to Long Island, where she and her children were killed by Indians in 1643.

While Anne Hutchinson's case was tied to theology and not to feminism, her fate was often cited as a warning to women. Governor Winthrop thought her "a woman of haughty and fierce carriage, of a nimble wit and active spirit, and a very voluble tongue more bold than a man, though in understanding and judgment, inferior to many women." She had strong convictions and she spoke her mind in an age when women were to be seen and not heard. Although she did not take up the banner of women's rights per se, Anne Hutchinson is considered by some feminist scholars today as the first martyr to the cause of women's liberation in America.

Colonial women had no political power. Even aristocratic women, who had had important rights in the old country, lost them here. Margaret Brent, one of the proprietors of Maryland, arrived in the colony with her sister Mary in 1638. They developed a thousand-acre estate and were technically enti-tled to the rights of lords of the manor, including the right to conduct trials, carry on business, and sign contracts. Margaret was the sole executrix of the will of colonial governor Lord Calvert. In 1648 she demanded the right to cast two votes in the Maryland assembly, one for herself and one as attorney for Calvert, but her demand was denied. The colonies did not recognize a class of free women with the right to sit alongside free men and decide the destiny of the community.

Colonial society also maintained a double standard of moral conduct. Legally, adultery was sinful whether committed by a man or a woman, but as a rule the New England adulteress suffered more than her male partner. Nathaniel Hawthorne's novel about colonial New England, *The Scarlet Letter*, describes how a "fallen woman" had to wear an "A" for adultery, while her partner protected himself from disgrace.

In some respects, however, women were more privileged in colonial America than in Britain. Provincial laws reflected the desire of men colonists to encourage women to migrate to the New World. Thus Virginia offered women land if they would cross the Atlantic. A Massachusetts law protected a wife against a wife-beating husband, protection she would not have had in England.

One surprising right a woman had in America as well as in England was that of abortion. While the church considered voluntary termination of pregnancy immoral, English common law (law derived from court decisions rather than statutes) considered it a matter of personal choice. In the *Abortionist's Case* (1348) a woman who was tried for killing a fetus was acquitted on the grounds that it was impossible to prove whether the fetus had died of natural or unnatural causes. In the absence of parliamentary legislation on the subject, this common-law right of abortion remained in effect in America through the eighteenth century.

Still, according to common law in both America and England, married women were practically nonpersons. When they exchanged marriage vows they suffered a civil death in the eyes of the court. When a woman married, she lost control over the property she had owned before marriage, income she might amass during marriage, and any debts owed her previously. She could not sign a contract, nor could she be sure of custody of her children in a divorce. On the other hand, widows had special protection. Part of the deceased husband's estate was automatically put aside to protect his widow against creditors' claims, and she had complete control over everything he left her. Regulations such as these made widows particularly eligible for remarriage.

But if a widow remarried, she died a second legal death. Martha Custis was a mature, capable, and extremely wealthy widow when she married George Washington, a young man of little means. Her former husband had left her a great deal of money, which became entirely Washington's, along with the dowry from her father. Washington also took complete custody of the fortune of Martha's daughter, who died shortly after her mother remarried. General Washington was in every way the lord and master of his home. He ordered his wife's clothes, picked out curtains and wallpaper, arranged furniture, and generally held tight control over the household.

Work and refinements in the eighteenth century

With the exception of domestic servants, women in the American colonies in the seventeenth century rarely worked away from home. It was almost unheard of for them to become writers, members of the clergy, or public officials. Yet in the eighteenth century many women worked at trades and professions where they did not compete too actively with men. Usually these women went to work because husbands or fathers had died. They worked mainly from the need to be self-supporting, not because society approved their right to independent careers.

A broad variety of careers was open to these women. They became governesses, school mistresses, seamstresses, and milliners. They sold all sorts of wares: crockery, musical instruments, nursery plants, hardware, farm products, groceries, cosmetics, drugs, and wines and spirits. In medicine they had practically unlimited freedom, for that profession still required no training. Women advertised skills at "physick" and "chirurgery" (surgery), midwifery, and nursing. Tavern keeping was commonly a woman's trade. Several women ran newspapers, tanneries, and other businesses. One woman, whose husband had died, con-

While women were considered fit to teach small children religion, reading, and writing, they were generally regarded as unsuited for intellectual pursuits.

tinued to run his gunsmith-blacksmith shop. Many women owned their own land, and in the South several were planters. The most remarkable was seventeen-year-old Eliza Lucas Pinckney (1723–1793), who managed three of her father's plantations near Charleston when he left to become governor of Antigua. In his absence she developed a commercially successful variety of indigo, which soon replaced rice as the major export crop of Carolina.

In the new Code of Laws . . . I desire
you would Remember the Ladies,
and be more generous and favourable
to them than your ancestors.
Do not put such unlimited power
into the hands of the Husbands.
Remember all Men would be tyrants
if they could. If particular care and
attention is not paid to the Ladies
we are determined to foment a Rebellion,
and will not hold ourselves bound by
any Laws in which we have no voice,
or Representation.

ABIGAIL ADAMS (1744–1818)
In a letter to John Adams, 1776

The idea of the wife as a "shining ornament" for her husband first began to make its appearance in the late eighteenth century as English middle-class values took hold in America. Women were expected to dress, furnish their homes, and arrange lavish entertaining in a manner that would uphold the class status of their husbands. Except on the frontier, women were spared as much as possible from manual labor and discouraged from intellectual pursuits. Their "purity" and "delicacy" were contrasted to their husbands' "baseness" and "crudeness." Girls

could attend dancing academies and female seminaries, where they studied subjects like music, French, and manners. They were not taught the classics, mathematics, philosophy, science, or other "masculine" disciplines.

Even language became more refined, at least for the upper classes. Four-letter words dating back to Elizabethan days gradually fell by the wayside, and conversations became more prudish. The French visitor Moreau de Saint-Méry observed that upper-class girls in eighteenth-century Philadelphia had a "ridiculous . . . aversion to hearing certain words pronounced." "American women," he added, "divide their whole body in two parts; from the top to the waist is stomach; from there to the foot is ankles."

Not all men thought that the "shining ornament" pattern of women's lives was admirable. Franklin printed several works which proposed a rational and humane education for women and a reciprocal relationship between husbands and wives. These ideas influenced Thomas Paine, who, as editor of *Pennsylvania Magazine*, published an essay in 1775 on the discrimination against women. His article was perhaps the first such commentary to reach a wide audience in the colonies.

It was the Revolution that gave women an opportunity to break with the conventional view that they should play no role in politics. During the boycott Boston women organized an anti-tea league. They brewed "Liberty Tea," made of substitutes instead of the imported product. The Daughters of Liberty was formed to parallel the Sons of Liberty. In 1777 patriotic Philadelphia women harassed wealthy merchants who hoarded valuable supplies; sometimes they seized their goods outright. Wives and daughters raised money for their menfolk in the Continental Army. They spun and wove cotton and sold clothing to help support the troops. Near the battlefronts women nursed the wounded. Debo-

Abigail Adams (1744-1818)

A MORE THAN EQUAL WOMAN

The Reverend William Smith and his wife of Weymouth, Massachusetts, did not believe that young John Adams would make a suitable husband for their eighteen-year-old daughter, Abigail. The suitor was only the son of a farmer-shoemaker, while Abigail was the daughter of a prominent clergyman and the granddaughter of a former Speaker of the Massachusetts House of Representatives. Not only was the girl well born; she was a voracious reader who had been educated at home by her mother and spirited grandmother in subjects ranging from sewing and music to philosophy and politics.

Despite her parents' doubts about John Adams, she was strong-willed and stood her ground. Abigail Smith and John Adams were married in 1764. The marriage was a love match. The devotion of John and Abigail Adams, famous even in its own time, is preserved in the many letters they exchanged during the years they were separated by the demands of his political responsibilities and her domestic duties. Their love and respect for one another never wavered. After more than ten years of marriage, she ended a letter to him, "Good night, friend of my heart, companion of my youth, husband and lover."

While John Adams was involved in the business of revolution, Abigail Adams was chiefly responsible for raising, educating, and even supporting their four children as well as managing their farm in Massachusetts. Meanwhile, she remained deeply interested in the problems of the emerging nation. Nor would she tolerate the idea that being a woman was a barrier to serious and intelligent thought. When her son John Quincy complained that American girls were shallow and gossipy, his mother replied that if they were shallow, it was because they lacked proper education, and also because men preferred them that way. Women, she added, were largely what men wished them to be. And when her husband and his colleagues met in the Continental Congress to shape the ideals of a budding nation, she asked whether they should not also consider the independence of women. "Do not put such unlimited power into the hands of the Husbands," she wrote. "Remember all Men would be tyrants if they could." Several months later she remarked, "I cannot say that I think you very generous to the Ladies, for whilst you are proclaiming peace and good will to Men, Emancipating all Nations, you insist upon retaining an absolute power over Wives."

If John Adams was a founding father and second president of the United States, Abigail Adams was certainly a founding mother not only of the nation but also of one of its most distinguished families. Given such a mother, it is hardly surprising that John Quincy Adams, in a speech in Congress in 1838, could publicly defend the unpopular view that, "The mere departure of woman from the duties of the domestic circle, far from being a reproach to her, is a virtue of the highest order, when it is done from purity of motive, by appropriate means, and the purpose good."

rah Gannett is said to have donned a uniform and disguised herself as a soldier for several years. When Molly Pitcher's husband, a cannoneer, was wounded at the Battle of Monmouth she took over his battle station. Meantime, in the absence of men, women managed farms and businesses as usual. While her husband was eluding the Tories, Abigail Adams kept a large, busy household running smoothly. Mercy Otis Warren was to write one of the best histories of the Revolution.

Thus the Revolutionary spirit made both men and women more conscious of women's capabilities. Yet the Revolution did not win more rights for women, and in fact few women claimed or demanded new rights. Men remained the heads of families and leaders of communities, and women remained their dependents.

Review

The role of women in early America involved caring for the home and family. In the seventeenth century both men's and women's work centered in and around the home. This closeness gave shape and meaning to the family unit. In New England the Puritan view of life dominated the character of the family. Laws were enacted to prevent immorality, in and out of marriage, and to keep the family intact and secure, but many of them were only loosely enforced.

The family was the basic group in colonial life, and it provided a stabilizing influence in a world filled with constant danger and hard work. Puritans did repress sex, but maybe not as strongly as we tend to think today. The family structure was generally nuclear and patriarchal, and it was common for couples to have many children. Within the family, lines were well drawn and expectations clear. Marriage did not take place until the man was able to support a family, and in many colonies the marriage ceremony was civil rather than religious. Puritans frowned on romatic love, and parents usually chose their children's mates.

The life cycle was different from the present-day pattern. Childhood was clearly defined, but there were no boundaries to mark off a period of adolescence. Responsibility came early in life and continued as an ongoing process into adulthood. Although schools existed, children received much of their basic education at home, and boys were often sent to learn a trade under the master-apprentice system.

On the plantations, the black family lived at the mercy of white masters. Of necessity, the bond between mother and children was the strongest.

Colonial settlements did not take hold until whole families and single women were transported to the New World. Special benefits, such as small land grants, were offered to women as inducements to settle in the colonies. Although American women had few political or legal rights, they were a little better off than their English sisters. Areas of work remained limited, but as the eighteenth century progressed, women did enter some trades that were not in competition with men. The model of the wife as an adornment for her husband also developed in the eighteenth century. A picture was just beginning to emerge of women as delicate, pure, and refined, unsuited both physically and intellectually to hard work. The active participation of women in the Revolutionary effort did not really change their role in society, nor did it win them any additional rights.

Questions

1. Describe the roles of the various family members in the colonial period.
2. Trace the changing role of women from seventeenth-century England through the American Revolution. Did they gain or lose ground?
3. Compare the similarities and differences between child rearing in the colonial period and in our own time. Do you think young people then grew up more secure than now? Which system seems better to you?
4. Describe some of the laws that hampered the rights of women. What were the rights of a single woman as contrasted with those of a married woman?
5. You have heard and read about the Puritans for many years. Is there anything in this chapter that surprised you or made you think of them differently?

New York's Hand-in-Hand Fire Company in action in the 1750s. Providing basic services to residents was a constant concern in the large cities.

7

7

Citty upon a Hill

A recent opinion poll taken in Detroit showed that half the people questioned would prefer to live somewhere else. Crime and urban decay influenced their decision. Surveys taken in other big cities have yielded similar results: the urban condition is an unhappy one for many people. Small towns seem to be making a comeback partly because of this big-city discontent.

The search for community is an ancient one. But what is community? Is it a place, a relationship, or a combination of both? Robert Nisbet's answer may be helpful, because it touches on psychological as well as social factors:

By community, I mean something that goes far beyond mere local community. The word as we find it in much nineteenth- and twentieth-century thought encompasses all forms of relationships which are characterized by a high degree of personal intimacy, emotional depth, moral commitment, social cohesion, and continuity in time. Community is founded on man conceived in his wholeness rather than in one or another of the roles, taken separately, that he may hold in the social order. It draws its psychological strength from the levels of motivation deeper than those of mere volition or interest, and it achieves its fulfillment in a submergence of individual will that is not possible in unions of mere convenience or rational assent. Community is a fusion of feeling and thought, of tradition and commitment, of membership and volition. It may be found in, or given symbolic expression by, locality, religion, nation, race, occupation, or crusade.

Each of the chapters on Community (7, 15, 23, 31, and 39) has two sections. One focuses on attempts to form ideal communities, including religious colonies and utopian communes. The religious seekers of the seventeenth and eighteenth centuries set the pattern. They were followed in the nineteenth century by refugees from the Industrial Revolution. The effort to overcome the worst aspects of urban-industrial society still continues in today's search for community.

The other section of each chapter centers on the city—its problems, government and planning, and culture. The rapid and largely unplanned growth of cities, the efforts to humanize life there, and the impact of urban growth on small towns are among the topics covered. The shift from rural to urban ways—a major change in American history—will be stressed in the later chapters on Community.

We must delight in each other, make each other's condition our own, rejoice together, mourn together, always having before our eyes our Communion and Community in the work, our Community as members of the same body.

JOHN WINTHROP (1588–1649)

New Plantations and Holy Experiments

Opening up the new continent

A complete inventory of community life in North America up to 1789 would include a great variety of social forms. Countless Indian villages dotted the landscape from the Atlantic to the Pacific, some of them fairly large. Spanish towns and missions were scattered from California and New Mexico to Florida. In Canada, French parishes and *rangs* (row villages) were strung out along the St. Lawrence River. Finally, English communities of varying sizes, shapes, and functions extended along the eastern coastline.

The early English communities were often founded with idealistic as well as economic goals. These communities were not haphazard collections of people and houses; they were settled and organized with a specific purpose. Many of them were inspired by religious ideals: John Winthrop's "Citty upon a Hill" in Massachusetts, Roger Williams' religious sanctuary in Rhode Island, Lord Calvert's haven for Catholics in Maryland, and John Davenport's new Zion in Connecticut, where the settlers had to make a "full and exact conformity to heavenly rules and patternes." James Oglethorpe planned to make Georgia a refuge for the poor of Europe, especially the persecuted German Lutherans. Even the settlements in Virginia were intended in part for the "Holy Business" of spreading the Gospel, although few people went there in search of religious liberty.

William Penn's "holy experiment" in Pennsylvania tried to create a model for putting religious ideals into action. To the Quakers, or Friends, community was a religious and moral idea rather than a physical, political one. They defined community in terms of fellowship instead of geography. As F. B. Tolles has noted, there was a "sense of Community among Friends transcending colonial and national boundaries." The fellowship of love and peace was to know no bounds. Still, the Quaker concept was tied geographically to the colonial proprietorship of William Penn.

Adventurers like Sir Walter Raleigh spearheaded the first English colonies. Roanoke, a

Attleboro, Massachusetts, was first settled in 1634 and incorporated as a town in 1694. Homes, public buildings, and the town's Congregational church centered around the commons.

colony sponsored by Raleigh in what is now North Carolina, vanished into thin air, leaving no clue to what had occurred there. Such ventures proved too risky for individuals. Soon afterward charter corporations like the Virginia Company of London, which received its charter from the crown, became the important agents of colonization. Their directors had the money to invest in such undertakings, and they had already financed expeditions to the Levant and to eastern Europe.

The communities established by the English may be grouped into three categories: towns, open-country neighborhoods, and plantations. Towns were located mainly in New England, while open-country neighborhoods appeared in the Middle Colonies. Most plantations were located in the South.

The New England town

The picture-postcard version of the New England town—with its village green, steepled church, picket fences, and green-shuttered cottages—is greatly idealized. But the real article was distinctive enough in its own right. The New England town (or township) had specific boundaries, and the streets and plots of land were often carefully laid out for maximum protection and convenience. It was an officially chartered community, and as such, it defined the legal rights and obligations of its residents. (In the seventeenth century any cluster of houses in a rural area, officially chartered or otherwise, was considered a "village." A "city" was a large town or community of any sort.)

The founders of early settlements were granted corporate charters and drew up church covenants among themselves. These documents were thought of as constitutions spelling out the civil and religious government of the new community, and the two were kept separate. The Mayflower Compact, for example, was a civil constitution. It was drawn up on board ship, off Cape Cod, and signed on November 11, 1620. When the Pilgrims aboard the *Mayflower* realized that they had landed outside the boundaries of the sponsoring company, they began to fear a revolt from the non-Pilgrims among them. To insure the future of their wilderness Zion, they agreed to abide by majority rule and were able to develop a stable government. Thanks to the iron discipline of Governor William Bradford and the colonists' own strong sense of religious purpose, Plymouth managed to survive its rocky beginnings.

The Puritans who founded Massachusetts Bay Colony got off to a surer start than their Plymouth cousins. They brought their own charter with them at the outset, making it more difficult for anyone to challenge their rule. It gave them the right to create a central government for a large territory that included many separate towns. They also had better financing, and, starting in 1630, one shipload after another of Puritan newcomers, some of them quite well to do, poured into the colonies.

The Puritans set out to build not merely good communities but the most perfect ones that they, who were stained by original sin, were capable of devising. To this end, they established their churches through covenants. That is, the members of the church, who were also the leaders of the community, promised with God's help to set up a religious commonwealth. Thus the church congregation came into being. Only the "holy and regenerate" signed the covenant and became members of the Congregational church, the established denomination. As others gave evidence of religious conversion, they too entered the church covenant.

Governor John Winthrop of Massachusetts hoped to build a "Citty upon a Hill" whose splendor would dazzle and set an example for the rest of the Christian world. The phrase referred not only to Boston or any other future metropolis but to the colony as a whole. Winthrop believed that God had chosen the Puritans from a nation of sinners (Anglican England) and had sent them on this "errand into the wilderness" with a complete and perfect set of instructions for their holy commonwealth—the Bible. This they planned to follow carefully. By contrast, Winthrop thought the Virginia colonists, who were Anglicans, "unfit instruments—a multitude of rude and misgoverned persons, the very scum of the people."

Church teachings required every Puritan to begin each day by asking, "What can I do for God this day?" The answer in part was to avoid idleness, to work at one's calling, and to be thrifty and sober. At one time or another Puritans officially prohibited swearing, Sabbath-breaking, snoozing during sermons, drinking in taverns, drinking at home for medicinal reasons, smoking, "profane and promiscuous dancing," and playing musical instruments. The list of taboos also included gaudy clothes, theatrical plays, shuffleboard, dice or cards, tightrope walking, beachcombing, bird hunting for sport, and long hair.

Not just anyone and everyone was invited to settle in the New England communities. The Puritans placed great value on harmony and uniformity. At their town meetings and church meetings they opposed any expression of views that differed from the general opinion. Dissenters were asked to leave.

In the seventeenth-century Bible commonwealths, people could spy on their neighbors under cover of "doing the Lord's work." If someone next door overstepped the bounds of proper behavior, a neighbor could call the tithing man, an official who watched over the moral conduct of ten families. This man could, if necessary, make the accused stand trial. The guilty paid a fine, spent time in the pillory or stocks, or were whipped, depending on the severity of the offense.

The early Massachusetts Saints constantly doubted themselves. By the end of the century they had already concluded that they had failed to create a perfect community. Instead, the backsliding and worldliness of their colony mocked and shamed them in the eyes of God. Cotton Mather told of the Massachusetts Bay minister who visited the northeastern New England settlements. There the minister urged a congregation to be "a religious people, [for] *otherwise they would contradict the main end of planting this wilderness: whereupon a well-known person, then in the assembly, cried out, Sir, you are mistaken . . . ; our main end was to catch fish."*

The Puritans' fear of failure, belief in conformity, and emotional repression reached a point of sickness in the Salem witch hunts of 1692. Not just New England Puritans, but almost everyone in the Western world believed in witches in the seventeenth century.

*If the devil will be heard against us,
and his testimony taken,
to the seizing and apprehending of us,
our liberty vanishes, and we are fools
if we boast of our liberty.*

THOMAS BRATTLE (1658–1713)
Writing on the Salem witch trials

Still, the affliction seemed to focus for a time on this small corner of Christendom. Many cases of witchcraft were brought to trial in New England, but the most bizarre and tragic events occurred at Salem. On the testimony of "afflicted" teen-age girls who had had "fits" brought on by "witches," 165 people were accused of witchcraft. The accused witches were generally eccentric middle-aged women who, it was said, indulged in wild feasts of food and drink. They were charged with consorting with the devil. Twenty were executed and scores imprisoned before the community finally came to its senses and ended the trials. The witch hunts at Salem hint at a profound unhappiness within the community of Saints.

New towns could be established in Massachusetts Bay Colony only with the permission of the colonial assembly, called the General Court. Usually a group of proprietors of good standing in the church applied for a grant of eight to ten square miles and promised to preserve order. All white males in a new community could participate in the town meeting, even if they were not church members. But in matters of selecting representatives to govern them, only male church members could vote. And only male church members controlled the congregation. Town meetings planted the seeds of participatory democracy, but the communities were not democracies.

Land distribution was always an important consideration. Only in Plymouth did the settlers own the land jointly, and this arrangement did not work out. After three years the land was divided up so that each adult received an acre of farmland. Later most settlers got a house lot of perhaps two to five acres and one or more farm lots for planting and mowing. In the earliest years farming at Plymouth was communal. Using the "open field" method, farmers cultivated each other's unfenced land. But this system did not last long, and soon each family put up fences and worked its own fields. A township normally kept some land for newcomers or the younger generation. "Common" land was also set aside for grazing.

The typical town centered around a "commons" or village green. Townspeople lived on house lots near the center of town and worked on farm plots in the surrounding countryside. In fact, Massachusetts law required that they live within five miles of the church. The commons served as a drill ground for the militia, a recreation area for strollers, and a pasture for sheep and cows. Around the commons stood the meeting house (where both church services and town meetings were held until separate buildings were erected), the minister's house, the school, other public buildings, and the marketplace.

New Englanders never lived in Indian wigwams or log cabins. House architecture evolved from crude mud hovels like those used by English shepherds, to thatched cottages, and finally to brick or frame houses. Stone masonry was less common because lime and mortar were scarce. Colonial architecture aped English models but used lumber and other native materials that were abundant. The low population density of the New England town, the limited area that it embraced, and the small size of buildings reinforced a feeling of community identity.

The growth of New England towns was generally peaceful and orderly in the seventeenth century. Still, the dwindling supply of new land frustrated the younger generation and ambitious newcomers. Since political rights were tied to church membership, those who were not members suffered distinct disadvantages. Also "strangers," "unregenerates," and religious dissenters undermined the old unity and authority. In the eighteenth-century towns arguments commonly erupted between newcomers and old-timers, big and small landowners, those who could vote and those who could not, parents and children. A historian of small towns in America has written, "It might be argued that quarreling was one of the principal causes of the expansion of New England."

After 1725 Massachusetts, Connecticut, and New Hampshire started selling large parcels of land to speculators. The speculators in turn either sold it to farmers or became absentee landlords. Some settlers simply left the villages and towns behind them and established themselves on isolated farms, going to town only to buy necessities. Thus the New England township evolved into an area of open neighborhoods, interlaced by towns.

The open-country neighborhood

In large parts of the English colonies there was no community focus at all, just people living on scattered farms sometimes miles away from the nearest neighbors. Usually these lands were settled sporadically by individual farm families who engaged in diversified small-scale agriculture. Seldom were official charters issued to the settlers; nor did church covenants often bind them together. These open-country neighborhoods, as they may be called, occurred most commonly in Pennsylvania, New York, and North Carolina. In New York Colony many such areas

An anonymous, primitive woodcut of a horse and wagon traveling through the countryside while a storm gathers overhead. Those who lived in the open country were often many miles removed from their nearest neighbors.

developed along the Hudson River when the old Dutch families divided their large manor estates, selling out or renting to tenant farmers. The families on these isolated farms sometimes came together for protection and recreation and were joined by bonds of friendship and marriage. But there were few towns as such, especially in the frontier regions of western Pennsylvania and the back country of the southern colonies.

Plantations in the South

At first the English used the term "plantation" to refer to a clearing of wilderness land or a distant colony of any sort. In America "plantation" gradually came to mean an estate on which servants and slaves produced staple crops, chiefly tobacco. Most of them were in the South. The tobacco economy of Virginia, with its dependent workers and headright system of acquiring land (see p. 31), invited community scattering. Also, the geography of Chesapeake Bay, with its numerous rivers, encouraged the tobacco planters to spread their properties throughout the Tidewater region so that each plantation could have its own private wharf and trade directly with oceangoing ships. Every plantation also had its own workshops, barns,

A typical Tidewater plantation, with slave quarters, a mill and warehouse, and, at the top of the hill, a mansion. Oceangoing ships, like the one shown in this painting, traveled inland along the numerous rivers of the Tidewater region to pick up tobacco or other plantation crops.

and storehouses. Whatever products it could not grow or produce, it could obtain by trade.

Plantations, then, were communities in miniature, based on the mutual dependence of those who owned the land and those who worked it. Masters relied on servants and slaves to make them prosperous. Servants and slaves relied on their masters for food and housing. If this link of interdependence broke down, there was a danger of rebellion and ruin. William Byrd II of Westover, Virginia, remarked, "I must take care to keep all my People to their Duty, to set all the Springs in motion and to make every one draw his equal Share to carry the Machine forward." His "People" numbered in the hundreds, and his "Machine" included large working estates and land totaling about 180,000 acres in Virginia and Maryland.

A large plantation was a community in another sense. It was the main center of economic and political activity for miles around. Scattered throughout the plantation areas were open-country neighborhoods with small farms belonging to independent farmers, including former white servants who had gained their freedom. Such small planters and farmers looked to the bigger ones for community leadership.

The planters of the South did not consider themselves irreligious, but they placed a higher value on wealth and conspicuous consumption than on frugality and sobriety. Far from wanting to recreate a biblical Zion, they sought the elegant life style of English country gentlemen. By the eighteenth century this meant living in roomy houses on large country estates which required an enormous amount of time and energy to keep up.

The typical plantation house stood on a rise overlooking an expanse of water or green lawn, not far from the slave quarters and the work yard and within a few hundred yards of the fields. When time permitted, the manor house was a social center where family and friends gathered for dancing jigs and reels, cock fighting, horse racing, gambling, and fox hunting. George Washington boasted that Mount Vernon was like "a well resorted tavern, as scarcely any strangers who are going from north to south, or from south to north do not spend a day or two at it." Many of his guests were "people of the first distinction." The consumption of food and drink was sometimes of heroic dimensions. In one year the Carters of Nomini Hall and their guests consumed 27,000 pounds of pork, 20 beefs, 550,000 bushels of wheat, 4 hogsheads of rum, and 150 gallons of brandy. No less than 28 fires were kept burning all winter in the massive house.

That the Tidewater population spread itself thinly over the countryside and did not congregate in towns or cities annoyed the crown officials. It complicated the problem of collecting taxes, convening courts, suppressing Indians, and repelling invaders. English officials repeatedly tried to lure rural Marylanders and Virginians into towns by promising them special land and tax privileges, but these offers fell on deaf ears. With the exception of Williamsburg and Annapolis, there were practically no towns in either Virginia or Maryland.

The county became an important administrative unit in the South during the colonial period. It often took care of poor relief. The court system of Virginia was also organized along county lines. County seats in Virginia often consisted of only an inn and a courthouse where cases were tried. Many of these county seats were not places were people lived or worked for any length of time. In the nineteenth century some of them became real towns.

The City, Center of Colonial Society

The urban scene

A city is a special form of community, not only larger than a town but different in kind. Precisely *how* it differs is hard to say, since there is no universally accepted definition of a city. The 1970 census calls all incorporated towns with a population of 2,500 or more urban areas. Others argue that 50,000 people is a more useful minimum figure. To those who reject statistics, the simplest definition of a city is a place where most people are not farmers.

Urban life first arose in various areas of the globe about 5000 B.C., when the division of labor and the surplus of goods allowed one segment of society to do something other than tend crops and domestic animals. Since that time the greatest cultural achievements have come from urban dwellers, whether in ancient Mesopotamia, China, Africa, Europe, or America. They have advanced learning, commerce, industry, religion, science, politics, warfare, theater, and the arts generally. It is not the farmer with a hoe or the shepherdess with a crook who lends sophistication to a nation, but the city man and woman.

The first cities on the American continent were constructed by Indians hundreds of years before the English or Spanish or French came to these shores. The Olmecs of Middle America constructed La Venta, a ceremonial center (800–400 B.C.). A related people founded Monte Albán, "one of the most beautiful open spaces conceived by man." This great plaza and surrounding dependent village system may have accommodated 250,000 people. In central Mexico the Aztec city of Tenochtitlán, founded in 1325 A.D. on the shore of Lake Texcoco, was in its time the world's most extensive urban center. The Aztec capital itself covered some 2500 acres and had a large tributary area, including highly productive farmland. To one of its largest market areas, twenty thousand buyers and sellers flocked daily along an intricate network of canals and roads. Its temples, markets, palaces, residences, and sacred places were all destroyed by the Spaniards in the name of civilization. In its place the Spaniards built Mexico City, a great metropolis at the time of the founding of the English colonies. In the middle of the seventeenth century, however, the silver mining center of Potosí in present-day Bolivia was the largest city in the hemisphere with a population of 160,000.

The five major colonial cities

Along the east coast of North America five cities arose during the seventeenth century: Boston, Newport, New York, Philadelphia, and Charleston. For commercial and cultural activity the English considered them on a par with Bristol and other British cities, excluding London.

City founders looked for specific advantages: protection against Indians, pirates, and enemy navies; an ample supply of fresh water and fuel; and access to the resources of the hinterlands. Above all, cities were important transfer points—strategic locations for shifting people and goods between land and ships. Each of the five major cities commanded a harbor, river, or bay with access to the Atlantic. Even inland towns and cities were located at natural transportation breaks—the edge of a river, the foot of a mountain pass, or the site of a waterfall that interrupted the flow of river traffic and provided power for industry.

The cities grew as their businesses flourished. But before about 1750, colonial cities had relatively little to do with each other. The main direction of trade was east and west across the Atlantic. The five American cities were the western frontier in England's trading sphere and the economic conduits that connected the New World and the Old. Each city specialized in one or more major resource such as lumber, fur, grain, tobacco, or naval supplies.

It is true that the towns and rural areas grew faster than the cities in the eighteenth century. In 1690 about one person in ten lived in cities, but the number declined to about one in twenty by 1775. Still, cities were far more important to colonial economic life than the population figures might indicate. Moreover, by the 1760s American cities rivaled provincial English cities in size and vitality. Philadelphia became not only the largest colonial city, but the second largest city in the British empire.

When Boston was four years old in 1634, it was described as an important administrative center: "This Towne although it be neither the greatest, nor the richest, yet it is the most noted and frequented, being the Center of the Plantations where the monthly Courts are kept. Here likewise dwells the Governour." It was a mediocre place for farming but was centrally located, on a small peninsula, with a harbor that could accommodate large ships.

In 1650 an observer wrote, "Now behold, in these very places where at their first landing the hideous Thickets in this place were such that Wolfes and Beares nurst up their young . . . the streets are full of Girles and Boies sporting up and downe." Boston was then twenty years old. By the 1660s one visitor called it a "Metropolis." It was "much frequented by strangers" and had numerous

State Street, the center of Boston's commercial district, in the seventeenth century. Peter Kalm, a Swedish visitor to Boston in 1750, wrote, "Its fine appearance, good regulations, agreeable situation, natural advantages, trade, riches and power, are by no means inferior to those of any . . . towns of Europe."

shops, wharves, and fairs. By 1730 it had become, with thirteen thousand inhabitants, the largest population center in the English overseas empire. Manufacturing, shipping, and the regional distribution of merchandise from all over the world were important enterprises.

The town of Newport, Rhode Island, overlooked Narragansett Bay, the best harbor between Boston and New York. Its oceangoing ships brought back valuable cargoes, including slaves from Africa. The wealthy merchants lived in a grand style that was imitated by other New Englanders.

Originally a Dutch settlement, New York City was absorbed by England with the rest of New Netherland in 1664. With its command of the Hudson Valley and access to the fur trade, New Amsterdam, as it was originally called, started out as a fur trading post, run principally by the Dutch West India Company. It had the finest harbor in the North Atlantic, with good protection from enemy vessels and anchorage for seagoing

ships. The Dutch, however, did little to exploit these advantages. Under the British the city began to flourish. New Yorkers developed the wheat-growing region of the hinterland, and flour milling grew up as a companion industry.

After a year of careful planning, William Penn selected a rise between the Delaware and Schuylkill rivers for Philadelphia. This assured it supremacy over Delaware Bay. Two decades after its founding, the "city of brotherly love" boasted ten thousand residents and was growing steadily. It surpassed Boston in population and cultural attractions in the middle of the eighteenth century. Actually, Philadelphia led all American cities in population, commercial activity, and social refinements. Penn arranged the streets in a grid, an economical but monotonous pattern which, unhappily, was later slavishly copied by numerous other cities in the West. To encourage settlement, those who bought town lots were given country lots as well. The surrounding countryside was divided into townships that were connected with the city. Thus Penn's original scheme represents the earliest regional planning in America.

By midcentury Philadelphia boasted fifty booksellers, numerous brick-paved streets and sidewalks, street lights, a library, a public college, a hospital, a regular night watch, and a thirty-man volunteer fire brigade. Franklin, its leading citizen, thought that everything was so well arranged in Philadelphia that one visit there would make a believer out of any atheist. It is said that the French philosopher Voltaire wanted to retire in Philadelphia, sight unseen. However, it was also observed that he would probably have found the Quakers too dour and humorless for his tastes.

The South lagged behind the rest of the nation in urban development. Savannah, Georgia, was considered a town of great potential, but the South's only pre-Revolutionary city was Charleston in South Carolina.

POPULATION OF MAJOR CITIES IN EARLY AMERICA

The population figures for colonial cities seem small by present standards, but at the time of the American Revolution Philadelphia was one of the largest cities of the British empire, exceeded only by London. The sharp drop in 1776, according to Carl Bridenbaugh, was due to the flight of people from all cities except Charleston in an effort to escape British occupation or the threat of its approach.

	1690	1760	1775	1776
Boston	7,000	15,631	16,000	3,500
Philadelphia	4,000	23,750	40,000	21,767
New York	3,900	18,000	25,000	5,000
Newport	2,600	7,500	11,000	5,299
Charleston	1,100	8,000	12,000	12,000

SOURCE: Adapted from Carl Bridenbaugh, *Cities in Revolt: Urban Life in America, 1743–1775*, p. 216.

I never was in a place so populous where the [zest] for public gay diversions prevailed so little.

DR. ALEXANDER HAMILTON (1712–1756)
Physician and social historian, on Philadelphia

It was considered the most aristocratic and elegant of the five major cities. Its wealth came from rice and indigo production and from lucrative commercial ties to the West Indies. The leading planters, merchants, and professionals built splendid homes, wore beautiful clothes, raced fast horses, and attended plays, open-air concerts, and fancy-dress balls. Their houses were filled with the finest silver, leather-bound books, silks, and furniture that money could buy in either London or America. The large number of Huguenot settlers gave the city a French flavor. Charleston's aristocracy was highly competitive and upwardly mobile. As a South Carolina newspaper wrote in 1773:

Their whole Lives are one continual Race in which everyone is endeavoring to distance all behind him; and to overtake or pass by, all before him; everyone is flying from his inferior in Pursuit of his Superiors, who fly from him, with equal alacrity. . . . Every Tradesman is a merchant, every Merchant is a Gentleman, and every Gentleman one of the Noblesse.

We are a Country of Gentry. . . . We have no such thing as a common People among us: The better Sort of Gentry, who can aim at no higher, plunge themselves into Debt and Dependence, to preserve their Rank.

Urban government and culture

By and large colonial cities were well governed. The merchants, professionals, and property owners took a steady interest in community problems. A city, by the very fact of its population density, has to pay more attention to social problems than does a small town or open-country neighborhood. Of necessity, night watch, fire watch, poor relief, animal regulation, garbage disposal, road repair, wharf expansion, and well digging were constant concerns in urban areas. All things considered, taxes were relatively light, yet the cities were generally able to provide basic services and maintain order and decency. Police and fire units were staffed by volunteers. The most well-to-do citizens supplied fire-fighting equipment and either personally manned the night watch or hired others to do so. Managing their own cities provided the town fathers with excellent schooling in self-government.

Leisure and culture reached rather high levels in the five leading cities. Here the colonists supported newspapers, libraries, schools, colleges, plays, booksellers, wig-makers, silversmiths, and furniture makers. Here the division of labor allowed for the greatest diversity of skills, professions, and services. Here the pace of travel was the quickest and news the most recent. Here the most learned people discussed the ideas of the Enlightenment. Here, in other words, was the "breeding ground of colonial culture."

The theater was a treat in most cities, although not in blue-nosed Boston, where an attempt to put on a play in 1750 caused a near riot. The New Hampshire legislature once expressed a sentiment held by many Puritans when it claimed that plays have "a peculiar influence on the minds of young people and greatly endanger their morals by giving them a taste for intriguing, amusement and pleasure." The titles of Shakespeare's plays were sugar-coated so as not to offend Rhode Islanders. *Othello* was billed as "a series of Moral Dialogues depicting the Evil Effects of Jealousy and other Bad Passions,

Founded in 1729, Baltimore grew slowly at first. In 1752, when this painting was done, it was a peaceful village of about 200. But by 1776 its population had risen to 6700. With its excellent harbor, Baltimore became an important shipping center.

and Proving that Happiness can only Spring from the Pursuit of Virtue." The play then passed muster. Other cities and towns were more tolerant, and by the 1760s Hallam's Company of Comedians made regular tours through most of the colonies.

Even the latter-day Puritans enjoyed taverns. Boston's seven thousand citizens in 1790 could choose from fifty-four licensed taverns in which to drink, socialize, or talk business. The Green Dragon and the Bunch of Grapes were notorious dives, where Sam Adams spurred people to revolt against England. Sam's cousin John Adams felt differently about taverns, where "the money, health, modesty of most that are young and of many old are wasted; here diseases, vicious habits, bastards and legislators are frequently begotten." But there were respectable taverns as well, and the proprietor of a Boston tavern was usually a pillar of the community. According to a personal count made by Benjamin Franklin in 1745, Phila-

delphia had one hundred taverns. There were taverns for all social classes and every social function from whoring to philosophical discourse, from high finance to gossip, from politics to dancing. Men's social, philanthropic, fraternal, and professional associations met there. Patrons read newspapers there and analyzed world events.

Smaller cities

As colonial society matured, numerous secondary cities that served as market centers for fishing and farming regions came into their own along the northeastern seaboard and its river network. Portsmouth in New Hampshire, Salem in Massachusetts, Providence in Rhode Island, and New London in Connecticut contained approximately five thousand people each on the eve of independence. Economically, the smaller ports subsisted by feeding goods to the major coastal cities and by sending their ships on

the less frequented trade routes, including those to the West Indies and other colonies. Portsmouth, for example, the capital of New Hampshire, had an excellent harbor on the Piscataqua River and was the focus of commercial activity for the entire colony. It specialized in supplying masts and spars for the Royal Navy. Of Virginia's few urban places Norfolk was one of the more promising. It had an excellent geographic location and an aggressive merchant community that dealt with the West Indies.

By the time of the Revolution some secondary cities in New England already showed the effects of stagnation. Because they could not compete with the nearest larger city and were dependent on its trade, their own growth was stunted. Their merchants tried to drum up new business, but to no avail. The sad story of the promising small town or city that shriveled on the vine would later become a familiar feature of American urban history.

The first strictly *inland* city was Lancaster, Pennsylvania, about sixty miles west of Philadelphia, over the mountains. Forty years after its founding in 1730, four or five thousand people lived there in six hundred houses. It specialized in the manufacture of saddles and guns for the fur trade and also benefited from the westward migration of pioneers.

Virginia's most appealing and prominent city was Williamsburg, which served as the colony's capital from 1699 to 1779. It was conceived by Governor Francis Nicholson, who had an unusually good eye for town planning and architecture. The recent reconstruction of colonial Williamsburg shows a varied street layout, a handsome governor's palace and legislative chamber, and many trees, lawns, gardens, shrubs, and open spaces. The College of William and Mary was established there, and the county court convened there every three months during "public times." On these occasions Williamsburg's normal population of about two thousand swelled, as planters, officials, traders, and moneylenders from all over the Chesapeake region gathered to settle their debts, drink, gamble, dance, argue politics, and deal in tobacco, slaves, and land. Most of the colony's leading families lived within fifty miles of Williamsburg. In Virginia, much of the Revolution was brewed in Williamsburg at the House of Burgesses and at Raleigh's Tavern.

The effect of the Revolution on cities

The Revolutionary War had an uneven effect on the cities. If the redcoats marched into town, those Whig residents who feared reprisals packed their belongings and fled. Philadelphia lost half of its population between 1775 and 1776, New York's population fell from 25,000 to 5,000, and Boston's from 16,000 to 3,500. Only Charleston's population held steady. Newport was occupied by British troops, later played host to French forces, and lost its commercial importance forever. Norfolk also suffered a permanent loss of vitality when, at war's end, Britain closed the West Indies to American shipping. Philadelphia served as the seat of the Revolutionary government for a time. The city was abandoned, recaptured, and again abandoned before the contest ended. Boston was heavily occupied for a short time until the British fleet sailed for New York.

New York City was devastated by fire during the Revolution. It remained a Loyalist stronghold until the evacuation in 1783. Those who stayed in the city fared well by selling supplies and services to the redcoats. The British army seized the property of Patriot New Yorkers and turned it over to Loyalists. It also abolished taxes and assumed the cost of running the city. As fighting spread to the countryside, farmers fled into New York for protection. At war's end, fifty thousand British soldiers and Loyalists sailed away for Nova Scotia or Britain. The Patriots poured back in, reclaiming their property and seizing the property of the exiles as well.

Community and the new nation

In 1789 Americans had strong ties to a state or geographical region rather than to the nation at large. Among the country's esteemed citizens were local landlords, merchants, planters, lawyers, and clergymen. The state assemblymen and local officials commanded the greatest respect. On the town or plantation or neighborhood level, the leaders and the followers were still linked by face-to-face relationships. Washington was a rarity in that he commanded interregional loyalties.

The framers of the Constitution had the job of pulling together all the small communities and forming one large one. This, of course, was a political community that did not destroy the other forms of community. Some men at the Philadelphia Convention, like Alexander Hamilton and Gouverneur Morris, had little if any feeling of identity with a specific part of the country and could be truly national in their allegiances. Morris, a Philadelphian, called himself "a representative of America," adding that "State attachments and State importance have been the bane of the Country. We cannot annihilate; but we can perhaps take out the teeth of the serpents." Most other delegates continued to see the national interest from the perspective of their own locale.

One colonial institution—the township—was destined to have an enormous influence on future efforts at community building. The Land Ordinance of 1785 translated the township idea into federal law. The public domain in the Northwest Territory (north of the Ohio River and east of the Mississippi River) was divided into townships precisely 6 miles square, with 36 sections of 640 acres each. One section in each township was set aside for the support of public schools; the rest was sold for private use. This national system of townships was an economical method for dividing public land, but a rigid one that ignored the irregularities of the landscape. To this day one can see, from a high-flying airplane or speeding auto, the roads that mark the township boundaries marching across Middle America.

While they were justly proud of their cities, some Americans harbored grave suspicions about them. In a letter to Madison after Shays' Rebellion and before the ratification of the Constitution, Jefferson wrote:

I think our governments will remain virtuous for many centuries; as long as they are chiefly agricultural; and this will be as long as there shall be vacant lands in any part of America. When they get piled upon one another in large cities, as in Europe, they will become corrupt as in Europe.

The antiurban bias expressed here by Jefferson later became powerfully fixed in the American imagination.

Review

Pre-Revolutionary North America included many forms of community, ranging from Indian villages to large colonial cities. The first English settlements, such as Roanoke, were business ventures financed by charter corporations. Colonies like Plymouth and Massachusetts Bay, on the other hand, were founded on idealistic and religious principles. They had compacts or covenants which bound their members into a disciplined unit with a single purpose. The Puritans set out to construct the most perfect communities possible, believing that God had appointed them to this task. The Saints emphasized community and conformity, but ultimately growing materialism made them feel that they had failed. The Quakers also had a sense of religious community, which was based on a fellowship of love and peace. There were three basic types of small community in the colonies: towns, open-country neighborhoods, and plantations. The plantations in the South featured a more elegant life style than the other two. They were largely self-sufficient communities based on an interdependence of masters and slaves.

The Anglo-American cities that grew along the eastern seaboard offered security from the dangers of the surrounding wilderness. The five main cities became rapidly expanding shipping points for people and cargo.

More than this, they were the jewels of colonial culture. By 1760 Philadelphia was the second largest city in the British empire. Smaller cities also arose, but the overwhelming majority of colonists lived in rural areas. Toward the end of the eighteenth century, America's strongest loyalties were still local rather than national.

Questions

1. Describe the function and geographical locations of (a) towns, (b) open-country neighborhoods, and (c) plantations.
2. How did Puritans conceive of their communities? Describe the purpose of church covenants, the concept of a "Citty upon a Hill," the religious spirit that prevailed, and the attitude toward conformity.
3. Discuss the Salem witch hunts. Knowing what you do about the colonial period, what conditions do you think allowed this to happen? Do you think anything like this could happen today?
4. List the five major cities of the colonial period, and either (a) briefly characterize each of these cities or (b) trace the history of Boston through this period.
5. Compare the New England town with the southern plantation.

Settlers cut back the forests to build new farms. The lumber obtained by clearing the land was put to many uses: planks for dwellings and barns, shingles for roofs, posts and rails for fences and storage bins, and birch bark for canoes. The abundant forests were also an important commercial resource in the colonies.

8

8

The Howling Wilderness

Few Americans can escape noticing today's environmental problems. We need go only as far as the nearest window to see some of the danger signals: the horizon clouded by pollution, the air filled with nerve-jangling noise, bulldozers carving up the countryside. To some, however, the charges of damage to the environment seem greatly exaggerated. They contend that concern over "saving the environment" is little more than a fad or an "in" topic of conversation. To others, the problems seem so vast and the outlook so gloomy that they give up all hope of finding any solutions. Neither extreme reaction is very productive. The issue is complex and troublesome but certainly not beyond human understanding or intervention. U.N. Ambassador Adlai Stevenson left the world a valuable metaphor when he said, "We travel together, passengers on a little space ship, dependent on vulnerable resources of air and soil; all committed for our safety to its security and peace; preserved from annihilation only by the care, and I would say, the love we give to our fragile craft."

What can studying past treatment of the environment tell us about today's crisis? Since most of the severe problems have become apparent only since 1945, is there much point in reaching back into the past? The answer is yes. Longstanding habits, values, and public policies explain what is happening now in our patterns of consumption and waste, in the corporate-industrial system, and in the government's action or lack of it. The chapters on Environment (8, 16, 24, 32, and 40) discuss Americans' view, past and present, of their natural surroundings and focus on such topics as natural resources, custodianship of the land, and the contest between aesthetic and utilitarian interests. Often the Environment chapters overlap with other themes in the book, such as economic growth, technology, and urbanism.

Most Americans are probably convinced that technology can solve our environmental problems. Specialists, however, are less optimistic. They realize that technology has caused the problems. And it is useless to blame them on our parents and grandparents, who, after all, consumed far less energy than we do. The important thing is to find reasonable solutions.

Ecology is the study of "living things in relation to their environment and to each other." Human ecology focuses on people's interaction with their environment. The word "ecology" first came into use in the 1870s. It stems from the Greek word *oikos*, meaning "house" in the sense of total surroundings. The term "conservation" generally refers to the preservation or protection of the environment, but it also has a specific political connotation that grew out of the Progressive movement (see Chapter 24). Conservationists include both those who believe in protecting natural resources for continued and efficient economic growth and those who wish to preserve wilderness for its own sake. The two groups are often in conflict. Our chapters on Environment will deal with both the general and the specific meaning of conservation as they discuss the impact of this concept on our history.

Before the Europeans

The virgin land of North America as it appeared to the Indians and to the first Europeans can be glimpsed today only in the fragments of wilderness still left in remote areas of Alaska, Canada, the Rocky Mountains, and northern Mexico. A third of the land mass was once covered with magnificent forests. To the west lay the grasslands, or "prairies," as the pioneers called them. In the Southwest were deserts. The continent teemed with wildlife of every description. It is estimated that North America contained some 800 varieties of birds, 400 different mammals, and 340 species of reptiles and amphibians. Also, there were over 800 different kinds of trees. Much of this plant and animal life was unknown elsewhere in the world.

A historian once suggested that the North American forests were so thick that a squirrel could have climbed a tree at Jamestown, Virginia, and traveled at treetop level for a thousand miles to the Mississippi River. The image was overdrawn, of course, for the forest was interlaced with natural meadows and clearings made by the Indians. Yet this picture points up the great expanse and density of the wooded region. And it is fact, not fiction, that sailors heading for America reported smelling pine trees a hundred miles off shore. The North American forests had stood for ten thousand years, from the end of the last ice age. They were in a stage of "climax," the term ecologists use to describe the period when a natural environment first becomes stable.

Archaeologists consider it likely that Stone Age peoples helped kill off more than a hundred animal species at the end of the last ice age. A "great dying" of mammoths, camels, giant sloths, and other creatures occurred under mysterious circumstances. Possibly the warming of the climate destroyed their natural habitats. But early people may well have been the major culprits. If so, then prehistoric times should serve as a warning of the damage that people can do and have done to the environment.

By comparison with these Stone Age peoples, the Indians who lived in the North American woodland after about 1000 A.D. were gifted conservationists. Their technology was limited, their numbers were small, and they worshiped nature. The Indians lived in harmony with the Earth Mother, who stood at the center of their universe. The people belonged to the land, not the land to the people. As the Iroquois chieftain Cornplanter said to George Washington, "The land we live on, our fathers received from God, and they transmitted it to us, for our children, and we cannot part with it. . . . where is the land on which our children and their children after them are to lie down?" The Indians mistrusted metal farming tools because they might harm Mother Earth. They continued to use their own wooden sticks instead of European implements.

Their concern for the earth carried over to the rest of nature. The Indians hunted furs for the tribe as a whole, not for themselves. Until the coming of the whites, they took pains not to wipe out wild animals or plants. Certain plants were sacred; they refused even to walk on a tobacco plant. The Navajos, among others, purposely left no trace on the desert, covering their trails and burying their camp refuse. Indians found it odd that whites liked to leave their mark on trees and rocks.

By concealing themselves within the skins of dead deer, Indian hunters could approach their prey without frightening them. They killed only as many as they needed and found a use for almost every part of the deer's carcass.

A Virgin Land to Conquer

Christianity and nature

Europeans had a completely different attitude toward the natural environment. Christianity had toppled all nature gods before the end of the Roman Empire. Christians believed that the Bible instructed them to conquer nature. Had not God given Adam and Eve "dominion over the fish of the sea, and over the fowl of the air, and over every living thing that moveth upon the earth"? Historian Lynn White, Jr., says, "To a Christian, a tree can be no more than a physical fact. The whole concept of the sacred grove is alien to Christianity and to the ethos of the west." Saint Francis of Assisi in the thirteenth century held the revolutionary belief that all creatures were equally precious in God's eyes. But his one-man rebellion, while it touched a sentimental chord in many people, had no lasting impact. Western technology—iron tools and weapons—contributed to the assault on nature. And the mercantilist economy (see Chapter 1) required that great quantities of natural resources—raw materials—be shipped back from colonies to the mother countries.

The earliest reports on America by the English in the sixteenth century tended to be highly favorable because they were used to attract financial backing. Returning from an exploration to the coast of North Carolina, Arthur Barlowe reported his findings to Sir Walter Raleigh:

We viewed the land about us, being, whereas we first landed, very sandie and low towardes the waters side, but so full of grapes, as the very beating and surge of the sea overflowed them, of which we found such plentie, as well there as in all places else, both on the sand and on the greene soile on the hils, as in the plaines, as well on every little shrubbe, as also climing towardes the tops of high Cedars, that I thinke in all the world the like abundance is not to be found.

Unlike Barlowe, those who set up beachhead colonies often expressed a more negative view, based on their fear of Indians and wild beasts and the hardships of coping with the environment. The Puritans envisioned America as a "howling wilderness." If they came to see it in a more favorable light, they interpreted its charms as a moral lesson from God for His favored but imperfect creations. The reason God had crammed such sublime beauty into nature, Jonathan Edwards thought, was as a mirror in which people could better view their own moral depravity.

Cutting and clearing the forests

British settlers were awestruck by the forests they encountered, for most of England had been cleared of timber during the previous centuries. The trees provided commercial and domestic resources. Logs (used for ships' masts), resins, and tars were vital for building sailing vessels. Pines that soared 180 feet high with diameters of 6 feet were common along the northern seaboard. White pine, along with fish and fur, headed the list of raw materials most wanted by the mother country. Trees also supplied everyday necessities, such as planking for homes, logs for the fireplace, rails for fencing, boards for cabinetry, and a hundred other uses— gunstocks, boat ribs, wagon hubs, canoes, tobacco pipes, baskets, chairs, spade and ax handles, oars, and cooking and eating utensils.

Farmers regarded trees as the best indicator of soil fertility. Samuel Sewell wrote, "Men . . . need not fear subsisting where Ash, Chestnut, Hazel, Oak & Walnut do naturally and plentifully grow." Even if farmers found a meadow, they preferred owning land with trees, which they cleared by girdling, chopping, or selective burning. They also used fires to scare out game, a hunting technique borrowed from the Indians. This was an unpredictable and dangerous method. By the end of the eighteenth century millions of board feet of lumber had gone up in smoke as a result of deliberate or accidental burning. Overcutting and burning in the hilly regions of Pennsylvania resulted in erosion and flooding in the eighteenth century. This was only a taste of conditions that would later prevail over half the continent.

Wholesale destruction of game and fish

The frontier existed in American life from the time of the first settlements to the end of the nineteenth century. It is still celebrated in song and legend. For most of the seventeenth century the colonists stayed close to the seaboard, east of the Appalachian Mountains. Then around 1690 fur trappers and traders and even pioneer farmers began chopping their way into the interior. Shooting Indians, cutting trees, and planting crops, they struggled up the Great Valley of Pennsylvania and the Shenandoah Valley of Virginia. In 1769

GEOGRAPHY OF THE CONTINENTAL UNITED STATES

Daniel Boone made his famous trip to the promised land of "Kentucke." In 1774 Boone opened the Wilderness Road, which was little more than a line of blazed tree trunks running west through the Cumberland Gap. It stretched some two hundred miles over steep mountains, weaving through dense cane thickets to the Kentucky River.

The coming of whites to America meant disaster for fur-bearing creatures. The combination of cold winters, heavy moisture, and dense forests created a perfect habitat for scores of species with thick, soft, lustrous fur. These pelts were highly prized by Europeans, who used the fur of otter, muskrat, weasel, mink, pine marten, wolverine, and fisher for coats and robes.

Seventeenth-century hatmakers found a simple method of bonding beaver fur to felt cloth, and in 1638 England's Charles I declared that only beaver would be used in hats. For the next three centuries it was the most sought-after wild animal in America. The beaver made its home almost everywhere except in the hottest desert and coldest tundra. The Hudson's Bay Company, chartered in 1670, sent trappers and traders roaming throughout Canada. In one month in 1743 the company sold the pelts of 26,750 beaver, 14,730 martens, and 1,850 wolves. Naturally, these animals thinned out. The retreat of fur-bearing creatures drew men deeper and deeper into the backlands.

It is worth recalling that most colonists killed game out of necessity—for self-protection or direct consumption rather than for sport or profit. Wolves, bears, and mountain lions preyed on cattle and sheep, so farmers set out to destroy them or drive them off. Colonial governments even offered bounties for predators' hides, a practice still followed in some states against certain predatory animals. Massachusetts pioneered this policy in 1630 when it offered one penny for every dead wolf.

The killing off of large predators brought

This place is a good climate, and probably not only very fertile, . . . but . . . otherwise furnished with furs and other desirable things.

DANIEL GOOKIN (1612–1686?)
Soldier and magistrate

relief to livestock growers, but in the long run it also had unhappy side effects. In a natural balance, predators keep small game populations in check. As their natural enemies were destroyed in large numbers, small game rapidly multiplied, creating new problems for the farmers.

The pioneers also trained their gun sights on game animals and birds. The passenger pigeon, heath hen, and quail—major items in the colonial diet—began to disappear from the dinner table as the eighteenth century wore on. The deer population rapidly declined, and the natural range of the wild turkey, today a Thanksgiving symbol of survival in the wilderness, was considerably diminished by colonial sharpshooters.

Many animals once common in the eastern forests either retreated to the Great Plains or mountain regions, eventually were placed in zoos and game preserves, or today remain only as pictures in books of rare fauna. Early settlers watched herds of buffalo wandering through the eastern woodlands. Mountain lions, now holed up in the Rocky Mountains and rarely seen by people, once preyed heavily on cattle in the Carolinas.

On sea as well as on land, the colonials vigorously attacked wildlife. New Englanders became famous for their fishing skills, catching innumerable cod and mackerel. Luckily, these species reproduced too fast to become endangered. The whale was less fortunate. New England whalers hunted their prey with such determination and skill that, by the time of the Revolutionary War, they had driven away the species known as the

Cod were heavily fished in the waters off New England. Here, fishermen are shown catching, dressing, and curing cod (upper right to left) and drying them (bottom). New England's economy was bolstered by exports of dried cod to the West Indies.

right whale from the North Atlantic. On the Atlantic beachline, hunters pursued the tasty green sea turtle relentlessly. It now survives only in the Caribbean. Since the coming of Europeans, two mammal and six bird species have become extinct: the sea mink and Steller's sea cow, Cooper's sandpiper, Townsend's bunting, the Labrador duck, the passenger pigeon, the Carolina parakeet, and the great auk.

The great auk, a large, flightless sea bird, was pursued for its delicious flesh and luxurious down feathers. Yankee fishermen sometimes dropped anchor at the bleak islands that housed the auk and, with a little coaxing, lured entire flocks up the gangplank to be slaughtered. As a result, these birds became very rare by the late colonial period and extinct by the middle of the next century.

Some early controls

Not all the colonists were blind to the effects of the destructive assault on the wilderness. Government agencies sometimes imposed restrictions, especially when proprietary, royal, or trading interests were threatened. Several New England townships passed strict laws to curtail forest fires, which endangered life and property. Plymouth Colony prohibited unauthorized timber exports and wood cutting on public lands. William Penn required Pennsylvanians to preserve an acre of forest for every five acres they cleared. Since the Royal Navy needed certain trees for masts, local officials in Massachusetts had to help preserve all pines and oaks which stood within three miles of the ocean and had twenty-four-inch trunks. Trees marked with the broad arrow of the Royal Navy were taboo, and ax men who cut them were fined. But they did it, nonetheless.

The disappearance of game brought some restrictions in hunting privileges. Massachusetts set up the first warden system to control hunting in 1739. Earlier, in the 1690s, it had established a closed season on deer hunting, and by the time of the Revolution all the other colonies had followed suit. New York declared a closed season on heath hens, grouse, quail, and turkey in 1708. As the area of settlement moved steadily west, however, the laws protecting the wilderness were easily violated.

The Myth of Superabundance

On the settled side of the frontier—on farms and in towns and cities—the colonials also altered their environment, although less radically. The relationship of the people to the land differed markedly from what it was in the Old World. Most of western Europe's forests had long since been cut and its bogs drained of water. By the sixteenth and seventeenth centuries Europeans had learned to preserve wooded areas, terrace hillsides, spread manure for fertilizer, build stone fences to protect crops against grazing animals, construct dikes, and alternate crops to replenish the soil. English agriculture in particular was "geared to the *flow* of nature, not to its sudden exhaustion."

In America the situation was reversed. New land was relatively abundant and cheap. The Chesapeake tobacco planters were faced with the continuous problem of using up the land, for tobacco is an acid crop that quickly exhausts the soil. By the eighteenth century, planters had opened new plots in the West, or were planning to do so. For them soil conservation was time-consuming and costly. The Germans of Pennsylvania perpetuated the old-fashioned habits of husbandry, but most other farmers, as they planted their crops, chopped down trees, shot birds out of the sky, or felled deer, had one eye on the horizon. There, they assumed, they would find more and better land and resources when the old land gave out. This created what Stewart Udall, a leading conservationist, calls the "Myth of Superabundance."

The spendthrift use of soil and other farm resources amazed the Swedish botanist Peter

A German artist's view of the bounty of colonial Virginia. Pictures such as this encouraged new settlers to come to America.

Kalm. On a visit to America in 1750 he noted:

[The] easy method of getting a rich crop has spoiled the English and other settlers. . . . in a word the grain fields, the meadows, the forests, the cattle, etc. are treated with equal carelessness; and the characteristic of the English nation, so well skilled in these branches of husbandry, is scarcely recognizable here . . . their eyes are fixed upon the present gain, and they are blind to the future.

Farming is essentially an effort to increase the food supply by controlling certain natural forces. Inevitably the process brings with it some negative results. Benjamin Franklin described one such situation:

In New England they once thought Black-birds useless and mischievous to their corn, they made [laws] to destroy them, the consequence was, the Black-birds were diminished but a kind of Worms which devoured their Grass, and which the Black-birds had been used to feed on encreased prodigiously; Their finding their Loss in Grass much greater than their savings in corn they wished again for their Black-birds.

Here is a classic instance of what biologist Barry Commoner would consider a violation of two basic laws of ecology: "Nature Knows Best" and "There Is No Such Thing as a Free Lunch."

City dwellers faced their own ecological problems. From the beginning, a water supply, home sanitation, and garbage collection were among the most troublesome aspects of city life. Only New York had a regular garbage collection system: hogs roamed the streets eating garbage and trash, and a hog-reeve patrolled them. Later, garbage collectors were hired to care for some streets, and men hauled away refuse in carts at the price of sixpence a load. Penalties existed for obstructing public thoroughfares with refuse or filth, but the laws were seldom obeyed. Drinking water came from wells that were often uncomfortably close to privies. In Newport and Charleston, privies sometimes emptied into the streets. Passersby complained of "Spoiling & Damnifying" their clothes, "especially in ye Night when people cannot see to shunn them." In nature there is no such thing as waste, but cities have the most difficult time coping with what Commoner terms "The Second Law of Ecology: Everything Must Go Somewhere." Nevertheless, European visitors found American cities astonishingly clean and healthy, with the exception of Charleston, which suffered from "country fever."

The vast majority of colonists were farmers who, despite their transgressions against the forest, remained very much in touch with nature and nature's rhythms. They were attuned to the change of seasons, to the shortening and lengthening of daylight. They perceived the readiness of the soil for planting, of the trees for pruning, and of the crops for harvesting. They sensed the smells, sounds, textures, and colors of the outdoors. The majority of towns retained a rustic aspect that pleased the townspeople of the eighteenth century. There were fish in the streams, wild birds in the treetops, and cattle and sheep — and sometimes deer — grazing on the meadows. The nation was still innocent of railroads, tenements, mill towns, and slag heaps. And science had not yet linked up with technology to produce the industrial-urban order that would profoundly change the landscape.

Review

Wilderness North America was clothed in magnificent forests, grasslands, and deserts. It teemed with animals and plants of great variety. The Indians were gifted conservationists who lived in harmony with their environment. The Christian invaders, however, believed they had a mission to conquer nature. British colonials exploited the abundant forests for commercial and domestic use. Overcutting and burning soon led to erosion and floods. Prized fur-bearing animals suffered wholesale slaughter. The beaver was a prime victim. Game birds and animals, as well as the large predators so necessary for ecological balance, were also destroyed. Animals fled their natural environment to escape from humans. Some species disappeared altogether. Most saltwater fish withstood the onslaught of colonial fishermen, but sea animals such as the right whale disappeared from the North Atlantic, and the once plentiful green sea turtle disappeared completely from the Atlantic shoreline. A few colonists and some government agencies sounded a warning, but it was largely ignored along the frontier. The cities' failures in sanitation and the farmers' misuse of the soil would have far-reaching effects. Dazzled by so much natural wealth and their own myth of superabundance, most colonists forgot their thrifty ways when dealing with the environment.

Questions

1. How did Europeans and Indians differ in their attitudes toward nature?
2. List some of the ways in which colonists reduced the forests, and describe the effects.
3. Describe measures taken by the colonials to protect the environment.
4. What environmental problems were posed by farms and cities?
5. The biologist Barry Commoner defines The Second Law of Ecology as "Everything Must Go Somewhere." How would this apply to the colonial period?

Selected Readings

OVERVIEW

A good starting point for practically any research project in American history is Frank Freidel and Richard K. Showman, eds., *Harvard Guide to American History* (Harvard U. Press, 1974). This comprehensive work is a mine of information with an enormous and useful index. The books cited below merely skim the surface of the sources available on the eight themes that comprise this textbook.

Students looking for general works on the colonial era have many books to consult. Richard B. Morris, *The New World* (Time-Life, 1974) is an easy-to-use survey. Louis B. Wright has published several readable accounts: *Glory, Gold, and the Gospel: The Adventurous Lives and Times of the Renaissance Explorers* (Atheneum, 1970); *The Cultural Life of the American Colonies: 1607–1763* (Harper & Row, 1957); and *Everyday Life in Colonial America* (Putnam, 1966). Samuel Eliot Morison's *The European Discovery of America: The Northern Voyages* (Oxford U. Press, 1971) is the work of an historian and sailor. For background see Wallace Notestein, *The English People on the Eve of Colonization, 1603–1630* (Harper & Row, 1954).* J. H. Parry's *Europe and a Wider World, 1415–1715* (Hillary, 1949) is an interesting survey. Richard Hofstadter, a distinguished historian, has captured a single year in print in his *America at 1750* (Random House, 1971).*

WEALTH

A wide sweep of economic history is covered by Stuart Bruchey, *The Roots of American Economic Growth, 1607–1861* (Harper & Row, 1968).* No stone is left unturned in Charles M. Andrews' *The Colonial Period of American History* (Yale U. Press, 1931),* of which the final volume deals with British imperial policy on the eve of the Revolution. Another impressive work is Lawrence H. Gipson, *The British Empire Before the American Revolution* (Knopf, 1958–1970). Oliver N. Dickerson, *The Navigation Acts and the American Revolution* (U. of Pennsylvania Press, 1974)* is a valuable study. Social classes and mobility are dealt with in Jackson T. Main, *Social Structure of Revolutionary America* (Princeton U. Press, 1963).* Michael Kammen, *Empire and Interest: The American Colonies and the Politics of Mercantilism* (Lippincott, 1970)* is a recent and valuable work on an important topic. America's "greatest success story" speaks for himself in *The Autobiography, and Other Writings of Benjamin Franklin*, Russel B. Nye, ed. (Houghton Mifflin, 1958).

* Available in paperback.

POWER

The political aspects of the Revolutionary War are covered by Edmund S. Morgan, *The Birth of the Republic: 1763–1789* (U. of Chicago Press, 1956)* and Bruce Lancaster and John H. Plumb, *The American Heritage Book of the Revolution* (Dell, 1958).* John C. Wahlke, ed., *The Causes of the American Revolution* (Heath, 1973)* presents conflicting points of view—an essential way to examine the question. Carl L. Becker, *The Declaration of Independence: A Study in the History of Political Ideas* (Random House, 1942)* is classic. John C. Miller, *Sam Adams: Pioneer in Propaganda* (Stanford U. Press, 1936)* is but one of many political biographies of the era.

Constitutional history is dealt with by Merill Jensen, *The Articles of Confederation* (U. of Wisconsin Press, 1940)* and Catherine Drinker Bowen, *Miracle at Philadelphia: The Story of the Constitutional Convention, May to September, 1787* (Little, Brown, 1966) and Charles Warren, *The Making of the Constitution* (Barnes & Nobles, 1967). See also *The Federalist* (available in many editions).* Jackson T. Main, *The Antifederalists: Critics of the Constitution, 1781–1788* (U. of North Carolina Press, 1961)* presents another side of the question.

WAR

An interpretative work covering centuries of military affairs is Walter Millis, *Arms and Men* (Putnam, 1967).* Two detailed studies dealing specifically with the period up to the formation of the new nation are Douglas E. Leach, *Arms for Empire: A Military History of the British Colonies in North America, 1607–1763* (Macmillan, 1973) and Donald Higginbotham, *The War of American Independence* (Macmillan, 1971). Much briefer is Howard H. Peckham, *The Colonial Wars, 1689–1762* (U. of Chicago Press, 1964)* and *The War for Independence: A Military History* (U. of Chicago Press, 1958).* Biographies exist for several generals, including, of course, the most important. See James T. Flexner, *George Washington* (Little, Brown, 1965–1972). *The American Heritage Book of the Revolution* (American Heritage, 1971) is a highly readable account.

RACE

There are innumerable books on Indians and Indian—white relations. Harold E. Driver, *Indians of North America* (U. of Chicago Press, 1969)* and Alvin M. Josephy, Jr., *The Indian Heritage of America* (Knopf, 1968) are excellent surveys. On the colonial period an indispensable new work dealing with interracial history is Gary B. Nash, *Red, White, and Black: The Peoples of Early America* (Prentice-Hall, 1974).* A useful specialized study is Alden T. Vaughan, *The New England Frontier: Indians and Puritans, 1620–1675* (Little, Brown, 1965).* As for white attitudes toward blacks, a valuable book of documents is Barry N. Schwartz and Robert Disch, eds., *White Racism* (Dell, 1970).* It also has a useful introduction. Winthrop D. Jordan, *White Over Black: American Attitudes Toward the Negro, 1550–1812* (U. of North Carolina Press, 1968) is unexcelled for its analysis of white racial sentiment in the colonial and early national eras. A valuable introduction to slavery as a whole down to 1860 is Kenneth Stampp, *The Peculiar Institution* (Random House, 1956).* A useful collection of documentary evidence is Leslie H. Fishel, Jr., and Benjamin Quarles, eds., *The Black American: A Documentary History*, 3rd edition (Scott, Foresman, 1976).*

NATIONALITY AND RELIGION

Practically every side of American religious history is covered by Sydney E. Ahlstrom's *A Religious History of the American People* (Yale U. Press, 1974)* and Winthrop S. Hudson's *Religion in America* (Scribner, 1973).* A standard reference is William W. Sweet, *Religion in Colonial America* (Cooper Square, 1942). Two religious biographies are Edmund S. Morgan, *Roger Williams: The Church and the State* (Harcourt Brace, 1967) and Edward H. Davidson, *Jonathan Edwards* (Harvard U. Press, 1968). Perry G. Miller's *Errand into the Wilderness* (Harper & Row, 1956)* is difficult but rewarding. Marcus L. Hansen, *The Atlantic Migration, 1607–1860* (Harper & Row, 1940)* is a standard account dealing with immigration. Sociologist Milton M. Gordon's work on *Assimilation in American Life: The Role of Race, Religion, and National Origins* (Oxford U. Press, 1964)* covers a great deal of American history in an insightful manner. Almost every ethnic group has had its historians. See, for example, Yves F. Zoltvany, ed., *The French Tradition in America* (Harper & Row, 1969).

WOMEN AND THE FAMILY

The best introduction to feminism, Eleanor Flexner's *Century of Struggle: The Woman's Rights Movement in the United States* (Atheneum, 1968),* has an introductory chapter on the colonial period and a useful bibliogra-

phy. A handy collection of documents is Aileen S. Kraditor, ed., *Up From the Pedestal* (Quadrangle, 1968).* Julia C. Spruill, *Women's Life and Work in the Southern Colonies* (Norton, 1972) is one of the few specialized treatments of women prior to 1789. Edmund S. Morgan, ed., *The Puritan Family: Religion and Domestic Relations in Seventeenth-Century New England* (Harper & Row, 1966)* and John Demos, *A Little Commonwealth: Family Life in Plymouth Colony* (Oxford U. Press, 1970)* are two brief readable and interesting accounts of family life, a subject much neglected by American historians.

COMMUNITY

William Bradford, *Of Plymouth Plantation* (Peter Smith, 1952) is a classic. It can be read along with George D. Langdom, Jr., *Pilgrim Colony: A History of New Plymouth, 1620–1691* (Yale U. Press, 1966). Samuel Eliot Morison, *Builders of the Bay Colony* (Houghton Mifflin, 1963) is a valuable account of early Massachusetts. A brief and readable interpretation of one community is Kenneth Lockridge, *A New England Town* (Norton, 1970).* An excellent survey of cities in the nation's development is Charles N. Glaab and A. Theodore Brown, *A History of Urban America* (Macmillan, 1967).* A penetrating sociological work is Ruth E. Sutter, *The Next Place You Come To: A Historical Introduction to Communities in North America* (Prentice-Hall, 1973).* Carl Bridenbaugh's *Cities in the Wilderness: The First Century of Urban Life in America, 1625–1742* (Oxford U. Press, 1971)* and *Cities in Revolt, Urban Life in America, 1743–1776* (Oxford U. Press, 1970)* are full-scale accounts of the five leading American cities.

ENVIRONMENT

Roderick Nash's full-length study, *Wilderness and the American Mind* (Yale U. Press, 1973),* and his edited book of documents, *The American Environment: Readings in the History of Conservation* (Addison-Wesley, 1968)* are good introductions to the subject. The latter has a handy bibliography. A readable and influential survey is Stewart L. Udall, *The Quiet Crisis* (Avon, 1964),* written by the Secretary of the Interior under Presidents Kennedy and Johnson. Perry Miller's *Errand into the Wilderness*, cited above, has an interesting chapter on the colonial view of nature.

San Francisco, about 1851.

II

Chronology

1789
George Washington inaugurated president (reelected 1792).

1800–1808
Jefferson's presidency.

1812–1815
War of 1812.

1828–1836
Jackson's presidency. First commercial railroad (1830).

1846–1848
War with Mexico.

1848
First women's rights convention.

1850
Compromise of 1850 begins a decade of crisis over slavery.

1861
Lincoln inaugurated president. Civil War begins (April 12).

1865
Lincoln assassinated. Civil War ends (April 19).

Our blood is as the flood of the Amazon, made up of a thousand noble currents all pouring into one. We are not a nation, so much as a world.

HERMAN MELVILLE   (1819–1891)

overview
A New Nation

In the seven decades between Washington's last year as president and Lincoln's assassination, many radical changes occurred in the new nation. The country's size quadrupled. The number of states in the Union almost tripled. The gold rush to California set off a massive transcontinental migration. The movement for women's rights emerged. Steam power was applied to transportation and manufacturing, starting a revolution in commerce and industry. And the great Civil War, which many consider the most important and most tragic episode in American history, was fought.

Setting a new government in motion

In 1789 George Washington was elected the first president under the Constitution. During his presidency the new government was organized. Washington appointed such able men as Thomas Jefferson (secretary of state) and Alexander Hamilton (secretary of the treasury) to serve as his department heads and to be members of his "cabinet"—a body of presidential advisers not mentioned in the Constitution. He sent his own program of laws to the Congress instead of waiting for Congress to send proposed laws to him, and he sent only *signed* treaties to the Senate for approval. He also supported the Federal Judiciary Act (1789), which organized the Supreme Court, circuit courts, and district courts, created the office of attorney general, and made it possible to appeal decisions of state courts to federal courts.

Disputes over the basic nature of the new government had begun during the struggle to ratify the Constitution and adopt the Bill of Rights. During Washington's administration such disagreements grew more heated. One of the stormiest disputes was over Hamilton's proposals for handling the national debt, national revenue, banking and currency, and tariffs. Their purpose was to give the new nation economic respectability, thereby winning it the support of the wealthy and powerful, and to create favorable conditions for the growth of commerce and industry.

Jefferson, on the other hand, believed that America's future depended on its being largely a nation of farmers, whose freedoms had to be preserved. He detested Hamilton's efforts to push America in new directions away from his own agrarian ideal. Jefferson argued that Hamilton's proposal for a national bank was unconstitutional. He championed "strict construction" (narrow interpretation) of the Constitution in an unsuccessful attempt to block Hamilton's scheme.

The rivalries and disagreements initiated by Hamilton's program sharpened in response to the French Revolution. When the French rebels stormed the Bastille in 1789 and destroyed that hated prison, all Americans cheered. The cause of liberty, equality, and fraternity in France seemed an extension of the American Declaration of Independence. But in 1793 the rebels executed Louis XVI and began a Reign of Terror that killed great numbers of people suspected of opposing the Revolution. In the same year France announced its determination to spread the ideals of the Revolution and declared war on Britain and Spain. Stirred by these alarming events, Americans voiced support for one side or the other. Jeffersonians—now called Democratic-Republicans or simply Republicans—sided with France. Hamiltonians—still called Federalists—backed Britain and opposed the French revolutionaries.

Undeclared war with France

By the Treaty of Alliance signed in 1778 America was technically supposed to help its French ally protect the French West Indies. But Washington refused to take sides with the new revolutionary government in France, and in a proclamation he forbade all Americans from participating "in any hostilities on land or sea with any belligerent powers."

But America could not stay completely out of a war that was becoming worldwide. In 1794 Jay's Treaty tried (with very limited success) to iron out the differences that had existed between the U.S. and Britain since the American Revolution. The treaty angered the French, who saw it as a sign that America really supported Britain. France dismissed the American ambassador to Paris and in the so-called XYZ Affair (1797) insulted the United States by demanding a bribe in exchange for a favorable treaty between the two nations. This spurred a war fever among Americans, and in 1798 the U.S. entered an "undeclared war" with France. Washington, whose presidency had ended in 1797, was called out of retirement to head the army. Harbors were fortified, new warships built, the Department of the Navy created, and naval battles fought.

President John Adams prevented the war with France from becoming even worse and from dividing Americans even more when, in 1800, he was able to reach a settlement with Napoleon. Adams' fight against the extreme positions of the War Hawks in his own Federalist party was his proudest accomplishment. But the Federalist Congress did attempt to suppress dissenting Republicans by passing the Alien and Sedition Acts of 1798. Republican leaders (Jefferson and Madison) responded on the state level with the Kentucky and Virginia Resolves (1798–1799), which claimed for states the right to nullify unconstitutional federal laws.

Political factions and Jefferson's election

By now America was divided into two political camps: Federalists and Democratic-Republicans, or Republicans (later to be called Democrats). The first signs of the split occurred at the time of the ratification of the Constitution but became more pronounced in the 1790s with the emergence of the Hamilton-Jefferson disputes during Washington's administration. The partisans of Hamilton's financial program (the Federalists) were strongest in commercial towns, in New England, and in the southern Tidewater region. They won the 1796 election with John Adams as their first presidential candidate. Opponents of Hamilton (the Republicans) supported Jefferson. This faction gained strength among farmers and artisans in scattered areas of the nation and was able to win a narrow presidential election in 1800.

Though some Federalists expected him to govern as an extremist, Jefferson in power was remarkably conservative. He did not undermine the Hamiltonian financial system or destroy the national bank. He did lower internal revenue taxes, including Hamilton's unpopular whiskey tax, and he did cut federal spending, including expenditures on naval construction and showy public functions. His purchase of the Louisiana Territory (1803) from France for $15 million was a far-reaching action which he knew to be unconstitutional (or at least not explicitly provided for anywhere in the Constitution). It directly affected the lives of fifty thousand Americans in the Ohio and Tennessee valleys and indirectly affected the entire nation—then and thereafter. Jefferson sent Meriwether Lewis and William Clark up the Missouri River to explore the new territory, and between 1804 and 1806 they trailblazed their way to the Pacific Ocean and back.

Jefferson's first administration was fairly routine. But the second term posed the challenge of how to respond to the warlike acts of feuding European powers against American shipping. Britain and France, their old competition made more intense by Napoleon's imperial ambitions, once again threatened to draw America into their endless duel. In June 1807 a British man-o'-war, the *Leopard*, fired at close range at the U.S. frigate *Chesapeake*. Twenty-one American seamen were killed or wounded, and four (the British claimed they were Royal Navy deserters) were "impressed"—that is, forced to serve in the British navy. War excitement again gripped the nation, but Jefferson tried to teach both Britain and France a lesson by imposing an embargo (December 1807) on all American shipping to Europe. As it turned out, this action hurt the U.S.

more than it hurt either warring power. America simply was not rich or powerful enough to cut off its trade with stronger nations or to expect to force them to mend their ways.

The War of 1812 and shifts in the political balance

In 1809 James Madison, who inherited Jefferson's headaches along with the presidency, supported a variety of restrictions on commerce as alternatives to America's being pulled into war. But Napoleon and his diplomats were too clever for both Madison and the British. French diplomacy, the slowness of the British to come to an understanding with America, and the belligerence of the western War Hawks in Congress finally led Madison, on June 1, 1812, to ask Congress for a war declaration against Britain.

American sentiment in favor of the War of 1812 was far stronger in the West and South than along the North Atlantic Coast. In fact, there was a threat of rebellion in New England because the war further damaged the ocean commerce on which the New Englanders depended. In December 1814 powerful Federalists in New England called a meeting, the Hartford Convention. They demanded basic changes in the structure of government, both to protect their interests and to bring an end to what they called the "Virginia dynasty" that had dominated American political life since the Revolution. By the time they ended their discussions, in January 1815, British and American delegations meeting in Ghent, Belgium, had signed a treaty ending hostilities. But the news did not reach the United States until after Andrew Jackson had won an amazing victory over the British at New Orleans. This ended the War of 1812 on a note of triumph for Madison's Republican administration, whose fortunes had been sagging throughout the conflict. Madison and Jackson became national heroes overnight, and the Federalist party was left with little prestige and few followers. By 1824 all the major candidates for the presidency were called Republicans.

But if the Federalists never regained power, they continued to influence American law and justice. John Marshall, a Federalist, served as chief justice of the Supreme Court from 1801 to 1835. He wrote over half of the Court's 1106 opinions in the course of a generation. His interpretations of the Constitution consistently fostered the rights of property owners—often business interests—and increased the power of the national government at the expense of the states. His overall impact was to make the Constitution an instrument of economic and social policy. One of his most important opinions (*Marbury* v. *Madison*, 1803) laid down the principle of judicial review, which held that the Supreme Court could declare acts of Congress unconstitutional. Another decision (*Fletcher* v. *Peck*, 1810) strengthened the force of private contracts by ruling that they could not be violated even by a state. In *McCulloch* v. *Maryland* (1819) Marshall ruled that, through powers *implied* in the Constitution, Congress had the right to charter the Bank of the United States and that states had no right to restrict the Bank's activities. His ruling in *Gibbons* v. *Ogden* (1824) held that no state could interfere with interstate commerce.

The westward movement

In the decades following the War of 1812, millions of settlers poured westward across the Appalachians to make permanent homes on new land. New farms, new towns, and even new cities arose. Indian tribes were forced out of the Old Northwest and the South. New states were created to swell the Union: Indiana (1816); Mississippi (1817); Illinois (1818); Alabama (1819); Missouri (1821); Arkansas (1836); Michigan (1837); Texas and Florida (1845); Iowa (1846); Wisconsin (1848); California (1850); Minnesota (1858); and Oregon (1859). In 1810 fewer than 300,000 settlers lived in the Old Northwest (the territory west of the original states, north of the Ohio River, and east of the Mississippi). By the Civil War there were more than seven million people there. In the popular mind the West had become a "safety valve" to ease the pressure of growing social problems in the older, more settled parts of America. In theory, if not in practice, the availability of free land would save Americans from class conflict and urban strife. So Americans "hitched their wagon to a star" and rode west.

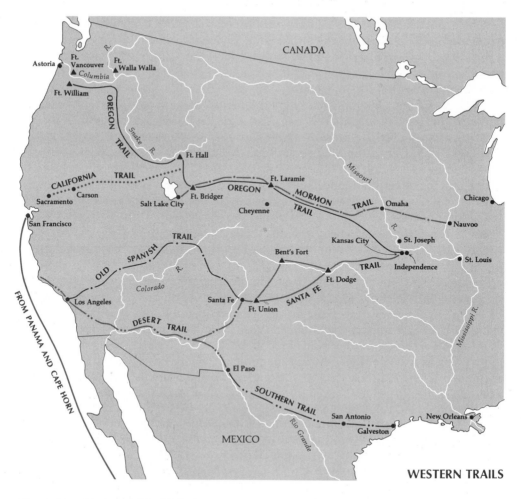

WESTERN TRAILS

The Jacksonian era

Until Andrew Jackson was elected in 1828, American presidents came from either Virginia or Massachusetts, and all Washington's successors had worked their way up through the cabinet. Jackson ended this "aristocratical" pattern and "toppled the Virginia-Massachusetts dynasty." Around the hero of New Orleans there formed a coalition of western farmers, city laborers, small bankers, tradespeople, and others who saw him as God's gift to the common people. They hoped to put him in the White House in 1824, and in the election of that year he did get the largest number of popular votes. But as Jackson's supporters saw it, a "corrupt bargain" between candidates John Quincy Adams and Henry Clay gave Adams the most electoral votes and the presidency. Adams then made Clay secretary of state.

Jackson—Old Hickory—succeeded in 1828 and was reelected president four years later. Jackson made good on the slogan "to the victors belong the spoils" by giving patronage jobs (positions filled by appointment) to his backers. He became the symbol of democracy at a time when the number of voters was expanding rapidly and when mobility—both social and geographical—was the keynote of American life.

Jackson waged two fierce contests as president. In one he tried to limit the activities of the federal government; in the other he greatly strengthened federal power. First, he destroyed the Bank of the United States, which had enjoyed special powers and privileges, and he placed its funds in state and local banks (1833). This pleased his backers, who wanted trade and finance to be free of central government control, but it helped cause a harsh economic depression in 1837. Second, he resisted South Carolina's attempt to "nullify" a tariff law that state disliked (1832–1833). This pitted him against Senator John C. Calhoun, a spokesman for the planter aristocracy of the Old South and for the idea that the states could declare federal laws unconstitutional. Jackson's victory in this nullification contest was a victory for centralism and the Union over "states' rights."

During Jackson's term the removal of Indians to the West became official government policy. The president ordered the Civilized Tribes of the Southeast moved to the "permanent Indian Frontier" beyond the Mississippi. Some went peacefully, making new treaties and getting some payment for giving up their homes. Others resisted, like the Cherokees, who took their case all the way to the Supreme Court, and the Seminoles, who fought on until 1843, inflicting many casualties on the U.S. Army. By 1839 the military had removed most of the southern tribes, but the cost was enormous—both in wasted human lives and in the growing moral burden created by such acts. For example, forced marches over the "Trail of Tears" killed about four thousand Cherokees and subjected the survivors to intense suffering from hunger and exposure.

The same sad story was played out in the North, where in the Black Hawk War of 1832 the Sac and Fox tribes of Illinois tried to return to their lands and were crushed by the state militia. This removed the last Indian barrier to white expansion in the Old Northwest. The Bureau of Indian Affairs, created in 1836 to administer Indian treaties, was more notable for becoming the most durable federal bureaucracy than for protecting the rights or meeting the needs of Indians.

Transportation and urban growth

From the beginning, transportation was a serious problem in America. Distance and terrain were obstacles that cut the farmer off from his market, the pioneer from his homestead, the traveler from his destination. In the early part of the nineteenth century numerous turnpikes were opened. The National Road, built with federal aid, stretched from Cumberland, Maryland, to Wheeling, West Virginia, by 1818. But overland travel remained slow and rough, and Americans looked to waterways. The Erie Canal in New York State, completed in 1825, was a great financial success and began a decade and more of canal building.

By then the age of steam was revolutionizing transportation. Robert Fulton's *Clermont* had splashed its way up the Hudson River in 1807, and it was soon evident that steam could power river boats dependably and profitably. By midcentury a thousand paddle-wheel steamboats were working the Mississippi River system, and steamers were beginning to capture the transatlantic trade. Meanwhile, overland travel had received a tremendous boost from the steam-driven railroad. Nine thousand miles of track were laid between 1830 and 1850, and 21,000 more in the next ten years. By the time of the Civil War much of the eastern half of the nation was crisscrossed by rails.

The growth of cities and industries kept pace. New cities sprang up and old cities grew bigger. New York City became the nation's leading metropolis. And the factory system made impressive gains even as economic progress was shaken by serious business depressions in 1819, 1837, and 1857.

American expansionism

Regionalism—divisions and differences between commercial North and agrarian South, between settled East and frontier West—was a constant factor in shaping the new nation. But so were nationalism and the American dream of expansion. John Quincy Adams, while secretary of state (1817–1825), had a vision of the U.S. stretching from ocean to ocean. He conducted a series of brilliant negotiations with Spain, which brought Florida under American control and gave the U.S. a clearer claim to lands bordering the Pacific north of California. And he helped write the Monroe Doctrine in 1823. There was a possibility that the great continental powers of Europe would seek to win back for Spain the Latin American republics that had established their independence, and Russia represented a threat to American ambitions in the Pacific Northwest.

In the Monroe Doctrine the U.S. proclaimed that Europe must not try to take back old colonies or grab new ones in the Americas. In turn, the U.S. would not take sides in any wars in the Old World. An important point about the Monroe Doctrine was that Britain also feared the intervention of the continental European powers in Latin America and lent its support to the newly stated policy of the United States. By its official words and actions, America seemed to be taking the stand that if there were to be any expansion in this part of the world, the U.S. would do the expanding. America was building an image of itself as a proud national state eager to grow larger.

By 1845 American expansionism was going into high gear. The press, politicians, and ordinary citizens had begun talking about the right of the U.S. to spread over the whole continent. Some saw American expansion as a plan of God or Nature and called it Manifest Destiny. Such a mystical idea suited a country whose population was growing fast and whose citizens were moving out to settle beyond the national boundaries. The U.S. tried to fulfill its Manifest Destiny by taking more and more land—some by annexation, some by peaceful agreements, some by war.

Texas, formerly a part of Mexico, had been an independent republic for a decade when, in 1845, it was annexed to the U.S. and quickly made a state. Next year the U.S. and Britain ended their joint occupation of the Oregon Territory by dividing it at the present Canadian-American border. The annexation of Texas led to the Mexican War (1846–1848), which not only settled the Texas issue but resulted in the American acquisition of what is now New Mexico, Arizona, Nevada, Utah, part of Colorado, and all of California, with its very valuable harbor at San Francisco. In only a few years the idea of Manifest Destiny had become the reality of an America stretching from sea to shining sea.

These same years were marked by the development of social movements and the spread of ideas about reforming and improving American life. The women's rights movement began in 1848 at a convention at Seneca Falls, New York, out of which came the famous declaration that "all men *and women* are created equal." Some other important movements that got started in America before the Civil War were organized labor, free public education, prison reform, pacifism, and temperance. The communitarian movement led to the establishment of colonies like Robert Owen's New Harmony in Indiana (1825–1828) and the Transcendentalists' Brook Farm in Massachusetts (1841–1847). Such experimental communities (or communes) differed radically in their philosophies but usually involved a small group working together to produce all they needed and sharing all they produced.

America creates a literature

Independence from British rule did not instantly create a distinctly American culture. That took time. But after 1815 a greater sense of national identity did begin to develop. And there soon emerged a literary culture that was not merely an echo of the European tradition.

From about 1815 to 1840 a number of writers based in New York City began exploring native American themes. Among them were Washington Irving,

William Cullen Bryant, and James Fenimore Cooper. Cooper's *Leatherstocking Tales*, published from 1823 to 1841, were the first important novels to use the frontier as a setting and to depict the contrast between civilization and the wilderness.

In the 1840s and 1850s New England became the scene of such extraordinary literary productivity—by poets, historians, novelists, and essayists—that the period came to be known as the New England Renaissance. This flowering of thought and letters was brightest in and around Boston. At Concord, Henry David Thoreau wrote *Walden* (1854), and at Salem, Nathaniel Hawthorne produced *The Scarlet Letter* (1850). Many of the better-known poets of the era were New Englanders: Henry Wadsworth Longfellow, Oliver Wendell Holmes, John Greenleaf Whittier, and James Russell Lowell. And at the heart of the intellectual ferment was the essayist Ralph Waldo Emerson, leader of the movement known as Transcendentalism. With its emphasis on the sacredness of the individual and the power of self-reliance, Transcendentalism suited the romantic spirit of the times.

Walt Whitman, who was born on Long Island, produced one of America's greatest literary classics, *Leaves of Grass* (1855). He was greatly influenced by Emerson's ideas, and his poetry goes far beyond that of his contemporaries in ignoring literary tradition and convention and relying on his own inspiration. Although his work shocked readers at the time, its informality, its outpouring of emotion, and its celebration of the common man all marked it as distinctively American.

Herman Melville, born in New York City, wrote about his experiences on American whaling ships and on the islands of the South Pacific. *Moby Dick* (1851), a failure in Melville's lifetime, has since become a world classic. It is a multilevel novel that, while describing the whaling industry in detail, explores the tragic and the heroic in human nature.

Although born in Boston, Edgar Allan Poe grew up in the South and worked there during much of his brief career. As literary critic, poet, and short story writer, he exerted a powerful influence both at home and abroad. One of Poe's benefactors was John Pendleton Kennedy, whose novel *Swallow Barn* (1832) presented a romantic picture of plantation life in Virginia. Augustus B. Longstreet and William G. Simms were two other southern writers who were well known in their time. Some of the most popular works about the South were the songs of a northerner, Stephen Foster.

The most popular novel of its time—also written about the South by a northerner—was *Uncle Tom's Cabin* (1852) by Harriet Beecher Stowe. Stowe condemned slavery for its cruelty and its destruction of black families. She made a whole generation of northerners concerned about what the South's "peculiar institution" (slavery) was doing to America. Although a huge amount of fiction was written by women for women in America, no other work had the influence of *Uncle Tom's Cabin.*

In 1835 a young French nobleman, Alexis de Tocqueville, published *Democracy in America.* Many still consider it the most remarkable book ever written about this country. For nine months Tocqueville journeyed throughout the nation, meeting citizens, both distinguished and ordinary. He seemed to notice everything—religion, marriage, prison management, vigilante justice, agriculture, the cities, the wilderness. Above all, he was impressed by the leveling trend in American life and by the strength and flexibility of popular government. Yet he did not fail to see some of the flaws in the democratic jewel. Slavery prompted him to make this gloomy forecast: either the country would grant full equality for blacks, which seemed unlikely, or it would crack open on the slavery issue. He saw early and clearly America's greatest problem.

Slavery: the great debate

At the time America won its independence, it seemed possible that the institution of slavery would gradually die out. But after the invention of the cotton gin, in 1793, southern agriculture was revolutionized. By the turn of the century production had increased nearly tenfold. After the War of 1812 great new territories were opened up that could be profitably worked by slave labor. The Missouri Compromise of 1820 prohibited the further expansion of slavery into the Louisiana Territory above the line of 36°30' north latitude. But the spread of slavery into the West became an issue that was more and more difficult to settle through political compromise. Crisis piled on crisis as southerners supporting slavery and northerners opposing it argued an issue on which they could never agree.

Southern resistance to ending slavery only increased as some slaves tried to free themselves and northerners began organizing a movement to abolish slavery. In Charleston a slave uprising led by Denmark Vesey in 1822 was crushed before it really got started—thirty-five slaves were executed. In 1829 David Walker, a free black, issued his *Appeal,* which called for all slaves to kill their masters. And in 1831 Nat Turner's slave rebellion took the lives of fifty-seven whites. In that same year, the white editor William Lloyd Garrison began publishing *The Liberator,* the era's main abolitionist newspaper.

After 1830 the South began thinking of itself as almost a separate nation based on slavery. Southern whites defended the system by saying it was economically necessary. And they argued that their way was better than that of the North, where white workers who could be hired and fired at will were free in name only. They claimed that many slaves in the South lived better, happier, more secure lives than poor whites in the North. The abolitionists disagreed violently and the ever harsher debate went on. The South reacted by denying freedom of expression to abolitionists. Those who spoke out were whipped and beaten. Schools, colleges, public forums, and the mails were denied to abolitionists. In 1836 southern congressmen even imposed a "gag resolution" that prevented the House from receiving antislavery petitions.

At no time did the abolitionists become a dominant political force. They remained a minority up to and during the Civil War. There were two camps. One, led by Garrison, called for immediate abolition. The other would accept a slower, more gradual ending of slavery.

Texas had been admitted to the Union as a slave state. But the vast territories acquired in the Mexican War raised again the whole issue of whether or not slavery would be allowed in new areas. Senator Henry Clay of Kentucky worked out the Compromise of 1850. This series of laws was supposed to bring about a peaceful and reasonable settlement of all disputes between pro-slavery and antislavery forces. It offered something for both sides. California was to join the Union as a free state; the settlers of New Mexico and Utah were to decide the slavery question through "popular sovereignty"—dealing with the issue locally, by and for themselves. The sale of slaves was to end in the District of Columbia, and there was to be a new fugitive slave law so that runaways could be seized in the North and returned to their southern masters.

Senator Daniel Webster of Massachusetts thought slavery was wrong, but he believed "the preservation of the Union" was the supreme issue, and so he favored the Compromise. Senator William H. Seward of New York opposed the Compromise because, to him, slavery was such a great moral wrong that any compromise would be equally wrong and vicious. Opinions were so sharply split on the matter that the Compromise of 1850 soon increased existing differences. The Fugitive Slave Act was openly violated in some northern cities, and the South felt deeply betrayed.

The next major crisis over slavery came in 1854 when Senator Stephen A. Douglas of Illinois proposed a bill that would allow the settlement of the last sections of the Louisiana Purchase under the system of "popular sovereignty." That is, the people of Kansas and Nebraska would assemble in convention and decide whether or not they wanted slavery. But slavery in these territories was forbidden by the Missouri Compromise of 1820. To many people this ban had become a fundamental constitutional principle. Nevertheless, Douglas pushed his bill through Congress. His personal objectives were to win support for a transcontinental rail line across the northern United States and to increase his own chances for the presidency. But the Kansas-Nebraska Act, with its built-in repeal of the Missouri Compromise, tore apart the Democratic party in the North. And violence soon broke out in "Bleeding Kansas," as proslavery and antislavery forces fought to gain control of the territory before it was admitted to the Union.

The Supreme Court threw a monkey wrench into the machinery of compromise in 1857. In the Dred Scott decision the Court declared that the Missouri Compromise line was unconstitutional; that Congress never had the right to prohibit slavery in the West; and that even a vote by the settlers of a territory was not a legal way to prevent the spread of slavery. The Court said that slaves were property and that the Constitution protected slave owners, along with all other property owners, from being deprived of their property. It was the first time since *Marbury* v. *Madison* (1803) that the Court had declared a federal law unconstitutional. Southerners were overjoyed, but Americans opposed to the westward expansion of slavery were furious.

The slavery issue split such important American institutions as political parties and churches. The largest church denominations divided along sectional lines. The "Conscience Whigs" joined with those Democrats who had been outraged by the Kansas-Nebraska Act and formed a new Republican party. In 1856 it ran the western explorer John C. Frémont in a losing bid for the White House against the Democrat James Buchanan. In 1860, with the Democrats hopelessly divided, the Republican candidate was Abraham Lincoln, a former Whig congressman who had always taken a moderate position on slavery.

With four candidates running, Lincoln was able to win the presidency with northern electoral votes alone, though he received less than 40 percent of the popular vote. The South, believing that Lincoln would not compromise on the slavery question and fearing his strong views on preserving the Union, would not accept his election. Southern states seceded and formed the Confederate States of America. Outgoing President Buchanan made ineffective efforts at compromise, and by the time Lincoln was inaugurated on March 4, 1861, civil war was unavoidable. On April 12, 1861, Confederate guns fired on Fort Sumter, a federal installation in Charleston Harbor. The Civil War had begun.

Civil War

The North had several advantages. In the course of the war some two million served in the Union forces, compared to about 750,000 for the Confederates. The Union's railroads, ships, and shipyards, its weapons production, farm output, and financial resources, and its civilian population all far outweighed the South's. But the Grays (the soldiers of the Confederacy) were fighting in defense of their homeland and had the advantage of shorter supply lines. And the Blues (the Union soldiers) had to defeat the South completely, while the Confederacy could win just by gaining a stalemate.

Early Union attempts to seize Richmond, the Confederate capital, failed, but Union armies fared better in the West. Under Ulysses S. Grant, they advanced along the Tennessee and Cumberland rivers from 1862 on, finally capturing Vicksburg in 1863. This opened the Mississippi River to Union ships and cut the Confederacy in two. But it took more than two years and some of the bloodiest warfare in history before the final northern victory. The gallant southern general, Robert E. Lee, finally surrendered the main Confederate army to Grant at Appomattox Court House, Virginia, on April 9, 1865. Five days later, an actor named John Wilkes Booth shot President Lincoln as he sat watching a play in a Washington theater. Lincoln died the next day.

The Union was preserved and the slaves were freed, but the price was awesome: 600,000 dead soldiers and many, many more gravely wounded, large portions of the South ravaged, the president slain, and a bitterness between the victorious and the defeated that would last for decades. The prayer of the fallen president for reunification was realized. He had hoped also, in his eloquent Gettysburg Address, "that this nation, under God, shall have a rebirth of freedom." Insofar as this referred to black Americans, achieving such a true rebirth of freedom would test the American Republic for generations—and tests it still.

A view of the locks joining the Champlain and Erie canals, painted by John Hill around 1835. The Erie Canal, completed in 1825, greatly reduced the time and cost of transporting goods between the Great Lakes and the Hudson River (and thus New York City). The huge success of the "Big Ditch" set off a canal-building boom across the nation.

9

9

A Go-Getter Nation

How does a nation become "developed"? How, in other words, does it acquire economic independence, modern equipment, and steady growth? This is an agonizing question in many world capitals today. The full answer is complex and has much to do with industrialization. In the United States, the feat of industrialization was accomplished before the Civil War. During the period between 1815 and 1860 America's economic potential became apparent. Some economic historians pin down the crucial turning point to the years 1843–1857. While the country's major output continued to be farm products, manufacturing rose so rapidly that by 1860 this country was second only to Britain in industrial production. Factories sprouted throughout the Northeast. The routes of clipper ships, steamboats, and railroads spanned great distances. California's gold rush was world news. The restlessness and aggressiveness of Americans were becoming legendary. By the early 1830s it was said that no American with an honest desire for work need ever be poor, but, in fact, explosive economic growth brought with it depressions and acute poverty.

In the past, historians have characterized America as an agricultural nation before 1865 and an industrial one afterward. Actually the effects of the Civil War on economic growth are debatable. Certainly the demands of the military did foster both large-scale manufacture and mass production. And the war brought on a spate of laws favoring capitalism. Wealth piled up in the hands of some financiers and manufacturers. Yet less cotton was used, fewer farm machines were wanted, building—a vital indicator of economic growth—slowed, and per capita income fell. Certainly the South was devastated by the war. The economy in general grew most rapidly before 1857. The war, like the depression which immediately preceded it, may actually have retarded growth.

The Economy of a New Nation

Questions of economic policy

The government of the United States was bankrupt in 1789. Enormous debts had piled up. It owed a total of $52 million to France, Holland, and Americans who had bought Continental bonds. It owed back pay and pensions to veterans (officers could claim full pay for five years or half pay for life). At the same time, the U.S. faced stiff competition in shipping, since it no longer enjoyed the protection of the Royal Navy. Pirates from North Africa's Barbary Coast captured U.S. merchant ships at will and held them for ransom. Worst of all, British ports in the Caribbean remained closed to American shipping. This denied Americans an important source of cash.

Even if the new government found new sources of revenue to keep its head above water, it still needed an overall economic policy. Who should pay taxes? How should tax money be used—and for whose benefit? Was it better to strengthen commerce and agriculture—both proven sources of income—or encourage manufacturing? Should the government grant businesses subsidies, special privileges, and monopolies? Or should it leave the market free to develop its own direction?

The Constitution was vital in assuring the future of capitalism. Certain provisions of the new framework of government had a direct bearing on economic growth. Article I gave Congress the power to levy taxes, thus providing a source of money to repay the government's war debts. It also allowed the federal government to take over the debts of the individual states, a policy that improved the government's standing with moneylenders at home and abroad. Thus the capitalists of Holland, Britain, and France could feel assured that further investments in America

might be worth the risk. The Constitution additionally gave the government the power to regulate coinage and money supplies. Congress also acquired the right to set tariff rates and improve international trade agreements. Commercial reprisals of one state against another were forbidden. Those who owned slaves—a valuable form of property—were guaranteed the return of runaways. The militia was strengthened to help put down domestic rebellions by debtors like Captain Shays. By allowing interstate court suits, the Constitution helped make commercial contracts binding. Aside from these specific provisions, the Constitution went a long way in establishing an overall climate of stability and order: the elimination of risks, the recognition of property rights, and the enforcement of contracts. This was a climate which business people found essential to their well-being.

Hamilton's system

Adoption of the Constitution paved the way for an economic policy devised by Washington's secretary of the treasury, Alexander Hamilton. On Congress' invitation he drew up a far-reaching blueprint for fiscal stability and economic growth. Hamilton's system was basically a modified form of mercantilism, where the government maintained certain controls over the economy.

Hamilton was an admirer of British institutions and a believer in law and order, discipline, and the theories of mercantilism. He wrote reports on public credit, manufacturing, and banking, and many of his proposals passed into law. He urged Congress to assume full responsibility for both the debts of the Continental and Confederation governments and for the states' debts. Both would be funded by issuing new, negotiable bonds, backed by the federal government, to holders of the old ones. The government would get money to pay the interest due on these notes by raising tariffs and enacting new excise taxes at home, particularly on whiskey (see p. 200). Finally, Hamilton pressed Congress to charter a national bank. It would be the country's master bank with power to regulate the monetary system and supply capital for private uses. All of these suggestions were adopted, but not without a fight.

Hamilton's program caused fierce arguments within Washington's administration. Thomas Jefferson, the secretary of state, tried hard to block the bill to charter the first Bank of the United States. He argued that the Constitution did not authorize such an institution. It would, he feared, put too much power in the hands of wealthy men, divert investment from farming to industry and speculation, and charge high interest rates that would benefit only the wealthy. Against Jefferson's "strict construction" of the Constitution, Hamilton argued a "broad construction." He maintained that the Constitution gave Congress implied power to set up any institution that would promote the general welfare.

The powers contained in a constitution of government, especially those which concern the general administration of the affairs of a country, its finances, trade, defense etc., ought to be construed liberally in advancement of the public good.

ALEXANDER HAMILTON (1755–1804)

Chartered in 1791, the Bank proved a success. In general, Hamilton's system greatly improved the credit rating of the United States abroad and made capital available for business.

A surge in economic growth

Even Thomas Jefferson, Hamilton's rival, believed in expanding the U.S. economy. When he became president, Jefferson retained much of Hamilton's program, including the first Bank of the United States. He adopted "broad construction" in authorizing the purchase from France of the Louisiana Territory, which brought the U.S. millions of acres of land and vast treasures of timber and natural resources. During the War of 1812, after his term in office, he came to see the advantages of promoting industrial growth as a way of ending America's dependence on English goods.

The three Republican presidents after Jefferson also favored Hamilton's program and encouraged economic growth. Madison approved the charter of the second Bank of the United States and the tariff of 1816. He authorized a survey of the West so that canals, turnpikes, and other improvements could be built. Monroe agreed to give $300,000 in federal money to the private Chesapeake and Delaware Canal Company. John Quincy Adams also signed measures backing federal roads and canals and a standard system of weights and measures. He granted land to Illinois and Indiana for state canals.

Numerous other federal measures aided economic growth. The government ran the post office. It granted public land to private owners and paid the Army Engineers to survey private transportation routes. It carved out military roads on the frontier and improved rivers and harbors. It subsidized steamships, codfisheries, and the first telegraph line. Interest-free loans on government contracts were offered to the makers of small firearms, and land was granted to the states for schools and state universities. The tariff of 1828 pushed the rates to their highest levels yet.

States and cities also supported business and overall economic growth. A favorite practice was to use state funds to establish corporations that would benefit the public in some way. Quasi-public organizations were set up to supply drinking water, erect docks, improve inland navigation, lay railroad tracks, and build bridges, turnpikes, and canals. In 1844 Pennsylvania alone had 150 such corporations. All told, over $136 million of state funds went into canal construction between 1815 and 1830. This accounted for about three quarters of the total investment in canals. Pennsylvania spent over $100 million on the Main Line canal and railroad system prior to the Civil War. In addition, states regulated the corporate charters of banks, insurance companies, and public utilities. In some cases they guaranteed corporate bonds, making them easier to sell. And cities participated in public improvement projects even more than did the states. In a scramble to attract railroads, Baltimore, Cincinnati, Milwaukee, and other cities made outright gifts to railroad companies totaling nearly $30 million by 1879.

The business corporation, whose presence we take for granted today, was just emerging in pre-Civil War days. At that time the average business was a partnership, an enterprise owned and operated by a group of relatives or close associates. But new enterprises like textile mills, railroads, and canals required more capital than most partners could supply. Promoters of these projects preferred to form corporations, which were state-chartered companies with a right to issue stock. Capital could then be raised from many investors. Another advantage of the corporation was its "limited liability." In the case of bankruptcy the personal property of each stockholder was safe from creditors, whereas if a partnership went under, the owners suffered "unlimited liability" and could lose all of their personal property.

To establish themselves, though, corporations had to overcome the strong popular sentiment that they were simply monopolies representing special privilege and, as such, would block free competition. In the Jacksonian period, corporation promoters met this problem by seeking charters which gave them no special privileges. This democratic move helped their cause. Another difficulty with the corporate operation was that the firm's directors were different from the owners and could sometimes cheat the stockholders. This happened frequently and was hard to stop.

Hamilton was indeed a singular character. Of acute understanding, disinterested, honest, and honorable in all private transactions, . . . yet so bewitched & perverted by the British example, as to be under thoro' conviction that corruption was essential to the government of a nation. . . .

THOMAS JEFFERSON   (1743–1826)

The Supreme Court helped the growth of corporations. The Charles River Bridge Case (1837) knocked down the claim of a bridge company to control the only right-of-way over the river and allowed other corporations to build competing bridges. In the long run this meant that old corporations could not block new ones from entering the market. The economy flourished with the competition.

Boom and bust cycles

In the years before the Civil War there were periods of depression as well as prosperity. Business panics struck in 1819, 1837, and 1857.

When the Constitution took effect, ocean trade was still in the doldrums. But the outbreak of war between France and Britain in 1793 tied up most European shipping and gave American firms a burst of energy that lasted until 1807. Desperate to obtain American goods, Britain dropped all trade regulations. The boom in trade was a stimulus to U.S. agriculture and the production of raw materials. Farmers suddenly found that their grains were in great demand on the wharves of Philadelphia, Baltimore, and New York, from which they were shipped to Europe. U.S. dollars spent overseas brought back abundant goods and capital. For the first time in years American ships were welcomed into the Caribbean, where they loaded up on sugar, coffee, cocoa, pepper, spices, and other tropical products. They carried these cargoes to Europe and exchanged them for finished goods. American cotton exports soared. Artisans worked full time. America was utilizing its resources to the best advantage.

In 1807 President Jefferson, reacting to both French and British conduct toward American ships, imposed an embargo on American trade with Europe. Initially, Jefferson had tried to steer a neutral course between the warring powers. But in blockading Britain, the French seized over two hundred U.S. ships. Not to be outdone, the British, while trying to stop shipping to France, seized over five hundred U.S. ships. With both nations attacking American ships, the president found it necessary to resort to the drastic remedy of embargo. This policy depressed American shipping all along the Atlantic coast from Boston to Charleston.

The War of 1812 between Britain and the U.S. had a positive effect on manufacturing, however. It encouraged investors to transfer capital from shipping to manufacturing. Mills for cotton textiles, wool, firearms, and clocks sprouted along New England's waterways. Pennsylvania, New York, and New

EXPORTS FROM THE U.S., 1790–1815

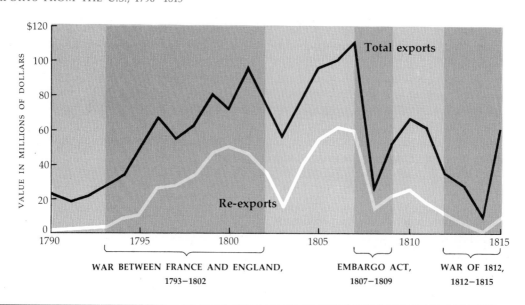

SOURCE: Adapted from Douglass C. North, *The Economic Growth of the United States, 1790–1860*, p. 26.

Wall Street on October 13, 1857. Overspeculation in railroads, real estate, manufacturing, and wheat during a decade and a half of prosperity and expansion led to the Panic of 1857.

Jersey boasted silk mills and factories that made shoes, hats, nails, and buttons. These manufactures temporarily eased America's dependence on Britain's factories. The investment in manufacturing in the U.S. stood at about $100 million in 1816. Still, when the war ended, British manufacturers dumped cheap finished goods on U.S. markets. This undercut prices and bankrupted numerous mills, causing havoc with the economy.

Manufacturing revived around 1820 with activity in processing industries like lumber, flour, and cornmeal and in light manufacturing including cotton and woolen goods, boots, shoes, and men's clothing. Production of iron machinery, steam engines, paper, glass, lead, sugar, molasses, and salt also picked up. The number of cotton spindles increased from 8000 in 1807 to 1.75 million in 1831. The first commercial steam engine was produced in 1805. Twenty-five years later 100 were manufactured in Pittsburgh and 150 in Cincinnati in a single year. As the Civil War neared, the U.S. was already the world's second greatest manufacturing nation.

In 1837 another panic struck, the result of years of too much land speculation in the West. Then from 1843 to 1857 the country experienced a major period of prosperity and was well on its way to becoming a truly industrial nation. In the eastern half of the country the railroads, canals, and steamboats were interconnected for the first time, so that the national market could be exploited. But in 1857 the speculation encouraged by expansion brought on another financial crash. As on previous occasions, the depression wiped out savings, disrupted productivity, and caused unemployment, poverty, and suffering.

The Industrial Revolution

Steam power and labor-saving inventions

Between the end of the eighteenth century and the middle of the nineteenth, science and technology merged to produce the Industrial Revolution. At its heart was the application of iron and steam to manufacturing and transportation. The machinery of the new age was hailed as a blessing that would relieve people of work, produce more goods at less cost, and generally make life safer and easier. Steamboats, railroads, cotton gins, and power looms caused the economy to spurt ahead.

In 1789 England was still far in front of the United States in technology. That was the year that an English factory mechanic, Samuel Slater, sailed for America, having memorized the design of British textile machinery. Anyone who exported machinery or mechanical plans could be fined or jailed, but there was no stopping the mechanics who carried their knowledge in their heads. In a few months Slater had set up America's first successful spinning mill at Pawtucket, Rhode Island. Even though Slater's mill was water powered, this event is often cited as the start of the Industrial Revolution in the U.S.

Mechanics in America developed the knack of modifying English equipment to make the best use of America's assets (abundant water power and natural resources) and to overcome its handicaps (primarily a labor shortage). Labor-saving machinery was one of America's main contributions to technology. One of the most successful early factories was Waltham Mills in Massachusetts. This textile firm specialized in "coarse sheeting," a cheap, low-grade cotton fabric that was scorned in England but widely used by frontier women for making clothes, sacks, and wagon covers. Waltham mechanics cleverly modified the English power loom to reduce the number of workers required to operate it. As a result, the firm survived the depression of 1816–1819 that devastated most manufacturing plants.

Eli Whitney topped the list of native inventors. It is doubtful whether any modern invention has had more immediate and dramatic economic impact than his cotton gin. Like many of his contemporaries, Whitney first learned about tools as a youngster in the workshed on his father's farm. As a teenager he repaired violins and manufactured nails. At one point he acquired a near monopoly on hat pins in this country. After graduating from Yale he went to Savannah, Georgia, to teach. There he was introduced to a group of men who wanted to develop a machine that would separate cotton fiber from the seed. It took him just ten days to develop the original model for his cotton gin. The machine consisted of a wooden drum studded with short spikes that caught the cotton seeds, and a comb that picked the fiber from the drum. By April 1793 Whitney had a working model in operation which would allow one worker to process fifty pounds of cotton a day. His invention revolutionized cotton production and changed American history. Until this time "upland" cotton—the type that grew inland from the Georgia and South Carolina coasts and offshore islands— was not a practical crop because of the difficulty of cleaning it. The gin opened the whole South, including the trans-Mississippi South, to cotton growing and enormously

One of my primary objects is to form the tools so the tools themselves shall fashion the work.

ELI WHITNEY (1765–1825)

increased the importance of slavery to the southern economy.

But Whitney was unable to defend his patent legally, and others quickly entered the market with copies of his machine. He turned his genius to a new area and obtained a government subsidy to manufacture firearms. Here he hit on the idea—possibly copied from others—of interchangeable parts as a means of mass production. Prefabricated rifle parts that were manufactured separately could be assembled by workers who were relatively unskilled. The new, efficient assembly method was immediately picked up by other manufacturers. Samuel Colt used the idea in making firearms and Eli Carey and Chauncey Jerome in producing clocks and watches. (Henry Ford later applied it to producing Model T cars.) By the mid-nineteenth century the United States was far ahead of Britain in labor-saving devices. The manufacture of standard, interchangeable parts by the factory method was generally known as "the American system."

The introduction of steam energy brought important changes in transportation. In 1807 Robert Fulton proved that steam could be used to power boats when he captained his hundred-ton *Clermont* up the Hudson River to Albany and down again to New York at five miles an hour. Improved models soon totally altered shipping along the Hudson, Ohio, Mississippi, and Missouri rivers by raising the volume of traffic and drastically lowering freight charges.

Steam power had even greater impact on the railroads. The first American-made commercial steam engine belonged to the Baltimore and Ohio line. Peter Cooper's *Tom*

M'CORMICK'S PATENT VIRGINIA REAPER.

McCormick designed his mechanical reaper in 1832 and patented it two years later. Many improvements were made over the years, including the addition of a seat for the driver, who, on earlier models, had to ride one of the team horses. By 1850 McCormick had built up a nationwide business.

Thumb, the pioneer engine, hauled cars over thirteen miles of B & O track in 1830. Philadelphia had four rail lines by 1849. Within ten years New York linked the northeast and middle Atlantic states by rail and had connections all the way to Chicago and the Mississippi River. By 1860 the eastern half of the country was interlaced with iron rails.

New machines also fundamentally changed farming. John Deere's "singing plow" solved a problem inherent in farming the prairie grasslands, where the loamy soil would pile up on the moldboard of wooden and cast-iron plows. Deere observed that a saw blade made of steel cleaned itself while cutting wood, and he reasoned that a steel plow might do the same in the ground. His new plow cut a smooth, straight, deep furrow and vibrated with a pleasant hum. Indeed, farmers using steel plows could plant far more wheat than they could harvest, for the crop had to be gathered by hand within two weeks or it would spoil. This problem was solved by Cyrus McCormick's mechanical reaper. The singing plow and the reaper

were only two of a hundred thousand different machines that were available to farmers. Agricultural methods that had remained essentially the same for a thousand years were rapidly being replaced.

Education for an industrial society

Before the Civil War most people learned by doing. Because American farms were isolated, farmers constantly had to devise ways to keep their equipment in repair. Many important innovations were the result of ordinary farmers improving their tools and craftsmen improving their products as part of the day's work. The American psychologist G. Stanley Hall, reminiscing about his mid-nineteenth-century New England childhood, observed that the household system of manufactures must have been the "best educational environment for boys at a certain stage of their development ever realized in history." And while boys helped their fathers, girls learned from their mothers to spin, weave, embroider, knit, darn, crochet, clean house, mend, and prepare and preserve food.

The well-to-do had always educated their children. Tutoring in the home was common and remained so in the South. Boys were sent to the best of the private colleges. There were about five hundred colleges by 1860. While most were founded to train preachers, they increasingly offered secular and practical training. Lecture series were popular with adults. Mechanics institutes for artisans, mechanics, manufacturers, and others were established in the 1820s in major cities. Various academies were open to middle-class youth. Unfortunately, the apprenticeship method of learning a craft was undermined by the growth of the factory system, which relied on unskilled labor.

Public education made slow progress in the United States, in part because free schools were at first known as paupers' schools. But by the middle of the nineteenth century, elementary schools supported wholly or partly by taxes were common outside the South, and in the South public education for whites had begun to make strides. The leading states in providing public high schools were Ohio, New York, and Massachusetts. Massachusetts was the home of America's pioneering educator Horace Mann, and it was there that school attendance was first made compulsory, in 1852.

Interdependent regions

Technology and skilled workers were two major factors that propelled the American economy forward between 1815 and 1860. The third, and probably most important, factor was regional specialization. As the North, the South, and the West specialized more and more in different economic areas, they became increasingly interdependent. The three-way regional specialization was assisted by the "transportation revolution" and resulted in a business efficiency that benefitted the nation as a whole.

The West specialized in corn, wheat, and livestock, which was sent mainly to the South (and to Europe). The South produced large quantities of cotton and corn, the former being utilized by northeastern mills and by England. The Northeast produced manufactured goods that were wanted in the West and South. The Northeast also supplied loans and investments for the other two regions. This new economic triangle paralleled the trade triangles that had sparked the growth of colonial America. Each region wanted what another was selling, and leftovers could be sent to Europe.

The regional triangle followed on the heels of a transportation revolution—a spurt of canal building, the introduction of steamboating on the Mississippi, Missouri, and Ohio rivers, and the spread of rail tracks as far west as the Mississippi Valley. Passengers and freight could cover greater distances more rapidly and cheaply than ever before. The Erie Canal, completed in 1825, moved goods east and west. The value of goods shipped on the canal rose from $10 million in 1836 to $94 million in 1853. It reduced the cost of shipping freight from 19¢ per ton-mile to about 1¢ per ton-mile. The steamboats of the Mississippi–Missouri–Ohio river complex made headway against the strong downstream current to deliver shipments from New Orleans. This meant that goods from the Northeast or Europe could be shipped into the interior by an all-water route. The Ohio Valley benefitted most by this innovation. Meantime, during the 1850s railways were developed that connected the larger cities and towns of the Northeast and West. Thus a network of commercial ties gradually bound together the vast land area of the United States, insuring a large and growing national market for American businesses. After 1840 the Gross National Product was growing at an annual rate of about 4.5 percent. That figure is close to the growth rate in modern times.

Work is not a curse, it is the prerogative of intelligence,
the only means to manhood and the measure of civilization.
Savages do not work.

PETER COOPER (1791–1883)
Industrialist and philanthropist

The gospel of success

Values inherited from colonial times—urging Americans to work hard, stay sober, and save their money—came in handy in the early nineteenth century. These years experienced some labor scarcity at a time when giant tasks had to be performed in forging mines, factories, farms, and cities. It is not surprising that the old maxims of Benjamin Franklin, first published in 1732, enjoyed new popularity a century later. Sermons, newspapers, wall plaques, political speeches, and schoolbooks all exclaimed that work was the means to success. "Work, work, be not afraid" began a poem in one of McGuffey's famous *Readers,* books read by millions of schoolchildren. "If you find your task is hard, Try, Try, Again; Time will bring you your reward," is another line from the *Reader.* "God helps them that help themselves," Franklin advised. There were religious overtones in the cult of success. The famous preacher Lyman Abbott declared that Jesus "approved of the use of accumulated wealth to accumulate more wealth." The Reverend Thomas P. Hunt stated his philosophy in the title of a book he published in 1836: *The Book of Wealth, in Which It Is Proved from the Bible that It Is the Duty of Every Man to Become Rich.*

The work ethic had changed in a subtle way since the time of the Puritans. Cotton Mather had wanted people to be content at their calling, whatever it may be, and he placed more importance on community spirit. The new message of success for young people, especially young men, was to "get ahead" by trying new and unfamiliar callings and not to be satisfied with a low station in life. It also placed the claims of the individual above those of the society at large.

Americans had long been famous for their competitive habits, but this theme was more noticeable in the mid-nineteenth century than ever before. "A people in motion," "a go-getter nation," "a materialistic people" were common descriptions of Americans, especially as seen by foreigners. Practically the first thing that Alexis de Tocqueville noticed here was the "prodigious commercial activity," and he had trouble finding words to "describe the avidity with which the American rushes forward to secure this immense booty that fortune offers. . . ." All things considered, American social values have remained remarkably stable over the years, for much of what Tocqueville saw in the 1830s can still be seen today.

In the Jacksonian era in particular, Americans praised democracy and equality, but it is not easy to measure how much of either existed in reality. Indeed, in some ways economic inequality—the gap between rich and poor—seemed to increase between 1830 and 1860. About 1000 New Yorkers had estates worth $100,000 to $800,000 in the 1840s, a time when $4000 was a princely income. In 1830, 75 Bostonians possessed $100,000 or more; ten years later 150 had risen to that level. The banker Stephan Gerard left a fortune of $6 million, and by 1845 John Jacob Astor had amassed $25 million in the fur trade. His fortune approached that of Baron Rothschild, generally considered the world's wealthiest person.

Popular belief held that the rich were born poor and worked their way up. In reality 95 of the 100 richest New Yorkers were born into wealthy families. Boston's richest 10 percent owned more than half the taxable wealth, precisely the same ratio as on the eve of the Revolution. In 1841 only 1 in 5 Brooklyn families had any taxable wealth at all. The poorest two thirds of the people in that city owned less than 1 percent of the wealth, while the richest 1 percent of the people owned 40 percent.

Industrialism and poverty

Americans believed that poverty was caused by divine will, migration from Europe, or habitual drunkenness or some other personal shortcoming. The accepted cures in the early part of the nineteenth century included moving west, working hard, avoiding alcohol, or experiencing a religious conversion. But industrialism brought increasing poverty in its wake. As industry grew, so did job competition, depressions, mass unemployment, and crowded slums. Nothing like this combination had existed in colonial times.

How should society treat its poor? One European theory advanced the idea that workers should receive only enough money beyond bare subsistence to enable them to have children. Wages over and above this level would lower investors' profits and unbalance the economy, according to this belief. If wealth were spread out among the poor, how could it be invested to create new wealth? Unless the wealthy could get a fat return on their money, why should they bother to invest it? This was known as "the iron law of wages," a theory that Karl Marx and other Socialists attacked in the 1840s and 1850s. Most Americans rejected both the "iron law" and the Socialists. Generally optimistic, they believed strongly in self-help and Christian charity.

Americans also thought that immigration was a major cause of poverty. Most newcomers arrived almost penniless. The Irish, for example, came here to escape famine during the 1840s and were hopelessly poor. Their willingness to work for almost any salary drove down the wages of natives and immigrants alike to a point where both could barely survive. The Boston Society for the Prevention of Pauperism complained about "the unwillingness of certain portions of the immigrants to leave the city, thereby causing a large surplus of laborers." By contrast, "the most enterprising and thrifty seek the country or the far west, immediately on their arrival" and leave the shiftless behind.

In the large cities notorious slums housed both immigrants and native-born factory workers. In one working-class neighborhood of Philadelphia (a model city in the eighteenth century) 253 people lived in 30 houses, none of which had even a privy. Chamber pots were emptied onto the docks or into the streets. While American cities were admired for their spaciousness and open look, the Five Points district of New York was already well known here and abroad as a horrifying slum. Charles Dickens, whose novels chronicled the ugliest facets of English factory slums, once visited the Five Points area with two policemen for bodyguards. There he saw slum dwellers crawling from their hovels "as if the judgment hour were at hand and every obscene grave were giving up its dead."

Private charities specialized in the care of certain "dependent paupers," such as orphans and widows with children. According to a New York City police report in 1852, there were about ten thousand abandoned, runaway, or orphaned youngsters in the city. Many of them lived by stealing, begging, or prostitution. The vast majority were totally illiterate. The Children's Aid Society did help many of these children out of the city and onto farms. Private charities sheltered the worst hardship cases in poorhouses,

supplied free meals, made home visits, gave free medical examinations, and offered moral tutoring.

Less fortunate paupers were handled by public bureaucrats known as "overseers of the poor." New York City's overseers farmed out paupers to labor contractors at a set price, auctioned them off to private employers who became responsible for their upkeep, or gave them small cash allotments. But the "poor rates" were meager in most cities, and a large part of the welfare money went to lawyers, judges, and constables for administrative costs. The farmed-out poor were often cruelly exploited by employers and had no legal recourse. State commissions investigated conditions among the poor, and missionaries and charities did what they could to help the needy. Although some laws improved hous-

ing conditions, poverty seemed to become more, not less, widespread.

Life in the mills

The first textile mills in America were comparatively pleasant places of work. The pace was slow, and physical labor was minimal, although workers were expected to put in as many as seventy hours a week. Factories were located in rural towns near waterfalls and often had an appealing physical appearance. Farm families, idled by the winter, earned extra income in factories, and mill owners often hired entire families. If every member over twelve or thirteen years of age worked at the spindles, a large family could earn a comfortable income. Prior to about

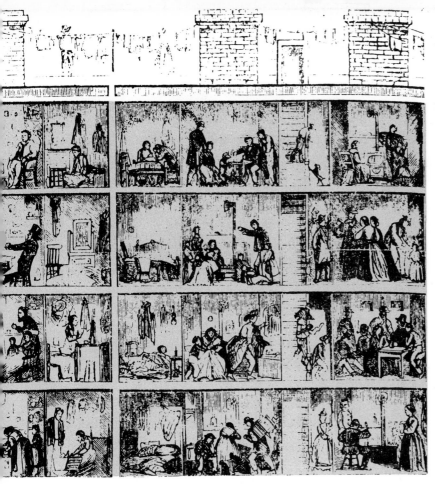

Tenements in New York and other large cities housed immigrant and native-born workers near their jobs. Extreme conditions of poverty and overcrowding bred crime, violence, and epidemic disease.

1840 most mill hands were female. The Boston Associates established a model mill at Waltham, Massachusetts, which employed mostly girls and women. They were housed in comfortable dormitories where their lives underwent rigid supervision by paternalistic managers. They earned about $2.50 a week but had to pay for their own board. Drinking and gambling were not allowed and curfew rang at ten o'clock sharp. When a group of women employed by the Associates tried to form a union to improve their conditions, they were coldly received.

Still, there were few "commercial utopias" like Waltham Mills. And even under the best of circumstances, most Americans considered wage work degrading. Wage workers, they felt, were slavishly dependent on their employers. Americans much preferred farm-ing or some other sort of independent life. Immigrants began to take over the mill jobs—in 1860 about half the New England mill workers were Irish. By midcentury many people compared the wages, living and work-ing conditions, and overall prospects for most factory hands to those of the southern plantation slave. In fact, southern planters claimed that they treated their slaves better than the mill owners treated their laborers. The average factory workday was twelve to fourteen hours, and people worked six days a week. Women and children made up two thirds of the work force in Pennsylvania's cotton mills (spinning was still considered women's work). They worked the same hours as men but for less pay—about one dollar a week in the 1830s. Children under the age of twelve worked the same hours for

Early textile mills offered relatively decent working conditions, but the situation worsened as more and newer machines were added to increase production. Most mill workers were women and children, who put in the same long hours as the men but received lower wages. Around 1840 immigrant workers began to replace women in the mills.

twelve cents a day—or, one cent an hour!

Factory life was run by whistles, clocks, and machines. In the steam-powered mills the engineer controlled the speed of the machinery. All the workers—both adults and children—had to keep pace. The *New York American* declared, "The 'personnel' of a large factory is a machine." The irony was that while labor-saving machinery was intended to liberate people, factory workers felt enslaved by it.

Laborers had few rights. Workers who quit had to give two weeks' notice, but employers could fire employees without any notice at all. Known agitators were quickly dismissed and "blacklisted" so that they could not get work in other factories. Workers could be fined for the smallest infractions, and children were manhandled or whipped. Even grown women were occasionally whipped when they were late or violated other rules.

Many factory workers lost hope. They saw themselves doomed to a life of poverty. Economic depression brought mass unemployment, and workers constantly feared losing their jobs. Thousands of laborers were unemployed in Philadelphia during the panic of 1819.

The first unions

The earliest trade unions arose to protect the skilled craftsman rather than the average factory worker. The Federal Society of Journeymen Cordwainers (skilled cobblers), organized in Philadelphia in 1792, was the first trade union in the U.S. Protesting a wage cut in 1805, the union members went on strike against the merchant-capitalists who employed them. The employers hired "scabs" as replacements, and the strikers retaliated by smashing windows. The strike was broken when eight strikers were arrested for conspiracy in restraint of trade, a criminal offense under common law. A jury of nine merchants and three masters found them guilty. A prominent Federalist judge ruled that the union was a criminal agency and the strike a criminal act against society. He fined the workmen eight dollars each. So ended the Cordwainers' Conspiracy Trial of 1805–1806, the first celebrated labor case in American law.

Following the Cordwainers' Trial the criminal conspiracy doctrine was applied in other labor cases and slowed the trade union movement. Finally, in 1842, in the case of *Commonwealth* v. *Hunt*, the Supreme Court ruled that unless there was proof of violence or intimidation by the workers, a union was a lawful organization. Nevertheless, many Americans looked on unions as interfering with the liberty of both employers and employees.

Skilled craftsmen often joined unions, but most unskilled factory hands did not. The 1819 depression idled many journeymen and temporarily slowed union activities. Boston carpenters and various skilled tradesmen in New York City struck in 1825 for a ten-hour day. The same issue, a shorter working day, led to the first city-wide trade union federation, the Philadelphia Mechanics of Trade Associations. In 1827 Philadelphia also saw the formation of the first American labor party.

While the unions fought mainly for better wages and hours, they also championed various social reforms. Partly through their efforts, all white men were given the vote in the 1820s in Massachusetts, New York, and other industrial states. Labor agitated for free public schools and against imprisonment for debt. Unions also favored fairer militia laws to reduce the heavy burden on wage earners. Finally, they advocated state control over banks, the end of convict labor, and mechanics' lien laws to protect employees' wages against crooked or bankrupt employers.

Farmers: Jefferson's Chosen People

The mixed blessings of farming

The standard advice to an unemployed factory worker was to go west. There, in "the garden of the world," the worker would become a farmer and grow food to nourish the hungry city dwellers. Urban Americans thought that farmers were better off than artisans or laborers and could always make ends meet. According to popular belief, farmers were independent, hard working, patriotic, God fearing, and responsible. "Those who labour in the earth," said the farmer's patron saint, Thomas Jefferson, "are the chosen people of

God if ever He had a chosen people."

But the farmers' life was hard, and they were often forced to fight for their rights in the 1790s. Hamilton's program to raise money to pay off the national debt included a tax on whiskey that led to a direct confrontation between the secretary of the treasury and the farmers on the frontier. Western Pennsylvania farmers preferred to convert their corn into whiskey rather than transport the raw grain over the twisting roads of the Alleghenies. The freight cost for corn was five to ten dollars per hundredweight, but the freight cost for a hundredweight of corn converted into whiskey was only one dollar. So they kept making whiskey and would not pay Hamilton's tax. Local courts refused to convict them. In 1794 Washington called out the militia and Hamilton, as second in command, led an army of thirteen thousand men over the mountains to "put down the insurrection." Jefferson condemned the spectacle of soldiers marching against "men at their plows." Four whiskey rebels were convicted of treason but were pardoned by President Washington. When Jefferson took over the White House, the tax was eliminated.

Give fools their gold, and knaves their power;
  Let fortune's bubbles rise and fall;
Who sows a field, or trains a flower,
  Or plants a tree, is more than all.

JOHN GREENLEAF WHITTIER (1807–1892)

For all their independence, farmers were increasingly caught up in a whirl of commercial forces over which they had little control. Foreign competition increasingly affected farm prices. As the value of land rose steadily, real estate became a more reliable source of profit than crops. So even if productivity was good, farmers were inclined to sell their land and move on if the price was right. Many farmers from coastal Virginia and Maryland left behind "wasted lands, abandoned fields, neglected stock, and shifting crops." New England farmers also turned their backs on thin, rocky soil and declining prices. Even in Kentucky, Tennessee, and Alabama, small farmers sold out to incoming planters and moved still farther west. Unlike the European farm, the American farm was eternally up for sale.

Distributing public land

Farmers had a vital stake in the basic land policies that were hammered out between 1785 and 1830. But other groups wanted land laws that would favor their own interests, and as Congress debated, a tug-of-war took place. Settlers wanted land at low prices, in small blocks, and on easy credit terms. Big speculators wanted large blocks at special discount rates, also on easy credit. Farmers made up the largest group in this struggle, and Congress needed their votes. But revenue for the treasury came more quickly from big land sales to speculators.

Pulling in another direction were prominent western politicians who urged Congress to hand the public domain over to the states. With the income from land sales, the states would then build roads, canals, schools, and other public facilities. Meanwhile, influential eastern merchants and industrialists opposed policies that made it easy for settlers to acquire western land, because they were afraid that population along the eastern seaboard would dwindle as a result. This would create a labor shortage, force up wages, and reduce the local market for finished goods. Finally, southern planters urged Congress to adopt a sales program that would bring the highest prices for public land. This income would fill the treasury,

Opportunities for obtaining cheap or free land lured Americans west. Homesteading was a hard life, but many people preferred it to working for wages in mills and factories because farming gave them greater independence.

and the government would not have to seek revenue by raising tariffs. The high tariffs that protected the products of other areas from competition simply meant higher costs for most of the South and reduced the ability of foreign customers to buy southern cotton.

Disposal of the public domain probably absorbed more of Congress' time and energy than any other kind of legislation. Land speculation became something of a national obsession. An English resident of the United States observed in 1862:

Speculation in real estate has for many years been the ruling idea and occupation of the Western mind. Clerks, labourers, farmers, storekeepers, merely followed their callings for a living while they were speculating for their fortunes. . . . The people of the West became dealers in land, rather than its cultivators.

Congress did not set a maximum size of purchase, but it did reduce the minimum purchase of land. The 640-acre minimum unit had come down to 80 acres by 1817, and by 1832 it stood at 40 acres. At first big land purchasers got special terms, while ordinary settlers had to pay two dollars an acre, a far steeper figure than most farmers could afford. Until 1819 Congress gave credit terms of up to four years, which eased the farmers' burden somewhat. But credit encouraged speculative buying, which took great blocks of land out of circulation. Since the law required only 5 percent down payment on public land, speculators could, by careful maneuvering, legally hold options on twenty times as much land as they actually intended to buy. And if they could not sell off the land, they lost only the down payment. But if farmers could not meet their payments under a credit arrangement, they stood to lose the basis of their livelihood.

Settlers demanded three basic land reforms, which Congress eventually provided. *Preemption* allowed squatters to settle on unclaimed public land before it went up for sale. Later they could buy their plot for a minimum price of, say, $1.25 per acre. "Squatting" was not yet a dirty word, and "squatters' rights" was a respectable concept. *Compensation* was paid for improvements that squatters made on public land that they later had to vacate. *Homesteads* were outright grants of farm-sized lots from the public domain.

Homesteading was seen as a safety valve for urban and industrial discontent. It was a means by which city artisans could improve their lot, especially in times of depression. Congress passed a homestead bill in 1860, but President Buchanan vetoed it. In the course of debate radical workingmen's organizations proposed that the land be given to homesteaders with no strings attached, but this was rejected as a violation of the work ethic. Lincoln signed the Homestead Act of 1862. Under this law every citizen (or alien who intended to become a citizen) who was a family head was eligible for a quarter section of land (160 acres) after he had lived on that piece of land for five years in a row.

In spite of the new land laws, rural Americans faced hard times. The number of tenant farmers was growing. In addition, a third of the farmers of the Mississippi Valley were farm laborers rather than farm owners before the Civil War. Railroad corporations and speculators were holding on to huge tracts of public land. And because this land was out of the reach of ordinary farmers and settlers, overall farm productivity was restricted and the growth of the new frontier communities was hampered. Land laws were confusing and contradictory, and the courts were jammed with conflicting claims. Because much land was opened before transportation was available or Indian claims were resolved, it was useless to permanent settlers. The actions of Congress did not reflect any concept of orderly western settlement but instead encouraged a helter-skelter rush to the frontier. This approach promoted the destruction of Indian nations and weakened the sense of community among whites. Even the public treasury would probably have profited more from slower land distribution.

Nevertheless, the American land system was liberal and flexible by existing standards. Settlers could buy parcels as small as forty acres at $1.40 per acre, and land offices were more and more accessible to purchasers. And despite increasing land tenancy, most farmers still owned some land. They were buying more livestock, applying machinery to the most difficult tasks, and harvesting larger crops each year. They enjoyed a comparatively good standard of living. And they had a sense of dignity and of belonging in their nation.

Review

The United States was deeply in debt in 1789, but by the middle of the next century the American economy was soaring. While still basically an agricultural nation at the outbreak of the Civil War in 1861, the U.S. by then was second only to Britain in manufacturing. The Constitution gave the federal government powers that paved the way for Alexander Hamilton's system of establishing credit and encouraging economic growth. The national government, as well as the states and cities, aided private enterprise. A

Supreme Court decision against monopoly spurred business competition. Although Jefferson's embargo of 1807 hurt the shipping industry and depressed overseas trade, it promoted investment in manufacturing. Mills and factories grew up in the East and helped end America's dependence on British-made goods.

With the arrival of the Industrial Revolution in the New World, devices like the labor-saving machines at Slater's spinning mill, the cotton gin, the steel plow, the mechanical reaper, and the principle of interchangeable parts revolutionized manufacturing and agriculture. The steam railroad and the steamboat helped open up the West and solidify interstate commerce. Technology seemed to assure America's success. At the same time, attitudes of competitiveness gave a new twist to the old work ethic.

But industrialism created conditions for poverty as well as for wealth. As America boosted the spirit of democracy, the gap between its rich and poor widened. Industrial growth brought with it subsistence wages, economic depressions, and mass unemployment. Slums, populated largely by immigrant factory workers, multiplied. Industrial workers constantly feared losing their jobs yet felt enslaved by machines. Finally recognized as lawful organizations, trade unions made some headway in reducing working hours and won some social reforms as well. Congress also enacted basic land reforms that gave urban workers an escape hatch: the option of moving west and becoming homesteaders. The Homestead Act culminated many years of agitation for better access to the public domain.

Farmers, like factory workers, were caught up in events beyond their control. They often found it more profitable to sell their land than to grow crops on it. But they were more independent and generally better off than urban workers. Certainly they had a stronger sense of being part of their country's destiny.

Questions

1. What part did the Constitution and Hamilton's system play in fostering capitalism and assuring the economic growth of the United States? How did federal and state governments help private enterprise?

2. What were the three main factors of economic growth between 1815 and 1860? How did each of these increase America's economic and industrial potential?

3. What did Americans believe were the causes of poverty? How did they deal with the poor? How did their beliefs and policies toward the poor compare with those of colonial Americans?

4. Discuss the problems raised by the sale of public land. What three land reforms did Congress provide?

5. Characterize the lives of factory workers and farmers. Which life would you have preferred for yourself?

power

The County Election by George Caleb Bingham.

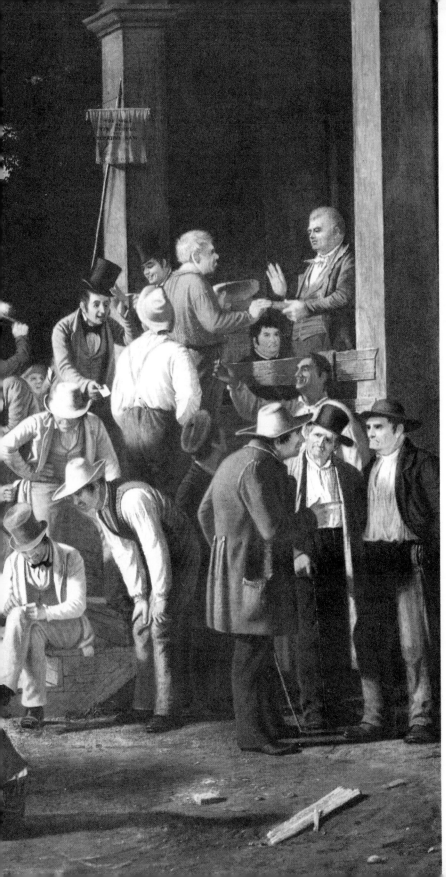

It is now for them to
demonstrate to the world
that those who can fairly
carry an election can also
suppress a rebellion; that
ballots are the rightful and
peaceful successors of bullets;
and that when ballots have
fairly and constitutionally
decided, there can be no
successful appeal back to
bullets.

ABRAHAM LINCOLN   (1809–1865)

10

10

A Sovereign Nation

The problem of power has shifted dramatically in the past century. Today it appears to involve struggles between the president and Congress and between the public and such special interest groups as big business, labor, and agriculture. Before 1860 the major power contests pitted the rights of states against the authority of the federal government, the "haves" against the "have-nots," the interests of one region against those of another, and the defenders of human freedom against the advocates of slavery.

The Civil War represented a climax of some of these power struggles. Although debate continues as to what the *primary* cause of the war was, there is no doubt that slavery was a big issue. As to the actual outbreak of violence, the two leading—and opposing—theories advanced in the past generation have been (1) that war was unavoidable, and (2) that it resulted from the ideological excesses and unstatesmanlike conduct of the "blundering generation." The American historian Charles A. Beard offered the strongest case for the theory that the war was unavoidable. He held that slavery was only a footnote to the story. According to Beard, the war resulted from an alliance between northern businessmen and western farmers who set out to destroy the power of southern planters. It was not slavery or the moral issue of emancipation that led to the conflict, but financial, commercial, industrial, and agricultural factors. Recently the underpinnings of this economic argument have been challenged by those who say that the differences between the capitalists and planters could have been settled peaceably. Historian Allan Nevins, in his monumental four-volume work on the Civil War, contended that it was the moral fervor on both sides that precipitated the fighting. Every generation adds its own interpretations, raises new questions, and seeks new explanations for this traumatic and tragic episode in

American history. No doubt this will continue to be true.

In America, political differences are supposed to be settled politically, through compromise, before they lead to bloodshed. And political parties have generally fostered such negotiated settlements. The pre-Civil War politicians created a party system that in some ways was remarkably flexible and functional. It was based on the idea of a large voting populace, two opposing parties, and a loyal opposition. But, as this chapter will show, that system failed to prevent the Civil War.

Power Blocs Before the Civil War

Aristocracy versus democracy

In the early years of the Republic the nation's best political minds continued to reflect on the meaning of power. The violence of the French Revolution and the demands for democratic reforms in this country seemed to confirm an early fear that too much democracy would threaten property and good order. In a series of articles for a Federalist newspaper, John Adams reaffirmed his support for republican government (in which the people rule without a king through elected representatives), but he warned of the dangers of majority rule. Even in the most extreme democracy, he believed, there would always be some who were smarter, richer, stronger, or more devious than others—a "natural and actual aristocracy"—and that they would acquire power over the rest. Here was the fatal flaw of democracy. "The fundamental article of my political creed," said Adams, "is, that despotism, or unlimited sovereignty, or absolute power, is the same in a majority of a popular assembly" as it is in any other form of government. It is "equally arbitrary, cruel, bloody, and in every respect diabolical." Since the "natural aristocracy" could not be gotten rid of, the government would have to balance the interests of the rich against those of the poor, even if it meant creating separate legislatures to express their interests.

In opposition to Adams' view, Jefferson believed that human improvement, if not human perfection, could be achieved through education and constructive laws. Another leading spokesman of the Democratic-Republicans, John Taylor of South Carolina, also fought a running word-battle with Adams. Taylor suspected Adams of wanting a new monarchy. He insisted there was nothing "natural" about aristocracy, that it was always built on corruption and violence. The only solution was to destroy the aristocracy and give power to the people. In short, Jefferson and Taylor believed that for a republic to retain its virtue, it *must* become democratic.

The spread of the frontier and the rise of industrialism brought democratic changes in America. As population moved westward and new states sought entry into the Union, more people demanded the right to vote. In the East, state constitutions were altered to allow all male taxpayers, not just male property owners, to vote and to serve in government. As bureaucracy grew, average men could choose careers in government. While Andrew Jackson was president, government jobs were filled with his supporters in accordance with the axiom of patronage, "To the victors belong the spoils." Any man, regardless of education or social status, could

Rough-and-tumble politics made an early appearance on the floor of Congress. In 1798 Federalist Roger Griswold disparaged the military record of Republican Matthew Lyon; Lyon responded by spitting in Griswold's face. In the ensuing brawl, Griswold attacked his adversary with a cane while Lyon grabbed the fireplace tongs, and the first congressional fistfight was under way.

hold a government job in a republic, he felt. Young men sought political careers as a way of fulfilling the American Dream. In older states like New York, wealthy gentlemen retired from politics, leaving the game to the new breed of young professionals.

A change in men's clothing symbolized the extension of democracy. Gentlemen had worn close-fitting velvet or satin breeches and coats of fine cloth to distinguish themselves from "ordinary" men, who wore long baggy pants and rough-cloth jackets. In the 1820s the dress of the "common man" became popular even with American gentlemen, who began wearing the long pants. John Quincy Adams was the first American president to dress in the new style, though the staunch conservative John Marshall, chief justice of the Supreme Court, wore knee-length breeches to the day he died in 1835.

The social leveling and its consequences were noted by Alexis de Tocqueville in his famous account, *Democracy in America*. The French traveler wrote:

When . . . the distinctions of rank are obliterated and privileges are destroyed, when hereditary property is subdivided and education and freedom are widely diffused, the desire of acquiring the comforts of the world haunts the imagination of the poor, and the dread of losing them that of the rich. The great advantage of the Americans is . . . that they are born equal instead of becoming so.

Tocqueville recognized the existence of America's upper class but observed, "Money is the only social distinction."

Strengthening the presidency and the Supreme Court

Both the executive and the judicial branch of government grew stronger in the first three decades of the nineteenth century. In the beginning, George Washington contributed most to the presidency by setting original precedents—such as suggesting legislation to Congress, forming a cabinet, and appointing able men to top positions. His firm command in foreign affairs also strengthened the office.

Andrew Jackson set the style that "strong" presidents have followed ever since. He used the veto more frequently, often in cases where he simply disagreed with Congress. Unlike other presidents before him, he did not confine its use to situations where he thought congressional action was unconstitutional. In England the veto power was a monarch's last weapon against an unruly Parliament. Thus Jackson's enemies began calling him "King Andrew."

The main political upheaval of Jackson's time concerned his veto of a bill to recharter the second Bank of the United States. This central bank, chartered by the government in 1816, had considerable authority over the national currency and over private bankers. Many Jacksonians, including frustrated small businessmen, saw the Bank as an evil force and made it a scapegoat for their anger. To Jackson it represented "monopoly power" at its worst, and in 1832 he refused to sign the congressional bill authorizing its recharter. The Bank closed its doors. The net result of the "bank war" was a weaker economy but a stronger executive power.

On one notable occasion Jackson ignored the Supreme Court. When Chief Justice John Marshall handed down a decision favorable to the Cherokee Indians in the case of *Worcester* v. *Georgia* (1832), the president is said to have remarked, "Well, John Marshall has made his decision, now let him enforce it!"

The Constitution created a federal system in which power was lodged in the states as well as the federal government and in which three branches of the federal government would check and balance one another. Inevitably the distribution of power among these levels of government was fluid. There were many centers of power in the country. During the years that Chief Justice John Marshall dominated the Supreme Court, from 1801 to 1835, questions pertaining to states' rights and to the powers of the three branches of federal government were constantly in the limelight.

Marshall, a Virginia Federalist, was in a special position to shape the future by participating in over one thousand Supreme Court cases and writing opinions and decisions in about five hundred of them. Time and again he emphasized a few basic principles. (1) The Constitution was "the *supreme* law of the land, superior to any ordering act of the legislative [branch]." (2) The Supreme Court had the power of judicial review. Marshall ruled in *Marbury* v. *Madison*

A legislative act contrary to the Constitution is not law. . . . It is, emphatically, the province and duty of the Judicial Department to say what the law is.

JOHN MARSHALL   (1755–1835)

(1803) that a law passed by Congress (the Judiciary Act of 1789) was invalid because it violated a clause of the Constitution. The Supreme Court's authority to declare laws unconstitutional, established by this decision, was a power not expressly granted in the Constitution. (3) A believer in American nationalism, Marshall held that the United States was a sovereign nation, not an alliance of states. (4) In *McCulloch* v. *Maryland* (1819) he ruled that Congress had "implied powers" under the Constitution. The case concerned an attempt by the state of Maryland to tax a branch of the second Bank of the United States, a federal institution. Marshall decided against the state, declaring that Congress had acted legally in chartering the Bank, even if the Constitution did not mention the Bank by name. If the general ends sought by Congress were legitimate, then "all means which are appropriate, which are plainly adapted to that end" are constitutional. Few court decisions made since John Marshall's time have had greater impact than those which established the principles of judicial review and implied powers.

Regionalism: the Northeast

Besides those who organized formal, constitutional power, there were also individuals and interest groups (Madison would have called them "factions") which exercised power informally. Between the time the Constitution was adopted and the Civil War erupted, the division of the country into three regions—the Northeast, the South, and the West—became increasingly apparent. It is in regional terms that social and economic changes can best be seen.

Most striking was the rising influence and power of industrialists and financiers in the Northeast. Merchants remained important. Many of the rich and influential belonged to families that had acquired their wealth in trade in the eighteenth century. But looming ever larger in power and prestige were manufacturers and financiers. Textile and iron manufacturers, railroad builders, and other big industrialists became prominent in political affairs. In Massachusetts, the most heavily industrialized state before the Civil War, fifteen Boston families controlled huge blocks of wealth in railroading, cotton spinning, banking, insurance, real estate, water power, and canals. These "Boston Associates," as they were known, influenced the press, clergy, schools, charities, and politics of New England. Among them, Nathan Appleton and Francis Cabot Lowell swayed many politicians on the local level and in Washington. Textile manufacturer Abbot Lawrence became Daniel Webster's patron in the 1840s and influenced his vote in the Senate on such matters as tariffs. In an age of

speculation, bankers controlled many economic destinies. Nicholas Biddle, for example, who headed the United States Bank during the crucial years of the bank war with Jackson, had extraordinary power.

In Washington, northern business leaders lobbied for federal laws concerning tariffs, currency, banking, and in some cases for federal support for roads, canals, and railroads. They pressured the government to encourage European laborers to immigrate to America. These same men also sought access to the land and resources in the public domain and, in the realm of overseas commerce, to world markets. They were especially concerned with tariffs in the 1850s. With prices depressed and with iron and textiles being stockpiled, northern businessmen wanted competition reduced from imported goods. The South's resistance to protective tariffs was especially irritating to them.

While "capital" was beginning to flex its muscles, "labor" was still scarcely heard from. Industrial workers were almost totally unorganized. Americans did not as yet recognize the "European" analysis of classes, which placed workers in opposition to employers. The basic class distinction in America was between the "producing" and the "nonproducing" classes. Those who worked for a living on farms, in shops, or in factories made up the first category. Speculators and bankers, especially those protected in any way by government "monopoly" or by "special privilege," comprised the second category. In Jackson's time Nicholas Biddle and the defenders of the second Bank of the United States epitomized this latter group.

The West

Americans from all walks of life made their way west between the return of Lewis and Clark in 1806 and the Civil War. They went there mostly to trap and trade fur, to speculate in land, to mine for gold, to buy and sell

. . . *from the sketchbooks of Lewis Miller*

Though a carpenter by training, Lewis Miller (1796–1882) is known today as an early American folk artist. His Chronicle of York, *begun in 1812 but spanning events throughout his lifetime, is a pictorial and written record of the daily lives of his fellow Pennsylvania Germans in York County. His sketches and the notes he wrote in their margins — at times in German and at times in broken English — combine to give us an unparalleled view of the commonplace occurrences and the momentous events, the details and the scope of life in the new nation.*

Above: Lewis Miller, Self-portrait.

Left: The yearly market or public fair, 1801. In a note added later Miller wrote, "In 1816 they prohibited the holding of fairs within the Borough of York and declared such holding a common nuisance," there having been "some dispute at Lewis Wampler's tavern . . . and at the same time at Eberhart tavern."

*All of [these] pictures . . . are true Sketches, I myself
being there upon the places and spot and put down what happened.*

Above: Dancing at the house of John Glessner, to the music of a violin and dulcimer, around 1800.

Right: The Court of Quarter Sessions and the Court of Common Pleas, 1801.

Far right: The inside of the Old Lutheran Church, 1800.

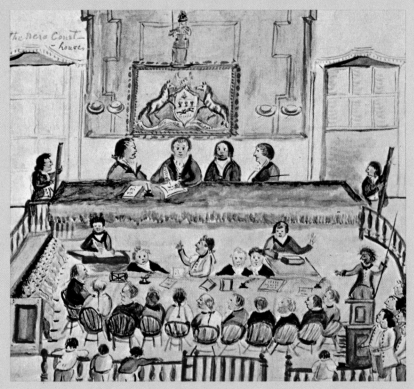

The Singing Choir, 1. Ludwig Miller, 2. John Barnitz, 3. George Snyder
4. Christopher Stoehr, 5. Daniel Lauman, 6. Lewis Shive, 7. William Hornschild
8. George Barnitz, 9. Steffe Horn, 10. George Miller, 11. Michael Eurich,
12. mis. Herman, 13. mis. Laub, 14. mis. Stoehr, 15. mis. Cramer, 16. Mis. Hay, the Organist John Morris. Charles Fisher.
Pastor, Rev. Jacob Goering,

Matthew. Mark. Luke. John. Paul. Peter. Joshua. Samuel. David. Luther. Goering.

In Side of the old Lutheran Church in 1800, York. Pa.
1. the Sexton, henry bannix, and his wife, the fire maker, old Brence 2.
3. John Hay Jr. president 4 Jacob Barnitz, Secretary. Jacob Hay, Nicles Dihl 6.
7. George Striebig, 8. Philip Kissinger, 9. Jacob Gardner, Michael Smyser, Martin Ebert 11.

mrs. Goster, mrs. Lamb, mrs. ... mrs. George Hay, mrs. Beard, and mrs. Eichelberger, not far from Town, the two last names ... old Style Cooking.

the Bake oven, bad Bread.

Smokeing and

No better and good cooks can be found no where to prepare victuals for the table. . . . They had plenty of raw materials to cook: beef, veal, lamb, mutton, pork, and fish, oysters, poultry, eggs, butter, cheese, milk, and honey. And all kinds of vegetables and fruit.

Old mrs. Hansman Killing a Hog and a b...

Above: A hotel cook baking bread, 1800.

Right: Old Mrs. Hansman killing a hog, 1802.

goods at remote trading posts, and, of course, to farm. The overwhelming majority of westerners were land-hungry farmers who at first intended to till enough land to make ends meet (subsistence farming) but hoped in a few years to produce a surplus that they could sell (commercial farming). They wanted "cheap money" (low interest rates on loans and mortgages), high prices for what they had to sell, and low prices for what they wanted to buy. Their desires for improved transportation and cheap land were frequently heard in Congress. Among the champions of the West were Congressman Henry Clay of Kentucky, a lawyer and land investor, and Senator Thomas Hart Benton of Missouri. Abraham Lincoln personified the pioneer farmer in some respects, with his firsthand knowledge of poverty, his reverence for "free labor," and his hatred of slave competition.

The South

For at least a generation before the Civil War the South nursed a separate society, with its own special interests. It underwent fewer changes in social or economic structure than the other regions. Southern society contin-

Before 1840 only fur traders penetrated to California, but the discovery of gold near Sacramento in 1848 started the gold rush, which brought the total population of the area to ninety thousand by 1850. This daguerrotype, taken in 1850, shows a group of prospectors (some with their families) at a gold mine near Marysville, California.

Put on the defensive because slavery was condemned throughout most of the civilized world, southerners tended to idealize the plantation as a happy feudal domain where slaves were humanely ruled by highborn gentlemen. They created idyllic pictures of a way of life that was all gentility and chivalry. But the paternalistic tradition was maintained at a high cost, for it led to a static society which resisted change.

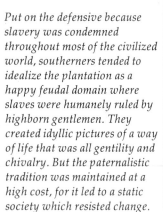

ued to be dominated by its planter class. After 1830 the planters of the lower Mississippi Valley had surpassed those along the Atlantic in land, wealth, slaves, and economic influence. Out of a total southern white population of around 5.4 million in 1860, only 25 percent owned any slaves at all. And only a small fraction of those owned large numbers of slaves. In 1860 7 percent of the whites owned nearly three quarters of the blacks.

The planters as a whole were not a hereditary class; many of the "cotton nabobs" were self-made men. Here, as in the North, success was measured by wealth. The small planters hoped to become big ones and often succeeded. Even small farmers hoped somehow to rise to the very top. The few industrialists were bankrolled by the rich planters' surplus capital or by northern capital. The poorest whites took comfort in knowing that no matter how hard times might be, they could never sink all the way to the bottom as long as slavery existed.

From the beginning, southern planters had enjoyed considerable power in all three branches of the federal government and in the Democratic party. From 1789 to 1832 all but two presidents (the Adamses) hailed from the South. Two southerners—Jefferson and Calhoun—served as vice-president during those years. From 1800 to 1864 the Supreme Court had two chief justices—Marshall from Virginia and Taney from Maryland. The Senate was a staunch bastion of southern power. Even though the South's voting strength was less in the House, its influence was still felt in Congress. In 1854, for example, Congress passed the Kansas-Nebraska Act, which restored the possibility of taking slaves into the western territories, where slavery was previously prohibited. The mere threat of secession enabled southerners to block legislation desired by others: protective tariffs, federally financed internal improvements, a centralized banking system, homesteads, and a federally supported program of immigration.

Rivalry over the economy and abolition

What was there in this mix that resulted in the Civil War? Why couldn't North-South differences be patched over? It is doubtful that economic differences alone could have caused a civil war, for northern businessmen and southern planters had much in common.

Yankee merchant-capitalists advanced credit to southern planters. They also insured a great deal of the South's cotton and shipped it to England. Yankee textile mills bought about 46 percent of the cotton grown in the South in 1849. The South's dependency on northern businessmen annoyed southerners. But the South had more to lose in dollars and cents than it had to gain from a North-South split.

Nor is it likely that the moral side of slavery was potent enough to bring on the war. Racism was almost as prevalent in the North as it was in the South. Northern workers feared the competition of free blacks as much as or more than the competition of slaves. The results of the election of 1860 showed clearly that a majority of the voters opposed abolition. The hesitant way in which Lincoln unveiled the Emancipation Proclamation reinforces this view.

The abolitionists conducted a campaign of subversion that unnerved the South. In 1830 the radical editor William Lloyd Garrison founded a newspaper, *The Liberator*, which called for an immediate — not a gradual — end of slavery. Abolitionists aided runaway slaves in defiance of the Fugitive Slave Act of 1850, which gave special federal commissioners the power to arrest fugitives and return them to their owners. Antislavery men and women also organized the Underground Railroad, a system for protecting and hiding escaped slaves and helping them to find refuge in the North or to reach Canada. In 1854 Garrison publicly burned a copy of the Constitution. He used this dramatic gesture to show that he would rather see the country broken up than continue to live with slavery.

In 1856, in the aftermath of the Kansas-Nebraska Act, the fiery abolitionist John Brown led a raid on Pottawatomie Creek, Kansas, killing five proslavery settlers. Three years later, in October 1859, Brown and a band of eighteen men attacked the federal arsenal at Harpers Ferry, Virginia, in an attempt to start a slave uprising. Brown was taken prisoner, tried, and hanged for treason.

The South saw the abolitionists as radical outsiders trying to overthrow their way of life. So the southern states took countermeasures to protect slavery. They restricted the mails and limited free speech on the question of slavery. Planters tightened their security arrangements to guard against rebellion. In fact, the abolitionists never seriously threatened slavery below the Mason-Dixon line (the "boundary line" between the northern and southern states). The antislavery crusade was conducted by only a tiny fraction of the white population.

Compromises

As one of the Founding Fathers, James Madison had foreseen that the nation's unity and integrity would be preserved only through compromises between conflicting groups. The question of slavery was a thorny issue that required concessions on both sides. Five major compromises were made on slavery, but after each one the situation worsened. The attempts to reconcile North-South differences on the issue began at the Constitutional Convention with the compromise that called for three fifths of the slave population to be counted in determining a state's federal tax liability and its representation in the House. They ended with the South's secession from the Union in 1860–1861.

Abolition proposes to destroy the right and extinguish the principle of self-government for which our forefathers waged a seven years' bloody war, and upon which our whole system of free government is founded.

STEPHEN A. DOUGLAS (1813–1861)

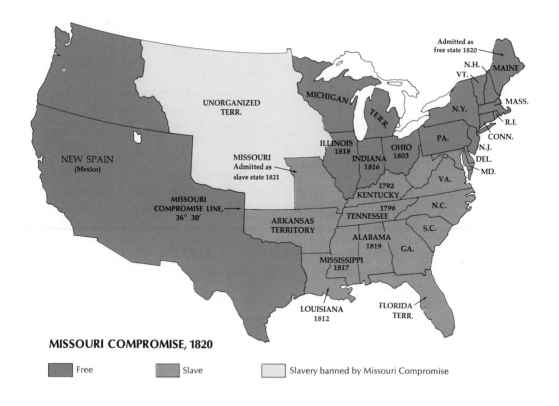

MISSOURI COMPROMISE, 1820

■ Free   ■ Slave   ☐ Slavery banned by Missouri Compromise

The Missouri Compromise of 1820 was the most enduring. When Missouri petitioned for admission to the Union as a slave state, northerners objected on political grounds. Thanks to the Three-Fifths Compromise, Missouri would receive more congressional representation than the North thought it deserved, and its entrance as a slave state would give the South an advantage in the Senate. A compromise finally was reached: the slave state of Missouri was admitted—along with the free state of Maine. As new states entered the Union, this pattern of pairing a slave state with a nonslave state continued. A central feature of the Missouri Compromise was the prohibition of slavery in the rest of the Louisiana Purchase above 36°30′ north latitude, the line of Missouri's southern boundary. This agreement held until about 1854.

The Nullification Controversy of 1828–

1832 concerned the conflicting economic interests of the North and the South more than it did slavery. South Carolina, hard hit by depression and losing its lead in the cotton trade, demanded tariff reform from Congress. High U.S. tariffs on imports from England had led England to place duties on cotton from the U.S., which put American cotton at a disadvantage in the competition for the English market. John C. Calhoun of South Carolina, vice-president under both John Quincy Adams and Andrew Jackson, presented the theory that a state could legally nullify a federal law it found to be unconstitutional, and in 1828 the South Carolina legislature resolved that the tariff was unconstitutional. In 1832 a new law lowered customs duties, but South Carolina, dissatisfied, called a special convention that declared the federal tariff null and void. President Jackson was prepared to order troops to

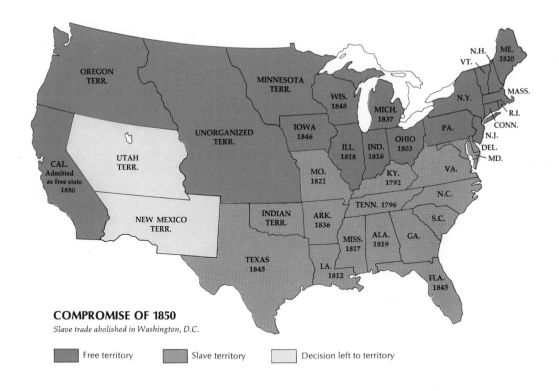

COMPROMISE OF 1850

Slave trade abolished in Washington, D.C.

Free territory   Slave territory   Decision left to territory

attack the "Nullifiers" and enforce the tariffs. To avoid such a confrontation, congressional leaders agreed on some further lowering of tariff rates. South Carolina thereupon repealed the nullification. While the bitter controversy ended in compromise, it reinforced a strong feeling in the South that "federal tyranny" must be opposed by the assertion of states' rights. And South Carolinians particularly saw the protariff forces and the abolitionists as partners in an evil alliance against the slave states.

The Compromise of 1850 was the result of a dispute over slavery in the vast area in the Southwest which the U.S. had acquired from Mexico. After long debate, Congress decided to admit California as a free state and to divide the rest of the region into the territories of New Mexico and Utah, which would enter the Union at some future time with or without slavery, as their settlers preferred. Con-

gress abolished the slave trade in the District of Columbia, but passed a stronger Fugitive Slave Act that denied runaway slaves the right to trial by jury. The main sponsors of this compromise, Senators Henry Clay and Daniel Webster, hoped it would last at least a generation, like the Missouri Compromise. But northern abolitionists immediately challenged it. They held public demonstrations and secured local laws to protect slaves from being captured and returned to the South.

The Kansas-Nebraska Act of 1854 reopened the question of whether to legalize or outlaw slavery in the territories and states carved out of the Louisiana Purchase, that vast region extending from just north of Texas all the way to the Canadian border. The act, authored by Illinois Senator Stephen A. Douglas, provided that the settlers themselves would decide the slavery issue in the new territories. The explosive feature of the

**KANSAS-NEBRASKA
ACT, 1854**

- ▓ Free territory
- ▓ Slave territory
- ░ Slavery question to be decided by people

promise). After being taken back to Missouri, Scott sued for his liberty, claiming that his stay in Wisconsin had made him a free man. The Court ruled that, as a slave, Scott was not a citizen and therefore could not sue in the courts. Furthermore, it declared the Missouri Compromise unconstitutional, stating that Congress had had no right to exclude slavery from the West. This was the first time in half a century that the Court had ruled a law unconstitutional, and in doing so it had thrown out a law which the North respected as a near equal of the Constitution. Finally, the Court had denied territories the right to ban slavery, since popular sovereignty in a territory clearly could not outweigh in legal authority a majority vote in the Congress of the United States. The Dred Scott decision outraged most moderates on the slavery question, but Democratic President Buchanan defended the ruling. It marked the point of no return along the road to the Civil War.

new law was that it repealed the Missouri Compromise, which had prohibited slavery north of 36°30'. Many northerners considered the Missouri Compromise sacred, so the outcry was loud and sharp. No sooner was the act signed into law than fighting broke out in Kansas between proslavery and antislavery factions. By now northerners simply would not accept any further extension of slavery into the western territories. With this crisis in "bleeding Kansas" many considered civil war a certain fate.

Feelings of outrage in the North were strengthened by the Dred Scott decision. In 1857 the Supreme Court decided a case involving a slave, Dred Scott, who was taken by his master from Missouri (a slave state) to Illinois (a free state) and then into Wisconsin Territory (free soil under the Missouri Com-

Free or slave labor in the West?

The North and the South both courted the West as a political ally. At first the South was the favored suitor, and western congressmen helped to fortify the political position of the southern states. Many westerners, including the Lincoln clan, had come from the South. In addition, the Mississippi River joined the West and the South, providing a natural route for commerce between the two regions. Yet as farming spread throughout the upper Mississippi Valley and a network of canals and railroads linked the Northeast to the West, the bond between the South and the West weakened. Slave owners kept expanding their operations westward into newer and cheaper lands that were also coveted by small farmers.

So the struggle seemed to hinge on the fundamental differences between western farmers, who supported "free labor, free soil, and free men," and southerners, who defended an economy and a way of life based on slavery. The crucial issue was a political one—which labor system would prevail in the West.

The South secedes

Between the first days of the new nation and about 1850 a shift in population had brought a corresponding shift of wealth and political power. In 1790 population in the North and the South was about equal. But by 1850 the North's population had risen to 13.5 million, while the South's stood at 9.6 million. This gave the North a significant edge in congressional representation and left the South with a feeling that its power was steadily diminishing—a feeling that at times verged on hysteria.

In 1860 Abraham Lincoln was elected president, promising to preserve the Union at all costs. He wanted to prevent the extension of slavery into the West, but not tamper with it in the South. Southern states, refusing to abide by the results of the election, began to withdraw from the Union. An eleventh-hour effort by Senator John J. Crittenden of Kentucky to achieve another compromise failed to win the vote in Congress. By now the middle ground had been cut away. Moderates who were quite indifferent to slavery had no political means of preventing secession or war. Seven southern states withdrew from the Union between December 20, 1860, and February 1, 1861. The president refused to recognize the right of the Confederate States of America to secede—the right to self-determination that the rebellious colonists had claimed in the Declaration of Independence. Had he done so, very probably there would have been no Civil War, at least not at this point.

Even before Lincoln was inaugurated, the seceding states held a convention in Montgomery, Alabama, to set up a provisional government and draft a new constitution. The Confederate Constitution of 1861 greatly resembled the U.S. Constitution except that it explicitly made slaves a form of property protected by law. It also guaranteed the individual states greater independence and freedom from federal controls. During the Civil War state sovereignty weakened the Confederate government's capacity to fight the more consolidated Union.

Mississippi's Jefferson Davis, a planter-politician known for his ardent support of slavery, became president of the Confederacy. He was a dedicated and energetic chief executive but a poor administrator, and he failed to win a popular following.

After the departure of southern senators and representatives from Washington in the secession winter of 1860–1861, Congress churned out many laws that had long been desired by northern and western interests but had been blocked by southerners. The Morrill Tariff Act (1861) raised tariff rates by almost 50 percent by 1865 and started a protectionist trend that would last for a generation. The Homestead Act (1862) offered loyal citizens—not Confederates—160 acres of public land, provided they occupied that land for five years. The Morrill Land Grant Act (1862) gave federal subsidies to state agricultural colleges. A companion law established the Department of Agriculture. Under the Pacific Railway Act (1862) Congress authorized a transcontinental railroad to be constructed with federal loans and outright grants of public land and resources. To meet wartime labor shortages, the Immigration Act of 1864 admitted foreign laborers contracted to work for railroad builders and industrialists. The National Banking Act of 1863 authorized a uniform currency and a system of connecting banks subject to federal controls. Those who had sided with the Republican party were well rewarded.

Party Politics and the Rise of Democracy

The need for political parties

As more and more citizens demanded — and received — the right to vote in America, a party system evolved based on the engagement of ordinary citizens in the election process. This political system generally involved the opposition of two major parties. About a dozen individual parties had come and gone by 1840, but the basic system has remained intact except during the Civil War years.

The new democratic political system had to overcome traditional prejudices. The Founding Fathers had strong convictions that parties were destructive and unnecessary. Moreover, in their day the masses were not considered fully ready to govern themselves; government should be left in the hands of those gentlemen who were most capable of governing rather than be entrusted to the common people. But as was already apparent in Washington's administration, basic questions concerning domestic policy created sharp divisions. The country was simply too large and too loosely knit for the government to operate successfully without the glue that political parties provided. At the same time, ordinary citizens were demanding a greater voice in government and were less content to let "gentlemen" have exclusive sway.

Federalists versus Republicans: the loyal opposition

The most important element in the growth of political parties in the U.S. was the principle of a loyal opposition. There can be no continuity in popular government unless the losing side in an election accepts defeat gracefully and becomes a responsible opponent, instead of resorting to guns. On the other hand, the winning party must let the losers oppose them in the next regular election.

There were no political parties in the first two presidential elections. Washington was unanimously elected in 1789 and was re-elected for a second term without party backing. (In the back of this book is a list of the presidents and the dates that they served.) Washington publicly denounced political parties. Yet from the moment that Hamilton submitted his financial program, Congress began to divide into different camps. From this division rose two political parties. Those who supported the administration and Hamilton's system called themselves "Federalists." Those opposed gradually acquired the name "Democratic-Republicans," often shortened to just "Republicans." Newspapers were started specifically to publish charges and countercharges. Caucuses were held in Congress to channel and block legislation. In some states partisans came together to help decide who would run for office and what they wanted to accomplish.

The political partisanship that started when Hamilton presented his financial scheme to Congress spread after the outbreak of the French Revolution. When revolutionary France declared war on Britain, the Federalists sympathized with Britain, while the Republicans, led by Madison and Jefferson, took the opposite side.

Washington first appointed men of varying political opinions to cabinet posts, including both Hamilton and Jefferson. He frequently declared his neutrality between contending factions. Yet the more he proclaimed himself politically neutral, the more he became in fact a staunch Federalist. He steadily alienated all the opponents of Hamilton's program, including Jefferson. Washington is remembered for warning in his Farewell Address against "the baneful effects of the spirit of party." Oddly enough, this section of the Address was probably ghost-written for him by Hamilton, the most partisan figure of his time.

Although not officially backed by Washington, the Federalists enjoyed a definite advantage as the first party in office and the one associated with the heroic president. They appealed strongly to merchants, financiers, manufacturers, and lawyers. Southern planters also supported them. But the Federalists never cultivated a mass following and were sharply divided among themselves. The more conservative branch, the "Low Federalists," centered around the merchants and financiers of New York and Philadelphia and hoped to make Hamilton president in 1796. The New England wing, sometimes known as the "High Federalists," successfully backed the moderate John Adams to become Washington's successor.

During John Adams' administration (1797–1801) the rift between Federalists and Republicans nearly destroyed the country. The Federalists feared that if Vice-President Jefferson and his Republican followers were not secretly sharpening a guillotine to behead their enemies, they were almost certainly conspiring to destroy private property and overthrow the government (and probably also Christianity). The Republicans, including Jefferson, believed that Hamilton was plotting to set up a monarchy and destroy liberty. In 1798 the Federalist-dominated Congress passed the Alien and Sedition Acts to crush "domestic treason" and "foreign subversion." The Alien Acts extended the number of years foreigners had to live in this country before they could apply for citizenship and authorized the president to deport political undesirables. The target of these new laws was the Republicans, since most immigrants tended to vote Republican.

Under the Sedition Act anyone who published "false, scandalous, and malicious" writing against the government could be prosecuted. Even speaking out against the government was punishable by fine or imprisonment. The Federalists jailed some Republican newspaper editors and printers for their antigovernment opinions.

Meanwhile many dedicated Hamiltonians tried to stir up a war between the U.S. and France. Their double purpose was to help Britain stamp out the French Revolution and to provide a pretext for attacking the "Republican rabble" in the U.S. Only Adams' determined opposition to dangerous foreign entanglements prevented the outbreak of war from 1797 to 1801.

During the uproar over the Alien and Sedition Acts, the Republicans maintained that these laws were unconstitutional. Led by Jefferson and Madison, they expressed their opposition in resolutions passed by the Virginia and Kentucky legislatures. These resolutions claimed that if Congress overstepped its power, the states had the right to decide whether or not they would obey or "nullify" an action by the federal government.

President Jefferson,
the loyal opponent

Some hotheads urged Jefferson to lead a southern secessionist movement and destroy the Federalist-dominated government in Washington. But Jefferson reasoned that the Federalist program for centralization would call for heavy taxes and high expenditures to pay for costly military actions. This, along with further clamps on civil liberties, would in time arouse powerful opposition among the people. There had gathered around Jefferson various anti-Federalist factions, including farmers, artisans, merchants, and planters, from New York, Pennsylvania, and Virginia. Jefferson reasoned correctly that a

Alexander Hamilton (1755-1804)

THE DUEL

"The will of a merciful God must be good. Once more Adieu, My Darling Darling Wife." With these words, Alexander Hamilton ended a farewell letter to his wife, Elizabeth, the night before his duel with Aaron Burr.

Bitter political opponents, Hamilton and Burr had long detested each other. When a tie vote in the electoral college threw the presidential election of 1800 into the House of Representatives, Hamilton, the Federalist leader, had finally helped Thomas Jefferson win the presidency over the other Republican, Burr. Indeed, one of the few things Hamilton and Thomas Jefferson ever agreed upon was that Burr was a scoundrel. And later, when Burr sought Federalist support in his attempt to become governor of New York State, his nemesis Hamilton went to great lengths to persuade members of his party to reject Burr.

Hamilton had made no effort to hide his belief that Burr was a rogue. His pronouncement that Burr was a "dangerous man, and ought not to be trusted with the reins of government" had been printed in a newspaper. Burr demanded a full apology for this insult as well as any others Hamilton might have made. When Hamilton refused, Burr challenged him to a duel.

Hamilton loathed dueling. It had already brought tragedy to his family. Three years earlier, in defense of his father's honor, Alexander Hamilton's oldest son Philip had died in a duel at the hands of a Burr supporter. Recently Hamilton had turned more and more to religion for consolation, and his faith forbade the taking of a human life. Now he felt forced to defend his honor by meeting Burr on the same New Jersey shore where his son had been shot down. But he was determined, he wrote, to "throw away" the first of the two shots allowed and perhaps to waste the second as well. He hoped that Burr would follow his example. In so doing Hamilton wanted the duel to stand as a protest against a practice he considered an uncivilized relic of the past.

Hamilton's hope was not to be realized. When the two men met at Weehawken on the morning of July 11, 1804, Burr fired, and Hamilton fell, mortally wounded. The dying man was carried to Manhattan, and his wife was summoned to his bedside. His death ended one of the most important public careers in American history. Alexander Hamilton had been a soldier, member of the Constitutional Convention, chief author of *The Federalist*, and founder of the Federalist party. As first Secretary of the Treasury he had created a national financial system at a time when the new republic had little nationhood and less financial strength or stability. The only good that might have come out of the senseless killing was that the public outcry raised at the news of Hamilton's death probably hastened the final outlawing of a barbaric custom.

coalition of these elements could eventually take over the government by legitimate means, for in 1800 he was elected president.

It is said that on the eve of Jefferson's inaugural, March 4, 1801, fearful Boston ladies hid their Bibles under their mattresses. But Jefferson amazed his listeners by soothing the opposition. "We are all Republicans, we are all Federalists," he declared. "If there be any among us who would wish to dissolve this Union or to change its republican form, let them stand undisturbed as monuments of the safety with which error of opinion may be tolerated when reason is left free to combat it."

Jefferson stood for older, agrarian values, which were threatened by Hamilton. Decentralized government, low taxes and minimal federal expenditures, restrictions on the military, elimination of special privilege and monopoly, and support for local government made up his platform. Yet when he took office he kept major portions of Hamilton's program, including the Bank of the United States. And despite his earlier protests against presidential powers, Jefferson greatly strengthened executive authority. He authorized the Louisiana Purchase, although he knew it was unconstitutional. But he decided to let the voters judge him at the polls, and they approved by reelecting him. Jefferson's moderation as president surprised some of his opponents and disappointed some of his followers. But retaining the Hamiltonian program was as essential to the preservation of the Union as had been his earlier decision against secession.

Jefferson was a contradictory figure. A planter by vocation, he considered small farmers God's chosen people. A believer in equality and democracy, he was nevertheless an owner of black slaves. Federalists considered him a wild-eyed revolutionary, yet he was a moderate liberal in office.

Jefferson's contribution to the American political system was twofold. First, he established a loyal opposition. Second, he set the pattern whereby a strong executive would lead the movement for moderate reform. He took a lively interest in the details of legislation, of appointments to office, and of the policies of administrators throughout the government. And he worked to build the machinery of the Republican party on the state and local levels.

Decline of the Federalist and Republican parties

Jefferson's Republican successors had a somewhat different concept of political parties and presidents. Madison, Monroe, and John Quincy Adams believed in a weaker chief executive and a stronger Congress. To their minds, parties were quarrelsome and only stirred up trouble. They should be allowed to fall by the wayside. As a result, the Republican party began to crumble on the national scene, although it still had some force in state politics and in Congress.

The Federalist party died a slow and agonizing death. Its ranks were never very large, and by opposing the War of 1812 it lost its limited following. By 1820 it could not even muster the energy to nominate a presidential candidate. President Monroe's nationwide trip in 1817 was reported in the press under the banner of "An Era of Good Feelings," a reference to the absence of Federalist opposition. Yet without an opposition to unify them, Republicans became caught up in political infighting. In 1824 four Republican candidates ran for president: Andrew Jackson, John Quincy Adams, Henry Clay, and William H. Crawford. By then the party was hopelessly split.

In 1824 the political system still teetered on a narrow base. Fewer than a half million voters went to the polls that year. There were still no party organizations in some states. Presidential nominees were selected by congressional caucuses. The party leaders in Congress met privately to select both the presidential candidates and the presidential electors committed to them. (Technically the electors were chosen by the state legislatures, and they were supposed to be free from political partisanship.)

The idea of a loyal opposition was perhaps the most solid political contribution of the first generation of politics, for it helped keep the country together at a crucial juncture. Such a system still appears necessary to maintain liberal institutions.

Democrats versus Whigs: the common man in politics

The arrival of grass-roots democracy in America is associated with the election of Andrew Jackson, the hero of New Orleans, in 1828. In the election of 1824 Jackson won more votes than the other two major candidates, Henry Clay and John Quincy Adams, but he lacked a majority. The runoff between Adams and Jackson was settled in the House of Representatives, and Adams was declared the winner. But Jackson's supporters charged that Clay threw his votes to Adams in return for the promise that he would be appointed secretary of state. This so-called corrupt bargain placed Adams in the White House, but it raised Jackson a notch in the eyes of his followers, who felt that he had been robbed of the presidency. If Jackson could mobilize the backwoods farmers, small planters, mechanics, and townspeople who supported him, he could be elected president in 1828.

The man who helped engineer Jackson's victory was Senator Martin Van Buren (1782–1862) of New York, the first of a new breed of public figure, the professional politician. Van Buren, the son of a tavern keeper in a remote New York township, had risen to the top by his bootstraps. As the protégé of the discredited Aaron Burr (who had killed Hamilton in a duel), Van Buren was the boss of the Albany Regency, a political faction that dominated New York politics. He was a career politician in the days when politics first became an avenue to success.

To boost Old Hickory for president, Van Buren formed an alliance of Virginians and New Yorkers. Van Buren's organizing skills and Jackson's popularity helped Jackson forge a winning coalition of farmers, small planters, manufacturers, western bankers, wage earners, unskilled laborers, artisans, and intellectuals. Jackson attacked special privileges, particularly those of the second U.S. Bank, headed by Nicholas Biddle. Like Jefferson, Jackson stressed simplicity and decentralized government. Two years of active party work brought Old Hickory into the White House amid scenes of wild inaugural joy in 1829. The Democratic-Republicans, soon to be known as Democrats, had produced a political coalition that would last until the late 1840s.

Jackson argued strenuously against the "hereditary" and "aristocratic" officeholders of John Quincy Adams' administration. According to Jackson, any voter was capable of holding any public office. "To the victors belong the spoils of the enemy," declared a Jackson man in 1832. The spoils system, whereby the winning party rewarded its favorites with government jobs, was actually invented by Jefferson but became institutionalized in Jackson's day. It became a vital cog in the machinery of politics.

Although a hero to some, Jackson also had scores of enemies. His opposition was drawn from the followers of John Quincy Adams, the states' rights Democrats of the South who embraced Calhoun's doctrine of nullification, certain western businessmen, southern planters, New England industrialists and merchants, and the supporters of Daniel Webster and Henry Clay. By 1834 these diverse groups fused into a new loyal opposition known as the Whig party.

A federal surplus of millions was accumulating in the second U.S. Bank when Andrew Jackson decided to chain the "Monster." In 1833 he ordered that the government's mounting deposits be placed in selective state banks, which the opposition quickly dubbed "pet banks." Beggars from the "Seventh Ward Bank," shown above, ask for "fiscal patronage." Jackson sits on surplus-fund bales, holding a scepter in one hand and a bag with $100,000 in the other.

The machinery of party politics

In the 1830s the major political parties for the first time had affiliates in all of the states and were using many of the tools of modern political organization. The Democrats met in state conventions. They also held a national nominating convention, a device adopted from a small anti-Jackson party. They used state legislative caucuses, like the Albany Regency, to help pick candidates. The Jacksonians, meanwhile, subsidized newspapers, and political journalism became a well-developed art.

Another innovation in politics in this era was the "city machine," a political faction whose "boss" or "bosses" ran urban government and had strong political ties on the national level. It originated with the Tammany Society of New York, which came on the scene in 1821 when voting qualifications were eased in New York State. The old aristocratic clans of the city abandoned politics to the common man, and the void was soon filled by members of a men's club which met in Tammany Hall. The Society's members

The election of 1840 brought out the largest number of votes yet seen; a whopping 78 percent of the electorate went to the polls. But during the election campaign sober argument got lost in a mighty outpouring of songs, torchlight parades, mammoth rallies, and log-cabin symbolism. In the end Harrison, the Whig candidate, scored a smashing victory over Democrat Van Buren.

invaded the new Democratic conventions and nominated and elected their own candidates to office. Tammany controlled about five hundred patronage jobs in federal, state, and city government in 1834. It was soon collecting kickbacks from city employees amounting to one million dollars a year. By the 1840s the Tammany Society was skillfully exploiting the immigrant vote. Similar political machines, usually (but not always) associated with the Democratic party, arose in other cities as well. City machines also devised primary elections for choosing convention delegates.

The first modern presidential campaign was the campaign of 1840, when the Whig candidate William Henry Harrison ran against Democrat Van Buren. The electorate numbered 2.4 million voters, who in most areas would choose the presidential electors directly. By now both parties were established everywhere, held national conventions, rallied behind a single leader, and engaged in campaign hoopla. The Whigs pioneered the use of parades, placards, floats, rallies, and songs, which made politics a form of mass entertainment. The jingle "Tippecanoe and Tyler too" that advertised the Whig ticket—Harrison and Tyler—reminded voters that Harrison had defeated the Indians at the Battle of Tippecanoe in 1811. Because Harrison was promoted as a man of the people (though he actually came from an aristocratic family and lived in a mansion), his supporters decorated their banners and buttons with coonskin caps, cider barrels, and log cabins. Harrison defeated Van Buren at his own game of politics.

While two parties have normally dominated American politics, third parties have frequently shown considerable strength. They have usually arisen over a single issue and stirred up the established parties. The Anti-Masonic party appeared around the time of the 1832 election. It opposed Jackson and Clay because they were Masons and therefore supposedly a threat to democracy. More important were the Liberty party (in the elections of 1840 and 1844) and the Free-Soil party (1848 and 1852). Both parties pushed for abolition of slavery. The platform of the Free-Soil party included "free soil, free speech, free labor, and free men." The anti-Catholic, anti-immigrant American party took part in the election of 1856. Because its members guarded the secrecy of their organization by claiming ignorance, it was called the "Know-Nothing" party.

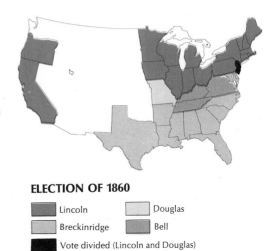

ELECTION OF 1860

■ Lincoln	░ Douglas
▨ Breckinridge	▧ Bell
■ Vote divided (Lincoln and Douglas)	

Origins of the GOP

Because the Whigs and Democrats both wanted the widest possible base of popular support, they tended to straddle the explosive issue of slavery. In the end this refusal to take a stand destroyed the Whigs and nearly wrecked the Democrats.

The Kansas-Nebraska Act of 1854 had opened a train of events that would split both parties. In that year antislavery Democrats and Whigs met with Free-Soilers in Michigan and Wisconsin. From these meetings came a new grass-roots organization — the Republican party (later called the GOP or Grand Old Party) — which scored immediate victories in the congressional elections. When the Democrats made concessions to the South in order to get James Buchanan into the White House in 1856, more northern members of the party shifted their allegiance to the Republicans. And when the Whigs chose not to mention slavery at all in their 1856 platform, their antislavery members — the so-called Conscience Whigs — took the same action.

The basic plank in the Republican platform was free soil and free labor — in short, keeping slavery out of the western territories. Beginning with the backing of midwestern farmers, the party gradually attracted large numbers of northern workers, both native born and immigrant, as well as businessmen, financiers, and others. At the Republican convention in 1856 the politically inexperienced western explorer John C. Frémont was nominated for president and went on to win 33 percent of the popular vote to Buchanan's 45 percent. (The Know-Nothing candidate took the rest.) Four years later the Republicans won the presidency with Abraham Lincoln.

Lincoln, a former Whig congressman from Illinois, was not the first choice of the GOP party regulars in 1860. They would have preferred the more outspoken William Seward of New York. But they felt that Lincoln stood the best chance of being elected precisely because he held moderate views on slavery. Lincoln swore to uphold the Union and to protect free soil in the territories, but he specifically disavowed any intention of freeing the slaves in the South. A sectional candidate, he failed to win a popular majority at the polls. But he won the electoral votes of the northern states. It was the immigrant vote of the Old Northwest that put him over the top. The GOP also won both houses of Congress. The South refused to recognize Lincoln's victory, and southern states began to secede in December 1860.

The sixteenth president of the United States was born in Kentucky in 1809, grew up in southern Indiana, and settled finally in Illinois. The lanky young man educated himself and practiced law in Springfield, Illinois. In 1846 he was elected to Congress on the Whig ticket as an opponent of the Mexican War (1846–1848). In 1856 he joined the Republican party. Two years later he opposed Stephen A. Douglas for the Senate, having denounced the Kansas-Nebraska Act and the Dred Scott decision. Lincoln's "House Divided" speech and his skillful debates with Douglas were not enough to win him the Senate seat. He arrived at the White House in 1860 at the most crucial juncture in the nation's history. President Lincoln proved an able politician and a gifted, if controversial, wartime leader. The man who had been a conservative on the issue of slavery in the South gradually became an abolitionist and approved the Thirteenth Amendment.

By 1865 the North looked on the Republicans as the party of loyalty, patriotism, freedom, and righteous victory. The Democrats were seen as the party of slavery, rebellion, treason, and defeat. But in the South the Democrats were regarded as the leaders of the Lost Cause—the Confederacy and the ideal of white supremacy. The war had given politicians, normally considered opportunists, an aura of statesmanship that they had not previously enjoyed.

The Civil War profoundly altered the country's power structure. Lee's surrender to Grant at Appomattox Court House in 1865 did more than stop the fighting on the battlefronts. It destroyed slavery, overthrew the Confederate government, broke the power of the big planters, and enthroned the GOP as the dominant political party. Its far-reaching effects prompted historians Charles and Mary Beard to say that "the so called civil war was in reality a Second American Revolution and, in a strict sense, the first."

For all practical purposes, the war also laid to rest the states' rights issue that had long embroiled many politicians. When the Union came together again in 1865 and the era of southern Reconstruction began, the U.S. government was far more centralized than anyone at the Philadelphia Convention of 1787 could have imagined. The old contest over states' rights and federal authority had been resolved in favor of the federal government.

Review

Leaders of the new nation were concerned with the problem of power—who should have it and how its excesses could be controlled. The presidency took firm shape under Washington, while the Supreme Court established its powers under the lead of Chief Justice John Marshall. As the Northeast, West, and South represented different interests and needs, there developed a three-way, regional contest for power. The Civil War, the most crucial power struggle in American history, resulted from this split. The main question was whether slavery would be allowed to spread to the new territories of the West. War was averted for a time by a series of compromises that tried to balance the interests of various groups. But the West continued to be a bone of contention. When Lincoln was elected president, solely by northern electoral votes, the South seceded from the Union. Lincoln refused to recognize the legitimacy of the Confederate States of America as a separate nation, and the battle lines were drawn. At the war's end, the South's defeat radically altered the distribution of power in the nation.

The Founding Fathers were opposed to political parties. But the deep split in Washington's administration soon opened the way for the two-party system. Jefferson developed the vital concept of a loyal opposition. When the Republican and Federalist parties outlived their usefulness, they gave way to a second party system. The Democratic party formed around Andrew Jackson, and his enemies joined forces to create the Whig party. The modern trappings of political contests now put in an appearance.

The westward movement spurred citizens to demand a larger stake in government. Voting rights were extended, and the old "aristocracy" in politics gave way to the middle class. Political parties became national organizations. In 1854 a new coalition emerged as the Republican party. Lincoln ran as the Republican candidate in the presidential election of 1860. He won the presidency in the electoral college, although he had failed to win a popular majority at the polls. But his Civil War leadership and his death by an assassin's bullet firmly established the Republicans as the dominant party in America. Meanwhile, the Democrats became entrenched in the South as the party of the Lost Cause.

Questions

1. What important contributions did Washington, Jefferson, and Jackson make to the presidency?
2. How did the decision in *Marbury* v. *Madison* strengthen the position of the Supreme Court? What new powers did Congress gain by the decision in *McCulloch* v. *Maryland*?
3. Describe the regional power blocs of the Northeast, West, and South in pre-Civil War America.
4. What do you think were the main causes of the Civil War? Do you think the war could have been, or should have been, avoided?
5. Trace the growth of political parties and the changing coalitions from Washington's administration to the end of the Civil War.

Civil War dead, outside Dunkard Church, Antietam, Maryland, September 1862.

We, on our side, are praying
to Him to give us victory,
because we believe we are
right; but those on the other
side pray to Him, look for
victory, believing they are
right. What must He think
of us?

ABRAHAM LINCOLN   (1809–1865)

11

229

11

In a "Century of Peace"

"Americans have found it rather more difficult than other peoples to deal rationally with their wars," writes Glenn S. Price. "We have thought of ourselves as unique, and of this society as specially planned and created to avoid the errors of other nations." Providence protected the U.S. against European diplomacy by placing it on the far side of a great ocean. God had seen to it that the new republic had no serious enemies in the Western Hemisphere. The nation was rich in land and resources and did not have to stray over the globe to seek an empire. All of this would make America strong and free with no need to wage war.

The United States arrived on the stage of history at a time when some profound thinkers claimed that war was disappearing and peace would be the normal state of affairs. The German philosopher Immanuel Kant forecast *Perpetual Peace* in his book of that title. The English philosopher Jeremy Bentham held that war would surely subside "as society progressed."

In actuality the nineteenth century was far from peaceful, for there were bloody wars and civil conflicts on all continents. It would be more nearly correct to say that the major European powers did not fight general or lengthy wars. After Napoleon was banished to the island of St. Helena in 1815, the major powers established a new balance of power which lasted, more or less undisturbed, until World War I. In this sense it appeared that nations had begun to find peaceful ways of resolving their differences.

In that age of supposed peace and harmony, America was unable to avoid either foreign or domestic conflict. Americans fought Indians for decades, went to war with the British in 1812, were involved in the Texas Revolution from 1835 to 1836, came close to another war with the British over Oregon in 1848, defeated Mexico's armies the same year, and from 1861 to 1865 engaged in one of the bloodiest civil wars of all time.

Trouble with England and France

Undeclared naval war with France

The first external threat to the nation was the war between Britain and France, which raged off and on from 1793 to 1815. The Hamiltonian Federalists tried to push the United States into a war with France that would aid Great Britain in squelching the French Revolution. Washington issued a statement of neutrality in the spring of 1793. Britain ordered its navy to seize American ships headed for France or for French West Indian ports and readied the troops at its military posts in the Northwest to attack American frontier settlements. Washington's response was to sign an agreement with Britain: Jay's Treaty of 1794. In effect, it did little to force the British out of their posts in the Northwest, and it did not stop the Royal Navy from seizing American cargoes bound for France. To westerners the treaty seemed a sellout to Britain. It also infuriated France, which seized over three hundred U.S. ships in 1796 alone. France demanded that the U.S. honor its obligations under the Treaty of Alliance (1778) by siding with France against its enemies in time of war. In his Farewell Address Washington warned against "the insidious wiles of foreign influence." He urged that it should be America's "true policy to steer clear of permanent alliances." The U.S. should make only temporary alliances in times of emergency. In context the Farewell Address was not an isolationist speech, but it was hostile to France.

In his first term John Adams was faced with the "undeclared war" against France from 1798 to 1800. When France continued its raids on the high seas, General Washington was called out of retirement, and the army was expanded. Some Federalists still hoped to provoke a war for political ends. But the supremely independent Adams, bucking the leaders of his own Federalist party, chose instead to arrange a settlement with France in 1800, by which time Napoleon was in power. This put a temporary halt to France's preying on American ships, ended America's "entangling alliance" with France, and, to Adams' great pride, avoided an actual war.

Causes of the War of 1812

When the war between France and Britain resumed in 1803, the British navy once again took to seizing American cargoes, American ships, and American seamen. Jefferson tried to avoid all-out war by imposing the Embargo Act of 1807. It prohibited any American ships from sailing for foreign ports, and it forced all foreign vessels to leave the U.S. without cargo. Unfortunately, the law crippled U.S. shipping and damaged the U.S. economy most of all. Jefferson's successor, James Madison, sought to persuade the combatants to respect the rights of American shipping by denying their merchant vessels access to U.S. ports. But he had equally bad luck, for Napoleon outmaneuvered him, and the British raids continued.

When Congress declared war against England in 1812, some called it "The Second War for Independence," a fight for national honor and survival. Britain still kept its military posts in the Northwest and seemed to be stirring up the Indians to harass American settlers. On the high seas the Royal Navy continued to impress American seamen and seize ships bound for France. A British blockade of European ports, set up under the British Orders in Council, remained in force. These measures greatly disrupted U.S. sea trade, which was the nation's most valuable economic asset.

Yet the New England shippers were against the war. They felt that they could weather the worst British shipping restrictions if the U.S. remained neutral. Despite the slogan "Free trade and sailors' rights," it was the farmers, not the shipping interests, who pressed for war. Westerners and southerners were in the midst of a severe agricultural depression, which they blamed on Britain's attacks on American ships. Besides, frontiersmen saw Canada and Spanish Florida as tempting farmland which the U.S. might grab in wartime. Those who shouted loudest for war in the Twelfth Congress (1811–1812) were the new western representatives, including Speaker Henry Clay of Kentucky. They bore the title "War Hawks" proudly.

Strike wherever we can reach the enemy, at sea and on land. But if we fail, let us fail like men, lash ourselves to our gallant tars, and expire together in one common struggle, fighting for free trade and seamen's rights.

HENRY CLAY (1777–1852)

The entire conflict could have been avoided if Madison had merely sought a *limited* war. The British Orders in Council, which the U.S. was protesting, were in fact suspended just five days after Congress declared war. But the pressure for all-out war against Britain was strong, and Congress had already voted for it.

The U.S. war campaign

The War of 1812 was poorly managed. The country talked a good fight but was ill-prepared for this war. The antimilitary legacy of the Revolution had reduced the regular army to a few tiny border patrols. The navy had only some twenty ships. Yet the main strate-gy was very ambitious — to seize Canada and to raid British shipping on the high seas until Britain changed its tune on U.S. shipping rights.

To snap up both Canada and Florida appeared an easy military task to the War Hawks. Britain's forces were heavily engaged in Europe fighting Napoleon's armies. As a result, fewer than 5000 British troops were posted in all of Canada. Spain had no troops at all in Florida. On paper at least, the U.S. military had a force of 700,000 officers and men in the state militias. The prowar faction predicted that "the Kentucky militia alone could take Canada." Yet comparatively few Kentucky recruits signed up to fight, and no more than 10,000 one-year volunteers were ever in arms in all the states combined. The armed forces never took Canada. But the successes of American warships in duels with British naval vessels surprised everyone. The navy also blocked a major invasion force from Canada by defeating a British fleet on Lake Champlain in 1814. At the same time, American privateers captured hundreds of British ships on the high seas.

In 1814, after defeating Napoleon at the Battle of Waterloo, Britain dispatched fighting men and ships to humble the upstart United States. In September an army of veterans landed at Chesapeake Bay. It drove out the U.S. government, including the president, and burned the Capitol and the president's official residence (later whitewashed and named the White House).

The last major battle of the war took place at New Orleans in January 1815. When General Andrew Jackson learned that a large British fleet had managed to move an army within striking distance of the city, he quickly organized his forces to meet the attack. Well dug in, Jackson's army of Indian fighters, pirates, and regulars successfully withstood the assaults of 7500 redcoats. In the process Americans killed, wounded, or captured more than 2500 enemy soldiers. Jackson's

The Battle of Queenston on October 13, 1812, ended in total victory for the British. An American force occupying Queenston, Ontario, near Niagara Falls, was supposed to be reinforced by the New York State militia. But the militiamen refused to cross the Niagara River into Canada, on the grounds that they were not required to fight outside their own state.

forces suffered only eight dead and thirteen wounded. Only later was it discovered that the Battle of New Orleans had taken place after the signing of the treaty that concluded the war. The War of 1812 ended at a bargaining table at Ghent in Belgium, not on the battlefield.

Wartime disunity and postwar nationalism

The War of 1812 came close to destroying the nation. Antiwar protest centered in New England, where the damage to trade was most severe. Here, Federalist leaders gave "Mr. Madison's war" minimum public support and maximum private resistance. The governors of Connecticut and Massachusetts refused to furnish militia to the federal government. In Massachusetts, where opposition was heaviest, Governor Strong sent a private emissary to the British to arrange a separate peace treaty for New England.

In December 1814 Massachusetts called a convention to consider ways of destroying the war effort. Delegates from five New England states met at Hartford, Connecticut. They called for constitutional amendments that would punish the prowar Republicans. Since the war had been sparked by westerners, they proposed making it harder for new western states to enter the Union. To break the hated "Virginia dynasty" (Jefferson, Madison, and Monroe) that seemed to have a permanent grip on the White House, they proposed a one-term presidency. They also tried to outlaw long embargoes. A few firebrand Federalists at the Hartford Convention even suggested that New England secede from the Union.

Had the war continued another year or so, it conceivably could have led to civil war. New Englanders might have joined the Royal Navy, signed a separate peace, and established a new, independent republic in the Northeast.

The War of 1812 became popular after it was all over. The Battle of New Orleans helped rally public support and made Andrew Jackson a national hero. The war inspired Francis Scott Key's "Star-Spangled Banner," produced the battle cry of the navy, "Don't give up the ship!" and sparked a new spirit of nationalism. But it did not win Canada or Florida for the U.S., and it did not guarantee America's neutral rights at sea. Nor did it force Britain to make even a gesture toward ending the impressment of American seamen. At home, the one sure outcome of the war was the total destruction of the Federalist party, which was now tainted as a party of secessionists and losers.

Stretching the U.S. Boundaries

The urge for more land

The boundaries of the United States were pushed out by the addition of vast new territory between 1803 and 1853. The Louisiana Territory was added in 1803, Florida in 1819, Texas in 1845, Oregon in 1846, the Mexican Cession in 1848, and the Gadsden Purchase in 1853. (See map, opposite.)

The Founding Fathers held opposing views as to how big the new nation should be allowed to grow. History seemed to teach that liberty survived best in small republics like ancient Athens or the Dutch Republic of the seventeenth century. Let a republic expand too much or dabble in empire, some felt, and it would invite the rise of dictators, who were the death of liberty. Yet their faith in America led them to think big. In fact, James Madison once asserted that the country must be large to protect its greatness. In a small republic the majority could easily destroy the minority. In a large republic opposing groups would limit each other's power. Still, in the early nineteenth century first the Mississippi River and then the Rocky Mountains seemed to be the natural western boundary.

The westward movement into Kentucky, Tennessee, and the Northwest Territory whetted Americans' appetite for more land.

Kentucky became a state in 1792, Tennessee in 1796, and Ohio in 1803. At first it was unclear whether newly acquired territories would remain mere colonies for an indefinite time or would become states and enter the Union on a basis of full equality with the original thirteen states. The fact that Congress, through the Northwest Ordinance of 1787, offered full equality to new states and their inhabitants promised an orderly expansion.

The motives for U.S. expansion were a tangle of idealism and realism. New land was needed to grow cotton and other staple crops. The search for markets for surplus farm products stimulated expansion. At the same time, Americans believed this country had a special mission to advance the cause of liberty and progress. Many felt that America must stand as a beacon of liberty to "the oppressed peoples of Europe." And others called for annexing Texas as a means of extending liberty to the American settlers who lived there under Mexican rule.

The Louisiana Purchase

With the stroke of a quill pen Jefferson doubled the land mass of the U.S. in 1803. The

Louisiana Purchase opened to Americans a vast unmapped territory stretching from the Mississippi River to the Rocky Mountains. Napoleon had secretly acquired Louisiana from Spain, hoping to fashion it into a granary for France. The idea that Louisiana would remain indefinitely in French hands enraged American westerners. Jefferson put out feelers to see if he could purchase New Orleans and possibly West Florida near the mouth of the Mississippi. This would assure the free flow of farm products from the Northwest into the world market. Then French-owned Santo Domingo (Haiti) was seized by rebellious slaves. The island was the keystone to Napoleon's plan for exploiting Louisiana, because ships bound for New Orleans needed a stopover on the way. When Napoleon lost Santo Domingo, he decided to sell all of Louisiana. His foreign minister offered it to American envoys Robert Livingston and James Monroe for $15 million. They snapped up his offer.

Jefferson had been a strict constructionist, arguing for a narrow interpretation of the Constitution. Now he found himself involved in a transaction that the Constitution could not be said to authorize according to any strict construction of its meaning. But he saw in Louisiana room "for a thousand years" of growth. And the Senate approved the purchase, despite constitutional arguments and other objections by suspicious easterners. Jefferson sent Meriwether Lewis and William Clark to investigate the new territory, which would eventually be carved into thirteen states.

Acquiring Florida

At the time of the Louisiana Purchase, Spain's Florida territory included all of the Florida peninsula plus land extending westward along the Gulf Coast. Americans nibbled away at Spanish West Florida by intrigue and diplomacy. In 1810 Yankee adventurers

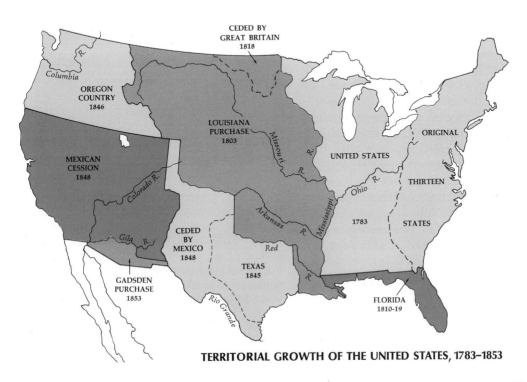

TERRITORIAL GROWTH OF THE UNITED STATES, 1783–1853

seized the western edge of Spain's possession, which bordered the Mississippi River. In league with President Madison they declared it an independent territory and offered it to the U.S. Madison accepted, although not before his advisers doctored vital documents to hide from Congress the president's involvement in the take-over. A slightly larger bit of West Florida was obtained by treaty a few years later. In 1819 Secretary of State John Quincy Adams foresaw a United States that stretched from the Atlantic to the Pacific. He arranged a treaty with Spain, the Adams-Onís Treaty, by which Spain ceded Florida to the U.S. and gave up its holdings in the Pacific Northwest, a concession to American interests there. Although the U.S. gave up all claims to Texas and the western edge of the Louisiana Purchase, its longterm outlook as a continental nation was well served by this treaty.

The Monroe Doctrine

Secretary Adams was also instrumental in drafting the Monroe Doctrine. Signed only by the United States, the policy statement was issued in 1823 as a warning to European monarchs who were toying with the idea of restoring the Spanish empire in Latin America, and to Russia's czar, whose traders were active in the Pacific Northwest and California. The wars of independence that had rumbled through Latin America since 1808 overthrew the Spanish crown and established a series of Latin American republics. The Monroe Doctrine supported republicanism and announced a "two-hemispheres" policy: America for Americans, Europe for Europeans. The Monroe Doctrine would have had no meaning at all, except that Britain, with the world's most powerful navy, also feared that the monarchs of continental Europe would intervene in Latin America and gave its full approval to President Monroe's policy. Latin Americans never showed the same fondness for the Monroe Doctrine as did Yankees, especially since the Yankees later used it to justify U.S. aggression in Latin America.

Manifest Destiny

In 1845 Democratic newspaper editor John L. O' Sullivan, in an article on Texas, declared that it is "the fulfillment of our manifest destiny to overspread the continent allotted by Providence for the free development of our yearly multiplying millions." The phrase "Manifest Destiny" became a popular cliché for expansion in the West in the 1840s and for overseas expansion in the 1890s. Poets, journalists, statesmen, clergymen, farmers, and artisans all sang the praises of Manifest Destiny. They proclaimed that God had designated North America as a refuge for Europeans seeking a new life and religious freedom. To the victims of foreign despotism here in North America (that is, the American settlers in Texas) this great nation must "extend the arm of liberty." The hardworking, thrifty, and pious American farmers would make "better use of the soil" than the Indian hunters and Mexican ranchers who must give way.

America's youthful exuberance and its greed for land were embedded in Manifest Destiny. "Land enough—land enough!" exclaimed a delegate to the New Jersey State Democratic Convention in 1844. He went on:

Make way, I say, for the young American Buffalo—he has not yet got land enough; he wants more land as his cool shelter in summer—he wants more land for his beautiful pasture grounds. I tell you, we will give him Oregon for his summer shade, and the region of Texas as his winter pasture. (Applause.) Like all of his race, he wants salt, too. Well, he shall have the use of two oceans—the mighty Pacific and the turbulent Atlantic shall be his. . . . He shall not stop his career until he slakes his thirst in the frozen ocean. (Cheers.)

Artists, poets, and journalists gave expression to the idea of America's "Manifest Destiny," as in this painting by John Gast. In a lecture delivered in 1844, Ralph Waldo Emerson declared, "The bountiful continent is ours, state on state, and territory on territory, to the waves of the Pacific sea: Our garden is the immeasurable earth. . . ."

Also behind this grasping for Oregon, Texas, and California lay a combination of economic motives. Eastern Texas and Oregon looked particularly green and inviting to midwestern farmers during the panic of 1837. California offered a magnificent natural harbor in San Francisco. Traders from the East had a large interest in the hide-and-tallow trade in California. They understood the commercial value of Pacific ports—not only San Francisco, but Monterey, San Diego, and the mouth of the Columbia River as well. Visionaries like Missouri Senator Thomas Hart Benton, one of the most powerful men in the Senate, could imagine a system of railroads, canals, and wagon routes spanning the continent to serve as a path for commerce between Europe and Asia. The Pacific ports would flourish as an outlet for farm produce as well as for manufactured goods from the Northeast. The old dream of a passage to the Orient would be fulfilled.

Polk adds Oregon and Texas

Democratic nominee James K. Polk won election as president in 1844 by promising to acquire new territory. He soon proceeded to make good his campaign promises. In his Inaugural Address he rejected the argument that if America became too large, it would sacrifice its liberties to empire. Polk insisted that, on the contrary, "our system may be safely extended to the utmost bounds of our territorial limits, and that . . . the bonds of our Union, so far from being weakened, will become stronger." He referred to the "extensive and profitable commerce with China, and other countries of the east" and stressed the value of Oregon and Texas for farming and business.

In an early move, Polk acquired Oregon. This he did through diplomacy, although not before rattling his sabre in a threat of war. In the Convention of 1818 with Britain, Secretary of State John Quincy Adams had arranged for joint British-American occupation of Oregon. President Polk demanded all of Oregon for the U.S. as far north as parallel 54°40'. "Fifty-four forty or fight!" became a popular slogan in the United States. By 1846 Britain was ready to negotiate a settlement. It had lost interest in the dwindling fur trade of the Pacific Northwest. Besides, Britain wanted to import more grain from America and devote its energies to industry. In the Treaty of Oregon the U.S. and Britain compromised on the 49th parallel. This line already marked the boundary of the U.S. and Canada east of Oregon and was now extended to the Pacific. The U.S. acquired that part of Oregon which was most heavily settled by Yankees.

Polk also annexed Texas. Despite their qualms about the potential threat of their Yankee neighbor, first Spain and later Mexico invited Americans into Texas to help develop its agriculture. The colonization proceeded smoothly until 1830. Then the Mexican government outlawed slavery and prepared to merge Texas with the state of Coahuila. Colonists in Texas began itching to establish an independent republic. In 1835 fighting broke out. The Texas Revolution was a short but bloody struggle for independence. A famous chapter of western derring-do occurred at the seige of the Alamo mission at San Antonio in March 1836. There fewer than two hundred Texans held off a force of some four thousand Mexicans. The Texans lost the Alamo—and their lives—but the Mexican army suffered heavy losses. "Remember the Alamo!" became the rallying cry of the Texas Revolution. Fighting against great odds, the Texans won their independence and established the Republic of Texas. It remained an independent republic for ten years. During this time the slavery question prevented the U.S. from annexing Texas. But in 1845, when Britain was working to keep Texas independent as a source of cotton for British mills, the U.S. made it a full-fledged state.

The world has nothing to fear from military ambition in our government.
JAMES K. POLK (1795–1849)

War with Mexico

Polk's aggression

The annexation of Texas was followed shortly by full-scale war with Mexico in a contest involving not only Texas but California and the entire Southwest. Mexico's refusal to recognize the U.S. annexation of Texas led to a border dispute on the southern boundary of the new American state. In addition, Polk was now eyeing other choice bits of Mexican territory—California and New Mexico—to fulfill his dreams of Manifest Destiny. Legally the United States had no claim to California, as it had, in part at least, to Oregon and Texas. When an attempt to buy California failed, Polk decided that the surest way to acquire that prize lay in war. Although the United States was under no serious military threat from Mexico, Polk made a warlike move by sending General Zachary Taylor into the border territory between the Nueces and Rio Grande rivers, an area claimed by both nations. There the U.S. forces built a fort that blocked the mouth of the Rio Grande to Mexican shipping. Mexican soldiers, now cut off from their supplies, attacked the Americans, killing eleven of Taylor's men and capturing others. Polk claimed, "Mexico has . . . shed American blood upon the American soil," and asked for a declaration of war.

The vote for a war declaration—174 to 14 in the House and 40 to 2 in the Senate—scarcely reflected the extent of congressional opposition. Few congressmen believed Polk's account of the trouble. They considered it suspicious that he allowed them no time to examine official documents and only two hours for House debate. Abraham Lincoln, the young Whig congressman from Illinois, made a telling point when he skeptically asked to be shown the exact spot on which "American blood had been shed on American soil." But those in Congress felt that if they voted against war, they would leave themselves open to the charge of abandoning American men on the field of battle. Even foes of the war like John Quincy Adams joined the stampede. Senator John Calhoun refused to vote without having more information and later said that not one in ten would have favored the war if they had first seen the official documents.

Antiwar dissent

Opponents of the war raised many objections. Some felt that Polk had violated the article of the Constitution that reserves to Congress the war-making power. Certain congressmen considered Mexico weak and unstable but totally harmless to the U.S. They charged that the president, by his orders to General Taylor and his manipulation of Congress, had started a war without provocation. There were Democrats who gloomily predicted that the army's top generals, Zachary Taylor and Winfield Scott—both Whigs—would soon become the prime candidates for president. Many characterized the actions against Mexico as a "slave owners' conspiracy" to acquire new soil for cotton plantations and new states for the South. The antislavery Whigs (Conscience Whigs) branded Polk's official explanation a "national lie." Calhoun and others protested that if the U.S. annexed too much of Mexico, the ensuing controversy over slavery in the new territory might destroy the nation.

Opposition again centered in the North-east. The dissenters included clergymen and writers, as well as politicians. Rather than support a war to help the "slave power," Henry David Thoreau refused to pay his poll tax and went to jail. "I cannot for an instant recognize that political organization as my organization which is the slave's government also," he later explained to a hometown audience. Thoreau's essay "Civil Disobedience" became the classic formulation of the philosophy of nonviolent resistance against unjust laws and immoral government policies. It greatly influenced the thinking of some twentieth-century leaders, most notably India's Mahatma Gandhi and Martin Luther King, Jr.

To the halls of Montezuma

Although overshadowed by the more dramatic events of the Civil War, the Mexican War still merits attention as military history. Here was the first conflict in which U.S. forces occupied a foreign capital. For the first time the army was led by professionals, members of the first graduating class of West Point. They led the troops to an unbroken string of victories against numerical odds.

Fighting proceeded on three fronts. First, at Santa Fe, New Mexico, and in California, Colonel Stephen Kearney established his authority with a minimum of resistance (January 1847). Second, in north central Mexico an outnumbered General Zachary Taylor defeated General Santa Anna at Buena Vista (February 1847). Third, General Winfield Scott landed at Vera Cruz on the Gulf Coast and fought his way inland, entering Mexico City in September 1847. Scott's eight-month campaign followed the route of the Spanish conquistadors three centuries earlier, ending up in "the halls of Montezuma."

Major atrocities were committed in the course of the Mexican War, especially under Taylor's command. His artillery deliberately

Naval and military units led by Commodore Robert F. Stockton and Colonel Stephen Kearney clashed with Mexican forces on the plains of La Mesa in January 1847. The Americans' victory brought Los Angeles under U.S. control and ended the war campaign in California. This sketch of the battle was done by a sailor serving under Stockton's command.

fired on civiliams at Matamoros. The worst crimes were at the hands of poorly disciplined volunteers, westerners who signed up to fight because they hoped to acquire Mexican booty. They burned and pillaged homes, vandalized churches, and murdered and scalped civilians. Outraged at the way Mexican Catholics were treated, scores of Irish Catholic volunteers in the U.S. Army deserted and joined the Mexicans. Recognizing the excesses of General Taylor's men, General Scott issued a special order condemning American war crimes and promising better treatment for civilians under his command.

Although the outcome of the war was never in doubt, Mexico's soldiers fought hard. Corrupt and incompetent generals, each less willing than the next to give in to the gringos, prolonged the agony, which lasted eighteen months.

Ending the war

Polk found it harder to stop the war than to start it. As American soldiers penetrated more deeply into Mexico, they stirred up pressure for the annexation of the whole country. But war weariness gradually took hold in the U.S. Conscience Whigs and antiadministration Democrats gained control of Congress in the off-year election of 1846 and were able to soften the peace terms. At the very least they squelched the impulse of the Polk Democrats to annex all of Mexico.

Under the terms of the Treaty of Guadalupe Hidalgo (1848), Mexico recognized the Rio Grande as the Texas border and ceded Upper California — territory which would become the states of California, Utah, and Nevada and parts of New Mexico, Arizona, Wyoming, and Colorado — to the United States. The United States paid $15 million for this Mexican Cession. Also, it assumed responsibility for $3 million in claims against Mexico by Americans who had suffered losses during the Mexican Revolution. The Gadsden Purchase of 1853 readjusted the boundary line with Mexico, adding to the U.S. a strip of land south of the Gila River in present-day Arizona and New Mexico. In the Mexican War, America fulfilled its "continental destiny" at the expense of Mexico, which lost half its territory.

South of the border the war is still remembered with deep bitterness. Mexicans are blunt in their view that the U.S. was an imperialist aggressor fighting a racist war. Feelings are still so fresh that until recently the maps in Mexican grade schools labeled the Mexican Cession as "Occupied Territory." Today Chicano separatists in the U.S. speak of "the redemption of Aztlán," of getting control of the original homeland of the Aztecs, which, according to legend, was located somewhere in the Mexican Cession.

A hidden cost of the Mexican War was that it heightened the slavery problem. In August 1846 Congressman David Wilmot of Pennsylvania proposed that slavery be prohibited in all territory taken from Mexico. Although the Wilmot Proviso failed, it was repeatedly introduced, each time causing greater bitterness over slavery. The Proviso struggle offered a grim foretaste of things to come.

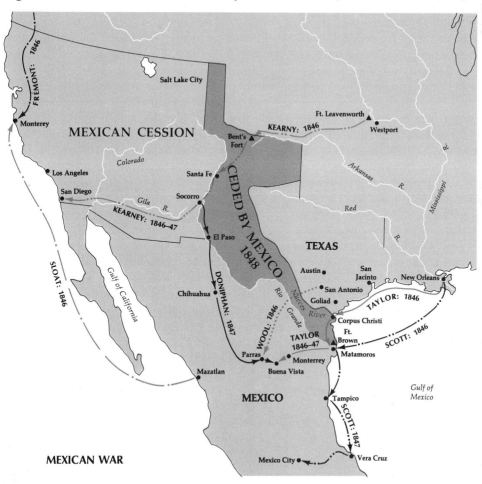

MEXICAN WAR

The Civil War

A country divided

All wars produce tragedy, but none more so than civil wars. They pit family against family and friend against friend and leave permanent scars. The American Civil War erupted at Fort Sumter on April 12, 1861, and tore the nation apart. In four years millions of men became soldiers, 600,000 died, and property worth millions of dollars was destroyed. The war freed the slaves, ended the Confederacy, and tested the mettle of a nation.

For a time in the early spring of 1861 it appeared that by some miracle war might be avoided. Eight of the fifteen slave states remained in the Union. Perhaps the seven that had seceded would reenter or would be allowed to go their way in peace. As late as February 1861 Lincoln declared that although he would use force to meet force, "there was no need of bloodshed and war." The showdown came at Fort Sumter on an island in Charleston Harbor. The president had already vowed to "hold, occupy, and possess" all federal installations in the South. Deliberately testing the Union's determination, Confederate forces fired on Sumter. On April 13 the Fort was forced to surrender. The president called for 75,000 volunteers, while four more slave states seceded. There was now no turning back.*

Basically Lincoln viewed the war as a defensive effort to preserve the Union. Despite his strong conviction that slavery was immoral, he had sworn not to interfere with it in the South. But in his oath of office he had

also sworn to uphold the Constitution, which meant to protect and defend the government. To Lincoln the Civil War was the supreme test of a democracy—still a relatively new and experimental form of government. A profound fatalist, he believed that God had willed the war, perhaps for purposes not yet revealed. Above all, Lincoln had an unconquerable faith in the Union—and in God.

In most ways the North enjoyed a huge advantage. It had a far larger population—20.7 million to the South's 9 million—and four times as many men of fighting age. It had more than double the railroad mileage. In industrial output, including the output of weapons, the North led the way. And it held a decided edge in bank deposits and coinage. Although the Confederacy was ahead in agriculture, much of what it grew was not food. The South produced more cotton, tobacco, rice, asses, and mules, but the North raised more corn, wheat, and oats.

Counterbalancing the North's material advantages to some extent was the fact that it had to extend itself far into enemy territory. If the Confederates had merely fought to a stalemate, perhaps they could have reentered the Union with slavery. To dictate the terms of peace, the North needed a decisive victory.

And in war, material factors are not always decisive. A nation's will to resist, the quality of its leadership, luck, and other vague factors often determine the outcome. Time was a factor in the Civil War. If the South had held out long enough, it might have gotten help from France and Britain. England was dependent on southern staples and offered

---

*The border slave states—Missouri, Kentucky, Delaware, and Maryland—did not secede. Northwestern Virginia separated from Virginia and was admitted to the Union as the state of West Virginia in 1863.

moral and financial support to the Confederates. In Britain the ruling class admired the southern aristocracy, though the people as a whole were pro-Union, and the government remained officially neutral during the war. It did not give the South military aid.

In the first flush of battle people on both sides expected a quick victory. To northerners the Confederate capital, Richmond, which lay just a hundred miles south of Washington, seemed an easy prize. At the first Battle of Bull Run (July 21, 1861), civilians rode down from Washington in their buggies to watch the fighting, as if going on a Sunday picnic. The contest ended with Union forces routed. Some civilians were killed while blocking the route of the fleeing soldiers. It became clearer that victory would take some time.

Organizing the war effort

Despite each side's confidence that it would win, the North and South faced large problems in organizing a victory. Many northerners were willing to die to save the Union but balked at the thought of putting their lives on the line to free the blacks. Those who opposed the war ("Copperheads") worked for a negotiated peace.

Both sides depended almost entirely on volunteer soldiers but passed conscription laws to stimulate enlistments. The Union draft law in 1863 resulted in the worst race riots ever seen in this country. The law allowed a draftee to find a substitute or to pay three hundred dollars to sit out the war at home. New York City's Irish immigrants considered the Conscription Act a rich man's

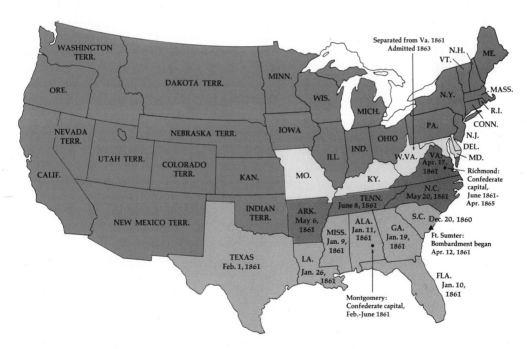

THE UNITED STATES ON THE EVE OF CIVIL WAR *(Dates of secession are given under state names)*

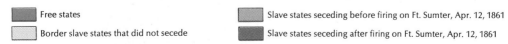

Free states

Border slave states that did not secede

Slave states seceding before firing on Ft. Sumter, Apr. 12, 1861

Slave states seceding after firing on Ft. Sumter, Apr. 12, 1861

(slavery abolished in territories: 1862)

Confederate volunteers in the First Virginia Regiment at the beginning of the war.

privilege and a poor man's obligation. When the draft lottery started in Manhattan in mid-July, mobs looted and burned the draft offices. Next they turned their wrath on free blacks, whom they considered their biggest rivals for jobs. The resisters also menaced wealthy whites. The police lost control, and a detachment of Union soldiers arrived from Gettysburg to subdue the week-long riot. An estimated one thousand persons were killed or injured in New York, and $2 million in property was destroyed.

The South had similar recruitment problems and enacted a draft law that met opposition. The desertion rate in both the Union and Confederate armies ran about 10 percent. As the war dragged on, defeatism increased on both sides.

The strong feeling for states' rights in the South prevented close cooperation with the new central government. Predominantly an agrarian society, the South deeply resented taxation, so essential for the proper management of the war. The financial program of the Confederate States of America was particularly chaotic and contributed to an eventual loss of morale.

Lincoln broadens the president's power

Lincoln, like Jackson before him (see p. 209), reshaped the office of the presidency. He was the first president to invoke the "Commander-in-Chief" clause of the Constitution (Article II, Section 2) during a national emergency. He held a low opinion of Congress for having failed to cope with the slavery crisis. Moreover, he believed the Constitution gave the president emergency powers greater than those of Congress, and he was willing to exercise those powers. Without waiting for congressional approval, he set up a blockade against the South, called up the militia, and suspended the writ of habeas corpus during wartime. Anti-Union rioting in Baltimore threatened to interfere with troop movements on the rail route from Philadelphia to Washington; Lincoln suspended habeas corpus in order to keep the rioters in jail. A year later, in 1862, over thirteen thousand persons were arrested when Lincoln proclaimed martial law in critical areas.

These actions brought charges of dictatorship. But Lincoln defended his actions as constitutional. His supporters argued that events justified his actions: desperate measures were needed to save the Union from collapse. Compared to Jefferson Davis, Lincoln for the most part used his powers with tact and firmness. But there is no question that he assumed extraordinary powers as president, setting a pattern for future wartime leaders.

Lincoln took extreme pains to hold on to the border states that remained in the Union—Missouri, Kentucky, Maryland, Delaware, and the newly created West Virginia. To pacify them, he held back the Emancipation Proclamation as long as he could. At the same time, he was aware that freeing the slaves would win his administration support in Europe, as well as among abolitionists. Lincoln waited for a military victory to announce emancipation. The Battle of Antietam on September 17, 1862, gave him the opportunity to take the plunge, which he did, five days later. Under the Preliminary Emancipation Proclamation (September 22), all slaves in Confederate-held territory were declared free as of January 1, 1863 (the official Emancipation Proclamation was issued January 1). Curiously, the thousands of slaves in the border states and in the areas held by Union troops remained in bondage. The practical effect of the Proclamation was negligible.

Generals and battles

For a civilian, Lincoln had an excellent grasp of the military situation. He made two crucial decisions early in the conflict. The first was to attack the Confederacy on many fronts at once, thereby making use of the North's greater troop strength. The second was to intercept the South's transatlantic supply lines by a blockade. This was a formidable task. The Confederacy controlled 3500 miles of seacoast, including 189 harbors and river mouths. And for several years the Union navy was a miscellaneous collection of ships poorly designed for blockade duty. Still, Lincoln's basic strategy was sound, although it took far longer to get results than anyone expected.

The verdict of history is that although the North won the Civil War, the South had the better generals. A succession of Union generals refused to take full advantage of the size and fighting power of the Army of the Potomac. On the other hand, the South's generals made maximum use of their smaller forces. Robert E. Lee, a West Point graduate and the son of a Revolutionary War officer, became commander of the Confederate forces in 1862. His skill, courage, and determination in carrying the war into the North and in defending the South made him the most revered man in southern history. Thomas J. (Stonewall) Jackson, Lee's brilliant lieutenant, was perhaps the best cavalry leader in the war.

The South's civilian leaders did not measure up to its commanders in the field. Jefferson Davis is honored for his honesty and energy, but he quarreled with his generals, with the members of his cabinet, and with Confederate governors. Considering the strength of local jealousies in the South, Davis' task was particularly difficult.

Lincoln had trouble finding a general who would use the large Union armies to best advantage. General George B. McClellan, a popular young officer, spent months training his troops but was overly cautious about taking them into battle. In 1864 Lincoln, after repeated disappointments, finally found the right general for the job—Ulysses S. Grant. Grant attracted attention through his determined campaigns along the Tennessee and Cumberland rivers. There he captured several Confederate forts, including Vicksburg, a major prize that helped cut the South's supply of Texas beef and secured the Mississippi Valley. It also secured the wavering border state of Missouri. Grant's motto summarized the art of modern war: "Find out where your enemy is. Get at him as soon as you can. Strike at him as hard as you can and as often as you can, and keep moving on."

Grant's capture of Vicksburg and Lee's

Robert E. Lee (1807-1870)

A Matter of Loyalties

As Colonel Lee guided his horse through the streets of Alexandria, Virginia, on April 19, 1861, one week after the firing on Fort Sumter, the town was buzzing with the news from the state capital. Virginia had seceded from the Union! At a drugstore, the pharmacist asked Lee what he thought of the news. The army officer replied, "I must say that I am one of those dull creatures that cannot see the good of secession." He then rode home to make the most momentous decision of his life.

Lee had just returned from Washington, where President Lincoln, acting through a mutual friend, had offered him command of the Union army, replacing seventy-five-year-old Winfield Scott. When Scott failed to persuade the younger man to accept, he sadly advised Lee to resign his commission. But Lee had made the army his life, and leaving it after thirty-two years of service would be painful.

Lee's conflict was not between serving the Union and serving the Confederacy, for as yet the Confederate States of America had no great meaning for him. Nor was he interested in defending slavery. Lee had freed his own slaves some time earlier, and he was angered to hear that the Confederacy was considering restoring the slave trade. He was torn rather by his deep attachment and loyalty to Virginia. In the Tidewater region were the homes, plantations, and graves of his ancestors going back to 1664. The Lees had intermarried with other prominent families, and doors opened to him along every road of the Old Dominion. His father, "Light-Horse Harry" Lee, had been a general in the Revolution. Virginia's part in the struggle for independence was not dead history to Lee, but living memory learned at his parents' knees.

After an agonizing evening of meditation and prayer the colonel wrote to the secretary of war, tendering his resignation from the army. Later he explained his decision in a letter to his sister: "With all my devotion to the Union and the feeling of loyalty and duty of an American citizen, I have not been able to make up my mind to raise my hand against my relatives, my children, my home. I have therefore resigned my commission in the Army, and save in defense of my native State (with the sincere hope that my poor services may never be needed), I hope I may never be called on to draw my sword."

In fact, Lee was called on by the Confederacy almost immediately. At the age of fifty-four he was entering not only upon the last decade of his life but upon a tragic civil war which his own military brilliance would prolong.

General Ulysses S. Grant (seated, in front of trees) and his staff officers confer during the Wilderness Campaign of 1864. Grant's army suffered heavy losses at the Battle of the Wilderness, but he continued to press forward. Lincoln remarked, "When Grant once gets possession of a place, he holds on to it as if he had inherited it."

failure to break through the Union lines at Gettysburg in July 1863 marked the turning point in the Civil War. Grant took command of all the Union forces in March 1864, and starting in May the Army of the Potomac began to press forward. Grant attacked Lee, who was protecting Richmond, while General William Tecumseh Sherman drove south from Chattanooga, Tennessee, to Georgia. Each of these two main Union armies had some 100,000 men. They opposed Confederate forces of about 60,000. In spite of this ratio, Lee inflicted severe losses on Grant at the Battle of the Wilderness (May 1864). But Grant kept moving forward. Casualties mounted, but the greater number of northern soldiers finally triumphed.

Although overshadowed by cavalry charges and infantry marches, the Union navy played a major role in the war, both on the western rivers and on the high seas. Its sea blockade began to hurt the South in 1863 and by January 1865 was quite effective. Daring blockade runners sneaked cotton cargoes through to Europe and brought back a few supplies, though these consisted mostly of luxury items. The South's military supplies

and daily necessities dwindled steadily. In the course of the war Confederate raiders, in particular the British-built *Alabama*, captured and destroyed many Union merchant ships. Submarines, ironclads, and torpedo ships were used for the first time. The Confederates fitted a captured frigate, the *Merrimack*, with iron plating and renamed it the *Virginia*. A memorable though indecisive battle took place off Hampton Roads in March 1862 between the *Virginia* and a Union ironclad, the *Monitor*.

The end of the war came in the spring of 1865. Grant kept stretching his line of attack farther and farther west, on the southern approaches to Petersburg and Richmond. Lee followed suit until the Confederate line became so thin and weak it could no longer hold. Lee was forced to surrender. The two generals met in the parlor of a farmhouse in the quiet village of Appomattox Court House, Virginia, on April 9, 1865. Grant dictated the terms of surrender. Fighting soon stopped on other fronts, and Jefferson Davis was captured a short time later. The Union was saved, the Confederacy had fallen, and the war was over.

The ruins of war

The Civil War represents a milestone in the history of warfare. The new steam-powered machinery of the Industrial Revolution — especially the railroad and river steamboat — played a direct role. The telegraph was used for the first time in war, sometimes with dramatic consequences. Factories produced unprecedented quantities of ammunition, clothing, and supplies. In the end, the exhaustion on both sides was more widespread than in the worst European wars of the previous century. Also, the South's defeat resembled the "total" defeat that accompanies fighting in the twentieth century. At Antietam (September 17, 1862) about twelve thousand "Billy Yanks" died in one day, as well as thousands of "Johnny Rebs." Frightful conditions in prison camps led to disease and death — at the rate of three thousand a month in the prison at Andersonville, Georgia. And more civilians found themselves directly in the path of Civil War armies than in earlier wars.

Most of the ten thousand separate military actions of the Civil War took place in the South. While the Union suffered greater casualties, more property damage occurred in the South. Southern railroads were destroyed and roads neglected. Farms were devastated: farmhouses, fences, and barns lay in ruins, fields were burned, horses and mules led off, and livestock slaughtered or turned loose to roam. In his march to the sea in late 1864, Sherman's army cut a fifty-mile ribbon of destruction through Georgia, in a deliberate effort to weaken and demoralize the enemy. There, according to one observer, the countryside "looked for many miles like a broad, black streak of ruin and desolation." Entire

Mathew Brady's photograph of Richmond, Virginia, capital of the Confederacy, after its fall in April 1865. As Lee evacuated Richmond and Grant marched in, the city was swept by fire.

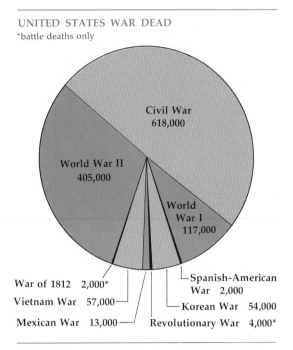

UNITED STATES WAR DEAD
*battle deaths only

Civil War
618,000

World War II
405,000

World War I
117,000

War of 1812   2,000*

Vietnam War   57,000

Mexican War   13,000

Spanish-American
War   2,000

Korean War   54,000

Revolutionary War   4,000*

towns were reduced to rubble. Charleston was "a city of ruin, of desolation, of vacant houses, of widowed women, of rotting wharves."

The South's economy suffered a terrible blow. Slave masters lost a billion-dollar investment when the slaves were freed without any compensation for their owners. The labor force was totally disorganized. The cotton crop was seized. Weak to begin with, southern industry lay in shambles at the end of the war. Financial institutions were bankrupt. And a "foreign" army occupied the Old South, which remained an economic colony of the North until the end of Reconstruction.

Lincoln's reconstruction plan

In his Second Inaugural Address Lincoln used the immortal phrase: "with malice toward none . . . with charity for all." He was referring to the treatment that the South should receive after the war. He had already devised a generous plan of reconstruction which assumed that only *individuals* and not states had left the Union. Any southern state could form a new government if only 10 percent of the number of voters in the election of 1860 would swear allegiance to the U.S.

The Radical Republicans proposed much harsher treatment of the postwar South. They wanted to treat the Confederate states like "conquered provinces" and to punish former slave owners by confiscating all their property. Ardent abolitionists, the Radical Republicans intended to make sure that slavery was permanently abolished. They tried to block Lincoln's renomination in 1864 because of his moderate views on abolition and reconstruction. Lincoln's assassination allowed them to impose a tougher plan of reconstruction which eventually prevailed.

Some form of amnesty has been granted after practically all American wars, but the terms have never been more generous than after the Civil War. Part of Lincoln's reconstruction plan was to grant complete amnesty to all but a few southern leaders. President Andrew Johnson followed through by offering amnesty to all Confederates with taxable property under twenty thousand dollars. Those who were excluded could petition for special pardons, which Johnson granted freely. Finally, in 1872, a congressional Amnesty Act cleared all but about five hundred of the most prominent southerners.

In his Gettysburg Address Lincoln eloquently asked "that this nation, under God, shall have a new birth of freedom." His precious Union was saved, but whether a genuine rebirth of freedom arose from the ashes of battle is open to question. Considering the oppression of blacks far beyond 1865 and the legacy of hate left by the Civil War and Reconstruction, there is reason to doubt that Lincoln's prayer was answered.

Review

Presidents Washington, Adams, and Jefferson all managed to sidestep actual war with France or England during their administrations. The War of 1812 might also have been avoided, for the British trade regulations which the U.S. was protesting were lifted just a few days after Congress declared war. This "Second War for Independence" created sharp political divisions and became popular only after it was over. Andrew Jackson's success at New Orleans in the last battle of the war brought him national fame.

The nation's boundaries expanded by stages from 1803 to 1853. An American claim to control the hemisphere was boldly expressed in 1823 in the Monroe Doctrine. By the 1840s the theory of Manifest Destiny and a vision of the U.S. stretching from ocean to ocean had captured the American imagination. After annexing Texas, President Polk forced a war with Mexico. The Mexican Cession made the U.S. a continental nation.

Hopes for avoiding civil war ended forever when Confederate troops fired on Fort Sumter in 1861. Both the North and South felt they would win quickly. The southern generals made good use of their smaller forces. Lincoln, who had a strong grasp of military tactics, set up an excellent overall strategy, but it was not followed by his generals until the mid-war appointment of General Grant. Lincoln was the first president to use the "war powers" clause of the Constitution to strengthen his authority as chief executive, setting a precedent for future wartime presidents.

The war's turning point came in 1863 with the Battle of Gettysburg. Two years later Lee surrendered to Grant, ending the most destructive war in American history. Both sides suffered terrible losses in human life and property, but physical and economic damage was much greater in the South. The Civil War was the first large-scale modern conflict fought with the weapons of the industrial age.

Questions

1. Discuss the outcomes, both positive and negative, of the War of 1812 and the Mexican War. Who were the "hawks" and "doves" in these wars and what were their motives?

2. Trace the geographical expansion of the United States from the Louisiana Purchase of 1803 to the Gadsden Purchase of 1853. How did each piece of new territory become part of the U.S.?

3. The Monroe Doctrine and Manifest Destiny were of major importance in forming national policy. Do you think they play any role in modern-day thinking? Explain.

4. What were the relative strengths and weaknesses of the North and South on the eve of the Civil War? Why did the South lose the war?

5. Describe Lincoln's attitudes toward the Union, the Civil War, and the presidency. Do you think his cause justified the actions he took? Is there anything he did that you strongly agree or disagree with?

Slaves working in the field, on an island off South Carolina, 1862.

Slaves sing most when they are most unhappy. The songs of the slave represent the sorrows of his heart; and he is relieved by them, only as an aching heart is relieved by its tears.

FREDERICK DOUGLASS (1817?–1895)

12

12
America's Color Scheme

Three basic racial types—"red, white, and black"—were already well established in America in 1789. In more precise terms this means that the nation's racial composition was Mongoloid (Indian), Caucasoid, and Negroid. Through conquest (the Mexican Cession) and migration (from Mexico and China) came two additional variants of the existing racial stock. The Mexicans were racially varied, but the most notable stock was mestizo, a mixture of Indian and European. The Chinese were a branch of the Mongoloid race. Thus the "brown" and "yellow" people were added to the spectrum. The multiracial society familiar in twentieth-century America existed, therefore, before the Civil War.

White Americans took for granted the "inferiority" of all "colored" races. Their assumption grew out of and helped maintain slavery, territorial conquest, and labor exploitation. Still, within the framework of racial supremacy whites made certain distinctions among nonwhites. They believed that racial groups differed along temperamental lines and that the Indians possessed a nobility lacking in the other groups. Lewis Agassiz, perhaps the leading American scientist of his time, declared in 1850, "The indomitable, courageous, proud Indian—in how very different a light he stands by the side of the submissive, obsequious, imitative Negro, or by the side of the tricky, cunning, and cowardly [Chinese]."

It is evident even from this quotation that in the mid-nineteenth century "race" was at best a confusing concept. The term was used to lump together such diverse elements as skin color, hair texture, facial features, heredity, culture, temperament, intelligence, achievement, nationality, and social graces.

Although white supremacy was taken for granted, two major questions concerning the origin of the different races were debated among learned whites in the early part of the century. One debate was whether heredity or environment had produced racial differences. Until midcentury most Americans who thought about the matter emphasized environment—at least until the ideas of Charles Darwin came into vogue in the 1860s. A second dispute was whether the human races had originated from a single species or from several. Those who emphasized racial differences defended the theory of multiple human origin, while those who stressed racial similarities turned to the single-species theory. The biblical account of the descent from Adam and Eve was cited to support the single-species argument.

Logically, those who considered environment the key factor and accepted the biblical justification should also have believed that an improvement in environment might at some future time equalize the status of all races. Actually, few went this far. As a practical matter most white Americans believed that the "colored" races had always been, were now, and would indefinitely remain, inferior. Racial distinctions were ingrained in American culture. Slavery for blacks was a reality. Cultural extermination and frontier warfare for Indians was a reality. Comparable realities awaited the Chinese and Mexicans.

Indians Along the "Trail of Tears"

White greed for Indian land

Of the thousands of cowboy-and-Indian movies made in Hollywood, the one that was never filmed shows the whites honoring a treaty "so long as the grass grows green." Imagine a script in which, after the peace pipe is smoked, the Indians establish a self-governing nation on their own land inside the United States, where they are free to follow their own traditions. They are assisted, of course, by the U.S. cavalry, which prevents white frontiersmen from raiding Indian land and Indian braves from attacking white settlements. This fantasy nearly became a reality in Indiana about 1812. Only the end of British rule there after the War of 1812 and the death of the great Shawnee chief Tecumseh prevented it from happening.

The United States in 1789 could not claim that it *owned the land* occupied by the Indians of the Old Northwest, but it did assert that it *held political sovereignty* there. As Washington's secretary of war, Henry Knox, explained: "The Indians being the prior occupants pos-

sess the right of the soil. It cannot be taken from them unless by their free consent, or by right of conquest in case of a just war." This peculiar relationship was reaffirmed later by the U.S. Supreme Court. The Court described Indian tribes as "distinct, independent, political communities" to be dealt with like all other foreign nations, according to the treaty provision of the Constitution. Although these "domestic dependent nations" occupied areas within the United States and were subject to its will, the Indians kept title to their land according to natural law. Secretary Knox hoped to deal with the Indians under this fair doctrine. But administration of the policy was placed in the hands of underlings and left up to the states or territorial governors to enforce. Here the system broke down. Pioneers cared little for the law and pressed to have the "hell hounds of death" removed by any means possible. So the border warfare continued.

The most troubled Indian-white frontier

Portrait of Tecumseh, or Shooting Star, one of the most extraordinary Indian figures in American history. The Shawnee chief was celebrated for his abilities as a warrior and administrator. He was also the leading Shawnee orator; according to an Indian biographer, "the Indians were raised to a perfect frenzy by his fiery eloquence."

was the Northwest Territory—the triangular region formed by the Ohio and Mississippi rivers and the Great Lakes. White settlers and speculators coveted the area and demanded government help. Beset by a variety of governmental difficulties, Presidents Washington and Adams moved haltingly in the matter of Indian affairs. The Indians, protected by British forts in the Great Lakes region, stoutly resisted white attackers. In 1791, at the headwaters of the Wabash River, various Indian tribes led by Chief Little Turtle, a Miami Indian, destroyed the six-

hundred-man army of General Arthur St. Clair. This remains the greatest single defeat ever suffered by the U.S. Army at the hands of Indians. Retribution came three years later at the Battle of Fallen Timbers, near present-day Toledo, Ohio. There General Anthony Wayne defeated the tribes of the Maumee River region and opened Ohio to settlement. The following year the main Indian tribes signed the Treaty of Greenville, which stripped them of much of what is now Ohio and Indiana, cut their alliance with Britain, and opened the Northwest Territory to white settlement. Ohio entered the Union as a state in 1803.

To obtain land U.S. treaty commissioners tried every trick in the book. Often they took advantage of the Indians' desire for muskets and rum. The government also played the Indian tribes off against one another. As General Harmer said, he liked to set the Indians "at deadly variance." Treaties were signed with the most willing Indian chiefs, often deliberately "mellowed" by whiskey or rum at the treaty powwow. But the treaties covered even those tribes that were not represented or had refused to sign. Sometimes Indians agreed to delayed purchases whereby they signed away their children's rights to the land but continued to occupy it during their own lifetime.

Jefferson began to shape a new policy. As a humane individual and a student of Indian languages and customs, he sympathized with their plight. "It may be regarded as certain," he wrote in 1786, "that not a foot of land will ever be taken from the Indians without their consent. The sacredness of their rights is felt by all thinking persons in America as much as in Europe." But his outlook changed when he became president in 1801. In organizing the Louisiana Territory, he encouraged a policy of Indian removal. And when Georgia began to move the Cherokees off twenty million acres of prime land and a Cherokee delegation came to protest to

*Where today is the Pequot? Where are the Narragansetts, the Mohawks, the
Pokanoket, and many other once powerful tribes of our people? They have vanished
before the avarice and the oppression of the White Man, as snow before a summer sun.*

TECUMSEH (1768? – 1813)

the Great White Father, Jefferson sided with
the state of Georgia.

Often when diplomacy failed to dislodge
the Indians, warfare followed. Sometimes
whites attacked the unyielding Indians.
Other times the Indians retaliated against
whites for breaking promises that were supposed to last "as long as the rivers shall run."
Indians who were determined to survive and
preserve their independence were faced with
a dilemma. If they accepted the white man's
payment and moved off the land, they soon
found that they were being pushed on again.
If they stood their ground, they needed other
tribes as allies. But these links were hard to
forge. Tribal feuding was the most difficult
barrier to overcome.

Tecumseh's attempt to unite
the Indians

The Indian leader who came closest to a solution was the Shawnee chief Tecumseh. Tecumseh tried to create a unified, independent Indian nation, centered in what is now
Indiana. He hoped it would serve both as a
buffer between the U.S. and British Canada
and as a permanent retreat for threatened
Indian tribes. He worked for a time with his
brother, Tenskwatawa, the Prophet, who
preached that Indians must give up whiskey
and other European "gifts" and return to
the ways of their fathers.

Tecumseh knew the Declaration of Independence and had a profound grasp of the
theory of the consent of the governed. He
argued that the land belonged to *all* Indians
and that no tribe could rightfully sell any of it
to the U.S. without the consent of all tribes:

No tribe has a right to sell, even to each other,
much less to strangers, who demand all, and will
take no less. . . . Sell a country! Why not sell the
air, the clouds and the great sea, as well as the
earth? Did not the Great Spirit make them all for
the use of his children?

A tireless organizer, Tecumseh traveled as
far east as New York and south to Florida
trying to enlist support for his pan-Indian
nation. War between the U.S. and Britain
seemed inevitable, and he wanted the Indians
to take advantage of it through concerted action. At the same time, he tried to restrain
impatient warriors from premature attacks
on whites that would lead to certain defeat.
Tecumseh faced the greatest resistance
among the Civilized Tribes of the South,
some of which were adopting white culture.
While he was away recruiting more tribes,
his brother let the warriors get drawn into
the Battle of Tippecanoe (November 7, 1811).
This battle against General Harrison's forces
had a demoralizing effect on the Indians and
undid much of Tecumseh's careful planning.

The War of 1812 was Tecumseh's final test.
Although his alliance was incomplete, he
recognized that the war was his last chance
to prevail against the "Long Knives," as the
Americans were called. He cast his lot with
the British, who at one point gave him command over a redcoat army. In battle he impressed both allies and enemies with his
courage and humanity. He never condoned
torture or cruelty. The flagging spirits of the
British regulars in the Northwest in 1813
enraged and disappointed him. He died on
the battlefield in September 1813, attempting
to lead the British to victory.

Another fateful contest in the War of 1812 occurred in the South. The Creek nation lapsed into violent civil war over how to handle the Americans. A party of anti-American Creeks fell upon Fort Mims in August 1813, killing over three hundred Americans. Two thousand Tennessee volunteers commanded by General Andrew Jackson, aided by a force of pro-American Creeks, retaliated. At the Battle of Horseshoe Bend in eastern Alabama Jackson's army killed nearly a thousand Creeks. Jackson then turned around and forced all the Creeks, friendly or otherwise, to give to the U.S. eight million acres, which amounted to two thirds of the Creek nation.

Thus the War of 1812 marked a steep decline in the fortunes of the Indians. In the North it destroyed forever the vision of a unified, independent Indian nation, while in the Southeast it opened the way for whites to push aside the established tribes. More and more Indians soon found themselves struggling for sheer survival.

The policy of Indian removal

In 1817 a congressional committee proposed that the Indian tribes clear out of the path of westward settlement *voluntarily*. Another alternative was for them to renounce "savagery" and become Christian farmers, following the Puritan Ethic. As the House of Representatives declared in 1819 while voting ten thousand dollars for a "Civilization Fund": "Put into the hands of their children the primer and the hoe, and they will naturally, in time, take hold of the plow . . . and they will grow up in habits of morality and industry." Soon the proposal of voluntary removal was switched to one of *forced* removal. Secretary of War John C. Calhoun and President James Monroe in 1825 recommended buying land from the eastern Indians and then removing them at government expense to open lands beyond the Mississippi. While

the Indians' interests must be cared for, Calhoun had once noted, "our opinion, and not theirs, ought to prevail, in measures intended for their civilization and happiness."

Tecumseh had prophesied wisely when he said that Indians who failed to unite and resist would be forced off their lands on a piecemeal basis. As chief architect of Indian removal, President Andrew Jackson, during eight years in office, signed no fewer than ninety-four Indian treaties. Millions of acres of Indian land were transferred to white owners for use as cotton plantations, farms, and mines. The Removal Act of 1830 supplied $500,000 to resettle the eastern tribes in the newly established Indian Territory (in present-day Oklahoma). It applied mainly to the Five Civilized Tribes of the Southeast—the Creek, Cherokee, Seminole, Choctaw, and Chickasaw nations of what is now Georgia, North and South Carolina, Florida, Alabama, and Mississippi. But it also affected the Sac and Fox, the largest surviving tribes of the Northwest Territory. The move in most cases involved an exchange of old land for new. A companion measure, the Reorganization Act of 1834, gave the military authority to "quarantine" Indians in other parts of the country and to prepare them for "civilization" in thirty years. In 1836, Congress created the Bureau of Indian Affairs as a branch of the War Department, to help "tame" and civilize the Indians. Speaking of the Indian removal program, Tocqueville wrote, "In this manner do the Americans obtain at very low prices whole provinces which the richest sovereigns of Europe could not purchase."

The so-called Black Hawk War of 1832 was the first fruit of the new laws. Remnants of the Sac and Fox tribes, vowing to live in peace with the whites, wandered east across the Mississippi into Illinois. The starving Indians were looking for farmland, not for a fight. Misreading the Indians' intentions, the settlers mobilized for action. The panicky militia destroyed nearly all the Indians, in-

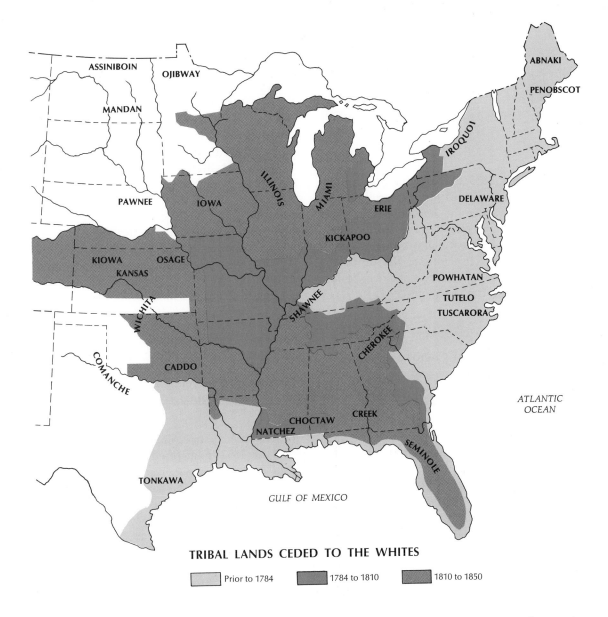

ASSINIBOIN
OJIBWAY
MANDAN
ABNAKI
PENOBSCOT
IROQUOI
PAWNEE
IOWA
ILLINOIS
MIAMI
ERIE
DELAWARE
KICKAPOO
KIOWA
OSAGE
POWHATAN
KANSAS
WICHITA
TUTELO
TUSCARORA
SHAWNEE
COMANCHE
CADDO
CHEROKEE
NATCHEZ
CHOCTAW
CREEK
ATLANTIC
OCEAN
SEMINOLE
TONKAWA
GULF OF MEXICO

TRIBAL LANDS CEDED TO THE WHITES

Prior to 1784   1784 to 1810   1810 to 1850

cluding women and children. Only a few small bands were left to go west.

At least one faction of each southeastern tribe signed a treaty and left peaceably. The Creeks, shattered by twenty years of white harassment, signed in 1832 and moved on. The removal law granted each family a land allotment (from acreage on which the Indians were then residing) that could be sold before departure. White landsharks defrauded the

Indians of these holdings. An official investigation of allotment procedures concluded that "a greater mass of corruption perhaps, has never been congregated in any part of the world."

The Seminoles fiercely resisted moving. Some were forced to leave Florida for land in the Indian Territory, but thousands of others joined the iron-willed Chief Osceola, who hid out in the remotest swamps of the Ever-

Your forefathers . . . sat down amongst us.
We gave them corn and meat;
they gave us poison in return.

RED JACKET (1758–1830)
Seneca chief

glades. From 1835 to 1842 the government spent $20 million and lost fifteen hundred officers and men in the Seminole War. Osceola was finally taken prisoner under a flag of truce. A peace treaty allowed some Seminoles to remain in Florida. Not until the 1960s did the United States make a formal settlement with the Seminoles.

The Creeks and the Cherokees

Even the Creeks and Cherokees, who conformed to Congress' idea of civilized Indians, were dispossessed. These tribes had mingled freely with British settlers since the early eighteenth century, intermarried and traded with them, worshiped their God, and adopted many of their customs. Alexander McGillivray, of Scottish, French, and Creek background, was the chief of the Creeks and Seminoles. He commanded some ten thousand warriors. The first Indian chief to visit an American president, McGillivray was an accomplished trader and diplomat. When he died in 1793, he was one of the wealthiest men in the South. Both the Creeks and the Cherokees patterned their system of government after that of the U.S., built schools and grist mills, lived in permanent villages, and raised cows. Creek women grew cotton and sewed their own European-style clothes. A Cherokee leader, Sequoya, devised a written alphabet which was used in a newspaper published by the nation. From their Indian background these tribes retained communal ownership of land and most of their ancient rituals. They had proved their willingness to adapt to white people's ways, and in return

they expected to preserve their lands and their nation.

In Georgia the Cherokees tried every legal avenue to prevent their forced exile, including appeals to the U.S. Supreme Court. The discovery of gold on their lands set off a rush of white settlers who harassed the Indians and treated them shabbily. Flaunting the doctrine of states' rights, the Georgia legislature declared all Cherokee laws void and tried to strip the tribe of federal protection. Georgia law asserted that Indians could not employ whites, could not testify in court against whites, and had to be tried by state courts, not tribal courts. The Cherokees appealed to Congress in 1835:

We are denationalized! We are deprived of membership in the human family. . . . Our cause is your own. It is the cause of liberty and justice. It is based upon your own principles, which we have learned from yourselves; for we have tried to count your Washington and your Jefferson our great teachers.

When Chief Justice Marshall, in *Worcester* v. *Georgia* (1832) reaffirmed federal jurisdiction over Indians, Jackson reputedly said, "John Marshall has made his decision, now let him enforce it!" Jackson simply sat on his hands while Georgia continued harassing the Indians.

By 1838 the Cherokees had exhausted all legal remedies and were forced off their land. They were granted new land in the Indian Territory, $5 million, and transportation costs, but they declared that "the original title and ownership of lands still rests in the Cherokee Nation, unimpaired and absolute." And with this they departed. The winter was bitter cold. Having received only light cotton garments and poor rations, they were stalked by illness and death all along the "Trail of Tears" to Oklahoma. About four thousand died on the way and during the first difficult months in the new territory. The government never acknowledged the

In this painting of the "Trail of Tears," Robert Lindneux shows with graphic impact the indignities and agonies suffered by Indians on the long trek from their homes to new territory in Oklahoma.

cruelty of removal. Apparently President Van Buren was serious when he told Congress that government handling of Cherokee removal was "just and friendly throughout; its efforts for their civilization constant, and directed by the best feelings of humanity; its watchfulness in protecting them from individual frauds unremitting."

Given the determination of white settlers, the force of state government, and the complicity of the president, nothing could halt the removal process. Slowly and surely the Indians were led away beyond the Mississippi: Choctaws in 1831, Seminoles in 1832, Creeks in 1836, and Cherokees in 1838. Whites hounded the departing columns, stealing the Indians' horses and possessions; they looted their homes and barns the min-

ute the owners left. Government contractors who were hired to oversee the removal skimped on supplies, food, and transportation facilities intended for Indians. (An appropriation of fifty thousand dollars to assist Choctaw removal was never used at all.) Over three hundred Creeks drowned in the sinking of a decrepit, overloaded ferryboat supplied by one contractor. Each summer from 1831 to 1836 cholera broke out on the removal trail, setting up a "belt of death" along the way. "We were drove off like wolves," one tribesman said, ". . . and our people's feet were bleeding with long marches. . . . We are men . . . we have women and children, and why should we come like wild horses?" Almost half the Creek nation perished on the way west.

Despite countless hardships and intertribal fights, the Civilized Tribes kept their integrity. Led by Chief John Ross, the Cherokees healed their differences and established schools, farms, ranches, and townships in the new land. By 1860 the new communities passed the test of progress: whites wanted what they saw and were clamoring for the government to uproot the Indians again and move them further west.

Pushing out the western tribes

With the Cherokee removal completed and the Seminole War slowly winding down, attention shifted to the tribes on the western side of the Mississippi. In the 1850s and 1860s speculators, miners, ranchers, and farmers demanded federal measures against the Indians. The army responded by restricting the range of native tribes through treaties and military action. Starting in 1854, warfare on the Plains and in the Rockies continued almost uninterrupted for two decades. The Indians of Kansas were forced to sign away nine tenths of their land. Soldiers drove the Navajos and Apaches to the Pecos River country of New Mexico in 1864 and permanently "quarantined" them. The Cheyenne-Arapaho War lasted from 1861 to 1864. At its end several bands of Indians were trying to surrender to the U.S. military when they came face to face with Colonel John Chivington's Colorado militia at Sand Creek. Chivington's volunteers killed over three hundred men, women, and children and mutilated many corpses, proudly displaying the human remains as trophies. It was the most brutal mass murder of Indians since the seventeenth century.

During the Civil War parts of the Indian frontier became a no-man's-land for the Union and Confederate armies. Indians served on both sides, although most of the Civilized Tribes sided with the Confederacy. For this the Union later punished them by taking away some of their reservation land. The time had long since passed when Indians could take advantage of a rift between whites.

Similarly, in gold-rush California, the largest concentration of Indians north of Mexico was being swiftly destroyed by disease, starvation, combat, slavery, and murder. A series of treaties signed in 1851 defrauded 119 tribes of half their land in California. It was just one more example of the white man's ruthless treatment of the Indians.

Slaves in an Age of Democracy

Repercussions of a slave rebellion
In August 1791 a bloody slave uprising occurred in Santo Domingo (later the Republic of Haiti) which had a decided effect on the future of slavery in America. In some ways it was a turning point in black-white relations in the United States. Napoleon sent 25,000 soldiers to retake the island, but even after they captured the rebel leader, Toussaint L'Ouverture, the rebellion continued. White America was terrorized by the event. Imports of slaves from the Caribbean fell. The idea of emancipation now evoked nightmares of black armies turning on their former masters and destroying the country in a rampage of arson, murder, and rape. Integrating blacks into white society became almost unthink-

able. Even Jefferson now believed that ex-slaves should be "removed from beyond the reach of mixture."

A wave of private emancipations that had swept the country during the era of the Revolutionary War came to an abrupt halt. Free Negroes in New England met with increasing discrimination, lost their voting rights if they had any to begin with, and had to pay special taxes. Southern slave codes hardened. In 1806 Virginia's free blacks were told to leave the state or suffer possible reenslavement within a year. In 1793 Congress had passed the first federal fugitive slave law. It allowed masters to reclaim runaways without even having to prove legal ownership.

The slave rebellion in Santo Domingo had another effect on American slavery. Napoleon discarded plans for establishing a new empire in America and sold the Louisiana Territory to the United States. The Territory gave the South ample new land on which to grow cotton, and that meant an expansion of slavery. The invention of the cotton gin by Eli Whitney in 1793 had revived slavery in America. Planters invested more heavily in slaves and grew more cotton. Small farmers bought or hired a few black hands and did the same. Much of South Carolina and Georgia raised nothing but cotton. The cheapest new land lay to the west, so planters took gangs of blacks and marched them to Tennessee and Alabama. Cotton production rose from 13,000 bales in 1792 to over 400,000 bales in 1817. New slave states entered the Union. The market for slaves quickened, and the price of field hands rose.

Free blacks in the early years of the country

The first U.S. census (1790) counted 750,000 blacks in the country. The number of slaves was 2 million in 1830, and it more than doubled in the next thirty years. Fewer than 60,000 blacks were free in 1790.

Free blacks became a distinct subculture in American life after the Revolution. They usually settled in towns and cities and worked as laborers, craftsmen, or preachers, but it was hard for them to get decent jobs. They could, as a rule, own property, but they were rarely allowed to vote, to testify in court against whites, or to serve in the army.

The free black community organized its own mutual aid societies and churches. In Philadelphia blacks chartered a separate branch of Masons and formed the Free African Society, which nursed the sick and dying—regardless of race—during the yellow fever epidemic of 1793. The Sons of Africa Society in Boston provided burial services for black families. During a Methodist Episcopal church service in Philadelphia two freedmen, Absalom Jones and Richard Allen, were ordered to move to the rear of the gallery. In response to this, Jones soon established an independent black Episcopal church, and Allen organized an all-black Methodist church (forerunner of the African Methodist Episcopal church). After the turn of the century, blacks also set up their own branch of the Baptist church.

Blacks fought in the War of 1812, as they have in all America's wars, but those who hoped it would earn them freedom were disappointed. After Washington, D.C., was burned, Philadelphia called on its leading black citizens—James Forten, Richard Allen, and Absalom Jones—to help recruit blacks for strengthening the city's defenses; more than 2500 blacks worked alongside whites for two days building earth works. Black naval seamen were commended for heroism in the Battle of Lake Erie. Free blacks in Louisiana were recruited for the Battle of New Orleans; they contributed greatly to the victory over the redcoats and were personally congratulated by Jackson.

Other blacks fled behind British lines in search of freedom, but the terms of the war settlement required the return of all property, including slaves, to rightful owners. Southern runaways sometimes found refuge among the Indians. Seminoles protected escaped slaves during the Seminole War.

Blacks took part in the westward movement. Some were taken in chains to Mississippi, Texas, and other new states of the Lower South. Others who were free or who escaped bondage went to the frontier looking for freedom and economic security. They worked as miners, carpenters, cowboys, barbers, and unskilled laborers. In 1820 George Bush, a black fur trapper, took a job with the Hudson's Bay Company and made several trips between Oregon and the Missouri River. He established the first grist mill on Puget Sound. The black trapper and scout Jim Beckworth learned to speak several Indian languages; Beckworth Pass over the Sierra Mountains commemorates his exploits. Mary Ellen Pleasant, known as Mammy Pleasant, owner of a notorious San Francisco hotel, contributed thirty thousand dollars to buy guns for John Brown's planned uprising. The Negro pioneer Clara Brown established a laundry in California. With the profits from her business she bought the freedom of relatives and friends and paid their way to California. The Reverend Darius Stokes, founder of fifteen Negro churches in gold-rush California, claimed that California blacks sent three quarters of a million dollars to the South for this purpose.

A black colony in Africa

In the early nineteenth century, some white Americans who considered slavery immoral but regarded abolition as unlikely began to toy with the idea of sending blacks back to Africa. The notion even appealed to some blacks. In 1815 the prosperous sea captain and free black of Massachusetts, Paul Cuffe, paid the way for thirty-eight blacks to go to Sierra Leone in Africa. Although the venture

failed, it promoted the idea of colonization. This seemed a possible solution to whites who wished to Christianize "heathen" Africa, to deal humanely with freed blacks, or to find a place for blacks captured in the illicit slave trade. In 1817 several prominent whites, including House Speaker Henry Clay, formed the American Colonization Society, which sought congressional and state aid, as well as church money, to finance sending blacks back to Africa. In 1822 Congress voted $100,000 to establish Liberia on Africa's west coast. In the end, only fifteen thousand American blacks moved to Africa. The majority favored integration into American life.

Nineteenth-century slavery

Technically the slave trade was ended in 1808, although slaves continued to be imported illegally until the Civil War. The interstate slave trade also continued. Estimates as to the number of Africans transported to the New World in 350 years varies from 9 to 15 million, with about 1 million going to the U.S. The price of slaves rose as fewer blacks were brought in from Africa and the Caribbean. By the 1850s a prime hand was worth about $1500 compared to $300 in the 1790s. Suppliers of animals, tools, and seeds took on slaves as another commodity, while auctioneers handled the bidding. Virginia was the main source of slaves.

From a strictly profit-and-loss viewpoint, slavery seems to have been a profitable form of business enterprise. At least those who owned the larger and better-managed plantations often made a return of 10 percent or better on their investment. But in terms of the overall efficiency of the southern economy, the difficulty with slavery was that it absorbed excessive capital. Too much money was invested in slaves and not enough in transportation and marketing facilities, which left southern planters at a disadvan-

Eyewitness testimony concerning conditions of slavery brought its abuses and cruelties to public awareness in the North and the West. As presented in such publications as the Anti-Slavery Almanac, it also provided effective propaganda for the growing abolitionist movement. This illustrated page contains accounts of alleged mistreatment of slave mothers and their infants.

1840.]   *Anti-Slavery Almanac.*   17

WOMEN AT WORK IN THE FIELD.

Mr. Lemuel Sapington, a native of Maryland, formerly a slave-trader, now a respectable citizen of Lancaster, Pa., in a letter dated January 21, 1839, speaking of slaves in the southern part of Virginia, says :—

" Among the gangs, are often young women, who bring their children to the fields, and lay them in a fence corner, while they are at work. When a child is three weeks old, a woman is considered in working order. I have seen a woman, with her child strapped to her back, laboring the whole day, beside a man, perhaps the father of the child, and he not being permitted to give her any assistance, himself being under the whip."

Rev. Francis Hawley, pastor of the Baptist church, Colebrook, Ct., who lived seventeen years in North and South Carolina, says :—

" Those who are with child are driven to their task till within a few days of the time of their delivery ; and when the child is a few weeks old, the mother must again go to the field. If it is far from her hut, she must take her babe with her. If the child cries, she cannot go to its relief; the eye of the overseer is upon her : and if, when she goes to nurse it, she stays a little longer than the overseer thinks necessary, he commands her back to her task. Brother, you cannot begin to know what the poor slave mothers suffer on thousands of plantations at the south."

Rev. Horace Moulton, of the Methodist Episcopal church, says :—

" Women are seen bringing their infants into the field to their work, and leading others, who are not old enough to stay in the cabins with safety. When they get there, they must set them down in the dirt and go to work. Some, who have *very young* ones, fix a little sack, and place the infants on their back and work. One reason is, the child will not cry so much when it can hear a mother's voice. Another is, the mothers fear the *poisonous snakes.* I never knew any place where the land is so infested with venomous snakes, as in the low lands round about Savannah. To secure their infants from poisonous snakes, females *often* work with their infants on their backs."

"'The South-west, by a Yankee," was published by the Harpers, N. Y., 1835. The writer takes great pains to impress his readers with the beauties of slavery. Yet he says, (vol. ii. p. 125,) " On most plantations females are allowed a month's cessation from FIELD labor before and after confinement. But it cannot be denied that on some plantations, nothing but *actual confinement* releases them from the field, to which the mother soon after returns, leaving an infant *a few days old* (! ! !) at the " quarters."

Race   265

Our warfare ought not to be against slavery alone, but against the spirit which makes color a mark of degradation.

HOSEA EASTON
Northern black minister

tage when it came to selling their slave-produced cotton.

Slavery changed very little during the nineteenth century. Although the planters boasted that their slaves were freer and happier than northern factory workers, the life of an average slave was probably much harder than that of a free wage-earner or farmer. Field hands worked from sunrise to sunset, with time off for lunch, half-days off on Saturdays, and sometimes all day off on Sundays or holidays. The sharply competitive planters of the Lower South were reputed to be the most heartless masters. Those of the Tidewater were the most humane.

As the slaves' value increased, the tendency to overwork them probably declined. Branding and similar cruelties became less common. By the same token, greater precautions were taken to prevent their escape. Masters retained the right to punish their own slaves for disobeying instructions or damaging tools or property. In a system which gave almost limitless power to the slave masters and practically none to the courts, extreme physical punishments—crippling, maiming, and even killing—certainly occurred. For minor infractions slaves were denied travel passes; for larger ones they were whipped: fifteen to twenty lashes was a common punishment. As a Virginia master said, "A great deal of whipping is not necessary; *some* is." For even more serious transgressions slaves were jailed, put in stocks, or shackled and collared. For revolting, they were branded or hanged.

For the most part, however, blacks and whites managed to get along under slavery. It could not be otherwise where people were dependent upon one another over the years. Wise masters offered Christmas bonuses, cash payments for special work (five dollars for four hundred pounds of cotton picked in one day), a special day of rest, or personal plots of ground on which slaves could grow crops or raise chickens for sale on the open market. Wise slaves found it useful to please their masters, if they could.

Yet to maintain the system of slavery required psychological as well as physical restraints. As Frederick Douglass explained, slaves were made to "know their place," to walk, talk, look, and behave submissively. Masters made their slaves feel totally dependent on them for food, shelter, and clothing. This they accomplished not only with the lash, but with words, gestures, and threats of sale "down the river"—that is, to a crueler master.

Black resistance to slavery

From all indications, the careful precautions used by planters to police the South and debase the individual slave were necessary. For American blacks resisted their slavery every way they could, short of mass armed uprisings, which occurred only rarely. Some became expert loafers and liars; others deliberately broke their masters' tools, stole their chickens and pigs, and burned their fields and barns. Slaves ran away or maimed themselves to gain freedom from toil. There were cases of parents who killed their own children rather than see them sold down the river. Most field hands probably worked below their full capacity and were more rebellious than slaves who worked as domestics.

The struggle against slavery produced its own black heroes and heroines. Among them are the few truly daring slave rebels. Denmark Vesey, a free black of Charleston, South Carolina, along with thirty-four others, was executed for plotting rebellion in 1822. Most of this group were city slaves: carters, porters, laborers, stevedores, mechanics, and lumberyard workers. The executions were intended, as the governor conceded, "to produce a salutary terror."

Nat Turner of Southhampton, Virginia, was the most famous slave rebel. He was a model slave and also a Baptist preacher, or "exhorter," who was moved by a vision: "I saw white spirits and black spirits engaged in battle, and the sun was darkened—the thunders rolled in the Heavens, and blood flowed in streams." In August 1831 Turner and fifty or sixty other blacks murdered nearly sixty whites. After being hidden by slaves for two months, he was captured, tried, and hanged. Scores of innocent Negroes were also executed as sympathizers. Turner's rebellion caused southern legislatures from Maryland to Louisiana to stiffen their slave codes, the laws governing the conduct of slaves. The South also restricted the movements of free Negroes and Negro preachers.

Proslavery in the South, antiblack in the North

After Turner's rebellion all talk of eventually freeing the slaves vanished in the South. Southern spokesmen declared slavery a positive good, a permanent feature of plantation life. They likened the South to ancient Greece, where slaves worked at manual labor while the masters created a splendid culture. Slaves were portrayed as happy and childlike. All publication of abolitionist tracts, pamphlets, and sermons in the South was banned. Such antislavery printed matter was destroyed by postmasters or sometimes publicly burned. Schools and colleges fired any faculty members and expelled any students who questioned slavery or the "southern way of life."

Oddly enough, while the North opposed slavery, northern prejudice against blacks was nearly as strong as in the South. Tocqueville observed that as slavery receded, racial discrimination became stronger. Free blacks were often severely restricted in the northern states that had abolished slavery. By 1860 about a quarter million free blacks lived in the North (about the same number as in the South). They lived in ghettos, held menial jobs, could not vote, were forced to use segregated travel accommodations, and were the victims of white mob action. Free blacks were considered to be lazy, often criminal, not very intelligent, and a threat to white womanhood. David Wilmot, author of the Wilmot Proviso, expressed a typical anti-Negro view when he said: "I plead the cause and the rights of white freemen. I would preserve to free white labor a fair country, a rich inheritance, where the sons of toil, of my own race and own color, can live without the disgrace which association with negro slavery brings upon free labor." For him, "men born and nursed of white women are not going to be ruled by men who are brought up on the milk of some damn negro wench!"

Voting reforms in Jackson's time brought no improvement for blacks. In fact, the laws were framed in ways to prevent Negroes from voting. It remains one of the great paradoxes of American history that freedom from slavery for blacks was won by the sacrifices of so many whites who did not really believe in racial equality at all.

Activities of the abolitionists

By 1840 there were hundreds of abolitionist societies in Massachusetts, New York, Ohio, and other northern states, with an overall membership of 150,000. They published newspapers, organized rallies, and raised funds to assist runaway slaves and freed blacks. They circulated antislavery petitions that were sent to Congress and tried to elect congressional representatives favorable to the cause. As southern proslavery sentiment hardened, abolitionists had declining influence in the South, but they continued to influence northern opinion until the adoption of the Thirteenth Amendment.

White antislavery societies normally excluded blacks from the decision-making process. So blacks formed their own abolitionist movement. Their first organization, founded in 1833, was the American Society of Free Persons of Color, an outgrowth of a nationwide Negro convention. Eventually there were some fifty antislavery societies organized by Negroes. Among the most noted black abolitionists were John B. Russwurm, Samuel Cornish, Harriet Tubman, John Mercer Langston, and Frederick Douglass. Langston, as president of the Ohio Anti-Slavery Society, had practically no direct contact with white abolitionists. His desire to end slavery at once, along with all racial discrimination, got a cool reception from the more moderate whites in the movement.

Frederick Douglass (1817–1895) was born in Maryland to a slave mother and a white man. He escaped to the North in 1838 and became a speaker at abolitionist gatherings in Massachusetts. In 1847, after publishing his autobiography, he founded and edited a periodical called the *North Star*. A gifted writer and speaker, he was able to describe to whites the personal reactions of a slave: "Those who enslave, rob and torment their cooks, may well expect to find death in their dinner-pots."

The Underground Railroad—a network of antislavery volunteers—assisted thousands of slaves to northern "depots" or to a safe destination in Canada. In the North sympathetic whites managed the Railroad. In the South, where the danger was greatest, it was run almost entirely by Negroes. The most successful "conductor" was Harriet Tubman, a woman of enormous inner strength, reportedly responsible for guiding three hundred slaves to freedom. In all, the Railroad liberated about two thousand slaves each year between 1830 and 1860, and perhaps fifty thousand altogether.

The one attempt by a white abolitionist to spark a southern insurrection failed dismally. John Brown's raid on Harpers Ferry, Virginia, in October 1859 was financed by a number of prominent white and black abolitionists. He intended either to seize arms for a general black uprising or simply to make a bold and dramatic gesture against slavery. With a party of sixteen white and five black followers, Brown assaulted the government arsenal. Some of the rebels were picked off by gunfire, while the rest were trapped and forced to surrender to troops led by Colonel Robert E. Lee. Denying any intention of causing wholesale bloodshed, Brown was tried for treason and conspiracy to incite slave revolt. He, along with six others, was hanged. Emerson said of him that he made the "gallows glorious like the cross." Although John Brown's raid was unsuccessful in starting a slave uprising, it brought the Civil War a step closer.

Blacks saw in the Civil War the immediate prospect of freedom and participated actively in their own behalf. Black spokesmen like Douglass and Langston urged the federal government to allow blacks to enlist. Acting independently, some Union generals accepted black volunteers, but the War Department barred blacks from service until 1862. Wherever the Union army penetrated the South, slaves flocked into Union camps. Since Lincoln refused to use runaway slaves as soldiers, they were returned to their masters as "contraband of war." But this merely helped the enemy solve manpower problems, and the Union army finally assumed control over the slaves. In 1863 they were given official

Harriet Tubman (1821?-1913)

UNDERGROUND CONDUCTOR

Harriet Tubman was on a northbound train when she overheard her name spoken by a white passenger. He was reading aloud from an ad which accused her of stealing $50,000 worth of property in slaves, and which offered a $5000 reward for her capture. She lowered her head so that the sunbonnet she was wearing hid her face. At the next station she slipped off the train and boarded another that was headed south, reasoning that no one would pay attention to a black woman traveling in that direction. She deserted the second train near her hometown in Maryland and bought two chickens as part of her disguise. With her back hunched over in imitation of an old woman, she drove the chickens down the dusty road, calling angrily and chasing them with her stick whenever she sensed danger. In this manner Harriet Tubman was passed by her former owner who did not even notice her. The reward continued to mount until it reached $40,000.

Born a slave in Maryland, the young Harriet was permanently injured when an iron weight, flung at another slave by an angry white man, struck her in the head. For the rest of her life she was subject to periodic blackouts. But she was strong and determined to be free.

Unable to persuade her husband, a free black, to move north, she escaped to Philadelphia in 1849. During the 1850s she led a brother, a sister with two children, and her aged parents from the South. In all, she risked her life nineteen times, returning again and again to bring out as many as three hundred slaves. Many of them she conducted all the way to Canada, so that they could not be returned under the Fugitive Slave Law.

The escape parties usually set out late on Saturday, because the slaves would not be missed ordinarily until Monday morning. Harriet Tubman dosed babies with paregoric so they would remain sleeping while the adults silently stole along the midnight roads, following the North Star to freedom. When her charges lost their nerve, Harriet Tubman is said to have cocked her gun and warned, "You go or die." Plantation owners, hearing of the "Moses" who was depopulating their slave quarters, offered thousands of dollars in rewards for her capture.

In time this illiterate black woman, who had financed her expeditions by working as a cook and scrubwoman in the North, became a heroine to abolitionists on both sides of the Atlantic. She spoke not only at antislavery gatherings but also before feminist groups. During the Civil War she served the Union army as a cook, nurse, scout, and spy. Yet when the war ended she had to travel to her home in Auburn, New York, in a baggage car. And though Queen Victoria sent her a medal, it was 1895 before she received a pension from her own government. Yet nothing could bend this strong woman who, throughout her long life, took pride in having been the star conductor of the Underground Railroad without ever having lost a passenger.

fighting status. Lincoln was immensely impressed by black support for the Union. About 186,000 blacks served in the Union army and navy, often with distinction. More than 37,000 died in the war.

The Emancipation Proclamation of 1863 had symbolic significance, but it did not overturn the whole system of slavery, since it applied only to slaves in the Confederacy. Of far greater consequence was the Thirteenth Amendment, approved by Lincoln and ratified in 1865, which outlawed slavery in the United States. Black abolitionists, although joyful at the turn of events, understood that abolition was only the first step in a long battle for full equality.

Absorbing the Mexicans

The Spanish-Mexican stamp on the Southwest

Anglo-Americans tend to see European civilization sweeping majestically westward from England to Jamestown and Plymouth Rock to the Golden Gate. They forget that it also came "north from Mexico in Spanish saddlebags." Catholicism, for example, was spread by Spanish soldiers, missionaries, and settlers, as they fanned out over the region now known to us as Florida, Texas, New Mexico, and California. While Plymouth and Massachusetts Bay colonies were struggling to survive, New Spain had over 150,000 residents. The University of Mexico predated Harvard by some eighty years.

Spain secured a foothold in Florida in the late 1500s and in New Mexico at the start of the seventeenth century. By the middle of the eighteenth century there were scores of Spanish missions and towns in Texas. California's first mission was founded in 1769. All of New Spain changed ownership in 1821, when Mexico won its independence.

Americans "discovered" the Spanish Southwest in the 1820s. Yankee settlers Moses and Stephen Austin took a party of settlers into Texas in 1821. At the same time, Yankee fur trappers roamed the West looking for beaver and other pelts, and Yankee traders opened up the Santa Fe Trail between New Mexico and the towns of the Missouri Valley. Still other Americans sailed from New England all the way around Cape Horn to buy leather hides and tallow in California.

Americans who went to Mexico developed a double vision of Mexican society. Those aspects of Mexican society which seemed "white, Spanish, and aristocratic" were quite attractive. Marriage to a senorita, especially the daughter of a wealthy don, was not out of the question. On the other hand, the Mexicans were a racially diverse people, and the Americans saw racial mixing as a great evil. The Mexicans were mostly mestizos, but there were also many mulattos, zambas (a mixture of Indian and black), and Indians, as well as Caucasians. According to the standard racial beliefs of Yankees in Mexico, the mestizos were cowardly, thieving, lazy, and superstitious—a combination of the worst elements in both the Indian and Spanish background.

Racial aftermath of the Mexican War

Both the Texas Revolution of 1836 and the Mexican War (see Chapter 11) had bitter

This watercolor illustration, done by William H. Meyers during his journey along the Pacific coast in 1838–1839, depicts a party scene in the Southwest. Entitled "San Maxymo at Xibara," it shows those aspects of Mexican society which seemed "white, Spanish, and aristocratic."

racial overtones that lasted for more than a generation. The term "greaser," which originated with Yankee soldiers in the Mexican War, expressed the Americans' contempt for Mexicans. The comparable term used by Mexicans to describe Yankees was "gringo." Senator John C. Calhoun, an oracle of southern racism, opposed annexing any part of Mexico except New Mexico or California, where the population was small and manageable. He could not conceive of granting equality to the Mexicans.

The Treaty of Guadalupe Hidalgo (1848) ended 150 years of Spanish-Mexican rule in the Southwest. With the Mexican Cession, the United States acquired some eighty thousand Mexicans—about 1 percent of Mexico's population. (About two thousand Mexicans migrated south into Mexico rather than join the hated Americans.) These were the charter members of the ethnic group now known as "Latinos," "Latin Americans," "Spanish Americans," "Mexican Americans," or "Chi-

canos." The 1970 census showed just over five million persons of Mexican descent in the United States, the second largest ethnic minority in the country.

The rush for gold in California

The wild scramble for gold in California after 1848 brought Yankees and Mexicans into sharp conflict in the Sierra mining regions. A great outpouring of Mexicans came from the border state of Sonora. Yankees treated them as hated foreign invaders. The California legislature passed a stiff foreign miners' tax, which effectively forced the Sonorans (also Chileans and Peruvians) out of the diggings. Also caught up in the turmoil were the Californios, the native-born Californians of Spanish-Mexican background. The treaty had made them U.S. citizens, yet they too were hounded out of the diggings, along with the "foreigners" from Latin America.

The Californios retreated to their ranches only to suffer other defeats. The Treaty of Guadalupe Hidalgo supposedly guaranteed them the "free enjoyment of their liberty and property." From 7,500 to 10,000 Californios owned thirteen million acres of land. But under the terms of a congressional land law of 1851, they had to prove the validity of their land claims. This was often difficult to do, and it was always costly. Squatters, taxes, lawyers' fees, and in 1864 a drought that killed innumerable cattle were further causes for loss of land.

After 1849 the Californios had relatively little power in the new state government. One of the last of their leaders was Pablo de la Guerra of Santa Barbara, who signed the state constitution in 1849 and was elected a state senator. His people, he once protested,

are unfamiliar with the prevalent language now spoken in their own country. They have no voice in this Senate, except such as I am now weakly speaking on their behalf. . . . I have seen old men of sixty and seventy years of age weeping because they have been cast out of their ancestral home. They have been humiliated and insulted. They have been refused the privilege of cutting their own firewood. And all those who have committed these outrages have come here looking for protection.

In spite of this plea, the wealth and land of the Californios fell into the hands of the American newcomers, and the unhurried and gracious style of the old families disintegrated. Californios became second-class citizens.

The bandidos

The Treaty of Guadalupe Hidalgo was followed by forty years of violence on both sides of the border, between Brownsville, Texas, and Stockton, California. American adventurers went "filibustering" south of the border to claim more land for the Stars and Stripes. Indian tribes from the U.S. raided Mexico despite America's pledge in the treaty to prevent such invasions. The Indians made the situation worse by skillfully playing off one nation against the other.

Numerous *bandidos* also roamed the troubled border. The mysterious Joaquín Murietta is alleged to have become a highwayman to avenge the rape of his sister by Yankees. Joaquín's story was first told by a Cherokee Indian journalist, John Rollin Ridge, or Yellow Bird, a crusader against Anglo-Saxon racism. Rangers later shot and killed a desperado said to be Joaquín. They cut off his head and preserved it in whiskey for some years afterward. Long after his death Joaquín's name lived on in legends.

More precise facts are available about Juan M. Cortina, a red-bearded *bandido* who was the terror of the Texas-Mexican border for a generation. Son of a prominent family of Brownsville, Texas, Cortina shot a U.S. marshal in 1859 for harassing an innocent Mexican. He then turned outlaw and battled the Yankees on a broad front. Cortina issued blazing pronouncements, planted the Mexican flag on American soil, destroyed the property of offending Yankees, and chastised Mexicans who aided the enemy. Eventually he became governor of the Mexican state of Tamaulipas and, along with Pancho Villa, the most celebrated folk hero of the border. *Corridos* (folk ballads) about him are still sung in the border area.

Mexican heritage

Mexican Americans are in some ways a unique minority. Like the Indians, they suffered military defeat. Yet the Mexicans were in theory granted complete equality, which the Indians were not. Like blacks, they were despised for their color, yet they were never slaves. Like Europeans, many came voluntarily. Yet because Mexico was so close, they could cross back and forth over the border. The majority never considered themselves immigrants at all, but natives.

The Southwest has made its mark on Anglo culture. Thousands of places still retain the names given them by Spanish and Mexican pioneers. Such Spanish words as *cañone*, *arroyo*, *mesa*, *barbacoas* (barbecue), and *patio* entered the English language in, or almost in, their original form. Similarly, such Indian products as cocoa, potatoes, tobacco, and tomatoes are called by their Spanish names.

The American cowboy's outfit—from his chaps and kerchief to his rope and saddle—is patterned after that of the *vaqueros*, his Mexican counterpart. The rodeo is a Spanish invention. Yankee settlers in the Southwest adopted Spanish mining techniques, architecture, furniture design, and ways of cooking, irrigating, grape growing, orchard planting, sheep ranching, and mule skinning. Elements of Spanish law on water, land, mining, and family rights were also absorbed into the culture of the Southwest.

Asian Americans: Trouble on Golden Mountain

Early American impressions of the Chinese

Americans in the eighteenth century held curious and inaccurate ideas about the Chinese. John Adams thought that China was no larger than one American colony. George Washington was surprised to learn that the Chinese were not white; he believed that they were "droll in shape and appearance." Washington sent the first American consul to China. Major Samuel Shaw, a Boston merchant, sailed there on the *Empress of China* and remained until 1794. American merchants, diplomats, and missionaries traveled back and forth to China beginning in the 1790s. The homes of wealthy Americans began to fill with ivory, jade, porcelain, and lacquer from the Orient. Protestant missionaries who were products of the Second Awakening (see p. 284) offered American readers a picture of immorality, vice, superstition, and religious indifference brought on by Confucianism. Other Americans wrote of the "bizarre" eating habits and dress, dishonesty in trade, cruelty, and despotic government of the Chinese.

Despite its long history and cultural achievements, China seemed a backward country to Americans. Even Ralph Waldo Emerson called it a "booby nation." "The Chinese Empire enjoys precisely a Mummy's reputation, that of having preserved to a hair for 3 or 4,000 years the ugliest features in the world."

Pseudoscientists claimed that the Chinese were an "inferior race." The brain capacity of whites was definitely larger than that of the Asians, they insisted, and so whites were obviously the more intelligent. By this reckoning all of the colored races were less intelligent than the white. And among the colored races the Asians had a low rating—almost as low as Africans.

Hard times for Asian immigrants

The first migration of Asians to the U.S. was in the nineteenth century. The U.S. census tabulated 3 Chinese in 1830, 8 in 1840, 758 in 1850. By 1852 some 25,000 Chinese had come to "Golden Mountain," as California was depicted in written Chinese characters. A decade later the figure reached 50,000 and was still rising. The majority were poor, uneducated, and unskilled peasants escaping from severe social upheavals in China's Pearl River delta. Most of them hoped to make their fortune in America and return home wealthy.

The first Chinese who arrived in San Francisco were considered a curious but welcome addition to the population. California's governor referred to them as "the most desirable of our adopted citizens" and recommended a system of land grants to encourage immigration. But this attitude changed as Chinese immigrants poured into the country. They worked for little pay, and whites soon came to fear them as job competitors. Whites felt much the same racial hatred for Chinese coolies as they did for blacks. Gangs of Americans drove the Asians out of the most profitable mines. And from less desirable diggings they were driven to the towns and cities. There they found work doing laundry, cooking, and keeping inns.

In the California social order the Chinese suffered from racial discrimination. Like other "coloreds," they were not permitted to testify in court against whites. Politicians found the "Chinese issue" an excellent vote-getter. For about a decade the state's largest source of public revenue was the foreign miners' tax of three or five dollars monthly, which was enforced against the Chinese as well as the Mexicans. Only the biggest employers like the Southern Pacific Railroad viewed the Chinese in a positive light. They continued to favor their immigration and offer them employment, and they tried to protect them against physical abuse from Yankee miners.

Chinese coolies and white Americans mining for gold in California in 1852. When Chinese immigrants started pouring into California in great numbers, white backlash, plus a foreign miners' tax imposed by the state, forced the Asians into towns and cities to do menial labor.

Review

According to its official policy, the United States would respect Indian rights and treat Indian tribes as sovereign nations. But the system never worked out this way. Pioneers wanted Indian land, and the government usually tried to oblige them. Tecumseh's attempt to create an independent Indian nation ended with his death during the War of 1812. President Jackson became the chief architect for Indian removal to the West. Even the Creeks and Cherokees, who had adopted white customs, were driven from their homes in the Southeast. Wherever the Indians relocated, white settlers seemed to follow, shouting for more land.

Instead of fading away as many whites expected, slavery grew stronger. As cotton acreage in the South expanded, the slave population increased. Even though the Constitution officially halted the slave trade in 1808, it continued on the sly until the Civil War. White fears aroused by the slave rebellion in Santo Domingo resulted in tighter laws against blacks, and slave rebellions in the U.S. caused further panic. Although blacks fought in the War of 1812, it did not bring them freedom. During the 1820s various groups, both white and black, proposed sending blacks back to Africa, but no mass exodus took place. To counter growing discrimination, free blacks formed their own mutual aid societies and became active abolitionists. During the Civil War blacks fought with the Union troops, although the government at first barred them from enlisting. Lincoln's Emancipation Proclamation had symbolic importance, but only the Thirteenth Amendment effectively ended slavery.

Americans first encountered Mexicans when they entered the Southwest as trappers, traders, and settlers. The newcomers were attracted to the Spanish missions and befriended the wealthy Spanish landowners. At the same time, they sneered at the natives of mixed parentage. Prejudice against Mexicans intensified during the Texas Revolution and the War with Mexico. During the California gold rush, the Californios were stripped of their land, wealth, and prestige and reduced to second-class citizens.

Americans held distorted views of the Chinese as far back as the 1700s. Because their heads were smaller, the Chinese were thought to be less intelligent. The first mass migration of Asians to the U.S. occurred during the California gold rush. Chinese immigrants were welcomed at first, but as American workers saw them flowing into the country in growing numbers, they became alarmed over the competition for jobs. The Chinese faced discrimination and harassment in the years that followed.

Questions

1. Identify the following: (a) Treaty of Greenville, (b) Removal Act of 1830, (c) Reorganization Act of 1834, (d) Trail of Tears, (e) Nat Turner's Rebellion, (f) Harriet Tubman, (g) Treaty of Guadalupe Hildalgo.
2. Explain Tecumseh's plan of pan-Indian nationalism. Why did it fail?
3. How did the rebellion in Santo Domingo alter slavery in the U.S.?
4. What was the foreign miners' tax? How did it affect the Spanish-speaking and Oriental miners?
5. Compare and contrast the conditions and treatment of Indians, blacks, Mexicans, and Chinese during this period.

Irish immigrants debarking in New York, 1847; detail from painting by Samuel B. Waugh.

At least three-fourths of the
people of the United States
derive their descent and
national sympathies . . .
from sects of respectable
exiles, by whom the basis of
the population was broadly
laid in principles and habits
of virtue, independence, and
toleration.

CHARLES J. INGERSOLL   (1782–1862)
Lawyer and public official

13

13

For God and Country

Prior to the Civil War most Americans felt highly optimistic about their future. To Ezra Stiles of Connecticut it appeared in 1789 that the Lord had "made his American Israel high above all nations." The subsequent expansion of the national borders reinforced the notion of America and Americans as a Chosen People. Americans felt certain that their governmental institutions were the freest in the world. Technology promised limitless material improvements.

Such optimism was clearly reflected in the history of immigration and religion. Millions of desperately poor Europeans looked to America as the Promised Land. As the American Protestants shifted to revivals and evangelism during the Second Awakening, they began to feel that every soul could be saved. Some Protestants believed in "perfectionism," the establishment of heaven on earth. These powerful stirrings among Protestants affected secular reform movements. Instead of dwelling on human depravity, many people became interested in improving the lot of humanity through women's suffrage, abolition of slavery, and temperance (these three topics are dealt with in other chapters of Part Two). The bloody Civil War and its aftermath was a sobering moment for idealists, although even that event could not completely dampen the country's self-confidence.

Baptist immersion, early 1800s.

The Frontier Melting Pot

The European emigration

Until 1815 European emigration was blocked by a series of wars on the continent so that only a few thousand newcomers trickled into the United States. Meanwhile, older immigrant groups like the Germans and Dutch became assimilated. By midcentury the foreign-born rarely spoke their native tongues, as they had in the late colonial period. Then the tide turned. Five million Europeans arrived in the U.S. between 1815 and the Civil War. Their number exceeded the total population of the U.S. in 1790. Most of these immigrants came from northwestern Europe. Over half were Britons, including two million Catholic Irish. The next largest group was German. Many thousands also came from Norway and Holland. Even Canada supplied a sizeable number after about 1837.

There were several reasons for the mass movement of Europeans. Europe's population had doubled in the century after 1750. In countries where land was scarce and opportunities limited, the younger generation was tempted to seek its fortune overseas. The major causes of emigration were the modernization of industry and the reorganization of farming that were sweeping through northern Europe. One country after another was caught up in the current of industrialism and large-scale farming. The small farmers, tenant farmers, and peasants were particularly affected in England, Scandinavia, Ireland, southwestern Germany, and the Scottish Highlands. Landlords in Scotland switched from growing crops to raising sheep, fenced in their land, and ousted their tenants and freeholders. Peasants who had survived by doing "home work" or domestic manufacture were gradually displaced by factories. Peasant families left their villages and flocked to the larger towns seeking facto-

ry work. Others simply fled to the United States (or other New World nations).

Ireland faced near devastation from 1845 to 1849 as a result of a potato famine. Half a million Irish had starved to death by 1847. Those who survived "walked like living skeletons," according to one eyewitness, ". . . the men stamped with the livid mark of hunger—the children crying with pain—the women too weak to stand." Hundreds of thousands took refuge in America. Arriving sick, dying, and without money, many became public wards in the port cities where their ships docked. Ireland, the most densely populated European country in 1815, lost 1.5 million people through migration during the years of the Great Famine.

Politics also contributed to emigration. Revolutions in France and Germany in 1848 created thousands of political émigrés. Among them were disillusioned liberals and socialists. The most famous of the German "forty-eighters," as the immigrants of that period were called, was Carl Schurz, who became a Republican senator and a cabinet member. Although most Germans are no longer considered a separate ethnic group, in those days their language and culture marked them off from the rest of society.

Passage to the New World

Europeans learned about fabled America from various sources. Few of the poorer emigrants had access to books or maps. Newspapers carried reports of amazing events in the U.S., and returned sailors told fascinating stories of American ports. Most important, though, were the letters that came back to the Old World and were passed from hand to hand. Through these accounts, the American Dream became etched upon the imagination of generations of Europeans. One letter could depopulate an entire village. Gjert Hovland's letters sent from Rochester, New York, to his village in Norway in 1835 set off widespread emigration. He described the schools, laws, religious freedom, soil fertility, and other attributes of America. "It is possible for all to live in comfort and without suffering want," he reported. "I do not believe that any of those who suffer under the oppression of others and who must rear their children under straitened circumstances could do better than to help the latter to come to America."

I have now been on American soil for two and a half years and I have not been compelled to pay a penny for the privilege of living. Neither is my cap worn out from lifting it in the presence of gentlemen.

Letter from a Swedish immigrant, 1849

But some offered an opposite view: "Dear friends and countrymen," a disgruntled Norwegian wrote in 1851, "consider carefully what you are doing before you decide to come here. Please do not expect to find roasted pigs, with knives and forks in their backs, ready for anyone to eat. . . . What you are quite sure to get here is a sickly body; Norwegians suffer particularly from the ague."

Crossing the Atlantic was cheap but hellish. At midcentury the cost of a steerage ticket from Liverpool, England, to New York was about forty dollars for adults and twenty dollars for children. This was a manageable sum. The low price resulted from the fact that eastbound ships carried heavy goods like cotton, grain, and lumber but returned with less bulky finished goods. This left space for extra passengers.

The crossing was hazardous. Ticket agents, food suppliers, and captains often lied about rations and space. Depending on weather conditions and the design of the ship, a trip could last from one to three months. Steerage passengers had to be strong in body and mind to endure the cramped and unsanitary living quarters. Food and water often ran low. Storms at sea threw people about in the dark hold of the vessel, sometimes for days at a time. Drunken sailors attacked women passengers. Captains ordered male passengers to swab decks and help hoist sails. Epidemics broke out, occasionally with tragic consequences. Thousands of Irish immigrants trying to escape famine at home died of ship's fever (typhus) in 1847. That year Congress passed a law regulating a few of the worst abuses, but it was poorly enforced. Overall, the voyage was more difficult than fatal. The death rate on shipboard over a period of several decades may have been less than 1 percent.

The difficulties of making a new life

Before the Civil War European immigration was an unorganized movement. Individuals and families planning to move to America took the plunge on their own. Often the result was chaos for the families and for the cities they arrived in. By taking no action, Congress left it up to the states to deal with immigration. The states and cities worried about the newcomers walking down the gangplank infected with diseases like smallpox, typhoid fever, and cholera, which could spread rapidly. Aside from checking on diseases, the states did little else.

The millions of incoming Europeans settled mostly in the northern United States. Many stayed in the cities where they docked or in a nearby town. Others pushed on west. Prior to the Civil War, access to land was the greatest boon to the newcomers. Aside from the Irish, the bulk of them made their way to farms. They shunned the Southeast, though, for land and jobs were less available there.

Even before the "greenhorns" set foot on land, they were beset by a horde of swindlers, known as "emigrant runners," who promised them the world. An agent "bought" an entire boatload of immigrants, paying the captain from one hundred to three hundred dollars to see the passengers through the quarantine area. He then "sold" them to another agent. This one put them up in boardinghouses, which were as filthy as they were expensive. He arranged to cart their baggage, which sometimes mysteriously disappeared. Ticket agents sold them railroad or steamboat tickets, which often took them nowhere. For a fee the immigrants were promised jobs, which rarely existed. Eventually the Irish and Germans formed their own immigrant aid societies to provide a smoother entry into the Promised Land.

When they arrived, the down-and-out immigrants often looked like the dregs of humanity. In their first years here they were weighed down by poverty. Driven by want and by the desire for familiar languages and faces, those who stayed in cities moved into the ghettos that developed in the 1830s and 1840s. Manhattan's Five Points slum was the city's Irish ghetto. Just to the north lay Kleindeutschland, home of 100,000 Germans.

The immigrant poor were anxious to succeed in the New World, though few came with skills, professional training, or investment capital. Their most saleable asset was muscle power. In 1855 half of New York's Irish working people were laborers, porters, waiters, and, of course, servants. The Irish servant girl was a fixture in every well-to-do home. Ten percent of the Irish were tailors or dressmakers. Many others took on heavy construction work, digging most of the canals and laying most of the railroad tracks in the eastern part of the country. In the 1840s the Irish gradually replaced native-born farm girls as unskilled workers in the New England textile mills.

The immigrants passed through a "brutal filter," to use Oscar Handlin's phrase. Those who settled here were cut off from their old lives and were never fully integrated into the Promised Land. They eased their transition into the new culture by forming mutual aid

The misery, poverty, destitution, wretchedness, and starvation, witnessed in the large capitals of Europe, are to be met with equally in all the large cities of America. . . . Fly from the large cities as from a plague.

Letter from an Irish immigrant, 1850

societies, fire brigades, militia companies, benevolent associations, social clubs, and church groups and by establishing their own schools and newspapers. The Germans made the strongest effort to retain their Old World ways. German ghettos supported their own churches, schools, restaurants, libraries, and beer halls. The 40 German-language newspapers in the U.S. in 1840 had increased to 133 by 1852. Immigrant parents sacrificed for their children. By helping them become Americanized and educated, they hoped their children would succeed where the parents may have failed.

Immigrants gave their votes to the party whose agents welcomed them at the dock and whose bosses supplied them with jobs, shelter, education, and police protection. Most adept in this form of social welfare, the Democrats picked up much of the urban immigrant vote. The Whigs, who leaned toward aristocracy, nativism, and temperance, were far less popular with immigrants. The Republican homestead plank appealed greatly to the Germans and Scandinavians of the Old Northwest, however, who helped form the party and elect Lincoln.

Nativism, a reaction against newcomers

The U.S. prided itself on being "the last best hope of mankind," a haven for Europe's oppressed. Yet free immigration was linked in the popular mind with social evils which might destroy the Republic: poverty, crime, radicalism, political corruption, and that old bugaboo, the Catholic church. These negative feelings encouraged the growth of nativism and distrust of immigrant newcomers.

In the 1790s the French Revolution awakened fears of foreign radicals. The Federalists suspected that European revolutionaries were sneaking into America to help the rival Jeffersonians undermine the Republic. In 1795 a panicky Federalist Congress extended from two to five years the period that an immigrant had to live here before attaining citizenship. During the anti-French hysteria of 1797–1798 the notorious Alien Acts gave the president sweeping powers to arrest and exile aliens suspected of subversive activity. Happily, John Adams did not use these powers. And neither the Alien Acts nor the Sedition Act, which was intended to silence Republican editors, subdued the opponents of Federalism. The legislation only rallied the immigrant voters behind the Republicans in 1800. The GOP victory that year was assisted by the Irish and French voters of New York City. Interestingly enough, the new Republican Congress restored the five-year probationary period for immigrants. The Republicans also felt uneasy about "dangerous foreigners," even though they bragged about making America an asylum for the wretched of the earth.

Radicalism was again cause for alarm after 1848. Radicals driven from Europe after the unsuccessful revolutions of 1848 angered many Americans with their talk of abolishing the U.S. Senate and presidency in order to democratize the Constitution.

Concern about the poverty and vice in the

Nativists (wearing beaver hats) resist militiamen called out to quell a riot between Catholics and non-Catholics in Philadelphia, 1844. Earlier, the editor of the Native American *had kindled nativist reaction by declaring: "The bloody hand of the Pope has stretched itself forth to our destruction. Our liberties are now to be fought for;—let us not be slack in our preparations."*

RIOT IN PHILADELPHIA

JUNE 7th 1844.

immigrant ghettos intensified in the 1830s and 1840s. Most irksome to many citizens was the thought that some European countries were deliberately dumping their "undesirables" on America. In fact, English parishes found it cheaper to send their poor to America than to support them for a year, and some European towns and cities unlocked their poorhouses and prisons, gave the inmates tickets, and waved farewell to them. Upon the arrival in Norfolk, Virginia, of a shipload of elderly paupers from England, *Niles' Weekly Register* in 1830 noted: "John Bull has squeezed the orange, but insolently casts the skins in our faces." Poor relief pushed up taxes, and poverty led to crime that threatened entire cities. Commissions were formed to look into slum conditions, but as long as America's ports remained open to all immigrants, nothing much could be done. Job competition from poor immigrants angered native-born Americans.

Nativists also charged the Europeans with Sabbath-breaking. The Germans loved a Sunday picnic or shooting festival, an afternoon in a beer garden, or an evening at the theater. Playing music, dancing, and drinking on Sunday, which was common in many European countries, threatened the quiet Sabbath customs in America. Many older communities strengthened their blue laws to control Sabbath-breaking. In time, though, the Europeans' notion "that it was a good thing to have a good time" began to influence American recreational habits.

In politics, immigrants often became associated in the public mind with corruption and bossism. In some big coastal cities newly landed foreigners were marched before compliant officials to be sworn in as citizens and then sent to the polls by politicians who told them how to vote. The native-born and many naturalized citizens were often angered by this subversion of the electoral process.

The hatred of Catholics that had burned in colonial times was rekindled. Imagining that the Ursuline convent in Charlestown, Massachusetts, was a den of vice, a mob burned it to the ground in 1834. The Reverend Lyman Beecher, one of the nation's most powerful Protestants, wrote a long tirade against Catholicism called *Plea for the West* (1834). He accused the pope of sending his "soldiers" (immigrants) to America to destroy the country's freedom. The West seemed particularly exposed, since it bordered on Catholic Mexico. Catholic demands for state aid to parochial schools and their protests against the use of the Protestant Bible in the public schools caused a violent reaction. During rioting in Philadelphia in 1844, fire destroyed two Catholic churches and numerous Irish homes. For three days a mob ruled the city. Thirteen persons died, and fifty were injured.

Lurid exposés of convent life, based largely on fantasy, inflamed the rioters in the "Protestant Crusade" against Catholicism. Rebecca Reed's *Six Months in a Convent* and Maria Monk's *Awful Disclosures of the Hotel Dieu Nunnery of Montreal* (1836) were the best-known works. *Awful Disclosures* and other equally fanciful works by the same author sold 300,000 copies by 1860.

Nativism reached new depths in the 1850s with the Know-Nothing party. This organization grew out of a secret patriotic group, the Supreme Order of the Star-Spangled Banner, which opposed immigration. Members, who used secret handshakes and tried to hide party membership, earned their name from their password, "I don't know." By 1854 the American, or Know-Nothing, party was strong enough to elect many governors, state legislators, and congressmen. They campaigned for a twenty-one-year naturalization law and other measures to keep the foreign-born out of politics and even out of the country. The nativist and anti-Catholic movement disturbed more sober and liberal Americans. Lincoln declared:

When the Know-Nothings get control, it [the Declaration of Independence] will read all men are created equal, except *negroes and foreigners and Catholics.'* When it comes to this I should prefer emigrating to some country where they make no pretense of loving liberty—to Russia, for instance, where despotism can be taken pure, and without the base alloy of hypocracy [sic].

After the 1856 elections, in which Fillmore was their candidate, the Know-Nothing movement evaporated into thin air.

The Kingdom of God in the New Republic

The Second Awakening

On August 6, 1801, Cane Ridge, Kentucky, witnessed the first great outdoor revival meeting since colonial days. Thousands gathered in this frontier town near Lexington. Most were unchurched, rough-spoken, whiskey-drinking, tobacco-chewing farmers, alongside gamblers, whores, and other frontier characters. Amid the scattered wagons and horses and makeshift tents and lean-tos were small clearings where preachers shouted their sermons from tree stumps or fallen logs. People swayed, twitched, jerked, danced, flopped, "barked," and ran as if pursued by the devil. Skeptics sneered at the wild conduct of some participants, but the meeting was a landmark in the history of American Protestantism. It was a vivid example of the spreading revivalist movement known as the "Second Awakening."

Associated with the spread of democracy in the United States, the Second Awakening recalled the religious excitement of the Great Awakening in the 1740s. The Second Awakening was not limited to the frontier. It seems to have begun in New England, and it certainly had strength in older Protestant congregations all along the eastern seaboard. The vitality of U.S. religious institutions and the close association of patriotic fervor with religious sentiment was noted by Alexis de Tocqueville. The mutual toleration among the Protestant churches seemed genuine. And even the Catholic church thrived on the principle of separation of church and state. True, some young Americans were abandoning Christianity under the influence of science, but most people remained believers. Furthermore, "religion exercises an immense power outside of the church," Tocqueville said, noticing what others have called "civic religion." Since the majority opinion wielded powerful pressure, a person had to at least *appear* to be a believer.

American Protestantism during the nineteenth century was different from what it had been in the seventeenth century. Gone were the days of dour Puritan righteousness, when only the Congregational church was permitted in some New England states. Connecticut and Massachusetts were the last two states to give up an established Congregational church. When that church was disestablished, the state no longer supported it with tax money. Religious liberty was a fact of life in the nineteenth century. Another change was the new emphasis given by Protestants to evangelicalism, the conversion of individuals during revivals. This aspect of Protestantism continued throughout the nineteenth and early twentieth centuries.

Spreading God's Word

The leading Protestant churches looked forward to a new and great Christian commonwealth. Denominations that had formerly warred with one another now joined hands in a unified crusade for the Lord. At every turn there were unrepentant sinners needing conversion. Beyond the Appalachian Mountains, beyond the Ohio River, and in the Lower South, the woods teemed with nonbelievers and backsliders: escaped criminals, debtors, runaway husbands, con artists, gamblers, prostitutes, and assorted sinners of every description. It was reported in the East that many westerners had never laid eyes on a Bible or even heard of Jesus Christ. Here was a fabulous realm for spreading the Gospel.

The Baptists and Methodists led the way in this exuberant religious outburst. Evangelists carried popular religion to rural America via camp meetings, circuit riders, and voluntary associations. Methodist circuit riders crammed their saddlebags with the works of the English preacher John Wesley and rode into remote wilderness clearings, exclaiming to startled pioneers, "The Kingdom of God is come nigh unto you!" Instead of circuit riding, Baptist preachers lived among their flocks, chopping wood, harvesting corn, and doing all the chores that their parishioners did. They thrived in New England and New York, where they filled the gap left by the dying off of older and sterner Calvinists.

The Baptists and the Methodists continued for decades to missionize the western fron-

Evangelicalism, the conversion of individuals during revivals, made camp meetings a common institution during the Second Awakening. Camp meetings were highlighted by much singing, shivering, shaking, shouting, praying, and even howling and barking. They usually ended when penitents came to the pulpit to embrace Jesus.

tier and the South. During the idle winter months or after the summer planting, evangelists summoned sinners (and curious onlookers) to camp meetings. There, from pulpits made of rough-hewn logs, fiery preachers called for sinners to repent and to seek salvation in Jesus. For days, rousing hymns, thunderous sermons, and emotional displays of a "willingness to accept Christ" broke the forest silence. Then the preachers moved on to other locations.

The Reverend Lyman Beecher was the first to organize voluntary associations, which later became a force in the revival movement. He discovered the usefulness of voluntary associations after the senseless duel between Alexander Hamilton and Aaron Burr. He preached against dueling, which he saw as a "great national sin," and formed a group to mobilize public pressure for a law forbidding it. Others soon began organizing voluntary associations for different causes. In 1816 Beecher proposed to supply "a bible for every family, a school for every district, and a pastor for every thousand souls." Over 23,000 Bibles were shipped to the Ohio Valley alone. Scores of societies started Sunday schools, distributed religious pamphlets, sold religious newspapers and journals, supported charitable causes, passed out hymnals, established schools and colleges, and, of course, organized churches and revivals. No two associations had the same membership, and almost all were nondenominational. The most ardent churchgoers were women, who figured prominently in these organizations.

The new sects

The Baptist minister William Miller created a stir by predicting that, according to the Bible, Christ would return to earth on October 22, 1844. Miller took by storm the Burned Over district in western New York State, a settled farm area repeatedly "burned" by religious excitement. As early as 1839 he had a large following, but after the "Great Disappointment," when Christ failed to appear, the Millerite movement subsided. Later, Mrs. Ellen G. White, who had been a teen-age convert of Miller's, reorganized the sect. It eventually became the Seventh-Day Adventist church, which sent missionaries all over the world.

The Unitarian church grew out of the liberal branch of Congregationalism. In a speech given in Baltimore in 1819 William Ellery Channing of Boston rejected the doctrines of the Holy Trinity, the depravity of man, and a vengeful God. From that time on he was the recognized leader of the new church. Channing de-emphasized the need for religious conversion on the grounds that people had to be free to work out their own salvation in their own way. Church membership, he thought, should be open and flexible. Regardless of what it may have been in the past, the purpose of Christianity was now "the perfection of human nature, the elevation of men into nobler beings." The Unitarians' watchword was "deeds not creeds." The sect won a strong following at Harvard and had an important influence on American philanthropy, humanitarianism, and social reform.

Channing was also a member of the Transcendental Club, a secular literary group with strong religious overtones. Transcendentalism began as an offshoot of Unitarianism when a Unitarian minister, Ralph Waldo Emerson, resigned from the church in 1836. He complained that it was a "corpse-cold" religion. Emerson's essay *Nature*, presented before the Transcendental Club of Boston that year, expressed his philosophical and religious viewpoint: The individual's perception of experience is sacred and unique. God expresses himself through the harmonies of nature, and an "oversoul" unifies all people. Each person can discover these harmonies outside of any church, through intuition and mystical experience. Many influential literary figures considered

Surrounded by his family — including several wives — a Mormon farmer poses in front · of his home near Echo City, Utah. A liberal land system based on religious sanctions made initial grants according to family size, and communal control of water resources permitted the development of an irrigation system essential to desert farming.

themselves Transcendentalists, including Henry David Thoreau, author of *Walden* (1854) and other essays.

Mormonism, America's most successful native religion, first sprang to life in 1830 in upstate New York. Its founder, Joseph Smith (1805–1844), based his beliefs on the *Book of Mormon*, which he claimed was a religious prophecy inscribed on golden plates and given him by an angel. Smith set up not only a church — the Church of Jesus Christ of Latter-Day Saints — but a cooperative society tightly ruled by a small group of men. Thousands of Mormons migrated from New York to Ohio, to Missouri, and then to Illinois. Their habit of voting as a political bloc and their rumored practice of polygamy created fierce local hatreds. In 1844 an anti-Mormon mob murdered Smith at Nauvoo, Illinois. Three years later his disciple Brigham Young (1801–1877) led sixteen thousand Mormons

to the Great Salt Lake, where they settled permanently. Young became governor of a new territory, in Utah, but the practice of polygamy and the Mormons' defiance of federal authority led to extreme, and sometimes violent, tensions with Washington. Territorial status lasted from 1850 to 1896. Early in their history Mormons started sending missionaries throughout the country and overseas. This practice continues to flourish.

By midcentury dissent took a hold on Protestantism. The harmony among denominations ended in the 1830s, when turmoil over the Mormons and Unitarians, among other things, created conflicts that lasted for a decade. Differences over slavery further divided Methodists, Baptists, and Presbyterians in the 1850s.

In their zeal for converts the Methodists and Baptists had surged ahead of the Congregationalists and Presbyterians to become, by 1850, the largest Protestant denominations in the U.S. Lutherans (mostly Germans and Scandinavians) were in fifth place. The Disciples of Christ, a relatively new sect, was sixth. But while America considered itself a nation of believers, the believers were still largely unchurched. Less than 20 percent of the population was officially enrolled in churches in the 1860s. Most churchgoers were women.

Growing numbers of Catholics

A twofold shift took place in the Catholic church in America at midcentury. First, it shifted from a "native" to an "immigrant" church, and second, it became the largest Christian denomination in Protestant America. At the time of Washington's inauguration most of the small number of American Catholics were native-born. As immigration increased, the faith came to be dominated by those of foreign birth, especially the Irish.

Only about 35,000 of the nearly 4 million Americans in 1790 were Catholics. A small, persecuted group, they lived mainly in the Middle Atlantic states and in the French villages beyond the Appalachians. Sixty years later, when the Catholic bishops of the U.S. held their first council in Baltimore, Roman Catholics numbered 2 million, lived in every part of the country, and took part in many phases of American life. Thirty-two bishops were the overseers of some 1400 priests, 1400 churches, 680 missions, and 6 archdioceses. The church had wide geographical scope, from Boston to Monterey, California, and from Texas to Oregon.

As an outgrowth of ethnic diversity, the Catholic church in America faced strong pressure from its members for more power in church affairs—a controversy known as "lay trusteeism." The French Catholics of Kentucky resented having Irish pastors, whereas in Louisiana the French scorned the Spanish clergy. Elsewhere it was Irish parishioners against the German priest or the priest of English descent. Because Protestant congregations controlled their own churches, local ethnic groups wanted a say in running the Catholic churches, especially the right to hire and fire priests. The bishops yielded to some demands, but not on appointing pastors. The conflict over lay trusteeism hit New York, Buffalo, and Philadelphia especially hard. The furor subsided in the 1820s but started up again later in the century.

While outsiders saw the Catholic church as an alien force, insiders saw it from a completely opposite point of view. Church leaders believed that Catholic schools, charities, orphanages, newspapers, presses, and pastoral councils all served to mold Catholics into good and loyal American citizens. The parochial schools, for example, exposed immigrant youngsters to native-born children. The first Catholic newspaper was issued in 1822 by Bishop John England of Charleston. Two decades later there were twenty different weeklies for English-speaking Catholics in the U.S. They published articles on the affairs of the immigrants' adopted country, explained Catholicism to outsiders, and countered the unending barrage of anti-Catholic sermons, tracts, pamphlets, books, newspaper reports, and rumors.

By contrast with its traditional role in Europe, the Catholic church stayed out of politics in America. It gracefully accepted democracy and allowed parishioners to take part in public life or not, as they wished. When the church did take a position, it generally held conservative political views and seldom supported radical causes.

German Jews bring the Reform Movement

The country's Jewish population rose from 2000 at the end of the colonial period to about 160,000 in 1860. The major influx of Jews started around 1836, when a depression in

Bavaria set off a mass migration of German Jews to America.

Most of the new arrivals were poor, and many were paupers. Unlike earlier Jewish immigrants, they did not settle in the northeastern cities but headed west or south. The Jewish peddler, burdened by a huge backpack or perched on top of a ramshackle wagon pulled by a bony horse, became a familiar sight on the frontier. As Jews had been denied land in Europe since the Middle Ages, few had a background in farming. They brought their old skills in trade and manufacturing with them to the new country. Throughout the West, from Ohio to California, the Jews bought and sold goods. During the gold rush they rose to the middle class in San Francisco.

Though anti-Semitism is thousands of years old, it did not acquire an active, organized status in America until late in the nineteenth century. Before then there were too few Jews in the country, and they were too widely dispersed. Besides, many American Protestant sects identified with the biblical Israel. In Cincinnati in the 1840s members of a small Christian sect (Nazarene Christians) traveled a hundred miles to view and converse with "the children of Israel, the holy people of God." Minor anti-Semitic incidents did occur, though. When General Grant occupied the Tennessee River Valley in 1863, northern businessmen followed closely in the wake of his army. Their sharp dealings in cotton brought loud complaints from resident southerners. Of all the businessmen involved, Grant blamed "the Israelites especially," and issued a general order expelling "the Jews, as a class" from the area covered by his command. Lincoln revoked the order.

German Jewish immigrants who came after 1824 introduced the Jewish Reform Movement to America. This was a scholarly movement initiated by rabbis who were influenced by the ideas of the Enlightenment. They modernized the old Orthodox prayer rituals and stressed progressive rather than traditional aspects of Jewish law. During religious services Reform Jews abandoned prayer shawls and chanting, played organ music, and used less Hebrew and more English or German in the prayers. Some Reform congregations even let the women sit with the men, a radical departure from the old ways. There was more interest in ethics and social justice than in ritual. Many of these changes offended the Orthodox congregations. From a social standpoint the Reform Movement helped the Jews assimilate into the middle class.

The most influential Reform rabbi in America was Isaac Mayer Wise (1819–1900), who arrived from Germany in 1846. Hoping to unify American Jews and spread the gospel of Reform, he founded English- and German-language journals and wrote a revolutionary work, *Minhag America* (American Ritual), in 1856. He also founded Hebrew Union College (1875), the first institution for training rabbis in the U.S. The Reform tradition was the dominant form of American Judaism until the massive influx of Orthodox Jews from eastern Europe after 1880.

Religious attitudes and the Civil War

The moral implications of slavery invaded the life of almost all religious communities. The evangelical fervor of Protestantism contributed to moralistic political debate on both sides of the Mason-Dixon line before the Civil War. Abolitionism was in many ways a religious movement. So too was the defense of slavery by southerners, who often referred to the Bible to justify slavery.

For a time Protestant denominations with national organizations tried to avoid coming to grips with the slavery issue, claiming that churches should steer clear of political matters. By the 1840s, though, the largest Protestant denominations—the Presbyterians, Baptists, and Methodists—split organizationally on the issue of slavery. Since these religious bodies were among the few institutions in this country that had nationwide scope, their division foreshadowed—some observers said "caused"—the Civil War.

Religious denominations that were basically regional (most Unitarians, for example, were located in the North) experienced no internal split. Those that were congregationally organized (controlled locally), such as the Disciples of Christ or the Jews, also avoided a split, since each community was free to go its own way. Jews were prominent in public and business affairs in both the North and South. Cleveland's Rabbi Wise steered a neutral course on slavery. Judah Benjamin of Louisiana, an ardent supporter of slavery and secession, became secretary of state in the Confederacy. Fifteen hundred Jews entered the Confederate army. Most sided with the North, however, and some six thousand Jews served with the Union army, including eight as generals. The banker Joseph Seligman raised $200 million for the Union and was asked by President Grant to serve as secretary of the treasury. He declined.

The Catholic church, with strong roots in both the South and the North, split at the time of secession. Slavery presented less of a problem for Catholics than did the break-up of the Union. Most Catholics seem to have accepted church doctrine, which held that slavery was not in itself an evil if the slave owners treated their slaves with "justice and charity." The slave trade was another matter and was declared immoral by Pope Gregory XVI in 1839. Catholic officials in America frowned on abolitionism. In 1841 Bishop Francis P. Kendrick declared that "nothing should be attempted against the laws nor anything be done or said that would make them [the slaves] bear their yoke unwillingly."

Catholic bishops and lay people lined up on both sides in the Civil War, and Catholic enlistment was heavy in both armies. Generals Pierre G. T. Beauregard in the South and William S. Rosecrans in the North were Catholics. At the time of the Emancipation about 100,000 Negroes, most of them in Louisiana, were Catholics. The church's conservative position on slavery prevented it from making black converts after Emancipation.

With secession came fresh outbursts of religious self-righteousness and a moral tone in sermons that had never been equaled before—or since—in America. The southern clergy supported secession almost to a man, while the northern clergy stood firmly behind the Union cause. Army chaplains in the North and in the South converted hundreds of thousands of soldiers through religious revivals. Leaders on both sides imbued the war with deep religious meaning. As the poet Robert Lowell has pointed out, Lincoln, in his Gettysburg Address, dwelled on "the Christian sacrificial act of death and rebirth" as no other president had done before. In his Second Inaugural the president suggested that God had willed the war upon the entire nation as a punishment for slavery, and it must suffer "until every drop of blood drawn with the lash shall be paid by another drawn with the sword."

Appomattox provided the theme for countless sermons—preachers searched out great moral lessons in the outcome of the Civil War. In the 1860s Memorial Day became part of the "civil religion," whereby Americans intermingle patriotism with religious observance. Millions of Americans in the North and in the South commemorated the deaths of those who had fallen in battle. In a spirit of reconciliation they recited the poem which said in part:

They banish our anger forever
When they laurel the graves of the dead:—
Under the sod and the dew
Waiting the Judgment Day;
Love and tears for the Blue
Tears and love for the Gray.

Review

Between 1815 and the Civil War five million immigrants poured into the country, more than doubling the existing population in 1790. Most settled in northern cities, although many were attracted to the farmlands in the West. Hungry to preserve elements of their Old World culture, these nationals huddled together and established their own aid societies, newspapers, clubs, and schools. They jammed the new urban ghettos. Most were unskilled workers whose dream was to educate their children and help them succeed. Politicians went after the immigrant vote. The naturalized citizens usually voted for the party or the boss that offered them the most protection or aid. The free immigration of Catholics revived old fears of "papist plots." Native Americans also worried about immigrant radicalism and job competition. These fears encouraged organized nativist movements, the most famous of which was the Know-Nothing party.

Nineteenth-century Americans enjoyed an exceptional degree of religious liberty. The separation of church and state was more than a theory in America. After 1806 the Second Awakening revived and united many Protestant sects in a battle against sin. This enthusiasm lasted until about midcentury, when respectable citizens turned more and more to secular causes such as abolition, temperance, and the women's movement.

By the 1850s the Catholic church had become a church of immigrants and was the largest single Christian denomination in Protestant America. It drew Catholic newcomers into the mainstream of American ways through its numerous church organizations, newspapers, and parochial schools. Ethnic differences caused trouble within the church, however, as various nationalities fought with each other for local control. Before the Civil War the official position of the church was that slavery was not in itself evil. Catholics were represented on both sides during the war.

America's Jewish population remained small until about 1836, when a depression in Bavaria caused a mass influx of German Jews. By 1860 there were 160,000 American Jews. Most new arrivals were poor; many became peddlers in the South and West. Those German Jews who migrated after 1830 introduced the Reform Movement that modernized Orthodox Judaism. Like members of the Christian denominations, Jews were found in both North and South during the Civil War. The ever widening division in most religious groups over slavery was a major warning signal of the war's approach.

Questions

1. Why did European immigrants come to the United States during this period?
2. Describe some of the major problems that immigrants faced upon their arrival. How did they attempt to overcome their difficulties and achieve their goals?
3. Why did nativism arise and what forms did it take? Why were Catholics in particular an object of hate?
4. Compare religious attitudes in nineteenth-century America with those of earlier times. What similarities and differences do you find?
5. What was the Jewish Reform Movement? How did it differ from Jewish Orthodoxy?

women and the family

The Emerson School, Boston.

Equality! where is it, if not in education? Equal rights! they cannot exist without equality of instruction.

FRANCES WRIGHT   (1795–1852)
Social reformer

14

293

14

All Men and Women Are Created Equal

"All men are created equal," announced the Declaration of Independence in 1776. Seventy-two years later a group of women dared challenge the sexism of the Founding Fathers. At the first women's convention, at Seneca Falls, New York, in 1848, they issued the Declaration of Sentiment, which said firmly, "All men *and women* are created equal."

The women's liberation movement has had three distinct phases. The first spanned the period from the 1830s to the Civil War, the second from about 1890 to 1920. The third began in the mid-1960s and has not yet run its course. What the pre-Civil War feminists had in their favor—in addition to their own courage and conviction—were the supporting ideals of Christian perfectionism, Jacksonian democracy, and the abolition movement. Each of these currents contributed to the feminist sweep. Over the generations the specific issues have varied: the right to equal education, to the vote, to entry into the professions, to equal pay for equal work, to legal abortions. But the underlying issue has remained the same for nearly two centuries: the improvement of the status of women in a society essentially dominated by men.

Nineteenth-century feminism must be considered against a background of family life. Women turned feminist not only because they were inspired by the idealism that came from Jacksonian democracy, abolition, or Christian perfectionism, but also because of the family situation in which they lived. The family of the Victorian age was strongly male-dominated and nuclear. It emphasized privacy, domesticity, and child rearing. Victorian attitudes created an image of woman as delicate and virtuous. Some women would not accept the role assigned to them and rebelled against it. This chapter describes new trends in nineteenth-century family life, especially as they concern women. But it is well to remember that family structure has always varied according to region, class, and racial and ethnic background.

The Family Scene

Farm families and pioneers

The farm family of the early nineteenth century had a unified structure, since to a large extent its members worked and played together. It was an economic as well as a social unit. In many cases the family produced most of the goods it consumed, and it supplied much of the education that children would acquire in life. Public schools were often nonexistent. All members of a farm family beyond infancy had important work chores suited to their abilities. The more isolated the farm, the more mutually dependent the family. This situation had a balancing effect on sexual roles.

Men and women pioneers had settled practically every frontier together, so it is not surprising that as the mining and farming frontiers moved to the Great Plains and then to California and the Pacific Northwest before the Civil War, women began to join the men who had blazed the path. In 1849 about 10 percent of the fifty thousand forty-niners who crossed the plains were women, and 5 percent were children. Soon more and more women were traveling west. By the 1860s the ratio of females to males was rapidly reaching parity. Most of the women were farm wives and daughters. Others were missionaries to the Indians, soldiers' wives, suffragists, actresses, barmaids, prostitutes, school teachers, or authors. Frontier women often enjoyed more property rights and freedom than their sisters in the East. And whether unmarried, married, or widowed, they often had the ability to support themselves.

Working-class families

Meanwhile, the quickening beat of industry and the rising flood of immigration gave a new aspect to family life in America's towns and cities. In the first phases of the textile industry some women did "home work"—made gloves, shawls, and other items of clothing in their own homes, with the aid of younger children. Later, the women and children were drawn into the work force and into the factories, particularly the textile mills. Spinning had always been considered "women's work," and the new machinery required relatively little strength. By 1850 over 200,000 women were factory workers, almost 25 percent of the factory work force. A large proportion of factory workers were under sixteen years of age.

Family life in and around the small industrial towns of the Northeast appeared less stable than it had been in earlier generations. Many of the immigrant workers of the 1850s and 1860s were desperately poor. Alcoholism, childhood deaths, juvenile delinquency, and other signs of troubled families increased. Immigrant communities had an excess of men compared to women. Widespread drunkenness and prostitution afflicted nearly all such communities at one time or another. Women, particularly new immigrants, often turned to prostitution in order to survive. A study of some two thousand prostitutes in New York City in 1855 found that 61 percent were born abroad and most lived in dire poverty.

Southern plantation families

The basic nineteenth-century ideal of the patriarchal family varied little on either side of the Mason-Dixon line, though northerners and southerners argued over which region best upheld the ideal. One southerner remarked in 1851 that slavery "increases the tendency to dignify the family. Each planter in fact is a Patriarch—his position compels him to be a ruler in his household. . . . The fifth commandment becomes the foundation of Society." Yet another southern writer, George Fitzhugh, who was one of the most important defenders of slavery, placed "the sanctity and purity of the family circle" at the center of the slaveholder's philosophy. "Slavery, marriage, religion, are the pillars" of society, said Fitzhugh. For him the ideal plantation family included not only the husband, wife, and children but also the slaves. Properly speaking, the family should be a paternalistic dictatorship, and he suggested that northerners, constantly interested in money matters and preoccupied with "individualism," had less family feeling than southerners.

Southern whites often felt that their slaves were part of the extended family. They inscribed the names of newborn slave babies in the family Bible and referred to their slaves as "the black family" or "our people." On the other hand, the tension created by the nearness of white women to black men explains in part the white man's creation of the myth of southern womanhood, an image of virginal perfection.

Northerners commenting on southern society often called southerners hypocrites, claiming that southern men, despite their professed loyalty to marriage and the family, were notoriously unfaithful to their wives. And white males, despite their avowed kindness to their "black family," were claimed by northerners to exploit black women sexually.

Rarely did plantation women talk about problems of family morality, but a diary entry by the plantation wife Mary Boykin Chesnut makes the point:

Under slavery, we live surrounded by prostitutes, yet an abandoned [white] woman is sent out of any decent house. Who thinks any worse of a Negro or mulatto woman for being a thing we can't name? God forgive us, but ours is a monstrous system, a wrong and an iniquity! Like the patriarchs of old, our men live all in one house with their wives and their concubines; and the mulattoes one sees in every family partly resemble the white children. Any lady is ready to tell you who is the father of all the mulatto children in everybody's household but her own. Those, she seems to think, drop from the clouds. My disgust sometimes is boiling over. Thank God for my country women, but alas for the men! They are probably no worse than men everywhere, but the lower their mistresses, the more degraded they must be.

Her parting shot about the men and their mistresses mirrors exactly what many northern women felt about northern men.

Raising children

The experience of childhood underwent a process of slow change. The increasing prominence of schools, the growth of towns and cities, the tempo of factory life, the replacement of child labor by farm machines,

On vast areas of the Great Plains where building stone and firewood were not to be found, pioneers put up sodhouses and burned buffalo or cattle chips. Here, a woman said to be Ella Sly, who lived near Garden City, Kansas, collects chips for fuel. Many women like her shared in the hard work of frontier life.

and, above all, the Victorian stress on the importance of child rearing—all of these influences had an effect on the life of the child in early nineteenth-century America.

The tendency to "permissiveness" in American families has been remarked upon by almost every social commentator in the last century and a half. European visitors in particular were struck by the "pampering" American parent and the "spoiled" child. An English observer, Anthony Trollope, in 1860 said: "I must protest that American babies are an unhappy race. They eat and drink as they please; they are never punished; they are never banished, snubbed, and kept in the background as children are kept with us."

In their teens boys were still fairly independent, certainly more so than girls. Most Americans of both sexes and of all classes did manual labor at some time in life. Poor children were sometimes sent away to work in order to supplement the family income. Even many wealthy children were used to working. The sons of New England mill owners and merchants worked in the family business from the age of eight or nine years. When their sons were sixteen or so, wealthy parents often sent them to sea to toughen them up. Farm boys often trained as craftsmen, moved from job to job, and were considered apprentices until they were about twenty-one. Meantime, they returned home for seasonal farm work. And, of course, some boys left home in their teens and became totally independent.

As schools multiplied in the early nineteenth century (by the 1850s most northern states had public schools), boys spent longer periods away from home. Master workmen were often forced by law to grant their apprentices one or two months of schooling yearly. Local communities created district common schools and winter schools designed for boys eight to twelve, but sometimes attended by young men. These schools became more and more prevalent in the

It must be woman's prerogative to shine in the domestic circle, and her appropriate duty to teach and regulate the opening mind of her little flock, and teach their juvenile ideas how to shoot forth into well improved sentiments.

HANNAH MATHER CROCKER
Observations on the Real Rights of Women, 1818

Northeast. Among prosperous farm families, boys were packed off to boarding school after the first frost and stayed there until time for the spring planting. They then returned home, and the schools closed until the following fall. Few boys continued in school after age twelve, since higher education was available only to the wealthy. Most young girls were still educated at home. Academic training for young women was rare, though higher education was beginning to be available for a select few before the Civil War.

Americans still did not identify adolescence as a separate and distinct stage of life. The period of "youth" extended from the age of eight all the way to the middle twenties. Society attached no special significance to the teen-age years. Adult responsibilities continued to unfold gradually throughout life. During the era of the Second Awakening, young Protestants were expected to have a religious "awakening," which could create emotional turmoil. But beyond this spiritual upheaval, a stormy "identity crisis" was not normally part of growing up. Perhaps the main reason is that in a society with limited occupational choices and well-defined sex roles, young people had relatively little conflict about their futures. For the vast majority of girls the "proper" calling was marriage; for boys it was farming or the life of an artisan.

Women and the Family **297**

The nuclear family

Monogamy was rejected in this period by a few religious and communitarian groups. The establishment of polygamy as part of Mormonism was a major cause of the violent opposition that drove the Mormons to seek refuge in Utah. Their charismatic leader Brigham Young at one time had fifty-six wives. The Mormans officially renounced polygamy in 1890.

The Oneida Colony of John Humphrey Noyes in New York State practiced group marriage. Husbands, wives, and children were shared on the theory that all moral persons could partake of one another and that monogamy was out of date. At the other extreme, members of Shaker communities had no sexual relations at all.

But the nuclear family continued to have the unwavering support of the vast majority of Americans. As in colonial times they thought that the ideal way to achieve personal happiness and social stability was through conjugal love. Was the ideal followed in practice? Tocqueville seemed to think so when he characterized the family in America. He attributed much of the country's social stability to its family stability:

There is certainly no country in the world where the tie of marriage is more respected than in America or where conjugal happiness is more highly or worthily appreciated. When the American [male] retires from the turmoil of public life to the bosom of his family, he finds in it the image of order and of peace. There his pleasures are simple and natural, his joys are innocent and calm. . . . the American derives from his own home that love of order which he afterwards carries with him into public affairs.

Mrs. Kiah Sewall, married in 1836, poses with her five children. Although some communal groups and a few early feminists rejected conventional marriage, the nuclear family remained a strong force in America.

The First Wave of Feminism

The cult of true womanhood

By midcentury there existed in the American mind an ideal type of woman, a sort of "mother-priestess." She was widely celebrated in sermons and speeches and in magazines and novels. According to the "cult of true womanhood," a phrase used by historian Barbara Welter, the ideal woman had to display "four cardinal virtues." *Piety* could be expressed through her attendance at Sunday church services, home prayer, and missionary activities. Men who let their own religious devotions slide could then take comfort in the observances of their wives. *Chastity* for women was an important virtue, for it counteracted male sexuality, which was considered a dangerous and disruptive force in society. In the novels of the time the women always suffered if they lost their virginity. *Submissiveness* to male authority was deemed vital to femininity. In return, of course, the male was expected to protect the female. *Domesticity* was also essential. The good woman kept an orderly household and nursed her family through all manner of illness and turmoil. Domesticity also meant bearing children, preferably sons.

The American woman was expected to exert a proper moral influence on her family. She was not to worry her head about politics or business or other worldly affairs, but keep to her own sphere—the home. There she had both power and virtue, whereas men in their sphere, which included the rest of the world, had only power. As one historian has expressed it, "America depended upon her mothers to raise up a whole generation of Christian statesmen who could say, 'All that I am I owe to my angel mother.'"

Women's dress styles among the middle class emphasized this concept of femininity. The grown female was weighed down by pounds of petticoats and laced up in corsets with whalebone stays, and her long skirts trailed to the ground. This gave her the desired feminine look but interfered with some essential functions like breathing.

Legal and social handicaps

Courts in the first half of the nineteenth century enforced sexist rulings. The growing number of cases where judges ruled against women finally caused the "legal death" of a married woman in most states. The woman who married had to turn control of her property over to her husband. She legally forfeited her dowry as well as any earnings or property she might accumulate during marriage. The law imposed severe penalties upon her as a divorcee. In a divorce the husband, even if he was the most brutal child-beater, ordinarily kept the children. A woman could not sue or bear witness in court or serve on juries. And, of course, she could not vote. In some parts of Virginia and New Jersey women property owners retained the right to vote for thirty years after the Revolution, only to lose it during Jackson's era.

The right to abortion by free choice was withdrawn by New York State in 1828 and by most other states shortly afterward. The change was justified primarily on the grounds of protecting women, since ending a pregnancy through surgery or drugs often led to the mother's death. The introduction of antiseptic surgery revolutionized medical practice toward the end of the century. But state laws against abortion remained in effect until a Supreme Court ruling in 1973.

Women faced endless job handicaps. In factories they were paid a quarter to a half of what men received and were denied training for higher-paying skilled jobs. Any literate woman could become a teacher, but teaching paid very little. Except as teachers, women were not welcome in the professions. The practice of medicine was becoming more and more professional—and this by definition meant that women were excluded. Except among Quakers and Baptists, women could not become ministers.

One of the few professions that opened up to women around 1830 was that of popular novelist. The so-called domestic novels sold up to 100,000 copies yearly, and the dominant popular literature of the century was written *by* and *for* women. According to historian Russell Nye, domestic novels were often part of "women's undeclared war against a male-oriented society" and had an "anti-husband" bias.

Leading educators described the female brain as incapable of absorbing real education. They warned that mental strain would produce a physical collapse. Only in French, dancing, manners, or other subjects designed to make them more gracious wives and mothers was education for women considered generally acceptable. Being black and female was a double handicap. A Negro girl belonged to both an "inferior" race and a "weak" sex. And she was always poor. In the South it was a punishable offense to educate slaves of either sex. Even in the North very few schools accepted black girls as students.

Mary Wollstonecraft, the founding mother

Feminism is not confined to the United States any more than is male dominance. The Englishwoman Mary Wollstonecraft, author of *A Vindication of the Rights of Women* (1792), was the founding mother of the women's movement. Man placed woman on a pedestal, she wrote, but he made her vain, brainless, docile, and slavishly dependent— all this merely to boost his own ego. A rebel by any standard, Wollstonecraft attacked monogamy as the means by which men trapped women for their own purposes, took

their property, controlled their children, and, in some cases, despoiled them physically. After a stormy life, she died at the age of thirty-eight of complications following the birth of a daughter conceived out of wedlock. (This daughter, Mary Shelley, wrote *Frankenstein*.) Because Wollstonecraft attacked marriage itself, most people rejected her beliefs out of hand. Had she lived a generation later, her influence might have been greater. Nevertheless, her ideas greatly inspired feminists.

Pioneers in education for women

It took years for radical feminist ideas to percolate among American women. The movement first arose in a moderate way, and without fiery rhetoric, in the struggle to improve educational opportunities for women. The pioneer women educators were determined individuals but not radicals like Wollstonecraft. Emma Willard hoped to place education for young women on the same high plane as that for young men. She opened the Troy Female Seminary in 1821. Here she trained women as teachers, instructing them in science, mathematics, philosophy, and even the taboo subject of physiology. Mary Lyon established Mount Holyoke Female Seminary in 1837 and accepted girls on the basis of their potential for intellectual growth. The school offered them a systematic three-year course. Another pioneer in education for women was Prudence Crandall, a Quaker, who battled gallantly to keep her school for black girls in Canterbury, Connecticut. It was burned by vandals.

Oberlin in Ohio was the first coeducational college. Established in 1841, its doors were open to anyone, regardless of race, color, or sex. It was the first school to offer women courses like those for men at Harvard or other top colleges. Even so, the first coeds had to take a watered-down, "literary" program that would not "overtax" their brains.

Abolitionism, training for feminism

The organized movement for equal rights for women grew out of the abolitionist crusade and was sustained by the zeal of Quakers and other radical Protestants. Sarah and Angelina Grimké, daughters of a prominent South Carolina family, toured New England in 1837–1838 to speak on the horrors of slavery. They were among the first American women lecturers. People came from miles around to hear their eyewitness accounts of men and women flogged, of mothers separated from their children on the auction block, and of black women assaulted by white men.

The strongest organized opposition to the women's movement came from preachers. The Massachusetts Congregational clergy sternly warned the Grimkés to stop making speeches, especially about things "which ought not to be named." They urged them to remember that "the Power of Woman is in her dependence." In her *Letters on the Equality of the Sexes and the Condition of Woman* (1838), Sarah Grimké replied to the offended clergy in their terms. The Bible, she insisted, did *not* support any notion that a woman was inferior to a man. "To me it is perfectly clear *that whatsoever it is morally right for a man to do, it is morally right for a woman to do.*" Besides, men were poorly suited for religious instruction: "I have suffered too keenly from the teaching of man to lead anyone to him for instructions."

Of the 100,000 abolitionists enrolled in over 1,000 abolitionist societies, half were women. They served as conductors in the Underground Railroad. They petitioned Congress to repeal the fugitive slave laws. In so doing they collected signatures and funds, arranged meetings, defied public opinion, and sometimes dodged sheriffs' posses. Through these organizational activities they received grounding in political action.

Following the path of the Grimké sisters, Lucy Stone devoted herself to the twin causes—abolition and women's rights. One of seven children from a poor farm family but an Oberlin graduate and teacher, she became the most famous woman orator of her time. For years she lectured on abolition Saturdays and Sundays and on women's liberation the rest of the week. She gave a series of talks that dealt with sex discrimination in industry, the courts, politics, education, and religious life.

In 1840 Lucretia Mott was among the women who were refused seats at a world antislavery convention in London because of their sex. She was forced to watch the proceedings from the gallery. In London she met Elizabeth Cady Stanton, who was on her honeymoon. Discussing the convention incident, they concluded that slaves were not the only ones who needed liberation. Mott, a Quaker minister and an outspoken abolitionist, had greatly influenced the Grimké sisters. She also inspired Stanton to take up the cause of feminism as a full-time career.

In July 1848 Stanton organized the first feminist convention at Seneca Falls, New York. The meeting was held in a Methodist church and was chaired by Lucretia's husband, James Mott. The group issued a declaration which said, "The history of mankind is a history of repeated injuries . . . on the part of man toward woman, having in direct object the establishment of an absolute tyranny over her." This was followed by a list of grievances, as in the Declaration of Independence. In a surprise tactic and without the support of the other leaders, Stanton moved that the convention adopt a resolution proclaiming that women should be allowed to vote. Only because the noted black abolitionist Frederick Douglass supported it did the resolution squeak through.

Other training grounds

Women learned to organize not only in abolitionist activities, but also while working in church groups, labor unions, and the temperance movement. In most Protestant denominations women took an active part in sewing and discussion circles, missionary activities, and charities. Female factory workers occasionally organized to protest the fact that they earned lower wages than men for the same work and were barred from the skilled trades. The Lowell Female Labor Reform Association, led by Sarah Bagley, included six hundred members in several New England factory towns. Their strikes usually failed dismally, but a well-organized petition campaign brought about an official investigation of working conditions for women.

What Woman needs . . . is as a nature to grow, as an intellect to discern, as a soul to live freely. . . . We would have every arbitrary barrier thrown down. We would have every path laid open to Woman as well as to Man.

MARGARET FULLER (1810–1850)

Still other women, including the greatest feminine organizer of all, Susan B. Anthony (1820–1906), came to feminism from the temperance movement. Alcoholism was a growing problem in cities. Many factories paid their workers a part of their wages in whiskey. Many workers spent the rest of the wages in saloons before staggering home to their wives and children. Women saw liquor as a source of their degradation. Susan Anthony started out as a professional temperance reformer, but when the men in the movement showed their resentment, she left in disgust to put her energy into women's rights.

The most creative thinker of the feminist movement was Elizabeth Cady Stanton (1815–1902). She and Anthony worked closely together for many years and provided much of the drive, direction, and continuity for the movement. Stanton explained:

In writing, we did better work than either could alone. While Susan was slow and analytical in composition, I was rapid and synthetic. I am the better writer—she, the better critic. She supplied the facts and statistics—I, the philosophy, and together, we have made the arguments that have stood unshaken through the storm of long years— arguments that no one has answered. Our speeches may be considered the united product of our two brains.

In the 1840s American feminists began rereading Mary Wollstonecraft and producing their own essays based on the condition of the American woman. Following in the tradition of the English radical feminists, Margaret Fuller published *Woman in the Nineteenth Century* (1845), one of the most important books in America's feminist literature. Highly educated by an exacting father, Fuller taught in a girls' school, preceded Ralph Waldo Emerson as editor of the Transcendentalist journal, *The Dial*, and became literary critic for the New York *Tribune*. *Woman in the Nineteenth Century* stressed the need for women to become less dependent on men. Otherwise, Fuller felt, they would always remain children. She denied that women were inferior to men intellectually or physically: "Those who think the physical circumstances of Woman would make a part in the affairs of national government unsuitable are by no means those who think it impossible for Negresses to endure field work even during pregnancy, or for seamstresses to go through their killing labors." Fuller's opinions and writings made her the first American woman intellectual to be widely recognized and accepted.

Three radical women

Amelia Bloomer (1818–1894) published the first newspaper issued expressly for women. She called it *The Lily*. Her fame, however, rests chiefly in dress reform. For six or eight years she wore an outfit composed of a knee-length skirt over full pants gathered at the ankle, which were soon known everywhere as "bloomers." Wherever she went, this style created great excitement and brought her enormous audiences—including hecklers. She was trying to make the serious point that women's fashions, often designed by men to suit their own tastes, were too restrictive, often to the detriment of the health of those who wore them. Still, some of her contemporaries thought she did the feminist movement as much harm as good.

Very few feminists hoped to destroy marriage as such. Most of them had husbands and lived conventional, if hectic, lives. And many of the husbands supported their cause. Yet the feminists did challenge certain marital customs. When Lucy Stone married Henry Blackwell, she insisted on being called "Mrs. Stone," a defiant gesture that brought her a lifetime of ridicule. Both she and her husband signed a marriage contract, vowing "to recognize the wife as an independent, rational being." They agreed to break any law which brought the husband "an injurious and unnatural superiority." But few of the radical feminists indulged in "free love" or joined communal marriage experiments. The movement was intended mainly to help women gain control over their own property and earnings and gain better legal guardianship over their children. Voting also interested them, but women's suffrage did not become a central issue until later in the century.

Many black women were part of the movement, including the legendary Sojourner Truth (1797–1883). Born a slave in New York and forced to marry a man approved by her owner, Sojourner Truth was freed when the state abolished slavery. After participating in religious revivals, she became an active abolitionist and feminist. In 1851 she saved the day at a women's rights convention in Ohio, silencing hecklers and replying to a man who had belittled the weakness of women:

The man over there says women need to be helped into carriages and lifted over ditches, and

Sojourner Truth urged feminists of her time to action. At one of the first women's rights conventions she attended, in 1850, she declared, "If women want any rights more than they got, why don't they just take them and not be talking about it?"

to have the best place everywhere. Nobody ever helps me into carriages or over puddles, or gives me the best place—and ain't I a woman? . . . Look at my arm! I have ploughed and planted and gathered into barns, and no man could head me—and ain't I a woman? I could work as much and eat as much as a man—when I could get it—and bear the lash as well! And ain't I a woman? I have borne thirteen children, and seen most of 'em sold into slavery, and when I cried out with my mother's grief, none but Jesus heard me—and ain't I a woman?

Changing the image and the reality

The accomplishments of a few women who dared pursue professional careers had somewhat altered the image of the submissive and

Rose O'Neal Greenhow and her daughter, Rose, in prison. Greenhow, a Confederate spy, based herself in Washington during the first year of the Civil War and relayed secret military plans to the South. She was arrested and tried for treason but never revealed how she got her information. Exiled to the South, she continued to work for the Confederate cause. In 1864 she was shipwrecked and drowned while trying to smuggle gold through the Union naval blockade.

brainless child-woman. Maria Mitchell of Nantucket, whose father was an astronomer, discovered a comet at the age of twenty-eight. She became the first woman professor of astronomy in the U.S. (at Vassar in 1865). Mitchell was also the first woman elected to the American Academy of Arts and Sciences and a founder of the Association for the Advancement of Women. Elizabeth Blackwell applied to twenty-nine medical schools before she was accepted. She attended all classes, even anatomy class, despite the sneers of some male students. As a physician, she went on to make important contributions in sanitation and hygiene.

By about 1860 women had effected notable improvements in their status. Organized feminists had eliminated some of the worst legal disadvantages in fifteen states. The Civil War altered the role—and the image—of women even more drastically than the feminist movement did. As men went off to fight, women flocked into government clerical jobs. And they were accepted in teaching jobs as never before. Tens of thousands of women ran farms and businesses while the men were gone. Anna Howard Shaw, whose mother ran a pioneer farm, recalled:

It was an incessant struggle to keep our land, to pay our taxes, and to live. Calico was selling at fifty cents a yard. Coffee was one dollar a pound. There were no men left to grind our corn, to get in our crops, or to care for our livestock; and all around us we saw our struggle reflected in the lives of our neighbors.

Women took part in crucial relief efforts. The Sanitary Commission, the Union's volunteer nursing program and a forerunner of the Red Cross, owed much of its success to women. They raised millions of dollars for medicine, bandages, food, hospitals, relief camps, and convalescent homes.

North and South, black and white, many women served as nurses, some as spies and even as soldiers. Dorothea Dix, already famous as a reformer of prisons and insane asylums, became head of the Union army nurse corps. Clara Barton and "Mother" Bickerdyke saved thousands of lives by working close behind the front lines at Antietam, Chancellorsville, and Fredericksburg. Harriet Tubman led a party up the Combahee River to rescue 756 slaves. Late in life she was recognized for her heroic act by being granted a government pension of twenty dollars per month.

Southern white women suffered more from the disruptions of the Civil War than did their northern sisters. The proportion of men who went to war or were killed in battle was greater in the South. This made many women self-sufficient during the war. Still, there was hardly a whisper of feminism in the South.

The Civil War also brought women into the political limelight. Anna Dickson skyrocketed to fame as a Republican speaker, climaxing her career with an address to the House of Representatives on abolition. Stanton and Anthony formed the National Woman's Loyal League to press for a constitutional amendment banning slavery. With Anthony's genius for organization, the League in one year collected 400,000 signatures in favor of the Thirteenth Amendment.

Once abolition was finally assured in 1865, most feminists felt certain that suffrage would follow quickly. They believed that women had earned the vote by their patriotic wartime efforts. Besides, it appeared certain that black men would soon be allowed to vote. And once black men had the ballot in hand, how could anyone justify keeping it from white women—or black women? Any feminist who had predicted in 1865 that women would have to wait another fifty-five years for suffrage would have been called politically naive.

Review

Before industrialism most Americans were involved in family farming, and the family unit worked together to produce goods. This had a balancing effect on sex roles. Education and chores centered around the home. The situation began to change with the coming of industrialism and urbanism. Men and women found work in factories and mills, while children went to school or also worked in factories. The family was also affected by the rise of democratic ideals. Although more public education became available, it was aimed mainly at boys. Most girls continued to be taught at home. Adolescence was not recognized as a separate stage of life. As choices of work and life styles were limited, young people did not face an "identity crisis." In spite of changing conditions, the family stayed a strong and stable force in the life of the nation.

The women's movement started at a time when the home was considered the only proper sphere for a woman. American women were expected to marry and have children. Married women still had limited legal and civil rights. Working women were at a serious disadvantage in most job situations; this was especially true of black women. As girls received little formal schooling, education was the first target of those who wanted to improve the status of women. The organized feminist movement grew out of the experiences of women abolitionists like the Grimké sisters. Women also had learned much from their work in churches, unions, and the temperance movement. In 1848 Elizabeth Cady Stanton organized the first feminist convention. This meeting opened the campaign for women's suffrage. The enormous contributions and sacrifices made by women during the Civil War helped change their image as helpless creatures.

Questions

1. Describe both the positive and negative effects that the westward movement had on women. How did the growing mill and factory systems change women's lives?
2. In the early nineteenth century young people had fewer decisions to make about their lives and their work than they do today. Do you think this made life harder or easier for them? Why?
3. What traits did the ideal woman have, according to "the cult of true womanhood"?
4. How did the women's movement grow out of the abolition movement? What part did the churches play in the rise of feminism?

"Your joy and gladness to express,
Come forth and dance in holiness!"

Singing and dancing were important
aspects of worship among the
Shakers, who established several
successful religious communes in
America.

15

15

Glimpses of a Better World

The decline of small, intimate, face-to-face institutions like the tribe, clan, family, or peasant village seems to be a long-term trend in human history. It has been accompanied by the growth of larger, more impersonal forms of community life, such as the city, the metropolis, and the nation. Early nineteenth-century America, which was in the midst of geographic expansion, rapid industrial change, and urbanization, experienced this institutional change more rapidly than most countries. Some Americans pinned their hopes on the new and larger communities, while others wanted to stop the clock, or even turn it back, to recapture the lost innocence of the era before the Industrial Revolution. In 1825 De Witt Clinton, the progressive governor of New York, looked forward exuberantly to the time when "the whole island of Manhattan, covered with habitations and replenished with a dense population, will constitute one vast city." John Humphrey Noyes, the radical reformer, turned away from this vision of the city in order to "catch a glimpse of a better world" in a small utopian community. Those who dreamed of future greatness for the commune and for the city were both part of the American scene in pre-Civil War days, and each is worth understanding.

New Orleans, 1803.

Chicago Historical Society

Utopias

Shaping the perfect community

Between the Revolution and the Civil War one thousand new communities may have been founded in the United States. Of these one hundred or so were utopian communes — ideal communities based on a principle of fraternity. The most active period for commune building was before the Civil War, from 1840 to 1860. The motivation was comparable to that of the colonial Puritans, except that these nineteenth-century planners held a more optimistic view of human nature. They focused on the good in people, not the evil. Many sought to recapture the lost innocence of bygone eras: the spiritual fellowship of the early Christians or the communal spirit of the towns, monasteries, villages, and guilds of the Middle Ages. The utopians believed that the general welfare required an atmosphere of mutual love and concern. The notion of an enlarged family was fundamental. Most of the communities were agricultural, not industrial. In some cases the members formed joint-stock companies, but most owned their property in common.

The two basic varieties of utopian communes are the secular and the religious. The long history of religious communes includes the monasteries and convents of the Middle Ages and some of Christian sects of the Reformation, which themselves looked back to the Christian communes of the New Testament era. The Bible records: "And all that believed were together, and had all things common; And sold their possessions and goods, and parted them to all men, as every man had need" (Acts 2:44–45). The Amish, who came from Switzerland to Pennsylvania beginning in 1727, the Pietists, who established the Ephrata Cloister in Pennsylvania in the 1730s, and the Moravian Brethren at Bethlehem, Pennsylvania, in the 1740s all followed the primitive Christian ideal of communal sharing that sprang up during the Reformation. Most of the religious communities interpreted the Bible literally, believed that an ideal life could be attained on earth, and looked for a return of Christ.

The Shakers

"Virgin Purity, Christian Communism, Confession of Sin, and Separatism from the World" was the motto of the Shakers, a religious sect that established remarkably long-lasting communes. Their ritual included a dance in which they attempted to "shake away" sin through their fingertips. Visitors commented on the joyous but disciplined air of their celebrations. The Shakers were a persecuted English sect founded by Mother Ann Lee, who arrived in America during the Revolutionary War. In 1776 they established their first church in Watervliet, New York. Mother Ann decreed strict celibacy for her followers, both male and female. Members of the opposite sex never even talked to one another except when someone else was present. This extreme purity was necessary, they felt, because the millennium was at hand.

The Shakers grew most rapidly during the Second Awakening and were hardiest on the New York and New England frontier. They owned property communally. Since they were adept at farming and handicrafts, they had no trouble supporting themselves. Their furniture is eagerly sought to this day. At their height, between 1830 and 1840, the Shakers numbered six thousand members in eighteen villages scattered throughout the Northeast. They have lasted into the 1970s, although their members have dwindled in number to a handful.

We have built us a dome
On our beautiful plantation
And we all have one home
And one family relation.

ONEIDA SONG

Oneida Colony led by Noyes

The most radical and controversial utopian community was Oneida Colony in New York, founded in 1848 by John Humphrey Noyes and his group of "Perfectionists." The Perfectionists, who started as a Bible study group in Putney, Vermont, believed that "Christ demanded and promised perfection on earth." More than two hundred people belonged to the commune at its peak.

The Oneida Colony practiced what Noyes referred to as "complex marriage" and others called free love. In a pamphlet on *Slavery and Marriage* he explained that exclusiveness in a love relationship was un-Christian. He also held that marriage was particularly demeaning to women because it forced them into unwanted pregnancy and menial work. Oneida couples agreed to have a child only if "Father" Noyes and a central committee agreed that the pair would create a superior offspring. Children were raised communally rather than by their natural parents. Unwanted pregnancy was prevented by male continence.

A new colonist had to transfer all property and all money to the community. Even clothing was communally owned. After a shaky start at farming, the colony turned to manufacturing steel traps, which became standard in the fur trade throughout the United States and Canada. Travel bags and silverware (the Oneida trademark is still in circulation today) contributed to their earnings, which in 1864 exceeded $61,000. Committees ran the businesses, with the members assigned to jobs and rotating from year to year. Everyone worked, women and children as well as men,

and workers were organized into small groups or teams called "bees." Plays, concerts, operettas, and other communal activities filled leisure time. To erase the "sin of pride" which led to individualism and interfered with group spirit, Noyes invented a system of public confession and mutual criticism called "mortification of the self."

In effect the Oneidans broke completely with middle-class values. Noyes and his followers believed they had created a tiny bright spot in the world. "Turn your eye toward it when you are tired of looking into chaos," Noyes advised, "and you will catch a glimpse of a better world." Outsiders ridiculed and damned their sexual eccentricities and eventually forced an end to their utopian experiment. The group stopped practicing complex marriage, gave up communal ownership of property, and became a joint-stock company in 1881. John Humphrey Noyes, under prosecution for adultery, had already fled to Canada.

Other religious communes

A few religious communes started as a matter of convenience, rather than from deep moral or spiritual conviction. These were started by German Protestant pastors who led their flocks to America. Their fellow villagers who wanted to emigrate with these pastors pooled their money to pay the fare to America. When the arrangement worked in getting them here, they continued it. The unity of the German peasant village worked in favor of the immigrant commune. The Ephrata Cloister in Pennsylvania was going strong until the death of its dynamic leader, Johann Conrad Beissel, in 1786. Christian Metz led six hundred Inspirationists to Buffalo in 1843 to escape persecution in Germany. A short time later the group moved to Amana, Iowa, where they established a very successful communal society. They became famous for their fine woollen goods and fertile farms. A remnant of the Amana Society still exists there, having become a cooperative corporation in 1932.

One of the strongest religious communes was the Harmony Society that George Rapp brought from Germany at the beginning of the century. Located first in Pennsylvania, then in Indiana, the Society later moved back to Pennsylvania. Rapp's commune amassed holdings of several million dollars. The Harmony Society held property in common and encouraged, but did not demand, celibacy. The organization of this and most other religious communes was highly autocratic. Rapp would appear without warning from underground tunnels to check on his followers. In the 1840s a rival to Rapp persuaded some of the Harmony members to break with the founder, and the community began to fall apart.

Owen's New Harmony, a secular commune

The most important secular commune in American history may have been Robert Owen's New Harmony in Indiana, founded in 1825. Before coming to America Owen was already famous for establishing a model textile mill and industrial town in New Lanark, Scotland. Most mill owners sweated their workers, even women and children, twelve hours a day for the meanest wages and housed them in grim barracks. Owen worked his mill hands only eight hours a day, provided good housing, and ran free schools for the children. During the day workers were entertained by musicians, and they were encouraged to dance in their off hours. Nor did he dock them a day's wages if they came to work ten minutes late, which

An architect's drawing of New Harmony, as Robert Owen envisioned it would be, with living quarters and large public buildings enclosing botanical gardens. But this futuristic complex was never built; Owen and his followers used the houses, dormitories, factories, and farms established by the Rappites.

was customary at other mills. An organizing genius, Owen amassed a huge fortune and gave much of it away to philanthropic causes. He was invited to address Congress upon his arrival in America. Before an enthusiastic audience that included President James Monroe, he outlined his objectives: "Make a man happy and you make him virtuous—this is the whole of my system. To make him happy, I enlighten his mind and occupy his hands, and I have so managed the art of instruction that individuals seek it as an amusement."

Like many seekers, Owen picked America for his cooperative experiment because it was a new and unspoiled country. He had purchased the Harmony Society colony in Indiana from George Rapp, staking four fifths of his fortune to do so. When he arrived at New Harmony on the banks of the Wabash River in the spring of 1825, the Rappites had already departed and eight hundred new colonists were waiting for him. The next year, on the fiftieth anniversary of the Declaration of Independence, Owen ended his personal ownership of New Harmony and turned over control of the colony to a series of committees. These groups took over the village with its regular streets and public buildings, hundreds of acres of improved land (out of a total thirty thousand acres), and orchards and vineyards. The machinery was there for making textiles, pottery, hats, boots, soap, candles, glue, and other products.

The project foundered almost at once. Owen's "Declaration of Mental Independence" on July 4th condemned not only private property but organized religion and marriage as well. This caused an immediate falloff in membership and public support. Also, no effort had been made to screen the Harmony colonists. Membership was on a come-one-come-all basis, which, as Owen's son wrote, drew a "collection of radicals, enthusiastic devotees to principle, honest lat-itudinarians and lazy theorists, with a sprinkling of unprincipled sharpers thrown in." Many gifted people were interlaced with a great deal of deadwood. Everyone enjoyed the lectures, the schooling, and the discussions, but the work projects went nowhere. Owen substituted one plan after another and then left to visit Britain before the colony's economic system had jelled. In his presence the wheels turned; in his absence they stopped. He never solved the dilemma of how to mold a cooperative society from a collection of individuals. Trying to avoid the taint of atheism and free love, splinter groups founded eighteen other Owenite colonies, but each collapsed in turn. The entire Owenite movement disappeared by 1830.

Robert Owen was a pioneer Socialist. Karl Marx considered him a "utopian" predecessor of his own more "scientific" brand of socialism. To this day the British labor movement and the cooperative movement revere his memory. In this country other utopian colonists regarded him highly.

Fourier and Brook Farm

A French Socialist philosopher, Charles Fourier, inspired the next wave of secular utopias in the 1840s. Where Owen had attempted through trial and error to find a practical formula for communal living, Fourier believed that he had discovered universal laws of human behavior which, when applied to communes, would put an end to competition, exploitation, and poverty. He theorized that people were driven by twelve basic senses and feelings: sight, sound, smell, touch, taste, love, hate, etc. These senses could be harmonized if people lived in "phalanxes," each consisting of 1,620 persons living on 5,000 acres devoted to farming and handicrafts. Fourier suggested that these groups cooperate in their buying, cooking, and housing. The colonies would be organized as joint-stock companies. Forty communes were formed in the U.S. more or less according to Fourier's notions, but the Fourierist movement declined after 1850.

George Ripley's Brook Farm, located nine miles from Boston, was not originally a Fourierist enterprise. Ripley, a Unitarian minister, and his wife put their whole fortune into a joint-stock community in which intellectuals and laborers would be united. There, each person could develop his or her talents fully. An "infant school" for children up to six years of age, an elementary school, and an academy were run by gifted teachers, who taught everything from the classics to manual skills. Pupil-teacher rapport was remarkable in this first American experiment in progressive education. Music by Mozart and Beethoven was performed for the first time in America at Brook Farm. Work was interspersed with play. Emerson, who was cool to collectivism, complimented Brook Farm by calling it a "perpetual picnic, a French Revolution in small, an Age of Reason in a patty-pan." Other Transcendentalists, including Margaret Fuller, supported the experiment. At its peak Brook Farm had about one hundred colonists, some of whom actually lived in Boston and commuted to the colony.

Brook Farm deserves high marks for developing human talent but not for practical management. Disorganization ran the fields and shops into the ground. The Brook Farm Association finally converted to Fourier's theories, but this did not help. The colony closed in 1847 after a disastrous fire. Nathaniel Hawthorne used Brook Farm as a background for his novel *The Blithedale Romance*, in which the main character seeks refuge in Boston from the pressures of communal living.

Although many religious communes operated for over a generation, none of the secular ones lasted that long. Modern Times, an anarchist commune founded on Long Island

I looked at everything with eyes of enthusiasm; and, for a time, the life there was wonderfully pleasant and hopeful to me. This, I think, is the common experience of intelligent and well-disposed persons who have joined the Brook Farm or other reputable community.

ROBERT OWEN (1771–1858)
On his first visit to Harmony

by Josiah Warren, who hoped to substitute a system of labor credits for money, lasted for fifteen years (1851–1866). Nashoba, in Tennessee, a communal experiment established by the radical Frances Wright and intended for ex-slaves, was short-lived. Of the one hundred or so communes established between the Revolutionary War and the Civil War only about a dozen lasted more than sixteen years. The average life span was less than four years. Those that survived probably benefitted most from having a system of shared work and belief, as well as strong personal leadership. Austere living and isolation—or perhaps persecution from the outside—also helped preserve some of the more durable communes.

The vast majority of Americans remained untouched by the utopians' efforts to reform society. Jacksonian equality created a favorable climate for communes, but the goal of individual success won out. High wages, cheap land, and Manifest Destiny had more appeal for most Americans than communal sharing. Other reform movements—abolition, temperance, the labor movement, and women's rights—competed with the communes for many of the same idealistic people. For each of these causes there were voluntary groups at work. At the same time, hundreds of conventional new communities were being formed. These new towns occupied the time and energy of most Americans.

The City: What Price "Progress"?

New York City in the lead

The proportion of urbanized Americans quadrupled between 1790 and 1860, rising from about 5 percent in 1790 to 9 percent in 1820 and to almost 20 percent in 1860. On the eve of the Civil War over 6 million Americans were urbanites, and the country had some 390 towns each with over 2500 people. Nine cities surpassed 100,000 in population, two exceeded 500,000, and the two separate cities of New York and Brooklyn created one metropolitan center that topped the million mark.

New York City nosed out Philadelphia in the early nineteenth century to become America's largest and most important city. Geography alone did not explain its supremacy, for New York's harbor and access to inland areas were little better than those of Boston, Philadelphia, Baltimore, or Norfolk. More significant was a series of brilliant and timely business innovations undertaken by the city's financiers and shippers.

First, they decided on a system of auctioning off imported goods, thereby eliminating several groups of middlemen. Auctions meant drastic discounts to wholesale buyers, so that merchants from all over the nation flocked to lower Manhattan to trade. Second,

New Yorkers set up the first *scheduled* transatlantic shipping lines. From 1818 the square-rigged packet boats of the Black Ball Line shuttled to and from Liverpool like clockwork, in raging blizzards or balmy weather, assuring the patronage of prime customers. Scheduled lines also served coastal ports. Third, they created the Erie Canal. Completed in 1825, it stimulated New York's growth by carrying farm produce from the Great Lakes region directly into lower Manhattan, where most of it was tagged, crated, and shipped off to Europe. Fourth, the city's financiers loaned money to southern planters and bought or insured their overseas cotton shipments. This made Manhattan the countinghouse of the cotton kingdom. Also, they extended credit to Latin American merchants who shipped goods to New York. And finally, New Yorkers dominated coastal shipping all the way to New Orleans. Thus New York City became, as one local booster explained, "the place where Capital and Brains, Import and Export, Buyer and Seller, . . . meet for exchange." New York's nearest rivals, Philadelphia, Boston, and Baltimore, failed in their attempts to break New York's commercial supremacy.

The city's population reached 200,000 in 1830 and four times that at the end of the Civil War. In 1864 alone over 200,000 immigrants debarked there. Most of them stayed in New York, moving into lower Manhattan. Real estate values skyrocketed. By 1865 the city had 15 daily newspapers, 10 public libraries, 400 churches, 5000 inns and hotels, 200 miles of paved streets, 800 miles of gas pipes, and 176 miles of sewers. No fewer than 20,000 horse-drawn vehicles jammed Broadway each day. Fourteen railroad lines and twenty ferry lines radiated out from Manhattan Island.

THE INCREASE IN CITIES, 1790–1860

Population of cities	1790	1800	1810	1820	1830	1840	1850	1860
500,000 to 1,000,000	—	—	—	—	—	—	1	2
250,000 to 500,000	—	—	—	—	—	1	—	1
100,000 to 250,000	—	—	—	1	1	2	5	6
50,000 to 100,000	—	1	2	2	3	2	4	7
25,000 to 50,000	2	2	2	2	3	7	16	19
10,000 to 25,000	3	3	7	8	16	25	36	58
5,000 to 10,000	7	15	17	22	33	48	85	136
2,500 to 5,000	12	12	18	26	34	46	89	163

SOURCE: *Historical Statistics of the United States, Colonial Times to 1957* (Washington, D.C., 1960), p. 14.

Many well-to-do New Yorkers moved to suburbs like Brooklyn Heights (shown in the foreground of this 1837 engraving), in the neighboring city of Brooklyn. In the distance, across the East River, is New York City, from Wall Street to Canal Street.

Washington as a planned capital

For about six decades after it was founded in 1781, Washington, D.C., struggled to live up to its role as the nation's capital. It was the federal government's only venture into city-making. Major Pierre L'Enfant, a gifted French engineer who had served on General Washington's staff, did his best to transform the malarial swamp, pawned off by land speculators, into a capital. His official plan placed the Capitol building on a hill overlooking the distant Potomac, with a view of the president's house. It called for many parks and monuments and long, wide boulevards for parades and public celebrations. Charles Dickens, who visited Washington, gave it a friendly ribbing when he called it

"the City of Magnificent Intentions." A more cynical newspaperman in 1861 saw it as "a great, little, splendid, mean, extravagant, poverty-stricken barrack for soldiers of fortune and votaries of folly."

Nevertheless, Washington was the administrative center of the nation, and it came to life during the Civil War. The city's population rose from 40,000 in 1850 to 200,000 by the summer of 1863. Officials, clerks, soldiers, lobbyists, contractors, and foreign diplomats crammed into the overflowing boarding-houses, hotels, bars, and restaurants. Construction derricks pierced the sky on every horizon. The completed Capitol dome was a source of national pride, but the Washington Monument stood only half finished.

A quieter pace in southern cities

Cities grew more slowly in the South than in the Northeast. In 1860 only 7 percent of southerners were urbanized as compared to 20 percent of the nation's population as a whole. Southern spokesmen often boasted of the superiority of rural life to urban living. Said one editor approvingly, the southerner "turns . . . from the bustle of cities . . . to the quiet and peaceful scenes of country life."

Lack of railroad track was a major drawback. While 21,000 miles of iron rails crisscrossed the Northeast and Midwest by the 1850s, only 9000 were laid in the South. Industrial development was also slower in the South than in the North. A cotton factory at Graniteville, South Carolina, employed nine hundred people in 1859, and Richmond and a few other cities had important mills. But so much of the South's capital was invested in slaves and land that the growth of factories, railroads, and cities was limited.

A handful of southern editors cursed the South's "cotton snobs" for preventing diversification in the South. These "aristocrats," critics said, were letting Charleston, Savannah, Mobile, and New Orleans stagnate while the merchants of northern port cities monopolized the carrying trade. But their message fell on deaf ears until about 1860, when it was used as an argument for secession. As a Charleston newspaper noted in 1860: "There are no people in the southern states who will gain so certainly by a dissolution of the Union as the merchants and mechanics of our city. At present Norfolk, Charleston, Savannah and Mobile are but suburbs of New York, Philadelphia and Boston."

A conspicuous feature of southern cities, especially to foreign visitors, was the number of blacks, both slave and free, who lived in them. With 28,000 Negroes, Baltimore had the largest black population of any U.S. city.

By custom, urban slaves could take jobs and keep some of their wages. Their personal lives were somewhat less restricted than those of plantation slaves. "City air makes free men" was a phrase applied to them.

Charleston, with its charm and grace, was the sentimental favorite of the Old South. As the cotton empire moved inland, Charleston's growth rate slowed, and the value of goods produced or shipped there fell. Baltimore followed a similar pattern. Meantime, life in Memphis, Louisville, and other inland cities quickened. New Orleans, the only southern city with over 100,000 people, appeared to European visitors the most sophisticated city in the country.

The Civil War brought an early flurry of prosperity to southern cities but in the end ruined them. The South's major railhead, Atlanta, along with Columbia and Charleston in South Carolina and Richmond in Virginia, were leveled by fire and shelling in the final months of fighting.

The urban frontier

Contrary to myth, it was the towns rather than the farms that spearheaded the westward movement. New towns often appeared sooner than new farm areas and helped stimulate growth on the western frontier. Many towns started as forts during the Indian fur trade or as speculative ventures. It was the towns that acquired the capital, railroads, canals, mills, shops, social amenities, and political leverage that built the West.

Land speculation in the West developed into a high art, especially in the early 1830s, a time of rapid expansion of canals, railroads, and turnpikes. Speculators sold urban home lots to easterners through cleverly designed propaganda. Maps and brochures pictured parks, railroads, canals, colleges, hotels, churches, and impressive boulevards with names like Broadway and Wall Street, when the real town may have been a few shacks

A wagon train in camp formation on a Denver street in the 1860s. John Simpson Smith and his Sioux Indian wife were the first to build their home on the site of Denver, in 1857. Other settlers from Georgia and Kansas came to the area the following year and established four small communities, out of which Denver grew. After a slow start, Denver became a boom town in the late 1870s and 1880s, when rich silver strikes were made nearby.

scattered over a stump-ridden clearing. Some easterners sank their modest savings into such towns, sight unseen, and were wiped out in the crash of 1837. Hundreds of towns shown on speculators' maps never materialized at all.

A handful of inland cities were beginning to prosper by 1830. St. Louis with 6000 residents was the base for the Rocky Mountain fur trade and the center of commerce for the upper Mississippi region. Cincinnati, founded in 1788 on the great bend of the Ohio River, had 25,000 people by 1830 and aspired to the title "Queen City of the West." Pittsburgh, the home of 12,000, already pulsated with the sounds of foundries, mills, and distilleries.

Not all frontier towns thrived the way their founders planned. Some quickly perished while others prospered for a time but then stopped growing. Lexington, Kentucky, started out smartly but lost its footing in the depression following the War of 1812. A landlocked city, Lexington's trade slipped away to Louisville, situated at a strategic spot for steamboat travel.

After 1830 western towns grew faster than any others. Rochester, Buffalo, Cleveland, Detroit, Chicago, and Milwaukee doubled their populations in two successive census counts. Most phenomenal was the rise of Chicago. A former fur trading post known to the Indians as "Stinking Onions," it had a population of 40 in 1830. Twenty-five years later there were 60,000 residents. Lots that sold for $75 in 1833 brought a whopping $7500 in 1837. A *daily* 25 percent increase in real estate values was not unusual that year.

Street vendors were a common sight in New York and other cities. The drawings on these two pages were done around 1840 and show a root beer seller, a boot cleaner, and a butcher.

Then the bubble burst, but the city recovered. Its meat-packing and flour-milling industries thrived in the 1840s, providing freight for the rail lines that spread out in all directions. By the Civil War Chicago, with 109,000 people, was the most promising rail hub in mid-America.

In the Far West San Francisco took a commanding lead after the gold discovery in 1848. Salt Lake City, Portland, Seattle, and Los Angeles remained villages when San Francisco became a metropolis. In only four months during 1849, the city's population zoomed from 6,000 to 40,000. The harbor was a forest of masts, as ships arrived from all parts of the world. When the Sierra gold-rush fever subsided in the mid-1850s, even richer discoveries of silver and gold were made at the Comstock Lode in Nevada. Through their investments in Nevada mines, San Francisco's speculators and financiers managed to capture much of Nevada's wealth. The completion in 1869 of the first transcontinental railroad to Sacramento, across San Francisco Bay, further stimulated the city's growth and prosperity.

The perils of city living

As America's cities grew larger, slums developed. Poverty and overcrowding bred crime, vice, violence, and other forms of social disruption. The worst conditions were associated with tenements—barrackslike apartment buildings constructed in the heart of town to house immigrant workers near their jobs. At 36 Cherry Street in New York City a five-story wooden tenement housed five hundred people in two-room apartments without running water or heat. When remodeled after ten years to include basement toilets, the building sheltered eight hundred people. In 1864 about five out of every eight people in Manhattan lived in tenements of various sizes and shapes. Some had such picturesque names as "Brickbat Mansion" and "Gates of Hell." Epidemics raged through the cities. Yellow fever, typhus, typhoid fever, and cholera were recurring menaces, and tuberculosis was a chronic threat. The germ theory of disease was not yet known, and a public health program hardly existed.

The slums spurred a heavy increase in crime and street disturbances. The 1830s began a period of "sustained urban rioting, particularly in the great cities of the Northeast." Gamblers, thieves, holdup men, prostitutes, pimps, and arsonists freely roamed the streets. New York City's Five Points district was crowded with rival gangs—the "Forty Thieves," "Shirttails," "Plug-uglies" (named for their bowler hats stuffed with wool and leather and worn as helmets), "Buckaroos," "Hookers," "Daybreak Boys," "Swamp Angels," and the notorious "Slaughter House Gang." In their periodic wars gang members hurled bricks and stones, fired pistols, and swung brass knuckles, clubs, and bottles. They broke windows, tipped over wagons, demolished fences, and injured and killed innocent bystanders as well as each other. Riots of all kinds broke out—food riots, bank riots, labor riots, election riots, antiabolitionist riots, anti-Negro riots, antirailroad riots, anti-Catholic riots, anti-German riots, antidraft riots, and even riots between rival groups of volunteer firemen.

City government, molded in the eighteenth century, was simply incapable of handling the disorder and violence. For one thing, the police were often part of the problem. A typical police force was untrained, underpaid, understaffed, and politically chosen. The first professional city police force was organized in Boston in 1838 in the aftermath of a riot between volunteer firemen and Irish immigrants. Still, in 1857 in New York City the mayor's own police fought a pitched battle with a metropolitan police squad. Since the men refused to wear uniforms, which suggested European autocracy, it was easy for them to melt into the mob and disappear at the first sign of a riot.

Competition in the arts

While the cities harbored the poor in grim-looking tenements, they also sheltered the rich in splendid mansions. Impressive brick residences costing from $50,000 to $200,000 lined New York's Fifth Avenue, as well as comparable boulevards in all major cities.

The wealthier or leisured classes of the cities often took the lead in developing local

cultural institutions. Academies of fine arts and of natural sciences, as well as private and public museums, were increasingly patronized by literate city dwellers. Bookstores and public or subscription libraries also had a following in the larger cities. Lyceums (lecture halls) were popular even in the smaller ones. Halls for the performance of plays, concerts, and operas were constructed in many big cities.

Newspaper editors boosted local cultural events. Each city tried to outdo the next in the arts. Jenny Lind, the "Swedish Nightingale," made 150 appearances around the country under the management of showman P. T. Barnum and earned one thousand dollars a performance. The Swedish violinist Ole Bull, the actors Edwin Booth and Edwin Forrest, and the most popular entertainer of all, Fanny Kemble, were among the super stars of the period. In 1849 rival gangs championing actors Forrest and William Charles Macready clashed on Astor Place in New York in a riot that killed twenty-two people.

Conflicting opinions on cities

American intellectuals, starting with Jefferson, have generally taken a dim view of cities. Jefferson disliked what he had seen of the crowded and ugly slums of Paris and London. He believed (as did most learned people of that time) that city air was unhealthy, a consequence of "miasmas," or noxious clouds that originated in filthy rivers and caused epidemic diseases like yellow fever. Jefferson also subscribed to the widely held belief that rural life was morally superior. In *Notes on Virginia* (1784) he declared, "The mobs of great cities add just so much to the support of pure government as sores do to the strength of the human body." Writing from his Virginia plantation at eighty years of age, he criticized New York and London as offering "all the depravities of human nature," while in rural Virginia "crime is scarcely heard of, breaches of order rare, and our societies, if not refined, are rational, moral and affectionate at least." Jefferson did temper his opinion somewhat during the War of 1812 when he saw that factory towns helped the country's economy, but he never became an enthusiastic supporter of cities.

Emerson, Melville, Poe, Thoreau, Hawthorne, and other authors of the Romantic era tended to agree with Jefferson. They linked small towns with America's lost innocence, and cities with depravity. Emerson's favorite place was the village. Thoreau liked the woods but made his home base near the village common. Hawthorne's major characters often came from cities but were always uncomfortable there because their environment was unnatural and impermanent. He once wrote, "All towns should be made capable of purification by fire or decay within each half century." Poe detested New York's commercialism and readiness to sacrifice trees, cliffs, and stately old mansions for wharves and warehouses. Of booming Brooklyn he said, "I know few towns which inspire me with so great disgust and contempt."

The clergy shared the writers' disapproving view of cities. References to Sodom and Gomorrah popped up regularly in their sermons about urban life. One preacher declared, "The most unnatural fashions and habits, the strangest eccentricities of intellect, the wildest and most pernicious in so-cial morals, and the most appalling and incurable barbarism, are the legitimate growth of city life."

It would be false to say that all American intellectuals were uniformly hostile to cities. While working among the poor, the Unitarian ministers Joseph Tuckerman and William Ellery Channing concluded that "the great cities need not be haunts of vice and poverty" and that the "purest and highest religious and moral influences could be found there." To them the city demonstrated both the worst and the best of human nature.

City politicians in the Jacksonian age, looking for votes wherever they could find them, were among the first public figures to proclaim the positive potential of cities. A radical Jacksonian, Amasa Walker, asserted that "great cities are not *necessarily* . . . 'great sores.'" They could also be "great fountains of healthful moral influence." Nor did the common people completely share the negative views of the Romantic writers. Most people were too optimistic — too willing to find the good mixed in with the bad.

City boosterism was popular in nineteenth-century America. The very commercialism that annoyed Poe was exciting to many people. Westerners especially favored cities, particularly those of the future that might grace their own region. William Gilpin, a western explorer, speculator, and politician, believed that one great city would rise in mid-America that would outshine all others. "The Great Basin of the Mississippi is the amphitheatre of the world . . . the most magnificent dwelling marked out by God for man's abode." A study of geography convinced him that the great city would be located on the Missouri River and that its glory would rival that of Jerusalem or Constantinople.

Westerners were not the only optimists. New York Governor De Witt Clinton, in promoting the "Big Ditch" (Erie Canal), prophesied that New York will, in course of time become the granary of the world, the emporium of commerce, the seat of manufactures, the focus of great moneyed operations, and the concentrating point of vast, disposable, and accumulating capitals, which will stimulate, enliven, extend, and reward the exertions of human labour and ingenuity. . . . And, before the revolution of a century, the whole island of Manhattan, covered with habitations and replenished with a dense population, will constitute one vast city.

Here was a vision of the future that most Americans probably found appealing at the time.

Review

Some of those who reacted against the country's rapid modernization sought to create utopian communities. The goal of most communes was to foster mutual care and cooperation, much in the manner of an extended family. These groups were mainly agricultural, and most owned their property in common. The two basic forms of communes were the religious and the secular; both tried to achieve perfection on earth. Most utopian communes were short-lived, but the religious ones tended to survive longer than the secular.

In 1830 only one tenth of the population lived in cities. By 1860 the percentage had risen sharply, due in part to immigration. The New York-Brooklyn metropolis with a million residents was the nation's largest urban area and its most important shipping center. The South remained more rural than the North. Southern cities, in a region of few railroads, little industry, and a slave economy, grew more slowly, although New Orleans was considered a sophisticated port city. Inland, as far west as the Mississippi, towns developed quickly. Chicago's rise was the most spectacular of all. In the Far West San Francisco boomed with the gold rush.

Cities seemed to contain the worst and the best in America. They produced slums, overcrowding, crime, violence, and epidemic disease. But they also produced libraries, museums, universities, and newspapers and introduced the arts in the United States. Many American intellectuals, and most clergymen, took a dim view of cities. In the Jacksonian era it was politicians and westerners who felt most optimistic about the city's future.

Questions

1. What differences and similarities can you find between New Harmony Colony and Oneida Colony?
2. What features helped ensure a commune's success? Why did some communes fail?
3. Explain the swift growth of eastern and frontier cities. Why did southern cities develop more slowly?
4. Describe some of the problems that accompanied the growth of cities.
5. Choose one of the following statements and develop arguments to support it based on what you've read in this chapter. (a) Rural living is better than urban living because the city is a place of crime, corruption, and frustration. (b) Urban life is better than rural life because the city offers more variety and opportunity for human growth and understanding.

Junction of the Yellowstone and Missouri rivers.

If the cause of the happiness
of this country was examined
into, it would be found to
arise as much from the great
plenty of land in proportion
to the inhabitants . . . as
from the wisdom of their
political institutions.

ALBERT GALLATIN   (1761 – 1849)
Diplomat and financier

16

16

The Fairest Portion of the Earth

In the first half of the nineteenth century the United States was still mostly wilderness—forests, prairies, deserts, and mountains—girded by farms, towns, and cities. Open land beckoned settlers to the West. Fuels and building materials were plentiful and cheap. Much of the wilderness was publicly owned and destined to pass into private hands. Those who penetrated the wilds—fur trappers and traders, pioneer farmers, miners, land speculators—gave little thought to the future of resources or of wilderness. They were too busy, as Tocqueville noted, "draining swamps, turning the course of rivers, peopling solitudes, and subduing nature." But as the forests were cut back, a tiny chorus of nature lovers was heard opposing the mindless destruction of the wilderness. With hindsight it is possible to fault the early Americans for squandering the land and its resources (and for destroying the native peoples who occupied the land), but at this juncture perhaps it is best simply to note that the pioneers who conquered the wilderness and those who tried to save the pieces were both in the American grain.

Prairie scene, Indiana.

The Wilderness as Public Resource

Abundance belies Malthus' theory

In 1798 the English preacher and political economist Thomas Malthus calculated that the world's population would someday outstrip its food supply. This would happen because human sexual passion was limitless, while the ability to grow food was limited. Or to put it more precisely, population tends to increase geometrically (like the series 2, 4, 16, 256), while the food supply tends to increase arithmetically (1, 2, 3, 4, 5). Eventually, when the competition for food became great enough, famine and warfare would occur on a grand scale, until population again dropped off. Although Malthus' prophecy haunts the twentieth century, most Americans who encountered it in the 1800s dismissed it as irrelevant. Their country possessed rich soil, green forests teeming with wildlife, and seemingly endless space for farms and settlements. As Lincoln said in the 1830s, "We find ourselves in the peaceful possession of the fairest portion of the earth, as regards extent of territory, fertility of soil, and salubrity of climate."

Even though the nation's population had doubled about every twenty-five years since colonial times, Americans had plenty of elbow room. Malthus himself admitted that the United States had the most favorable people-to-land ratio of any major nation. In 1790 population density in the U.S. averaged 4.5 persons per square mile. Before the Louisiana Purchase Jefferson said confidently that the country had "room enough for our descendants to the thousandth . . . generation." With the addition of the Louisiana Territory the U.S. land area more than doubled, lowering still further the density of population. Territory added during the next half century brought the figure to 1.9 billion acres for 31.5 million people by 1860, a ratio of roughly sixty to one. Those concerned with population pressure in the early nineteenth century were assured that the frontier offered a safety valve that would be good for decades to come.

Beginning with the Lewis and Clark expedition (1804–1806) and continuing almost to the end of the century, Americans luxuriated in the immensity of their nation, with its vast natural resources and public land. Over half of America's nearly two billion acres was in the public domain in 1853. Small wonder that Americans put their faith in the abundance surrounding them and not in Malthus' grim prophecy.

The impact of the lumber industry

Already a timber-rich country in colonial times, America's forest resources became even greater in the first half of the century with the addition of lands around the Great Lakes, in the Rocky Mountains, and in the Far West. Timber for fuel and fencing, for construction and tools, and for numerous household uses was readily available in most parts of the country. Only the Great Plains region beyond the Mississippi and the southwestern desert were largely devoid of lumber. Today most people would agree that the *reduction* of forest land is an inevitable feature of the spread of civilization. They would probably also agree that the indiscriminate *elimination* of forests impoverishes society. In the nineteenth century the superabundance of timber in the United States made it hard to see the truth of this idea, and the cutting was often careless and wasteful.

The most far-reaching ecological shifts were taking place in the eastern forests. Here occurred the first systematic ungreening of America. The lumber industry became better

Balloon-frame houses were easy to assemble, requiring no more than a hammer, saw, nails—and a good supply of lumber. Resulting in part from the invention of techniques for the mass-production of nails, the balloon frame was invented in Chicago in 1833. It quickly spread throughout the Midwest and later over the nation as a whole.

organized and more methodical, attacking first Maine, then upper New York State, and later the Great Lakes region. The broad axes of the lumberjacks had felled the choicest hardwoods along the East Coast by the time of the War of 1812. Twenty years later they had stripped Maine and New York of their best spruce and pine forests. Many lumberjacks were farm boys making extra money in the "pineries" during the winter. Their cry was, "Let a little light into the swamp!" Trees crashed down, opening land for farms and supplying timber for export, for paper mills, for ships, and, most important, for the building industry.

In the early nineteenth century the "balloon-frame" method of house construction came into general use. House carpenters no longer had to hew heavy posts and beams,

lift them into place, and join them. Instead they created a cage of two-by-four lumber with studs spaced sixteen inches apart and fastened by nails. This type of construction was easier and faster—and a boon for growing cities—but it required more wood than the old method.

U.S. lumber production was 850 million board feet in 1829 and rose tenfold in the next thirty years. William Bingham of Philadelphia purchased two million acres of Maine woods for two and a half cents an acre and made a handsome fortune. He typified the new breed of timber barons. When most of Maine's white pine had vanished into the sawmills, the lumberjacks shouldered their axes and headed west for Michigan and Wisconsin. Large segments of the original forests remained and made a second-growth comeback within fifty years. But so much of the highly prized white pine had been cut the first time around that it would not grow again.

Fur companies and mountain men

After the Lewis and Clark expedition and the War of 1812 the American fur business shifted westward, centering its activity in the Rocky Mountains. Like the lumber industry, the fur trade became more methodical than it had been in the previous centuries, and the destruction of wildlife was probably therefore greater. Competition was keen among American fur companies and between the Americans and the British Canadians. In some parts of North America the fur companies deliberately killed all the furbearing animals they could. In the Utah-Idaho-Oregon region the Hudson's Bay Company tried to "keep the country closely hunted" so as to create a "Fur Desert" and thereby beat out the American competition. In 1805 the Northwest Company of Canada shipped to Europe the pelts of 77,500 beaver, •51,033 muskrat, and 40,440 marten, along with 1,135 buffalo hides. The yield of American fur companies in the next years was comparable.

John Jacob Astor's American Fur Company, which just about monopolized the fur trade between 1812 and 1840, organized the fur business to perfection. Controlling his operation from New York and from Europe, Astor became the first American millionaire.

The new Rocky Mountain fur business, headquartered in St. Louis, was conducted in the field largely by white trappers (many of them were actually of racially mixed background) instead of by Indians, as in colonial times. These mountain men used superior traps made of iron. The baited beaver trap was set under water and drowned any animal caught in it. The trappers considered six dollars a pelt a fair price. They gathered

yearly in June and July at prearranged locations in the Rockies known as rendezvous, which proved to be a highly efficient method for collecting furs and shipping them to market, sometimes as far away as Europe. Having been paid for their yearly hauls, the trappers turned the rendezvous into an orgy of gambling, brawling, and lustful encounters with Indian women.

The tough, buckskin-clad mountain men knew the western wilderness better than any whites before or since. On various trapping expeditions between 1826 and 1836 Jedediah Smith traveled farther and saw more of North America than Lewis and Clark had. Kit Carson became a legend in his own time. Hundreds of other mountain men were known for amazing exploits.

In the life of a mountain man a broken twig, a cut-off birdcall, or an unusual smell might signify mortal danger. Like the Indians whom they frequently fought, trappers were constantly attuned to nature's ways. Their self-discipline and rugged individualism, their endurance of physical hardship, and their incredible bravery have long appealed to the American imagination. It was true, however, that they used their skills primarily to decimate fur animals—and, quite often, Indians. By the time beaver hats went out of fashion in the 1840s, beaver was almost extinct in many parts of the country. Fur companies began shifting their attention to buffalo skins and robes.

Whale hunting and an early fuel crisis

Like fur trappers, whalers also hunted their prey relentlessly and without regard for preserving the species. At midcentury whaling was second only to cotton weaving as Massachusetts' leading industry. In 1846, 740 whaling ships, employing 20,000 men, sailed out from New Bedford and Nantucket and from lesser whaling ports such as New London and Sag Harbor. (The hardships and adventures of the whale hunt were described in a classic American novel, Herman Melville's *Moby Dick* [1851].) The harpooners searched out the sperm whale, whose oil was used for lamps and lubrication. When the commercial supply of sperm whale dwindled, the right whale became their main target. This huge sea creature was valuable not only for its oil but also for its long flexible mouth bones (baleen) that were used as stays and hoops in women's garments. The right whales in the North Atlantic had been destroyed during colonial times, so in the 1800s the men and ships hunting them sailed the world over on trips lasting two or three years. American whalers entered Pacific waters in the 1790s and were hunting off the Japanese coast in the 1820s. By midcentury—the golden age of whaling in this country—they reached arctic waters.

Around 1850, when society was becoming dependent on whale oil, the supply began giving out until a "fuel crisis" loomed. The shortages, price hikes, and search for new sources of fuel were not unlike the sequence of events in the 1970s. Demand for sperm-whale oil kept outstripping supply until the problem became critical. The price of this product, the "premium" oil of those days, rose from $.43 a gallon in 1823 to $2.55 a gallon in 1856. As *Scientific American* observed in 1857: "The whale oils which hitherto have been much relied upon in this country to furnish light are yearly becoming more scarce, and may in time almost entirely fail, while the rapid increase of machinery demands a large portion of the purest of these oils for lubricating."

Happily, a black ooze floating on the ground in Pennsylvania—known as "rock oil," "Indian oil," or "petroleum"—saved the

Whalers harpoon a sperm whale in the final stage of the chase. This 1835 engraving tries to capture the drama of the perilous battle put up by the wounded whale against the small, oar-propelled boats.

day. The first oil well was drilled in Titusville, Pennsylvania, in 1859. It was soon discovered that petroleum could be distilled into byproducts for heating, lighting, and lubrication. By 1863 three hundred firms were refining crude oil into kerosene and other products. Whale lamps were discarded, and kerosene became the main source of light. Science and technology—and a generous Nature—had saved the machine age from a potentially crippling disorder.

Moving into the prairies and deserts

"Old America seems to be breaking up and moving West," wrote Morris Birkbeck, an English immigrant, in 1817. Birkbeck had journeyed from the East Coast to Illinois and established the town of New Albion to attract other English settlers. His popular book of travels drew attention to the Illinois prairies. From the end of the War of 1812 to the Civil War large numbers of Americans— trappers and miners, farmers and city people—trekked their way west. By 1860 the frontier had shifted beyond the Mississippi River, halting a little west of the Missouri River. Maps of the West showed a winding frontier line stretching down from Minnesota to Texas, falling mostly between the ninety-fifth and the one-hundredth meridian. Another frontier line, on the Pacific Coast side of the continent, ran through the interior of California, Oregon, and Washington. Settlements were also located along the Rio Grande River near Salt Lake. Substantial portions of the western half of the country, including the Great Plains and Rockies, still appeared on the maps as white areas marked "Undeveloped," or "Indian Territory," or "Unsettled." In ecological terms, the frontier had moved out of the eastern forests and into new forests and new climatic zones (the grasslands and deserts).

The first serious efforts to tame the prairies occurred before the Civil War. Pioneers entered northern Indiana, central Illinois, and eastern Kansas, where glacial deposits and decayed grass had created probably the most fertile topsoil in all of North America. In its natural state the prairie consisted of endless stretches of tall bluestem grass, brilliant wild flowers, and reeds and marsh grass in the swamps. The land teemed with wildlife. This environment posed difficulties for the settlers. Little wood was available for fences, fuel, or home building. Wagon wheels sank in the marshes and swamps, which had to be drained before they could be planted. Although the native grasses made excellent forage, they posed a fire hazard in dry spells. Worst of all, the sod, an iron-tight mesh of grass roots, would break an ordinary plow.

The Great Plains, an extension of grasslands which lay to the west, seemed especially forbidding to whites at this time. In this region communication was difficult, fuel and building materials were hard to come by, and Indians were a constant menace. To some extent settlers were held at bay by official government reports that described the area between the Missouri River and the Rocky Mountains as a trackless wasteland. After an expedition in 1805–1806, Lieutenant Zebulon M. Pike predicted that "these vast plains of the western hemisphere may become in time as celebrated as the sandy deserts of Africa; for I saw in my route . . . tracks of many leagues where the wind had thrown up the sand in all the fanciful forms of the ocean's rolling waves, and on which not a speck of vegetable matter existed." Reporting on a similar expedition in 1820 which explored the Platte River basin, Major Stephen H. Long reinforced the myth by using the term "Great American Desert." Pike and Long implied that the Great Plains grasslands and deserts were good only for Indians and runaway thieves. Their reports probably discouraged settlement of the trans-Mississippi West until after the Civil War.

In the Southwest stretched the desert. This climatic zone was noted for its sun-baked sands, its cactus and mesquite, its exotic desert birds, insects, and rodents, and its barren-looking landscape. Indians, Spaniards, and Mexicans had long ago adjusted to this environment. The Mormons, too, made a stunning conquest of the desert around Salt Lake. But most people heading west preferred the friendlier climate and terrain of the Far West.

The landscape altered by the Industrial Revolution

In the era of the Industrial Revolution Americans visibly altered the landscape by clearing forests for farms and cities, digging canals, mining for fuels and precious metals, and laying tracks for railroads. Unquestionably the advantages of changing the natural environment to suit human needs outweighed any inherent disadvantages. On the other hand, such ecological changes led to measurable difficulties and required human adjustments.

Railroad directors and railroad projectors are no enthusiastic lovers of landscape beauty. . . . Their business is to cut and to slash, to level or deface a finely rounded field and fill up beautifully winding valleys.

DANIEL WEBSTER (1782–1852)

In the Hudson and Mohawk river valleys of New York, for example, the forests had been cut down to make way for wheat farms. The original forests had been a stable biome—that is, a major ecosystem consisting of plant and animal communities with similar structure. Plants, insects, birds, animals, fungi, minerals, water, and sunlight bal-

anced each other. Clearing the forests to open the land for wheat farming created a new ecological environment that was less stable, for the natural balance was thrown off. The wheat attracted insects and parasites. The midge, Hessian fly, chinch bat, and mildew or blight stunted the stems and kernels of the crop. Farmers desperately tried different remedies, but many finally abandoned their farms altogether. They headed west, leaving their land to new-growth forests.

Canals opened great wounds in the surface of the earth. But the wounds soon healed, and the scars were easy to live with. The Erie Canal, for example, blended into the natural scenery a few years after its completion. Horses and mules trudged along the tow paths, pulling the barges slowly and quietly through the surrounding farmland. Passengers lounging on the decks passed their days in restful travel, strumming guitars, singing, reading, playing cards, sketching, and talking to local farmers.

The effect of railroads on nature was perhaps more jarring than that of canals. In the 1840s everyone was fascinated by the "iron horse." Train travelers wrote glowing accounts of the scenery they viewed. Artists included trains in pastoral scenes. Poets sought to capture the power and roar of the great engines in their verse. But the coming of the railroads marks a distinct increase in the effects of industrialization on nature. Trains belched smoke and ashes, frightened animals and birds, and generally disrupted the placid countryside. Unlike canal boats or horses and wagons, steam locomotives devoured huge quantities of wood—and coal, a fuel that was essentially irreplaceable.

Worst of all was the effect of mines and steam mills on their surroundings. In California and Nevada the gold and silver rushes left piles of debris, open pits, eroded banks, and other scars that are still visible a century later. Factories were first seen as evidence of

America's genius for technology and organization. But after two or three decades, mill towns became ugly and unpleasant to live in. While mills driven by water wheels caused relatively little environmental damage, steam mills muddied brooks and streams, killed off fish, made fierce noises, and darkened the sky with smoke. In addition, the mines, mills, and factories often created health hazards for the people who worked in them. Happily, only a small part of the American work force was employed in industry, for in 1812 Dr. Benjamin Rush noted some curious effects of chemical pollution. Lead workers suffered from "mill-reck," a disease that caused them to bite and tear at their own flesh. Workers who used indigo blue became "peevish and low spirited," while those who handled scarlet dyes felt uncommonly cheerful. Yet most Americans felt that the advantages of technological progress far outweighed any drawbacks. A general optimism led people to think that the disadvantages of progress could be overcome.

The Wilderness Through Rose-Colored Glasses

Romanticizing nature

In its broadest sense "wilderness" can be defined as the opposite of civilization. The term has various applications which narrow its meaning — wilderness is an empty plain or desert, a pathless forest of trees, a portion of land growing wild, even an ocean. To primitive peoples the wilderness teems with supernatural beings, while to the ancient Hebrews it was a cursed and barren desert. To early Anglo-Saxons it contained horrible beasts. To some early Christians it was the devil's abode; to others it was a refuge, a place in which to become pure. Early American settlers viewed the wilderness as a threat to survival and hence a place to be conquered: Governor William Bradford of Plymouth Colony used a typical epithet, "hideous and desolate wilderness."

There came a time, in the late eighteenth and early nineteenth centuries, when Americans stopped using phrases like "howling wilderness" and began glorifying wild nature. This change of attitude resulted from the Romantic movement in literature, art, and philosophy that occurred in Europe and America. The new scientific perception of a "vast, complex, and harmonious" universe bestowed a sense of pleasure in nature, rather than the old feelings of terror and awe. Some philosophers wrote that God was responsible for nature's harmony. Others emphasized the benefits of primitivism — the life of the noble savage. Where better to study God than in wild natural surroundings? And what more natural surroundings were there in the world than the American wilderness?

In America the Romantics celebrated the glories of nature along with equality and democracy. The American forests were more "natural," the mountains more "manly," and the rivers more "grand" than those in the Old World. The birds sang more lyrically, the sun shone more brightly. Our wilderness lay to the west, which seemed like the charmed point on the compass. "Westward the course of empire takes its way," said England's Bishop Berkeley, coining a phrase that became especially popular in America. Pride in the wilderness became a form of patriotism.

> *Life consists with wildness. The most alive is the wildest.*
> *Not yet subdued to man, its presence refreshes him.*
>
> HENRY DAVID THOREAU (1817–1862)

The Romantic approach to nature appealed most to bookish individuals. Soon the most talented American writers were exploring nature in poetry, fiction, and essays. James Fenimore Cooper, Ralph Waldo Emerson, Henry David Thoreau, Herman Melville, and Walt Whitman were among the leading literary Romantics. One of the earliest American writers interested in nature themes was the poet and newspaper editor William Cullen Bryant. His poem "A Forest Hymn" (1835) remarks that "the groves were God's first temples." Throughout life he retreated from time to time to worship there.

Ralph Waldo Emerson's essay *Nature* (1836) gave expression to a mystical reverence for nature. He wrote:

In the woods . . . a man casts off his years, as the snake his slough, and at what period so ever of life is always a child. In the woods is perpetual youth. . . . Standing on the bare ground — my head bathed by the blithe air and uplifted into infinite space — all mean egotism vanishes. I become a transparent eyeball; I am nothing; I see all; the currents of the Universal Being circulate through me; I am part or parcel of God.

Inevitably the celebration of the *American* wilderness produced heroes and legends. Daniel Boone became the country's first folk hero (even before George Washington). Much of what we know of him is drawn from a fanciful biography written by John Filson in 1833. Boone came from a Pennsylvania Quaker family, pioneered alone at Blue Lick in the Yadkin Valley of North Carolina, and helped open the land west of the Appalachians, including Kentucky, around the time of the Revolution. He was a two-sided figure. A loner who liked to ramble in the forest with his gun, his dogs, and an Indian companion, he moved on whenever he could see smoke from a neighboring cabin. The other Boone was a highly civilized and responsible agent of speculators and politicians.

Daniel Boone's legend was embroidered in innumerable stories, poems, etchings, and sculptures. After his death in 1820, he became the model for the hero of James Fenimore Cooper's five *Leatherstocking Tales* (1823–1841). Their hero, Natty Bumppo, or "the Deerslayer," spends much of his time with an Indian friend, Chingachgook, quietly stalking the woods in close touch with nature. He acts with courage, patience, and a sense of justice. Bumppo-Boone is not a wanton killer or a reckless destroyer of wildlife but an ethical man with a deep respect for nature. (Other western heroes, real or fictional, were generally more brutal. Davy Crockett boasted of shooting 105 bears in one season.) Boone and Natty Bumppo, as described by Filson and Cooper, awakened a wanderlust in the American soul. They reinforced the desire to cut loose from old ties and head for wild mountains and woods.

Another popular writer, Washington Irving, famous for his stories of old New York, associated himself with wilderness themes. His history of *Astoria* (1836), the far western fur outpost, and *The Adventures of Captain Bonneville, U.S.A.* (1837), written as the journal of an early western explorer, helped to preserve in print, as he said, "the romance of savage life."

Landscape painters also tried to capture the essence of the American wilderness. The Catskill Mountains of New York and unmarred scenes of New England were favorite subjects of the Hudson River School, founded by Thomas Cole of Greenwich Village, New York. Explaining his painting *The*

Oxbow, a panoramic view of the Connecticut River, Cole delighted in the fact that in an American landscape "you see no ruined tower to tell of outrage, no gorgeous temple to speak of ostentation," but only "the abodes of plenty, virtue and refinement."

"Appreciation of wilderness," Roderick Nash has observed, "began in the cities: among men of letters who never had to swing an axe, fire a gun, or milk a cow for a living." Some noticed that as civilization pushed forward, the natural landscape began to lose its luster and needed protection. Among these early "conservationists" were novelists, essayists, philosophers, painters, and naturalists.

John James Audubon, the French-born naturalist, became famous for his *Birds of America* (1827–1838), a book of magnificent color plates and accompanying scientific text. It spurred an interest in studying and protecting the great variety of birds that existed on the continent. Bird fanciers later named their protectionist organization the Audubon Society. Less well known is Audubon's book on four-legged animals in America. He denounced the mindless "destruction of the forest" and the overkill of deer in the East and of mink and marten in the West.

Another graphic illustrator of wild nature was George Catlin. In 1829 he went west to paint Indians of the Plains and Rockies in their own surroundings. His *North American Indians* (1841) is a detailed and fully illustrat-

Mandan Indian village, painted by George Catlin. Regarding his purpose in visiting and painting Indian tribes, Catlin stated that "the results of my labors will doubtless be interesting to future ages, who will have little else left from which to judge of the original inhabitants of this noble race of beings who require but a few years more of the march of civilization and death to deprive them of all their native customs and character."

ed description of Indian life and customs based on eight years of travel. Catlin had the germ of an important idea when in 1832 he proposed that "a nation's Park" be established to preserve both the wildlife and the Indians of the West. But it was twenty-five years before Congress created the first national park.

Henry David Thoreau, who spent much of two years alone at Walden Pond near Concord, Massachusetts, must be considered a major influence on the wilderness movement. In *Walden* he described his deliberate withdrawal from the artificial world of human affairs. Relying on ingenuity, he lived a satisfying life of hiking, meditating, studying nature, and writing. "In Wildness," he wrote in 1851, "is the preservation of the World," a statement which has become the slogan of the wilderness movement.

Thoreau believed that in wild nature one could restore a weary body and sense the harmonies of the universe. He was not a hermit or a frontiersman but preferred to live, as he said, in "a sort of border life," in a "partially cultivated country" that lay between wilderness and civilization. In his essay "Walking" he expressed the almost mystical preoccupation with the West that was typical of his time:

When I go out of the house for a walk, uncertain as yet whither I will bend my steps, and submit myself to my instinct to decide for me, I find, strange and whimsical as it may seem, that I finally and inevitably settle southwest, toward some particular wood or meadow or deserted pasture or hill in that direction. . . . the future lies that way to me, and the earth seems more unexhausted and richer on that side.

The earliest conservationists

Often it was a trip abroad that prompted an American to see the meaning of wilderness. Thus it was in a book entitled *Glances at Eu-rope* (1851) that the journalist Horace Greeley exclaimed: "Friends at home! I charge you to spare, preserve and cherish some portion of your primitive forests; for when they are cut away I apprehend they will not easily be replaced."

Worldwide travel and study also influenced George Perkins Marsh's *Man and Nature* (1864), the first book-length study to stress the need for protecting the American environment. Marsh (1801–1882), a successful lawyer, businessman, scholar, and diplomat, pointed out that in ancient times excessive lumbering had destroyed wood supplies and water resources in the Near East, as well as in parts of Europe. Entire civilizations had crumbled as a result. He feared the same was happening in America:

We have now felled forest enough everywhere, in many districts far too much. Let us restore this one element of material life to its normal proportions, and devise means for maintaining the permanence of its relations to the fields, the meadows, the pastures, to the rain and the dews of heaven, to the springs and rivulets with which it waters the earth.

A man of practical intellect, he believed that the government should scientifically manage the nation's forests and reclaim arid areas. Marsh must be considered one of the earliest and most influential American conservationists.

Marsh was interested particularly in saving the Adirondack Mountains of New York as a wild preserve. A contemporary of his in this battle was Samuel H. Hammond, an Albany lawyer. Hammond admired the march of civilization, but he also valued the wild forests. His answer was to have the government "mark out a circle of a hundred miles in diameter, and throw around it the protecting aegis of the Constitution." Let this territory remain "a forest forever" in which "the old woods should stand . . . always as God made them."

Another forerunner in the environmental field was Frederick Law Olmsted (1822–1903), the landscape architect and city planner. As the owner of a model farm on Staten Island and a great believer in nature's restorative and spiritual values, Olmsted argued that parks could make cities habitable. New York City's Central Park, an eight-hundred-acre oasis of lawns, trees, ponds, brooks, rock outcroppings, and promenades in the midst of a congested city, was largely his inspiration. Later Olmsted was appointed a commissioner of a park in Yosemite Valley for the state of California. Congress had turned over this park of about ten square miles to the state for safekeeping. To do it justice, Yosemite must be kept in its natural state "for the free use of the whole body of the people forever." Said Olmsted: "The first point to be kept in mind then is to the preservation and maintenance as exactly as is possible of the natural scenery [and] the restriction . . . of all artificial constructions . . . markedly inharmonious with the scenery." Like Marsh, Olmsted left a mark on the next generation of wilderness advocates.

Review

The vast American wilderness began to fall back as settlers pushed ever westward. Abundance of resources kept the pioneers from giving much thought to conservation. America was blessed with cheap and plentiful fuel, rich forests, teeming animal life, and huge stretches of land in the public domain. The first organized ungreening of America took place in the eastern forests. Trees were felled to provide lumber barons with timber for export, paper mills, and construction. Competing fur companies killed hundreds of thousands of animals for their pelts. On the high seas the whaling industry followed a similar pattern. As people tampered with nature, they created new environmental problems. Railroads altered the American landscape and consumed huge amounts of energy. Mills and factories polluted the land, sky, and water around them, but not many people worried about the consequences. Americans' belief in technological progress far outweighed their concern over unpleasant side effects.

As Americans came to control more of the "howling wilderness," they began to glorify nature. Worship of the landscape was part of the Romantic movement, which produced heroes, real and fictional, whose closest ties were to nature. Many famous writers, artists, and philosophers of the time, including Emerson, believed that wild nature was a key to physical and spiritual restoration. Strangely, the first warnings that the land was becoming scarred by the new technology came largely from city people. Their concern sounded an early call for conservation.

Questions

1. How did Americans view their environment in the first part of the nineteenth century? Why weren't they more worried about their changing environment?
2. Does Malthus' theory have any relevance today?
3. This chapter cites what happened in the Hudson and Mohawk valleys, where the forests where cut down and the land was used for growing wheat. Can you give any modern examples where altering the environment has created problems?
4. How did the Romantic movement affect the way Americans viewed their environment?
5. Identify the following: (a) John Jacob Astor, (b) Daniel Boone, (c) Henry David Thoreau, (d) George Catlin, (e) John James Audubon, (g) George Perkins Marsh.

Selected Readings

OVERVIEW

Probably the best single overview of American life is Alexis de Tocqueville's *Democracy in America* (available in a number of editions).* This account by a young French aristocrat, based on a visit to the U.S., describes and analyzes innumerable facets of American life. Another valuable travel account is Harriet Martineau's *Society in America* (Peter Smith, 1837).

WEALTH

Curtis P. Nettles, *The Emergence of the National Economy* (Holt, Rinehart, 1962); Stuart Bruchey, *The Roots of American Economic Growth* (Harper & Row, 1968);* and Douglas C. North, *Growth and Welfare in the American Past* (Prentice-Hall, 1973)* are three general works dealing with early economic evolution. An introduction to labor is Foster R. Dulles, *Labor in America* (T. Y. Crowell, 1966). A good survey of pre-Civil War agriculture may be found in Paul W. Gates, *The Farmer's Age* (Harper & Row, 1968).* Constance M. Green, *Eli Whitney and the Birth of American Technology* (Little, Brown, 1956)* deals with an important American inventor. George R. Taylor, *The Transportation Revolution, 1815–1860* (Harper & Row, 1968)* is readable and thorough. A particular era is covered by Peter Temin, *The Jacksonian Economy* (Norton, 1967).* Social structure and related themes are dealt with by Stephen Thernstrom, *Poverty and Progress* (Harvard U. Press, 1964)* and Edward Pessen, *Jacksonian America* (Dorsey, 1969).*

POWER

The troubled political era of the 1790s has had many interpreters. Richard Hofstadter, *The Idea of a Party System* (U. of California Press, 1969) is excellent. Charles A. Beard, *The Economic Origins of Jeffersonian Democracy* (Macmillan, 1915) has been much criticized for its methodology but remains an influential interpretation of the Federalist–Republican split. The parallel between the formation of the U.S. and of new nations in the twentieth century is traced by Seymour N. Lipset, *The First New Nation* (Doubleday, 1963).* Merrill D. Peterson, *Thomas Jefferson and the New Nation* (Oxford U. Press, 1970) is also valuable. George Dangerfield, *The Era of Good Feelings* (Harcourt Brace, 1963)* is a highly

* Available in paperback.

readable account of the politics after the War of 1812.

The Whig–Democratic era is covered by Richard P. McCormick, *The Second American Party System* (U. of North Carolina Press, 1966).* Robert V. Remini, *The Election of Andrew Jackson* (Lippincott, 1963)* is brief and scholarly. *The Emergence of the Nation, 1783–1815* (Scott, Foresman, 1972)* by John C. Miller describes political, economic, and social events from the Confederation to the War of 1812.

The number of books dealing with politics on the eve of the Civil War is practically limitless. A taste of the drama can be gotten from biographies, such as David Donald, *Charles Sumner and the Coming of the Civil War* (Knopf, 1960); George F. Milton, *The Eve of Conflict: Stephen A. Douglas and the Needless War* (Octagon, 1963); and David M. Potter, *Lincoln and His Party in the Secession Crisis* (Yale U. Press, 1942).* Kenneth M. Stampp, *And the War Came* (Louisiana State U. Press, 1950)* is also enlightening on the origin of the conflict.

WAR

General analyses of the meaning of war in American history are hard to come by. Merlo J. Pusey, *The Way We Go to War* (Houghton Mifflin, 1971),* covers constitutional war-making power up to the Vietnam War. Three distinguished historians, Samuel Eliot Morison, Frederick Merk, and Frank Freidel, have teamed up to write *Dissent in Three American Wars* (Harvard U. Press, 1970).* A useful survey of diplomacy is Thomas A. Bailey, *A Diplomatic History of the American People* (Prentice-Hall, 1969).

Harry L. Coles, *The War of 1812* (U. of Chicago Press, 1965)* and Charles J. Dutton, *Oliver Hazard Perry* (Longmans, 1935) deal with the "Second War for Independence." Seymour V. Conner and Odie B. Faulk, *North America Divided: The Mexican War, 1846–1848* (Oxford U. Press, 1971) is a thorough study of an important war. Bernard De Voto, *The Year of Decision: 1848* (Houghton Mifflin, 1950) examines the major strands of American history in a single year.

The most carefully studied war of all is the Civil War. David Donald, ed., *Why the North Won the Civil War* (Louisiana State U. Press, 1960) is an anthology covering a fascinating question. Bruce Catton, *Centennial History of the Civil War* (Doubleday, 1961–1965) is reliable and readable. David M. Potter's *Division and the Stresses of Reunion, 1845–1876* (Scott, Foresman, 1973)* interprets the basic causes of the Civil War, the war it-

self, and Reconstruction. Concerning the life of ordinary soldiers, see Bell I. Wiley, *The Life of Johnny Reb
and The Life of Billy Yank* (Doubleday, 1971). Douglas S.
Freeman has written a four-volume study: *R. E. Lee*
(Scribner, 1935). Clement Eaton, *History of the Southern
Confederacy* (Free Press, 1965)* is a reliable treatment of
the South as an independent nation. J. G. Randall, *Lincoln the President* (Peter Smith, 1945–1955) covers presidential leadership in time of crisis.

RACE

A useful collection of essays on race relations is Gary B.
Nash and Richard Weiss, eds., *The Great Fear: Race in
the Mind of America* (Holt, Rinehart, 1970).* Alvin M.
Josephy, Jr., *The Patriot Chiefs: A Chronicle of American
Indian Resistance* (Viking, 1961)* has chapters on Te-
cumseh, Osceola, and Black Hawk. Also useful are two
specialized studies: Reginald Horsman, *Expansion and
American Indian Policy, 1783–1812* (Michigan State U.
Press, 1967) and Francis P. Trucha, *American Indian Pol-
icy in the Formative Years* (U. of Nebraska Press, 1970).*

John Hope Franklin, *From Slavery to Freedom: A History of American Negroes* (Random House, 1969)* is a
comprehensive history. The South's most able scholar
of slavery is Ulrich B. Phillips, *Plantation and Frontier,
1649–1863* (B. Franklin, 1969). Louis Filler, *The Crusade
Against Slavery, 1830–1860* (Harper & Row, 1960) is a
helpful study of the abolitionist movement. Eugene D.
Genovese, *The Political Economy of Slavery* (Random
House, 1965)* is a sophisticated analysis. Much can be
learned from Harriet Beecher Stowe's influential *Uncle
Tom's Cabin* (available in a number of editions).*

Concerning the Mexicans, see Leonard Pitt's *Decline
of the Californios: A Social History of the Spanish-Speaking Californians* (U. of California Press, 1968).* Rudy
Acuña, *Occupied America: The Chicanos Struggle Toward
Liberation* (Canfield Press, 1972) argues that Chicanos
are a colonized people in the United States. Many in-
sights into racial thinking can be found in Stuart C.
Miller, *The Unwelcome Immigrant: The American Image of
the Chinese, 1785–1882* (U. of California Press, 1972).

NATIONALITY AND RELIGION

The works by Hansen and Gordon, cited on p. 167, are
useful for a study of immigration before the Civil War.
Maldwyn A. Jones, *American Immigration* (U. of Chicago
Press, 1960)* is another helpful survey. Carl Wittke,
We Who Built America (Press of Case Western Reserve,

1967) is a sympathetic account of the immigrant contribution. The distribution of newcomers is studied by David Ward, *Cities and Immigrants* (Oxford U. Press, 1971).*
A readable account of immigration in a single city is Oscar Handlin's *Boston's Immigrants* (Atheneum, 1968).*

Many reform movements whose roots lie deep in religious history are covered by Alice F. Tyler, *Freedom's
Ferment* (Harper & Row, 1962).* Whitney R. Cross, *The
Burned-Over District* (Harper & Row, 1956)* deals with
the religious excitements in upstate New York. *The
Autobiography of Peter Cartwright* (Books for Libraries,
1856) is a firsthand account of the revivalist movement
by an important preacher. Timothy L. Smith's *Revival-
ism and Social Reform* (Harper & Row, 1957)* covers a
great deal of ground on the nineteenth century. A biography that analyzes the origins of Mormonism is Fawn
M. Brodie, *No Man Knows My History: The Life of Joseph
Smith* (Knopf, 1971). Ray A. Billington, *The Protestant
Crusade, 1800–1860* (Quadrangle, 1964) deals with the
organized attacks on Catholicism.

WOMEN AND THE FAMILY

The books by Flexner and Kraditor, cited on p. 167,
present much material on this era. See also Anne F.
Scott, *The Southern Lady: From Pedestal to Politics, 1830–
1930* (U. of Chicago Press, 1972).* Gerda Lerner, *The
Grimké Sisters from South Carolina* (Schocken, 1971)* is a
biography of two women who confronted male chauvinism as well as slavery.

COMMUNITY

Oneida, the Shakers, Brook Farm, and other religious
communes are dealt with in Tyler, cited above. A socio-
logical look at both new and old utopias is Rosabeth M.
Kanter, *Commitment and Community: Communes and
Utopias in Sociological Perspective* (Harvard U. Press,
1972).* Arthur E. Bestor, Jr., *Backwoods Utopias* (U. of
Pennsylvania Press, 1971)* describes sectarian and
Owenite communes. Edward D. Andrews describes *The
People Called Shakers* (Dover, 1953).* Maren L. Carden,
Oneida: Utopian Community to Modern Corporation (Harper & Row, 1971)* is a survey of the famous New York
society. Charles Nordhoff, *The Communistic Societies of
the United States* (Dover, 1966)* is a history of dozens of
communities, written by a firm believer in the Utopian
movement.

The general surveys of urban history mentioned in
Part One (p. 167) are pertinent here. Two landmark

studies by Richard C. Wade are *The Urban Frontier, The Rise of Western Cities, 1780–1830* (Harvard U. Press, 1959) and *Slavery in the Cities: The South, 1820–1860* (Oxford U. Press, 1967).* Robert G. Albion and J. B. Pope, *The Rise of New York Port* (Scribners, 1939) tells how New York City rose to great prominence. A well-illustrated and fascinating work on the origins of many American cities is John W. Reps, *The Making of Urban America: A History of City Planning in the United States* (Princeton U. Press, 1965).

ENVIRONMENT

Hans Huth, *Nature and the American: Three Centuries of Changing Attitudes* (U. of Nebraska Press, 1972)* focuses on the growing awareness of natural beauty in the nineteenth century. An introduction to environmental history is William R. Van Dersal's *The American Land* (Oxford U. Press, 1943). The romantic painters are treated by Frederick A. Sweet in *The Hudson River School and the Early American Landscape Tradition* (Art Institute of Chicago, 1945). Literary historians have dealt at length with the meaning of the wilderness and the frontier. One of them, Henry Nash Smith, has written a penetrating study, entitled *Virgin Land: The American West as Symbol and Myth* (Random House, 1957).* A book which first called the nation's attention to environmental problems is *George Catlin and the Old Frontier* (Dial, 1959) by Harold McCracken. Many earlier explorers contributed to a deepening awareness of the environment. See, for example, Paul R. Cutright, *Lewis and Clark: Pioneering Naturalists* (U. of Illinois Press, 1969).

epilog
Reconstruction 1865-1877

The end of the Civil War meant that armies of Americans no longer clashed in battle. It did not mean that the differences that had torn North and South apart had miraculously disappeared. Even after the Thirteenth Amendment, outlawing slavery, was ratified in December 1865, the question of the place the former slaves would occupy in American society remained unanswered. And the South itself—was it an enemy state that had been defeated, or a part of the family that had temporarily gone astray? There was continuing disagreement about these matters, but a dozen years after the war ended, two facts seemed clear. Neither North nor South believed in racial equality. And if southern society could not return to its antebellum ways, neither could the North force changes upon the South that conflicted with its strongest convictions and deepest prejudices.

Presidential plans for reconstruction

From the first there were two very different approaches to the problem of re-building, or reconstructing, the nation. One approach, shared by President Lincoln and his successor, Andrew Johnson, was to take the former Confederate states back into the Union as quickly and as painlessly as possible, asking only a pledge of allegiance and acceptance of abolition. Lincoln sought to readmit states on this basis while the war was in progress. After the war's end and Lincoln's assassination, Johnson moved quickly to restore the South to its old place.

In both cases, Congress refused to recognize the new governments and the elected representatives of the southern states. The Radical Republicans, who had fought for the abolition of slavery and who believed that the South should be punished for its rebellion, were particularly outraged when the states to be brought back into the Union under Johnson's plan elected to office many of the men who had been their leaders in the Confederacy. The Radicals were also dissatisfied with readmission plans that demanded no guarantees of the civil rights of former slaves. And northerners in general were irritated, if not aroused, when state after state in the South enacted "Black Codes" that deprived blacks of many rights and forced them into a laboring caste that would serve the needs and the convenience of whites.

Republicans had another reason for opposing the speedy readmission of the former Confederate states under the generous Johnson plan. The Constitution based congressional representation on "the whole Number" of each state's "free Persons," plus three fifths of "all other Persons" in the state—that is, its slaves. But now slavery was abolished. The southern states could therefore count all their residents. Their representation in Congress would be increased, and they would end up more powerful than they had been before the war.

Congressional reconstruction

For a variety of reasons, then—idealistic and emotional, political and practical—Congress rejected the results of the presidential plans and launched its own reconstruction program. Early in 1866 it passed a bill continuing the Freedmen's Bureau as a protection to former slaves threatened by the Black Codes. President Johnson, himself a southerner, vetoed the bill. Congress passed a bill conferring citizenship on all black Americans. Johnson vetoed it. Congress passed both bills over his veto and went on to propose the historic Fourteenth Amendment. Its first clause defined American citizenship so as to include blacks and denied states the right to abridge the privileges of citizenship or "deprive any person of life, liberty, or property, without due process of law." The second clause called for the congressional representation of a state to be reduced if it denied the vote to any of its adult males. (The South could thus choose between permitting black men to vote and losing power in Congress.) The third barred any former officeholder who had joined the Confederacy from again holding federal or state office until pardoned by Congress.

Clearly Congress was out to discipline the South. President Johnson, still fighting for his own reconstruction plan, tried to block the amendment by speaking out against ratification. But in the congressional elections of 1866 the Republicans won large majorities in both House and Senate. This indication of public support made the Radicals even more ready to brush aside presidential vetoes. When ten former Confederate states refused to ratify the Fourteenth Amendment, the Radical bloc believed itself strong enough to discipline both the South and the president.

Beginning in March 1867, Congress took aim at both targets. With a series of Reconstruction Acts it divided the South into five districts headed by military governors. Their duty, in addition to safeguarding the rights of all citizens, was to register voters, including adult black males but excluding many white men who had served the Confederacy. The registered voters were then to elect representatives to state constitutional conventions. The new constitutions, which had to give the vote to black males, also had to win congressional approval. And the state legislatures elected under the new constitutions had to ratify the Fourteenth Amendment. Although the white South dug in its heels, a year later the return of the southern states was under way. In another year the Fourteenth Amendment was ratified.

Impeachment of a president

Also in May 1867, Congress passed the Tenure of Office Act, denying a president the right to fire without Senate approval any official whose appointment the Senate had had to approve. By this means the Radicals intended to keep in office one of their allies in the administration, Secretary of War Edwin M. Stanton, who had originally been appointed by Lincoln. President Johnson challenged the constitutionality of the act by dropping Stanton and thereby gave Congress the excuse it had been looking for. The House voted to impeach the president, and in May 1868 thirty-five of fifty-four senators voted to convict. But this was one vote short of the two-thirds vote required for conviction, and the first attempt in American history to remove a president from office by impeachment ended in failure.

The Republican Congress remained very much in the saddle, however. In addition to overturning a succession of presidential vetoes and taking control of Reconstruction out of the president's hands, it had passed legislation to prevent the Supreme Court from interfering with its program. In the fall of 1868 Ulysses S. Grant, commander of the Union armies during the Civil War, was elected president on the Republican ticket. Unlike Johnson, Grant was quite willing to let Congress run the show.

Reconstruction triumphant

Meanwhile in the South, Reconstruction was proceeding. Voters—both black men and white—were registered. Constitutional conventions were held, with both blacks and whites taking part. Blacks and whites were elected to legislatures, and the new state governments functioned. In South Carolina the lower house of the legislature had a black majority. Blacks were elected to all levels of local and state government except governorships, to the federal House of Representatives, and to the Senate.

These first state governments under Reconstruction were Radical Republican—Black Republican, they were called. Besides blacks, Republicans in the South in the Reconstruction period included "carpetbaggers" from the North and white southern "scalawags." To the majority of southern whites, these were the villains of the piece, along with the occupation forces. But the occupation forces were far too few for a real occupation, and by no means all the Republicans were villainous. Among the blacks who were elected to office were those best qualified, and most proved to be hard-working moderates. Among the carpetbaggers were men sincerely dedicated to improving the lot of black Americans. Among the scalawags were men who believed that in working with the Republicans they were doing what was best for the South.

The new state governments built schools and roads and made other public improvements on a scale never before known in the South. A great deal of money was spent. Some was wasted, and some was stolen. Many legislators, both black and white, were sadly lacking in experience. Some were fools, and some were thieves. But that was also true of legislators in the North. And some of the southern thieves were white Democrats. In this Gilded Age, as the postwar period was later called, there was corruption in politics from the Capitol in Washington to townhalls and county courthouses. If Reconstruction began to come apart in a very few years, it was not primarily because of black incompetence or carpetbagger corruption or scalawag treachery or military brutality. It came apart because the white South was overwhelmingly opposed to it and because support for it in the white North ran out of steam.

Backlash in the South

In February 1869, Congress proposed the Fifteenth Amendment, which stated that no American citizen could legally be denied the vote because of "race, color, or previous condition of servitude." Grant had been narrowly elected with black votes in 1868, and the Republicans were determined to ensure that their candidates would continue to have this support at the polls. The amendment was ratified in 1870, after arousing considerable opposition in some northern states. Once ratification was achieved, many white supporters of the rights of blacks decided that the fight was over, that their cause had triumphed.

Ironically, it was after the denial of voting rights had been outlawed by constitutional amendment that the campaign to deny the vote to black Americans picked up speed in the South. The Ku Klux Klan and other secret organizations increased their efforts to terrorize blacks who dared go to the polls or act in other ways like free and equal citizens. Other southern whites disdained hiding behind hoods and masks and carried on their harassment of blacks publicly. Most effective of all was the withholding by the white establishment of jobs and credit. It worked to keep other whites from voting Republican and to keep blacks from voting at all, or except as instructed.

For a while Congress fought back. Force Acts were passed in 1870 and 1871 to combat the intimidation of black voters and to shore up the remaining Republican state governments. (By 1870 several had already been voted out of office.) For a while President Grant was ready to dispatch troops to enforce the voting laws, but public support of such action waned in the North as public interest lagged. In 1872 Congress granted amnesty to all but a few hundred former Confederates, and the political strength of the South increased. During the 1870s the Democrats were frequently in control of the House of Representatives. The two parties were approaching stalemate—or fundamental agreement.

The compromise of 1877

In the presidential election of 1876 the Democratic candidate, Samuel J. Tilden, received a quarter of a million more votes than the Republican, Rutherford B. Hayes. But Tilden's apparent victory was challenged in Louisiana, South Carolina, and Florida, the only southern states that still had Republican governments. (Louisiana and South Carolina were also the last states to be occupied by federal troops.) An electoral commission voted along party lines and gave all three states to Hayes, making him the winner. But Congress still had to conduct the official count of electoral votes, and some Democrats were angry enough to block the proceedings. In the end southern Democrats refused to join in a filibuster and Hayes was named president, just two days before inauguration. A month later the new chief executive removed the few remaining federal troops from the South, and Reconstruction was ended.

The so-called Compromise of 1877, by which the Republicans won the cooperation of the southern Democrats, involved more than troop removal. Hayes had previously favored such a move. There was also to be a southerner in his cabinet, and there was supposed to be federal support for a railroad from Texas to the Pacific. This was the era of big business and big money, and the South was eager to have its share.

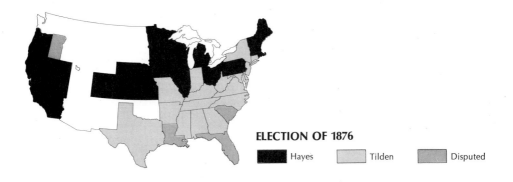

ELECTION OF 1876

Hayes   Tilden   Disputed

The reconstruction of black citizenship

As for the former slaves, the North was more than ready to leave that problem to the South, and the South seemed to have it well in hand. Blacks worked as hired hands and servants. Some blacks were sharecroppers. Often debt placed them in permanent economic bondage. Although they had finally been granted the right to vote, both political parties had used them shamelessly at the polls, and now they were in the process of losing their voting rights for decades. They had gained schools, but their schools would become completely separate and anything but equal. They had gained citizenship, but for them citizenship had been reconstructed. It had been made second-class.

THE DECLARATION OF INDEPENDENCE
In Congress, July 4, 1776

The unanimous Declaration
of the thirteen united States of America,

When in the Course of human events, it becomes necessary for one people to dissolve the political bands which have connected them with another, and to assume among the Powers of the earth, the separate and equal station to which the Laws of Nature and of Nature's God entitle them, a decent respect to the opinions of mankind requires that they should declare the causes which impel them to the separation.

We hold these truths to be self-evident, that all men are created equal, that they are endowed by their Creator with certain unalienable Rights, that among these are Life, Liberty and the pursuit of Happiness. That to secure these rights, Governments are instituted among Men, deriving their just powers from the consent of the governed, That whenever any Form of Government becomes destructive of these ends, it is the Right of the People to alter or to abolish it, and to institute new Government, laying its foundation on such principles and organizing its powers in such form, as to them shall seem most likely to effect their Safety and Happiness. Prudence, indeed, will dictate that Governments long established should not be changed for light and transient causes; and accordingly all experience hath shown, that mankind are more disposed to suffer, while evils are sufferable, than to right themselves by abolishing the forms to which they are accustomed. But when a long train of abuses and usurpations, pursuing invariably the same Object evinces a design to reduce them under absolute Despotism, it is their right, it is their duty, to throw off such Government, and to provide new Guards for their future security.— Such has been the patient sufferance of these Colonies; and such is now the necessity which constrains them to alter their former Systems of Government. The history of the present King of Great Britain is a history of repeated injuries and usurpations, all having in direct object the establishment of an absolute Tyranny over these States. To prove this, let Facts be submitted to a candid world.

He has refused his Assent to Laws, the most wholesome and necessary for the public good.

He has forbidden his Governors to pass Laws of immediate and pressing importance, unless suspended in their operation till his Assent should be obtained; and when so suspended, he has utterly neglected to attend to them.

He has refused to pass other Laws for the accommodation of large districts of people, unless those people would relinquish the right of Representation in the Legislature, a right inestimable to them and formidable to tyrants only.

He has called together legislative bodies at places unusual, uncomfortable, and distant from the depository of their Public Records, for the sole purpose of fatiguing them into compliance with his measures.

He has dissolved Representative Houses repeatedly, for opposing with manly firmness his invasions on the rights of the people.

He has refused for a long time, after such dissolutions, to cause others to be elected; whereby the Legislative Powers, incapable of Annihilation, have returned to the People at large for their exercise; the State remaining in the mean time exposed to all the dangers of invasion from without, and convulsions within.

He has endeavoured to prevent the population of these States; for that purpose obstructing the Laws for Naturalization of Foreigners; refusing to pass others to encourage their migrations hither, and raising the conditions of new Appropriations of Lands.

He has obstructed the Administration of Justice, by refusing his Assent to Laws for establishing Judiciary Powers.

He has made Judges dependent on his Will alone, for the tenure of their offices, and the amount and payment of their salaries.

He has erected a multitude of New Offices, and sent hither swarms of Officers to harass our people, and eat out their substance.

He has kept among us, in times of peace, Standing Armies without the Consent of our legislatures.

He has affected to render the Military independent of and superior to the Civil Power.

He has combined with others to subject us to a jurisdiction foreign to our constitution, and unacknowledged by our laws; giving his Assent to their acts of pretended Legislation:

For quartering large bodies of armed troops among us:

For protecting them, by a mock Trial, from Punishment for any Murders which they should commit on the Inhabitants of these States:

For cutting off our Trade with all parts of the world:

For imposing taxes on us without our Consent:

For depriving us in many cases, of the benefits of Trial by Jury:

For transporting us beyond Seas to be tried for pretended offences:

For abolishing the free System of English Laws in a neighbouring Province, establishing therein an Arbitrary government, and enlarging its Boundaries so as to render it at once an example and fit instrument for introducing the same absolute rule into these Colonies:

For taking away our Charters, abolishing our most valuable Laws, and altering fundamentally the Forms of our Governments:

For suspending our own Legislatures, and declaring themselves invested with Power to legislate for us in all cases whatsoever.

He has abdicated Government here, by declaring us out of his Protection and waging War against us.

He has plundered our seas, ravaged our Coasts, burnt our towns, and destroyed the lives of our people.

He is at this time transporting large armies of foreign mercenaries to compleat the works of death, desolation and tyranny, already begun with circumstances of Cruelty & perfidy scarcely paralleled in the most barbarous ages, and totally unworthy the Head of a civilized nation.

He has constrained our fellow Citizens taken Captive on the high Seas to bear Arms against their Country, to become the executioners of their friends and Brethren, or to fall themselves by their Hands.

He has excited domestic insurrections amongst us, and has endeavoured to bring on the inhabitants of our frontiers, the merciless Indian Savages, whose known rule of warfare, is an undistinguished destruction of all ages, sexes and conditions.

In every stage of these Oppressions We have Petitioned for Redress in the most humble terms: Our repeated Petitions have been answered only by repeated injury. A Prince, whose character is thus marked by every act which may define a Tyrant, is unfit to be the ruler of a free people.

Nor have We been wanting in attentions to our British brethren. We have warned them from time to time of attempts by their legislature to extend an unwarrantable jurisdiction over us. We have reminded them of the circumstances of our emigration and settlement here. We have appealed to their native justice and magnanimity, and we have conjured them by the ties of our common kindred to disavow these usurpations which, would inevitably interrupt our connections and correspondence. They too have been deaf to the voice of justice and of consanguinity. We must, therefore, acquiesce in the necessity, which denounces our Separation, and hold them, as we hold the rest of mankind, Enemies in War, in Peace Friends.

We, therefore, the Representatives of the united States of America, in General Congress, Assembled, appealing to the Supreme Judge of the world for the rectitude of our intentions, do, in the Name, and by authority of the good People of these Colonies, solemnly publish and declare,

That these United Colonies are, and of Right ought to be Free and Independent States; that they are Absolved from all Allegiance to the British Crown, and that all political connection between them and the State of Great Britain, is and ought to be totally dissolved; and that as Free and Independent States, they have full power to levy War, conclude Peace, contract Alliances, establish Commerce, and to do all other Acts and Things which Independent States may of right do. And for the support of this Declaration, with a firm reliance on the Protection of Divine Providence, we mutually pledge to each other our Lives, our Fortunes and our sacred Honor.

JOHN HANCOCK	GEO. TAYLOR
BUTTON GWINNETT	JAMES WILSON
LYMAN HALL	GEO. ROSS
GEO. WALTON	CAESAR RODNEY
WM. HOOPER	GEO. READ
JOSEPH HEWES	THO. M'KEAN
JOHN PENN	WM. FLOYD
EDWARD RUTLEDGE	PHIL. LIVINGSTON
THOS. HEYWARD, Junr.	FRANS. LEWIS
THOMAS LYNCH, Junr.	LEWIS MORRIS
ARTHUR MIDDLETON	RICHD. STOCKTON
SAMUEL CHASE	JNO. WITHERSPOON
WM. PACA	FRAS. HOPKINSON
THOS. STONE	JOHN HART
CHARLES CARROLL	ABRA. CLARK
of CARROLLTON	JOSIAH BARTLETT
GEORGE WYTHE	WM. WHIPPLE
RICHARD HENRY LEE	SAML. ADAMS
TH. JEFFERSON	JOHN ADAMS
BENJ. HARRISON	ROBT. TREAT PAINE
THOS. NELSON, JR.	ELBRIDGE GERRY
FRANCIS LIGHTFOOT LEE	STEP. HOPKINS
CARTER BRAXTON	WILLIAM ELLERY
ROBT. MORRIS	ROGER SHERMAN
BENJAMIN RUSH	SAM'EL. HUNTINGTON
BENJA. FRANKLIN	WM. WILLIAMS
JOHN MORTON	OLIVER WOLCOTT
GEO. CLYMER	MATTHEW THORNTON
JAS. SMITH	

THE CONSTITUTION OF
THE UNITED STATES OF AMERICA

We the People of the United States, in Order to form a more perfect Union, establish Justice, insure domestic Tranquility, provide for the common defence, promote the general Welfare, and secure the Blessings of Liberty to ourselves and our Posterity, do ordain and establish this Constitution for the United States of America.

ARTICLE I.

Section 1.

All legislative Powers herein granted shall be vested in a Congress of the United States, which shall cõnsist of a Senate and House of Representatives.

Section 2.

The House of Representatives shall be composed of Members chosen every second Year by the People of the several States, and the Electors in each State shall have the Qualifications requisite for Electors of the most numerous Branch of the State Legislature.

No Person shall be a Representative who shall not have attained to the Age of twenty five Years, and been seven Years a Citizen of the United States, and who shall not, when elected, be an Inhabitant of that State in which he shall be chosen.

Representatives and direct Taxes shall be apportioned among the several States which may be included within this Union, according to their respective Numbers, which shall be determined by adding to the whole Number of free Persons, including those bound to Service for a Term of Years, and excluding Indians not taxed, three fifths of all other Persons.[1] The actual Enumeration shall be made within three Years after the first Meeting of the Congress of the United States, and within every subsequent Term of ten Years, in such Manner as they shall by Law direct. The Number of Representatives shall not exceed one for every thirty Thousand, but each State shall have at Least one Representative; and until such enumeration shall be made, the State of New Hampshire shall be entitled to chuse three, Massachusetts eight, Rhode-Island and Providence Plantations one, Connecticut five, New-York six, New Jersey four, Pennsylvania eight, Delaware one, Maryland six, Virginia ten, North Carolina five, South Carolina five, and Georgia three.

When vacancies happen in the Representation from any State, the Executive Authority [2]thereof shall issue Writs of Election to fill such Vacancies.

The House of Representatives shall chuse their Speaker and other Officers; and shall have the sole Power of Impeachment.

Section 3.

The Senate of the United States shall be composed of two Senators from each State, chosen by the Legislature thereof, for six Years; and each Senator shall have one Vote.

Immediately after they shall be assembled in Consequence of the first Election, they shall be divided as equally as may be into three Classes. The Seats of the Senators of the first Class shall be vacated at the Expiration of the second Year, of the second Class at the Expiration of the fourth Year, and of the third Class at the Expiration of the sixth Year, so that one third may be chosen every second Year; and if Vacancies happen by Resignation, or otherwise, during the Recess of the Legislature of any State, the Executive thereof may make temporary Appointments until the next Meeting of the Legislature, which shall then fill such Vacancies.[2]

No Person shall be a Senator who shall not have attained to the Age of thirty Years, and been nine Years a Citizen of the United States, and who shall not, when elected, be an Inhabitant of that State for which he shall be chosen.

The Vice President of the United States shall be President of the Senate, but shall have no Vote, unless they be equally divided.

The Senate shall chuse their other Officers, and also a President pro tempore, in the Absence of the Vice President, or when he shall exercise the Office of President of the United States.

The Senate shall have the sole Power to try all Impeachments. When sitting for that Purpose, they shall be on Oath or Affirmation. When the President of the United States is tried the Chief Justice shall preside: And no Person shall be convicted without the Concurrence of two thirds of the Members present.

Judgment in Cases of Impeachment shall not extend further than to removal from Office, and disqualification to hold and enjoy any Office of honor, Trust or Profit under the United States: but the Party convicted shall nevertheless be liable and subject to Indictment, Trial, Judgment and Punishment, according to Law.

Section 4.

The Times, Places and Manner of holding Elections for Senators and Representatives, shall be prescribed in each State by the Legislature thereof; but the Congress may at

---

[1]"Other Persons" being black slaves. Modified by Amendment XIV, Section 2.

[2]Provisions changed by Amendment XVII.

any time by Law make or alter such Regulations, except as to the Places of chusing Senators.

The Congress shall assemble at least once in every Year, and such Meeting shall be on the first Monday in December, unless they shall by Law appoint a different Day.[3]

Section 5.

Each House shall be the Judge of the Elections, Returns and Qualifications of its own Members, and a Majority of each shall constitute a Quorum to do Business; but a smaller Number may adjourn from day to day, and may be authorized to compel the Attendance of absent Members, in such Manner, and under such Penalties as each House may provide.

Each House may determine the Rules of its Proceedings, punish its Members for disorderly Behaviour, and, with the Concurrence of two thirds, expel a Member.

Each House shall keep a Journal of its Proceedings, and from time to time publish the same, excepting such Parts as may in their Judgment require Secrecy; and the Yeas and Nays of the Members of either House on any question shall, at the Desire of one fifth of those Present, be entered on the Journal.

Neither House, during the Session of Congress, shall, without the Consent of the other, adjourn for more than three days, nor to any other Place than that in which the two Houses shall be sitting.

Section 6.

The Senators and Representatives shall receive a Compensation for their Services, to be ascertained by Law, and paid out of the Treasury of the United States. They shall in all Cases, except Treason, Felony and Breach of the Peace, be privileged from Arrest during their Attendance at the Session of their respective Houses, and in going to and returning from the same; and for any Speech or Debate in either House, they shall not be questioned in any other Place.

No Senator or Representative shall, during the Time for which he was elected, be appointed to any civil Office under the Authority of the United States, which shall have been created, or the Emoluments whereof shall have been encreased during such time; and no Person holding any Office under the United States, shall be a Member of either House during his Continuance in Office.

Section 7.

All Bills for raising Revenue shall originate in the House of Representatives; but the Senate may propose or concur with Amendments as on other Bills.

Every Bill which shall have passed the House of Representatives and the Senate, shall, before it become a Law, be presented to the President of the United States; If he approve he shall sign it, but if not he shall return it, with his Objections to that House in which it shall have originated, who shall enter the Objections at large on their Journal, and proceed to reconsider it. If after such Reconsideration two thirds of that House shall agree to pass the Bill, it shall be sent, together with the Objections, to the other House, by which it shall likewise be reconsidered, and if approved by two thirds of that House, it shall become a Law. But in all such Cases the Votes of both Houses shall be determined by yeas and Nays, and the Names of the Persons voting for and against the Bill shall be entered on the Journal of each House respectively. If any Bill shall not be returned by the President within ten Days (Sundays excepted) after it shall have been presented to him, the Same shall be a Law, in like Manner as if he had signed it, unless the Congress by their Adjournment prevent its Return, in which Case it shall not be a Law.

Every Order, Resolution, or Vote to which the Concurrence of the Senate and House of Representatives may be necessary (except on a question of Adjournment) shall be presented to the President of the United States; and before the Same shall take Effect, shall be approved by him, or being disapproved by him, shall be repassed by two thirds of the Senate and House of Representatives, according to the Rules and Limitations prescribed in the Case of a Bill.

Section 8.

The Congress shall have Power To lay and collect Taxes, Duties, Imposts and Excises, to pay the Debts and provide for the common Defence and general Welfare of the United States; but all Duties, Imposts and Excises shall be uniform throughout the United States;

To borrow Money on the credit of the United States;

To regulate Commerce with foreign Nations, and among the several States, and with the Indian Tribes;

To establish an uniform Rule of Naturalization, and uniform Laws on the subject of Bankruptcies throughout the United States;

To coin Money, regulate the Value thereof, and of foreign Coin, and fix the Standard of Weights and Measures;

To provide for the Punishment of counterfeiting the Securities and current Coin of the United States;

To establish Post Offices and post Roads;

To promote the Progress of Science and useful Arts, by securing for limited Times to Authors and Inventors the exclusive Right to their respective Writings and Discoveries;

To constitute Tribunals inferior to the supreme Court;

To define and punish Piracies and Felonies committed on the high Seas, and Offences against the Law of Nations;

To declare War, grant Letters of Marque and Reprisal, and make Rules concerning Captures on Land and Water;

To raise and support Armies, but no Appropriation of

---

[3]Provision changed by Amendment XX, Section 2.

Money to that Use shall be for a longer Term than two Years;

To provide and maintain a Navy;

To make Rules for the Government and Regulation of the land and naval Forces;

To provide for calling forth the Militia to execute the Laws of the Union, suppress Insurrections and repel Invasions;

To provide for organizing, arming, and disciplining, the Militia, and for governing such Part of them as may be employed in the Service of the United States, reserving to the States respectively, the Appointment of the Officers, and the Authority of training the Militia according to the discipline prescribed by Congress;

To exercise exclusive Legislation in all Cases whatsoever, over such District (not exceeding ten Miles square) as may, by Cession of particular States, and the Acceptance of Congress, become the Seat of the Government of the United States, and to exercise like Authority over all Places purchased by the Consent of the Legislature of the State in which the Same shall be, for the Erection of Forts, Magazines, Arsenals, dock-Yards, and other needful Buildings;—And

To make all Laws which shall be necessary and proper for carrying into Execution the foregoing Powers, and all other Powers vested by this Constitution in the Government of the United States, or in any Department or Officer thereof.

Section 9.

The Migration or Importation of such Persons as any of the States now existing shall think proper to admit, shall not be prohibited by the Congress prior to the Year one thousand eight hundred and eight, but a Tax or duty may be imposed on such Importation, not exceeding ten dollars for each Person.

The Privilege of the Writ of Habeas Corpus shall not be suspended, unless when in Cases of Rebellion or Invasion the public Safety may require it.

No Bill of Attainder or ex post facto Law shall be passed.

No Capitation, or other direct, Tax shall be laid, unless in Proportion to the Census or Enumeration herein before directed to be taken.

No Tax or Duty shall be laid on Articles exported from any State.

No Preference shall be given by any Regulation of Commerce or Revenue to the Ports of one State over those of another: nor shall Vessels bound to, or from, one State, be obliged to enter, clear, or pay Duties in another.

No Money shall be drawn from the Treasury, but in Consequence of Appropriations made by Law; and a regular Statement and Account of the Receipts and Expenditures of all public Money shall be published from time to time.

No Title of Nobility shall be granted by the United States: And no Person holding any Office of Profit or Trust under them, shall, without the Consent of the Congress, accept of any present, Emolument, Office, or Title, of any kind whatever, from any King, Prince, or foreign State.

Section 10.

No State shall enter into any Treaty, Alliance, or Confederation; grant Letters of Marque and Reprisal; coin Money; emit Bills of Credit; make any Thing but gold and silver Coin a Tender in Payment of Debts; pass any Bill of Attainder, ex post facto Law, or Law impairing the Obligation of Contracts, or grant any Title of Nobility.

No State shall, without the Consent of the Congress, lay any Imposts or Duties on Imports or Exports, except what may be absolutely necessary for executing its inspection Laws: and the net Produce of all Duties and Imposts, laid by any State on Imports or Exports, shall be for the Use of the Treasury of the United States; and all such Laws shall be subject to the Revision and Controul of the Congress.

No State shall, without the Consent of Congress, lay any Duty of Tonnage, keep Troops, or Ships of War in time of Peace, enter into any Agreement or Compact with another State, or with a foreign Power, or engage in War, unless actually invaded, or in such imminent Danger as will not admit of delay.

ARTICLE II.

Section 1.

The executive Power shall be vested in a President of the United States of America. He shall hold his Office during the Term of four Years, and, together with the Vice President, chosen for the same Term, be elected, as follows:

Each State shall appoint, in such Manner as the Legislature thereof may direct, a Number of Electors, equal to the whole Number of Senators and Representatives to which the State may be entitled in the Congress: but no Senator or Representative, or Person holding an Office of Trust or Profit under the United States, shall be appointed an Elector.

The Electors shall meet in their respective States, and vote by Ballot for two Persons, of whom one at least shall not be an Inhabitant of the same State with themselves. And they shall make a List of all the Persons voted for, and of the Number of Votes for each; which List they shall sign and certify, and transmit sealed to the Seat of the Government of the United States, directed to the President of the Senate. The President of the Senate shall, in the Presence of the Senate and House of Representatives, open all the Certificates, and the Votes shall then be counted. The Person having the greatest Number of Votes shall be the President, if such Number be a Majority of the whole Number of Electors appointed; and if there be more than one who have such Majority, and have an equal Number of Votes, then the House of

Representatives shall immediately chuse by Ballot one of them for President; and if no Person have a Majority, then from the five highest on the List the said House shall in like Manner chuse the President. But in chusing the President, the Votes shall be taken by States, the Representation from each State having one Vote; A quorum for this Purpose shall consist of a Member or Members from two thirds of the States, and a Majority of all the States shall be necessary to a Choice. In every Case, after the Choice of the President, the Person having the greatest Number of Votes of the Electors shall be the Vice President. But if there should remain two or more who have equal Votes, the Senate shall chuse from them by Ballot the Vice President.[4]

The Congress may determine the Time of chusing the Electors, and the Day on which they shall give their Votes; which Day shall be the same throughout the United States.

No Person except a natural born Citizen, or a Citizen of the United States, at the time of the Adoption of this Constitution, shall be eligible to the Office of President; neither shall any Person be eligible to that Office who shall not have attained to the Age of thirty five Years, and been fourteen Years a Resident within the United States.

In Case of the Removal of the President from Office, or of his Death, Resignation, or Inability to discharge the Powers and Duties of the said Office, the Same shall devolve on the Vice President, and the Congress may by Law provide for the Case of Removal, Death, Resignation or Inability, both of the President and Vice President, declaring what Officer shall then act as President, and such Officer shall act accordingly, until the Disability be removed, or a President shall be elected.

The President shall, at stated Times, receive for his Services, a Compensation, which shall neither be encreased nor diminished during the Period for which he shall have been elected, and he shall not receive within that Period any other Emolument from the United States, or any of them.

Before he enter on the Execution of his Office, he shall take the following Oath or Affirmation:—"I do solemnly swear (or affirm) that I will faithfully execute the Office of President of the United States, and will to the best of my Ability, preserve, protect and defend the Constitution of the United States."

Section 2.

The President shall be Commander in Chief of the Army and Navy of the United States, and of the Militia of the several States, when called into the actual Service of the United States; he may require the Opinion, in writing, of the principal Officer in each of the executive Departments, upon any Subject relating to the Duties of their respective Offices, and he shall have Power to grant Reprieves and Pardons for Offences against the United States, except in Cases of Impeachment.

He shall have Power, by and with the Advice and Consent of the Senate, to make Treaties, provided two thirds of the Senators present concur; and he shall nominate, and by and with the Advice and Consent of the Senate, shall appoint Ambassadors, other public Ministers and Consuls, Judges of the supreme Court, and all other Officers of the United States, whose Appointments are not herein otherwise provided for, and which shall be established by Law: but the Congress may by Law vest the Appointment of such inferior Officers, as they think proper, in the President alone, in the Courts of Law, or in the Heads of Departments.

The President shall have Power to fill up all Vacancies that may happen during the Recess of the Senate, by granting Commissions which shall expire at the End of their next Session.

Section 3.

He shall from time to time give to the Congress Information of the State of the Union, and recommend to their Consideration such Measures as he shall judge necessary and expedient; he may, on extraordinary Occasions, convene both Houses, or either of them, and in Case of Disagreement between them, with Respect to the Time of Adjournment, he may adjourn them to such Time as he shall think proper; he shall receive Ambassadors and other public Ministers; he shall take Care that the Laws be faithfully executed, and shall Commission all the Officers of the United States.

Section 4.

The President, Vice President and all civil Officers of the United States, shall be removed from Office on Impeachment for, and Conviction of, Treason, Bribery, or other high Crimes and Misdemeanors.

ARTICLE III.

Section 1.

The judicial Power of the United States, shall be vested in one supreme Court, and in such inferior Courts as the Congress may from time to time ordain and establish. The Judges, both of the supreme and inferior Courts, shall hold their Offices during good Behaviour, and shall, at stated Times, receive for their Services, a Compensation, which shall not be diminished during their Continuance in Office.

Section 2.

The judicial Power shall extend to all Cases, in Law and Equity, arising under this Constitution, the Laws of the United States, and Treaties made, or which shall be made, under their Authority;—to all Cases affecting

---

[4]Provisions superseded by Amendment XII.

Ambassadors, other public Ministers and Consuls;—to all Cases of admiralty and maritime Jurisdiction;—to Controversies to which the United States shall be a Party;—to Controversies between two or more States;—between a State and Citizens of another State;—between Citizens of different States,—between Citizens of the same State claiming Lands under Grants of different States, and between a State, or the Citizens thereof, and foreign States, Citizens or Subjects.[5]

In all Cases affecting Ambassadors, other public Ministers and Consuls, and those in which a State shall be Party, the supreme Court shall have original Jurisdiction. In all the other Cases before mentioned, the supreme Court shall have appellate Jurisdiction, both as to Law and Fact, with such Exceptions, and under such Regulations as the Congress shall make.

The Trial of all Crimes, except in Cases of Impeachment, shall be by Jury; and such Trial shall be held in the State where the said Crimes shall have been committed, but when not committed within any State, the Trial shall be at such Place or Places as the Congress may by Law have directed.

Section 3.

Treason against the United States, shall consist only in levying War against them, or in adhering to their Enemies, giving them Aid and Comfort. No person shall be convicted of Treason unless on the Testimony of two Witnesses to the same overt Act, or on Confession in open Court.

The Congress shall have Power to declare the Punishment of Treason, but no Attainder of Treason shall work Corruption of Blood, or Forfeiture except during the Life of the Person attainted.

ARTICLE IV.

Section 1.

Full Faith and Credit shall be given in each State to the public Acts, Records, and judicial Proceedings of every other State. And the Congress may by general Laws prescribe the Manner in which such Acts, Records and Proceedings shall be proved, and the Effect thereof.

Section 2.

The Citizens of each State shall be entitled to all Privileges and Immunities of Citizens in the several States.

A Person charged in any State with Treason, Felony, or other Crime, who shall flee from Justice, and be found in another State, shall on Demand of the executive Authority of the State from which he fled, be delivered up, to be removed to the State having Jurisdiction of the Crime.

No Person held to Service or Labour in one State, under the Laws thereof, escaping into another, shall, in Consequence of any Law or Regulation therein, be discharged from such Service or Labour, but shall be delivered up on Claim of the Party to whom such Service or Labour may be due.

Section 3.

New States may be admitted by the Congress into this Union; but no new State shall be formed or erected within the Jurisdiction of any other State; nor any State be formed by the Junction of two or more States, or Parts of States, without the Consent of the Legislatures of the States concerned as well as of the Congress.

The Congress shall have Power to dispose of and make all needful Rules and Regulations respecting the Territory or other Property belonging to the United States; and nothing in this Constitution shall be so construed as to Prejudice any Claims of the United States, or of any particular State.

Section 4.

The United States shall guarantee to every State in this Union a Republican Form of Government, and shall protect each of them against Invasion; and on Application of the Legislature, or of the Executive (when the Legislature cannot be convened) against domestic Violence.

ARTICLE V.

The Congress, whenever two thirds of both Houses shall deem it necessary, shall propose Amendments to this Constitution, or, on the Application of the Legislatures of two thirds of the several States, shall call a Convention for proposing Amendments, which, in either Case, shall be valid to all Intents and Purposes, as Part of this Constitution, when ratified by the Legislatures of three fourths of the several States, or by Conventions in three fourths thereof, as the one or the other Mode of Ratification may be proposed by the Congress; Provided that no Amendment which may be made prior to the Year One thousand eight hundred and eight shall in any Manner affect the first and fourth Clauses in the Ninth Section of the first Article; and that no State, without its Consent, shall be deprived of its equal Suffrage in the Senate.

ARTICLE VI.

All Debts contracted and Engagements entered into, before the Adoption of this Constitution, shall be as valid against the United States under this Constitution, as under the Confederation.

---

[5]Clause changed by Amendment XI.

This Constitution, and the Laws of the United States which shall be made in Pursuance thereof; and all Treaties made, or which shall be made, under the Authority of the United States, shall be the supreme Law of the Land; and the Judges in every State shall be bound thereby, any Thing in the Constitution or Laws of any State to the Contrary notwithstanding.

The Senators and Representatives before mentioned, and the Members of the several State Legislatures, and all executive and judicial Officers, both of the United States and of the several States, shall be bound by Oath or Affirmation, to support this Constitution; but no religious Test shall ever be required as a Qualification to any Office or public Trust under the United States.

ARTICLE VII.

The Ratification of the Conventions of nine States, shall be sufficient for the Establishment of this Constitution between the States so ratifying the Same.

done in Convention by the Unanimous Consent of the States present the Seventeenth Day of September in the Year of our Lord one thousand seven hundred and Eighty seven and of the Independence of the United States of America the Twelfth[6] IN WITNESS whereof We have hereunto subscribed our Names,

GEORGE WASHINGTON,
President and Deputy
from Virginia

[6]The Constitution was submitted on September 17, 1787, by the Constitutional Convention, was ratified by the conventions of several states at various dates up to May 29, 1790, and became effective on March 4, 1789.

New Hampshire
JOHN LANGDON
NICHOLAS GILMAN
Massachusetts
NATHANIEL GORHAM
RUFUS KING
Connecticut
WILLIAM S. JOHNSON
ROGER SHERMAN
New York
ALEXANDER HAMILTON
New Jersey
WILLIAM LIVINGSTON
DAVID BREARLEY
WILLIAM PATERSON
JONATHAN DAYTON
Pennsylvania
BENJAMIN FRANKLIN
THOMAS MIFFLIN
ROBERT MORRIS
GEORGE CLYMER
THOMAS FITZSIMONS
JARED INGERSOLL
JAMES WILSON
GOUVERNEUR MORRIS

Delaware
GEORGE READ
GUNNING BEDFORD, JR.
JOHN DICKINSON
RICHARD BASSETT
JACOB BROOM
Maryland
JAMES MCHENRY
DANIEL OF ST. THOMAS
  JENIFER
DANIEL CARROLL
Virginia
JOHN BLAIR
JAMES MADISON, JR.
North Carolina
WILLIAM BLOUNT
RICHARD DOBBS
  SPRAIGHT
HU WILLIAMSON
South Carolina
J. RUTLEDGE
CHARLES C. PINCKNEY
PIERCE BUTLER
Georgia
WILLIAM FEW
ABRAHAM BALDWIN

AMENDMENTS TO THE CONSTITUTION

[AMENDMENT I]

Congress shall make no law respecting an establishment of religion, or prohibiting the free exercise thereof; or abridging the freedom of speech, or of the press; or the right of the people peaceably to assemble, and to petition the Government for a redress of grievances.

[AMENDMENT II]

A well regulated Militia being necessary to the security of a free State, the right of the people to keep and bear Arms, shall not be infringed.

[AMENDMENT III]

No Soldier shall, in time of peace be quartered in any house, without the consent of the Owner, nor in time of war, but in a manner to be prescribed by law.

[AMENDMENT IV]

The right of the people to be secure in their persons, houses, papers, and effects, against unreasonable searches and seizures, shall not be violated, and no Warrants shall issue, but upon probable cause, supported by Oath or affirmation, and particularly describing the place to be searched, and the persons or things to be seized.

[AMENDMENT V]

No person shall be held to answer for a capital, or otherwise infamous crime, unless on a presentment or indictment of a Grand Jury, except in cases arising in the land or naval forces, or in the Militia, when in actual service in time of War or public danger; nor shall any person be subject for the same offense to be twice put in jeopardy of life or limb; nor shall be compelled in any criminal case to be a witness against himself, nor be deprived of life, liberty, or property, without due process of law; nor shall private property be taken for public use, without just compensation.

[AMENDMENT VI]

In all criminal prosecutions, the accused shall enjoy the right to a speedy and public trial, by an impartial jury of the State and district wherein the crime shall have been committed, which district shall have been previously ascertained by law, and to be informed of the nature and cause of the accusation; to be confronted with the witnesses against him; to have compulsory process for obtaining witnesses in his favor, and to have the Assistance of Counsel for his defence.

[AMENDMENT VII]

In Suits at common law, where the value in controversy shall exceed twenty dollars, the right of trial by jury shall be preserved, and no fact tried by a jury, shall be otherwise re-examined in any Court of the United States, than according to the rules of the common law.

[AMENDMENT VIII]

Excessive bail shall not be required, nor excessive fines imposed, nor cruel and unusual punishments inflicted.

[AMENDMENT IX]

The enumeration in the Constitution, of certain rights, shall not be construed to deny or disparage others retained by the people.

[AMENDMENT X]

The powers not delegated to the United States by the Constitution, nor prohibited by it to the States, are reserved to the States respectively, or to the people.[7]

[AMENDMENT XI]

The Judicial power of the United States shall not be construed to extend to any suit in law or equity, commenced or prosecuted against one of the United States by Citizens of another State, or by Citizens or Subjects of any Foreign State.[8]

[AMENDMENT XII]

The Electors shall meet in their respective states, and vote by ballot for President and Vice-President, one of

---

[7]The first ten amendments were all proposed by Congress on September 25, 1789, and were ratified and adoption certified on December 15, 1791.

[8]Proposed by Congress on March 4, 1794, and declared ratified on January 8, 1798.

whom, at least, shall not be an inhabitant of the same state with themselves; they shall name in their ballots the person voted for as President, and in distinct ballots the person voted for as Vice-President, and they shall make distinct lists of all persons voted for as President, and of all persons voted for as Vice-President, and of the number of votes for each, which lists they shall sign and certify, and transmit sealed to the seat of the government of the United States, directed to the President of the Senate;— The President of the Senate shall, in the presence of the Senate and House of Representatives, open all the certificates and the votes shall then be counted;—The person having the greatest number of votes for President, shall be the President, if such number be a majority of the whole number of Electors appointed; and if no person have such majority, then from the persons having the highest numbers not exceeding three on the list of those voted for as President, the House of Representatives shall choose immediately, by ballot, the President. But in choosing the President, the votes shall be taken by states, the representation from each state having one vote; a quorum for this purpose shall consist of a member or members from two-thirds of the states, and a majority of all the states shall be necessary to a choice. And if the House of Representatives shall not choose a President whenever the right of choice shall devolve upon them, before the fourth day of March next following, then the Vice-President shall act as President, as in the case of the death or other constitutional disability of the President.—The person having the greatest number of votes as Vice-President, shall be the Vice-President, if such number be a majority of the whole number of Electors appointed, and if no person have a majority, then from the two highest numbers on the list, the Senate shall choose the Vice-President; a quorum for the purpose shall consist of two-thirds of the whole number of Senators, and a majority of the whole number shall be necessary to a choice. But no person constitutionally ineligible to the office of President shall be eligible to that of Vice-President of the United States.[9]

[AMENDMENT XIII]

Section 1.

Neither slavery nor involuntary servitude, except as a punishment for crime whereof the party shall have been duly convicted, shall exist within the United States, or any place subject to their jurisdiction.

Section 2.

Congress shall have power to enforce this article by appropriate legislation.[10]

---

[9]Proposed by Congress on December 9, 1803; declared ratified on September 25, 1804; supplemented by Amendments XX and XXIII.

[10]Proposed by Congress on January 31, 1865; declared ratified on December 18, 1865.

[AMENDMENT XIV]

Section 1.

All persons born or naturalized in the United States, and subject to the jurisdiction thereof, are citizens of the United States and of the State wherein they reside. No State shall make or enforce any law which shall abridge the privileges or immunities of citizens of the United States; nor shall any State deprive any person of life, liberty, or property, without due process of law; nor deny to any person within its jurisdiction the equal protection of the laws.

Section 2.

Representatives shall be apportioned among the several States according to their respective numbers, counting the whole number of persons in each State, excluding Indians not taxed. But when the right to vote at any election for the choice of electors for President and Vice-President of the United States, Representatives in Congress, the Executive and Judicial officers of a State, or the members of the Legislature thereof, is denied to any of the male inhabitants of such State, being twenty-one years of age, and citizens of the United States, or in any way abridged, except for participation in rebellion, or other crime, the basis of representation therein shall be reduced in the proportion which the number of such male citizens shall bear to the whole number of male citizens twenty-one years of age in such State.

Section 3.

No person shall be a Senator or Representative in Congress, or elector of President and Vice President, or hold any office, civil or military, under the United States, or under any State, who, having previously taken an oath, as a member of Congress, or as an officer of the United States, or as a member of any State legislature, or as an executive or judicial officer of any State, to support the Constitution of the United States, shall have engaged in insurrection or rebellion against the same, or given aid or comfort to the enemies thereof. But Congress may by a vote of two-thirds of each House, remove such disability.

Section 4.

The validity of the public debt of the United States, authorized by law, including debts incurred for payment of pensions and bounties for services in suppressing insurrection or rebellion, shall not be questioned. But neither the United States nor any State shall assume or pay any debt or obligation incurred in aid of insurrection or rebellion against the United States, or any claim for the loss or emancipation of any slave; but all such debts, obligations and claims shall be held illegal and void.

Section 5.

The Congress shall have power to enforce, by appropriate legislation, the provisions of this article.[11]

[AMENDMENT XV]

Section 1.

The right of citizens of the United States to vote shall not be denied or abridged by the United States or by any State on account of race, color, or previous condition of servitude.

Section.

The Congress shall have power to enforce this article by appropriate legislation.[12]

[AMENDMENT XVI]

The Congress shall have power to lay and collect taxes on incomes, from whatever source derived, without apportionment among the several States, and without regard to any census or enumeration.[13]

[AMENDMENT XVII]

The Senate of the United States shall be composed of two Senators from each State, elected by the people thereof, for six years; and each Senator shall have one vote. The electors in each State shall have the qualifications requisite for electors of the most numerous branch of the State legislatures.

When vacancies happen in the representation of any State in the Senate, the executive authority of such State shall issue writs of election to fill such vacancies: *Provided,* That the legislature of any State may empower the executive thereof to make temporary appointments until the people fill the vacancies by election as the legislature may direct.

This amendment shall not be so construed as to affect the election or term of any Senator chosen before it becomes valid as part of the Constitution.[14]

[11]Proposed by Congress on June 13, 1866; declared ratified on July 28, 1868.

[12]Proposed by Congress on February 26, 1869; declared ratified on March 30, 1870.

[13]Proposed by Congress on July 12, 1909; declared ratified on February 25, 1913.

[14]Proposed by Congress on May 13, 1912; declared ratified on May 31, 1913.

[AMENDMENT XVIII]

Section 1.

After one year from the ratification of this article the manufacture, sale, or transportation of intoxicating liquors within, the importation thereof into, or the exportation thereof from the United States and all territory subject to the jurisdiction thereof for beverage purposes is hereby prohibited.

Section 2.

The Congress and the several States shall have concurrent power to enforce this article by appropriate legislation.

Section 3.

This article shall be inoperative unless it shall have been ratified as an amendment to the Constitution by the legislatures of the several States, as provided in the Constitution, within seven years from the date of the submission hereof to the States by the Congress.[15]

[AMENDMENT XIX]

The right of citizens of the United States to vote shall not be denied or abridged by the United States or by any State on account of sex.

Congress shall have power to enforce this article by appropriate legislation.[16]

[AMENDMENT XX]

Section 1.

The terms of the President and Vice President shall end at noon on the 20th day of January, and the terms of Senators and Representatives at noon on the 3d day of January, of the years in which such terms would have ended if this article had not been ratified; and the terms of their successors shall then begin.

Section 2.

The Congress shall assemble at least once in every year, and such meeting shall begin at noon on the 3d day of January, unless they shall by law appoint a different day.

[15]Proposed by Congress on December 18, 1917; declared ratified on January 29, 1919; repealed by Amendment XXI.

[16]Proposed by Congress on June 4, 1919; declared ratified on August 26, 1920.

Section 3.

If, at the time fixed for the beginning of the term of the President, the President elect shall have died, the Vice President elect shall become President. If a President shall not have been chosen before the time fixed for the beginning of his term, or if the President elect shall have failed to qualify, then the Vice President elect shall act as President until a President shall have qualified; and the Congress may by law provide for the case wherein neither a President elect nor a Vice President elect shall have qualified, declaring who shall then act as President, or the manner in which one who is to act shall be selected, and such person shall act accordingly until a President or Vice President shall have qualified.

Section 4.

The Congress may by law provide for the case of the death of any of the persons from whom the House of Representatives may choose a President whenever the right of choice shall have devolved upon them, and for the case of the death of any of the persons from whom the Senate may choose a Vice President whenever the right of choice shall have devolved upon them.

Section 5.

Sections 1 and 2 shall take effect on the 15th day of October following the ratification of this article.

Section 6.

This article shall be inoperative unless it shall have been ratified as an amendment to the Constitution by the legislatures of three-fourths of the several States within seven years from the date of its submission.[17]

[AMENDMENT XXI]

Section 1.

The eighteenth article of amendment to the Constitution of the United States is hereby repealed.

Section 2.

The transportation or importation into any States, Territory, or possession of the United States for delivery or use therein of intoxicating liquors, in violation of the laws thereof, is hereby prohibited.

Section 3.

This article shall be inoperative unless it shall have been ratified as an amendment to the Constitution by

conventions in the several States, as provided in the Constitution, within seven years from the date of the submission hereof to the States by the Congress.[18]

[AMENDMENT XXII]

Section 1.

No person shall be elected to the office of the President more than twice, and no person who has held the office of President, or acted as President, for more than two years of a term to which some other person was elected President shall be elected to the office of the President more than once. But this Article shall not apply to any person holding the office of President when this Article was proposed by the Congress, and shall not prevent any person who may be holding the office of President, or acting as President, during the term within which this Article becomes operative from holding the office of President or acting as President during the remainder of such term.

Section 2.

This article shall be inoperative unless it shall have been ratified as an amendment to the Constitution by the legislatures of three-fourths of the several States within seven years from the date of its submission to the States by the Congress.[19]

[AMENDMENT XXIII]

Section 1.

The District constituting the seat of Government of the United States shall appoint in such manner as the Congress shall direct:

A number of electors of President and Vice President equal to the whole number of Senators and Representatives in Congress to which the District would be entitled if it were a State, but in no event more than the least populous State; they shall be in addition to those appointed by the States, but they shall be considered, for the purposes of the election of President and Vice President, to be electors appointed by a State; and they shall meet in the District and perform such duties as provided by the twelfth article of amendment.

Section 2.

The Congress shall have power to enforce this article by appropriate legislation.[20]

---

[18]Proposed by Congress on February 20, 1933; declared ratified on December 5, 1933.

[19]Proposed by Congress on March 24, 1947; declared ratified on March 1, 1951.

[20]Proposed by Congress on June 16, 1960; declared ratified on April 3, 1961.

[17]Proposed by Congress on March 2, 1932; declared ratified on February 6, 1933.

[AMENDMENT XXIV]

Section 1.

The right of citizens of the United States to vote in any primary or other election for President or Vice President, for electors for President or Vice President, or for Senator or Representative in Congress, shall not be denied or abridged by the United States or any state by reason of failure to pay any poll tax or other tax.

Section 2.

The Congress shall have the power to enforce this article by appropriate legislation.[21]

[AMENDMENT XXV]

Section 1.

In case of the removal of the President from office or his death or resignation, the Vice President shall become President.

Section 2.

Whenever there is a vacancy in the office of the Vice President, the President shall nominate a Vice President who shall take the office upon confirmation by a majority vote of both houses of Congress.

Section 3.

Whenever the President transmits to the President pro tempore of the Senate and the Speaker of the House of Representatives his written declaration that he is unable to discharge the powers and duties of his office, and until he transmits to them a written declaration to the contrary, such powers and duties shall be discharged by the Vice President as Acting President.

Section 4.

Whenever the Vice President and a majority of either the principal officers of the executive departments or of such other body as Congress may by law provide, trans-mit to the President pro tempore of the Senate and the Speaker of the House of Representatives their written declaration that the President is unable to discharge the powers and duties of his office, the Vice President shall immediately assume the powers and duties of the office as Acting President.

Thereafter, when the President transmits to the President pro tempore of the Senate and the Speaker of the House of Representatives his written declaration that no inability exists, he shall resume the powers and duties of his office unless the Vice President and a majority of either the principal officers of the executive department or of such other body as Congress may by law provide, transmit within four days to the President pro tempore of the Senate and the Speaker of the House of Representatives their written declaration that the President is unable to discharge the powers and duties of his office. Thereupon Congress shall decide the issue, assembling within 48 hours for that purpose if not in session. If the Congress, within 21 days after receipt of the latter written declaration, or, if Congress is not in session, within 21 days after Congress is required to assemble, determines by two-thirds vote of both houses that the President is unable to discharge the powers and duties of his office, the Vice President shall continue to discharge the same as Acting President; otherwise, the President shall resume the powers and duties of his office.[22]

[AMENDMENT XXVI]

Section 1.

The right of citizens of the United States, who are 18 years of age or older, to vote shall not be denied or abridged by the United States or any state on account of age.

Section 2.

The Congress shall have the power to enforce this article by appropriate legislation.[23]

---

[21]Proposed by Congress on August 27, 1962; declared ratified on January 23, 1963.

[22]Proposed by Congress on July 6, 1965; declared ratified on February 10, 1967.

[23]Proposed by Congress on March 23, 1971; declared ratified on June 30, 1971.

PRESIDENTS AND VICE-PRESIDENTS

President and Vice-President	
George Washinton (F)	1789
J. Adams	'89
John Adams (F)	1797
T. Jefferson (R^J)	'97
Thomas Jefferson (R^J)	1801
A. Burr (R^J)	'01
G. Clinton (R^J)	'05
James Madison (R^J)	1809
G. Clinton (R^J)	'09
E. Gerry (R^J)	'13
James Monroe (R^J)	1817
D. Tompkins (R^J)	'17
John Quincy Adams (NR)	1825
J. Calhoun (R^J)	'25
Andrew Jackson (D)	1829
J. Calhoun (D)	'29
M. Van Buren (D)	'33
Martin Van Buren (D)	1837
R. Johnson (D)	'37
William H. Harrison (W)	1841
J. Tyler (W)	'41
John Tyler (W and D)	1841
James K. Polk (D)	1845
G. Dallas (D)	'45
Zachary Taylor (W)	1849
M. Fillmore (W)	'49
Millard Fillmore (W)	1850
Franklin Pierce (D)	1853
W. King (D)	'53
James Buchanan (D)	1857
J. Breckinridge (D)	'57
Abraham Lincoln (R)	1861
H. Hamlin (R)	'61
A. Johnson (U)	'65
Andrew Johnson (U)	1865
Ulysses S. Grant (R)	1869
S. Colfax (R)	'69
H. Wilson (R)	'73

Rutherford B. Hayes (R)	1877
W. Wheeler (R)	'77
James A. Garfield (R)	1881
C. Arthur (R)	'81
Chester A. Arthur (R)	1881
Grover Cleveland (D)	1885
T. Hendricks (D)	'85
Benjamin Harrison (R)	1889
L. Morton (R)	'89
Grover Cleveland (D)	1893
A. Stevenson (D)	'93
William McKinley (R)	1897
G. Hobart (R)	'97
T. Roosevelt (R)	'01
Theodore Roosevelt (R)	1901
C. Fairbanks (R)	'05
William Howard Taft (R)	1909
J. Sherman (R)	'09
Woodrow Wilson (D)	1913
T. Marshall (D)	'13
Warren G. Harding (R)	1921
C. Coolidge (R)	'21
Calvin Coolidge (R)	1923
C. Dawes (R)	'25
Herbert Hoover (R)	1929
C. Curtis (R)	'29
Franklin D. Roosevelt (D)	1933
J. Garner (D)	'33
H. Wallace (D)	'41
H. Truman (D)	'45
Harry S. Truman (D)	1945
A. Barkley (D)	'49
Dwight D. Eisenhower (R)	1953
R. Nixon (R)	'53
John F. Kennedy (D)	1961
L. Johnson (D)	'61
Lyndon B. Johnson (D)	1963
H. Humphrey (D)	'65

Richard M. Nixon (R)	1969
S. Agnew (R)	'69
G. Ford (R)	'73
Gerald R. Ford (R)	1974
N. Rockefeller (R)	'74

Party affiliations: D, Democratic; F, Federalist; NR, National Republican; R, Republican; R^J, Republican (Jeffersonian); U, Unionist; W, Whig.

POPULATION OF THE UNITED STATES: 1800–1880

Division and State	1800	1810	1820	1830	1840	1850	1860	1870	1880
UNITED STATES	5,308,483	7,239,881	9,638,453	12,866,020	17,069,453	23,191,876	31,443,321	39,818,449	50,189,209
New England	1,233,011	1,471,973	1,660,071	1,954,717	2,234,822	2,728,116	3,135,283	3,487,924	4,010,529
Maine	151,719	228,705	298,335	399,455	501,793	583,169	628,279	626,915	648,936
New Hampshire	183,858	214,160	244,161	269,328	284,574	317,976	326,073	318,300	346,991
Vermont	154,465	217,895	235,981	280,652	291,948	314,120	315,098	330,551	332,286
Massachusetts	422,845	472,040	523,287	610,408	737,699	994,514	1,231,066	1,457,351	1,783,085
Rhode Island	69,122	76,931	83,059	97,199	108,830	147,545	174,620	217,353	276,531
Connecticut	251,002	261,942	275,248	297,675	309,978	370,792	460,147	537,454	622,700
Middle Atlantic	1,402,565	2,014,702	2,669,845	3,587,664	4,526,260	5,898,735	7,458,985	8,810,806	10,496,878
New York	589,051	959,049	1,372,812	1,918,608	2,428,921	3,097,394	3,880,735	4,382,759	5,082,871
New Jersey	211,149	245,562	277,575	320,823	373,306	489,555	672,035	906,096	1,131,116
Pennsylvania	602,365	810,091	1,049,458	1,348,233	1,724,033	2,311,786	2,906,215	3,521,951	4,282,891
South Atlantic	2,286,494	2,674,891	3,061,063	3,645,752	3,925,299	4,679,090	5,364,703	5,835,610	7,597,197
Delaware	64,273	72,674	72,749	76,748	78,085	91,532	112,216	125,015	146,608
Maryland	341,548	380,546	407,350	447,040	470,019	583,034	687,049	780,894	934,943
Dist. of Columbia	8,144	15,471	23,336	30,261	33,745	51,687	75,080	131,700	177,624
Virginia	886,149	983,152	1,075,069	1,220,978	1,249,764	1,421,661	1,596,318	1,225,163	1,512,565
West Virginia	....	....	....	....	....	....	....	442,014	618,457
North Carolina	478,103	555,500	638,829	737,987	753,419	869,039	992,622	1,071,361	1,399,750
South Carolina	345,591	415,115	502,741	581,185	594,398	668,507	703,708	705,606	995,577
Georgia	162,686	252,433	340,989	516,823	691,392	906,185	1,057,286	1,184,109	1,542,180
Florida	....	....	....	34,730	54,477	87,445	140,424	187,748	269,493
East South Central	335,407	708,590	1,190,489	1,815,969	2,575,445	3,363,271	4,020,991	4,404,445	5,585,151
Kentucky	220,955	406,511	564,317	687,917	779,828	982,405	1,155,684	1,321,011	1,648,690
Tennessee	105,602	261,727	422,823	681,904	829,210	1,002,717	1,109,801	1,258,520	1,542,359
Alabama	1,250	9,046	127,901	309,527	590,756	771,623	964,201	996,992	1,262,505
Mississippi	7,600	31,306	75,448	136,621	375,651	606,526	791,305	827,922	1,131,597
West South Central	....	77,618	167,680	246,127	449,985	940,251	1,747,667	2,029,965	3,334,220
Arkansas	....	1,062	14,273	30,388	97,574	209,897	435,450	484,471	802,525
Louisiana	....	76,556	153,407	215,739	352,411	517,762	708,002	726,915	939,946
Oklahoma	....	....	....	....	....	....	....	....	....
Texas	....	....	....	....	....	212,592	604,215	818,579	1,591,749
East North Central	51,006	272,324	792,719	1,470,018	2,924,728	4,523,260	6,926,884	9,124,517	11,206,668
Ohio	41,365	230,760	581,434	937,903	1,519,467	1,980,329	2,339,511	2,665,260	3,198,062
Indiana	5,641	24,520	147,178	343,031	685,866	988,416	1,350,428	1,680,637	1,978,301
Illinois	....	12,282	55,211	157,445	476,183	851,470	1,711,951	2,539,891	3,077,871
Michigan	....	4,762	8,896	31,639	212,267	397,654	749,113	1,184,059	1,636,937
Wisconsin	....	....	....	....	30,945	305,391	775,881	1,054,670	1,315,497
West North Central	....	19,783	66,586	140,455	426,814	880,335	2,169,832	3,856,594	6,157,443
Minnesota	....	....	....	....	....	6,077	172,023	439,706	780,773
Iowa	....	....	....	....	43,112	192,214	674,913	1,194,020	1,624,615
Missouri	....	19,783	66,586	140,455	383,702	682,044	1,182,012	1,721,295	2,168,380
North Dakota	....	....	....	....	....	....	....	4,837	36,909
South Dakota	....	....	....	....	....	....	....	11,776	98,268
Nebraska	....	....	....	....	....	....	28,841	122,993	452,402
Kansas	....	....	....	....	....	....	107,206	364,399	996,096
Mountain	....	....	....	....	....	72,927	174,923	315,385	653,119
Montana	....	....	....	....	....	....	....	20,595	39,159
Idaho	....	....	....	....	....	....	....	14,999	32,610
Wyoming	....	....	....	....	....	....	....	9,118	20,789
Colorado	....	....	....	....	....	....	34,277	39,864	194,327
New Mexico	....	....	....	....	....	61,547	93,516	91,874	119,565
Arizona	....	....	....	....	....	....	....	9,658	40,440
Utah	....	....	....	....	....	11,380	40,273	76,786	143,963
Nevada	....	....	....	....	....	....	6,857	42,491	62,266
Pacific	....	....	....	....	....	105,871	444,053	675,125	1,148,004
Washington	....	....	....	....	....	1,201	11,594	23,955	75,116
Oregon	....	....	....	....	....	12,093	52,465	90,923	174,768
California	....	....	....	....	....	92,597	379,994	560,247	864,694
Alaska	....	....	....	....	....	....	....	....	....
Hawaii	....	....	....	....	....	....	....	....	33,426

CREDITS AND ACKNOWLEDGMENTS

The author and publisher acknowledge with gratitude permissions to reprint or adapt the following materials. The numbers shown below refer to the pages of this text.

Literary Permissions
818*c*: Poem, "For Brother Malcolm" by Edward S. Spriggs. From *For Malcolm: Poems on the Life and Death of Malcolm X*, edited by Dudley Randall and Margaret G. Burroughs. Copyright © 1967 by Broadside Press. Reprinted by permission of the author. 818*d*: Fragment of poem, "Back to/Back to" by Victor Hernandez Cruz. From SNAPS, by Victor Hernandez Cruz. Copyright © 1968, 1969 by Victor Hernandez Cruz. Reprinted by permission of Random House, Inc.

Maps, Charts, and Tables
65: Table from *A Diplomatic History of the American People* by Thomas A. Bailey, 9th Edition © 1974, page 24, Prentice-Hall, Inc., Englewood Cliffs, N.J. Adapted with permission. 90: Table from Donald B. Cole, *Handbook of American History*, Harcourt Brace Jovanovich, Inc., page 50. Adapted with permission. 107: Table from Winthrop S. Hudson, *American Protestantism*, Chapter 5, Chart 2, "Congregations in 1775," page 4, The University of Chicago Press. Reprinted with permission. 148: Table from Carl Bridenbaugh, *Cities in Revolt: Urban Life in America, 1743–1776*, page 216, copyright 1938, © 1955, Alfred A. Knopf, Inc. Reprinted with permission. 188: Charts from Douglas C. North, *The Economic Growth of the United States, 1790–1860*, page 26, © 1961, Prentice-Hall, Inc., Englewood Cliffs, N.J. Adapted with permission. 504: Map, Where the Buffalo Roamed. Adapted from J. A. Allen, "The American Bison, Living and Extinct," *Memoirs, Museum of Comparative Zoology*, Vol. 4, No. 10, Harvard University Press, 1876. 505: Maps, Virgin Forest, 1620, 1850, 1926. Adapted from *The Influence of Geography on Our Economic Life* by Ridgley & Ekblaw, Gregg Publishing Co., 1938, pp. 528–529. Used with permission of McGraw-Hill, Inc., Gregg Division; and of the Department of Agriculture. 524: Chart, Mass Communications, 1929–1945. Adapted with permission of *Editor & Publisher*; and the National Broadcasting Company.

Illustration Credits
PART I 1: I. N. Phelps Stokes Collection, Prints Division, The New York Public Library, Astor, Lenox and Tilden Foundations. 17: engraving by Wm. and Thomas Birch, The Free Library of Philadelphia. 23: Courtesy of The New York Historical Society. 24: detail from *Poor Richard Illustrated*, engraving by O. Pelton, 1859. 29: The First National Bank of Boston. 33: Library of Congress. 34: Arents Collections, The New York Public Library, Astor, Lenox and Tilden Foundations. 37: The Historical Society of Pennsylvania. 41: detail from Speeds' *Theatrum Imperii Magnae Britanniae*, 1676, The British Library. 42: The Historical Society of Pennsylvania. 44: Courtesy, American Antiquarian Society. 45: illustration to J. W. Barber: *Interesting Events . . .*, The Metropolitan Museum of Art, Bequest of Charles Allen Munn, 1924. 46: Courtesy of The Newberry Library. 48: Colonial Williamsburg Photograph. 56: The Maryland Historical Society, Baltimore. 59: Library of Congress. 66: Courtesy of The New York Historical Society. 67: Anne S. K. Brown Military Collection, Brown University Library. 70: The Gilbert Darlington Collection. 73: Courtesy of The Henry Francis du Pont Winterthur Museum. 74: The Metropolitan Museum of Art, Bequest of Charles Allen Munn, 1924. 76: "American Soldat," The Metropolitan Museum of Art. 79: David Muench. 83: David Muench. 84: Courtesy of The Newberry Library. 88: Hernandez: *Nova Plantarum . . . 1651*. 91: Courtesy, American Antiquarian Society. 93, 94: Library of Congress.

PART II 168, 182: Courtesy of The New York Historical Society. 189: Museum of the City of New York. 192: State Historical Society of Wisconsin. 196: *Frank Leslie's Illustrated*, July 1, 1865. 198: Yale University Art Gallery, Mabel Brady Garvan Collection. 201: Collot, *Voyage Dans L'Amerique . . . Paris 1826*. 204: City Art Museum of St. Louis. 208: Library of Congress. 211: Historical Collection, Title Insurance and Trust. 212: Olivier Plantation, Louisiana State Museum. 223: Stephan Lorant from *The Glorious Burden: The American Presidency*. 224: Franklin D. Roosevelt Library. 228: Library of Congress. 233: Royal Ontario Museum, Toronto, Canada. 237: Collection of Harry T. Peters, Jr. 240: Franklin D. Roosevelt Library. 244: Cook Collection, Valentine Museum, Richmond, Va. 247: Library of Congress. 248: U.S. Army Photograph. 252: Courtesy of The New York Historical Society. 256: Field Museum of Natural History. 261: Woolaroc Museum. 265: The Newberry Library. 271: William H. Meyers Diary, 1838–39, Manuscripts and Archives Division, The New York Public Library, Astor, Lenox and Tilden Foundations. 274: California State Library. 276: Museum of the City of New York. 278: Pavel Svinin, ca. 1812, The Metropolitan Museum of Art, Rogers Fund, 1942. 282: Library of Congress. 285: Courtesy of The New York Historical Society. 287: Union Pacific Rail Road Co. 292: Metropolitan Museum of Art, Gift of I. N. Phelps Stokes, Edward S. Hawes, Alice Mary Hawes, Marion Augusta Hawes, 1937. 296: Kansas State Historical Society. 298: Maine Historical Society. 303: The Sophia Smith Collection, Women's History Archive, Smith College. 304: Library of Congress. 306: Worcester Art Museum. 311: Library of Congress. 315: Eno Collection, Prints Division, The New York Public Library, Astor, Lenox and Tilden Foundations. 317: Denver Public Library Western Collection. 318: Museum of the City of New York. 322: Library of Congress. 324: Book-page engraving of the George Winter painting "Prairie Scene, Indiana," courtesy of The Indiana Historical Society Library. 326: Metropolitan Museum of Art, Harris Brisbane Dick Fund, 1934. 328: Courtesy of The New York Historical Society. 333: Courtesy of The American Museum of Natural History.

PART III 341: Carnegie Library of Pittsburgh. 357: Byron Collection, Museum of the City of New York. 359: Library of Congress. 361: Courtesy of The New York Historical Society. 365: Photo by Lewis Hine, George Eastman House Collection. 371: Brown Brothers. 374: Courtesy of the Caterpillar Tractor Co., Peoria. 379: From the Collection of R. L. Dodd, Kosciusko, Miss. 383: Library of Congress. 384: Culver Pictures. 386: Underwood & Underwood. 392: *Harper's Weekly*, October 20, 1877. 395: U.P.I. 399: National Archives. 400: U.S. Signal Corps. 406, 408: Library of Congress. 413: National Archives. 415: U.P.I. 416: National Archives. 421: Library of Congress. 425: Montana Historical Society, Helena. 426: National Archives. 427: Jack R. Williams. 434: Library of Congress. 437: History Division, Natural History Museum of Los Angeles County. 441: Courtesy, The Bancroft Library. 445: The Bettmann Archive, Inc. 446: George Eastman House Collection. 447: Museum of the City of New York. 451, 455: Brown Brothers. 459: Natural History Museum of Los Angeles County. 463: The Bettmann Archive, Inc. 464: American Telephone & Telegraph Co. 466: David R. Phillips. 468: Courtesy of The Chicago Lawn Historical Society. 474: Brown Brothers. 475, 481: Library of Congress. 482: Library of Congress. 484: Montana Historical Society, Helena. 486: Photo by Jacob A.

Riis, The Jacob A. Riis Collection, Museum of the City of New York. 487: Photo by Lewis W. Hine, George Eastman House Collection. 489: Frederic Lewis. 491: Culver Pictures. 493: Library of Congress. 499: The Darius Kinsey Collection. 500: Collection of Robert E. Cunningham. 503: Library of Congress. 506: The Huffman Pictures, Miles City, Montana. 512: Photo by William Henry Jackson, Metropolitan Museum of Art. 513: Denver Public Library. 514: Courtesy of The Sierra Club, Photo by Joseph Le Conte.

PART IV   521: Brown Brothers. 535: U.P.I. 542, 546: Brown Brothers. 548: *Collier's*, October 10, 1936. 552: Wide World. 554, 557: U.P.I. 559: Brown Brothers. 562: The Bettmann Archive, Inc. 563, 570: Brown Brothers. 573: Wide World. 578: National Archives. 584, 585: U.S. Coast Guard. 586: Underwood & Underwood. 589: Margaret Bourke-White, Time-Life Picture Agency, © Time Inc. 592: Energy Research and Development Administration. 595: Dorothea Lange/National Archives. 598: Photoworld. 602: Duncan Schiedt Archive. 607: Wide World. 608: Culver Pictures. 613: Underwood & Underwood. 616, 618: Brown Brothers. 619, 622: Wide World. 627: U.P.I. 628: Franklin D. Roosevelt Library. 633: Culver Pictures. 635: Underwood & Underwood. 637: Culver Pictures. 641: Photoworld. 644: U.P.I. 648: Brown Brothers. 653: Library of Congress. 657: Brown Brothers. 659: Underwood & Underwood. 665: Mrs. Henry Rhoades. 666: Frederic Lewis.

PART V   671: Donald C. Dietz/Stock Boston. 681: Bill Owens. 686: Cornell Capa/Magnum. 693: Charles Harbutt/Magnum. 696: Burk Uzzle/Magnum. 699: Marc Riboud/Magnum. 704: Nicholas Sapieha/Stock Boston. 714: Lawrence Fried/Magnum. 719: Cornell Capa/Magnum. 727: Wide World. 729: Robert Phillips/Black Star. 737: Photri. 732: Wide World. 739: Charles Gatewood. 744: Charles Moore/Black Star. 749: George Ballis/Black Star. 759: George Gardner. 763: Karen Preuss/Jeroboam. 771: Charles Gatewood. 775: Jeanclaude Lejeune. 778: Bill Owens. 782: Ellis Herwig/Stock Boston. 789: Arthur Tress. 793: George Gardner. 796: Archie Lieberman. 803: Burk Uzzle/Magnum. 808: Larry Keenan, Jr./Nest. 812: Optic Nerve/Jeroboam. 813: Elihu Blotnick/BBM.

PART I—ADDITIONAL CREDITS   96: Abby Aldrich Rockefeller Folk Art Collection. 98, 99: Courtesy Museum of Fine Arts, Boston, Bequest of Maxim Karolik. 102, 103: Rare Book Div., New York Public Library, Astor, Lenox and Tilden Foundations. 105: Local History and Genealogy Div., The New York Public Library, Astor, Lenox and Tilden Foundations. 109: The American Philosophical Society. 111: Courtesy Commission on Archives and History, The United Methodist Church. 118, 119: Connecticut Historical Society. 122: Radio Times Hulton Picture Library. 123: Courtesy of the Trustees, The British Museum. 125: Connecticut Historical Society. 126: Ann Parker. 131: Rare Book Div., The New York Public Library, Astor, Lenox and Tilden Foundations. 136, 137: I. N. Phelps Stokes Collection, Prints Div., The New York Public Library, Astor, Lenox and Tilden Foundations. 140: Courtesy of the Newberry Library. 143: Library of Congress. 144: The Metropolitan Museum of Art, Gift of Edgar William and Bernice Chrysler Garbisch, 1963. 147: The Massachusetts Historical Society. 150, 151: I. N. Phelps Stokes Collection, Prints Div., The New York Public Library, Astor, Lenox and Tilden Foundations. 154, 155, 158, 164: Rare Book Div., The New York Public Library, Astor, Lenox and Tilden Foundations. 162: Map Division, The New York Public Library, Astor, Lenox and Tilden Foundations.

Photographic Essays
CHRONICLE: EARLY EXPLORATION 82*a:* "The Manner of Their Fishing" (John White). 82*b*–*c:* Clockwise from lower left: (1) Florida Sandhill Crane (William Bartram), (2) Little Brown Lark (Bartram), (3) Great Yellow Bream (Bartram), (4) Swallow-tail butterfly (John White), (5) Portuguese Man-of-War (White), (6) Flying fish (White), (7) Green Heron (Bartram), (8) Coachwhip snake (Bartram), (9) Savannah Pink, Imperial Moth (Bartram), (10) Diamond-back Terrapin (White); center artwork, "The French Reach Port Royal" (Jacques Le Moyne, engraving by Thomas de Bry). 82*d:* "The Conjurer," "A Woman of Florida," "Village of Secoton" (all by John White). All drawings by John White: courtesy of the Trustees, The British Museum. All drawings by William Bartram: by permission of the Trustees of The British Museum (Natural History). Painting by Jacques Le Moyne: from the Rare Book Division, The New York Public Library, Astor, Lenox and Tilden Foundations.

CHRONICLE: LIFE IN THE NEW NATION 210*a*–210*d:* Drawings and watercolors by Lewis Miller from the collection of the Historical Society of York County, York, Pa.

CHRONICLE: THE WILDERNESS 338*a:* (top) Library of Congress; (bottom) Collection of The Oakland Museum, Gift of Miss Marguerite Laird in Memory of her parents, Pinkston Wade Laird and Flora McCloskey Laird. 338*b*–338*c:* U.S. Department of the Interior, National Park Service. 338*d:* The Berkshire Museum, Pittsfield, Mass.

CHRONICLE: A HARD LIFE TO SWALLOW 527: (top) Dorothea Lange Collection, The Oakland Museum; (bottom) Library of Congress. 528: (top, right) Dorothea Lange Collection, The Oakland Museum; (bottom) Library of Congress; (left) Library of Congress. 529: Dorothea Lange Collection, The Oakland Museum. 530: (top and bottom) Dorothea Lange Collection, The Oakland Museum.

CHRONICLE: MUSEUM OF THE STREETS 818*a:* (top) Alex Webb/Magnum; (bottom) "La Raza de oro" by José G. Gonzalez. 818*b:* (top) Peter Menzel/Stock Boston; (middle) Elihu Blotnick/BBM; (bottom) Jerry Sloan; (center page) Erich Hartmann/Magnum. 818*c:* (top) Gianni Tortoli/Photo Researchers; (bottom) John Running. 818*d:* (top) Frank Muller-May/Magnum; (bottom) Elihu Blotnick/BBM.

Biographical Illustration Credits
27: Courtesy Newberry Library, Chicago. 133: Brown Brothers. 220: White House Collection. 246: Reproduced from the Collections of the Library of Congress. 269: Schomburg Center for Research in Black Culture, New York Public Library, Astor, Lenox and Tilden Foundations. 353: Mark Twain Memorial, Hartford, Conn. 510: M.I.T. Historical Collections. 541: U.P.I. 566: Photoworld/FPG. 591: Photoworld/FPG. 727: Wide World. 743: U.P.I.

INDEX

Abbott, Lyman, 194
Abolition movement, 92, 95, 97, 179, 212–213, 215, 225, 245, 250, 264, 267–268, 289–290, 294, 301, 303, 305, 313
Adams, Abigail, 94, 132, 134; biography, 133
Adams, John: administration 171–172, 219, 256, 282; on China, 273; in Congress, 48; Declaration of Independence, 12, 49–50; foreign policy, 231, 251; peace treaty, 75; on politics, 56; on slavery, 94; on taverns, 150; vice-president, 15; on violence, 46
Adams, John Quincy, 133, 208, 212, 214, 401; administration, 175, 186, 221, 222; election, 222; Mexican War, 239; in government, 176, 236, 237
Adams, Sam, 11, 24, 44–45, 46, 48, 49, 56, 150
Africa, 3, 7, 15, 22, 63, 69, 80, 146, 185; slave trade, 89, 90–91, 92, 95, 97, 148, 264
Agassiz, Lewis, 254
Alcoholism, 302. *See also* Temperance movement
Algonquin Indians, 63, 64, 68, 85
Alien and sedition acts, 172, 219, 282
Allen, Richard, 263
Amana Society, 310–311
American party, 225
American Revolution, *see* Revolutionary War
Amherst, Jeffrey, 85
Amish, 103, 309
Anarchists/-ism, 100, 313
Anthony, Susan B., 302, 305
Anti-Masonic party, 224–225
Apache Indians, 262
Appleton, Nathan, 210
Architecture: colonial, 124, 143; family, 121, 124; lumber, 326; plantation, 145
Ardrey, Robert, 60
Army: blacks in, 263, 268, 270; cavalry, 255; chaplains, 290; desertion from, 240, 244; imperialism of, 239–240; Indian wars, 175, 255–256, 257, 258, 260, 262, 264, 272. *See also* Confederacy, military; Military; Union, military
Arnold, Benedict, 71

Articles of Confederation, 14, 50–52, 54, 57, 69
Asian Americans, 80, 273–274, 275. *See also* China, emigrants
Astor, John Jacob, 194, 327
Attucks, Crispus, 11, 46, 94
Audubon, John James, 333
Austin, Moses and Stephen, 270
Automobile industry, 191
Aztec Indians, 2–3, 4, 62, 146, 241

Bacon, Nathaniel, 42
Bagley, Sarah, 302
Barlowe, Arthur, 159
Baltimore, Lord, 112
Banks/bankers/banking: Bank of the United States, 173, 175, 186, 209, 210, 221, 222; colonial 21, 43; controls, 199, 217; Hamiltonian, 171, 185; Jacksonian, 175, 209, 210; political power, 175, 210
Banneker, Benjamin, 94
Barnum, P. T., 319
Barton, Clara, 304
Battles: Antietam, 245, 248; Boston Massacre, 11, 45–46, 94; Boston Tea Party, 11, 46; Bull Run, 243; Bunker Hill, 12, 49, 94; Fallen Timbers, 256; Gettysburg, 247, 251; Horseshoe Bend, 258; Lake Erie, 263; Monmouth, 134; New Orleans, 173, 175, 222, 232–233, 234, 251, 263; Sand Creek, 262; Tippecanoe, 257; the Wilderness, 68, 247; Yorktown, 13, 72, 95. *See also* Army, Indian wars; War; *and individual wars*
Beard, Charles A. and Mary, 206, 226
Beauregard, Pierre G. T., 290
Beckworth, Jim, 264
Beecher, Lyman, 283, 286
Beissel, Johann Conrad, 310
Benjamin, Judah, 290
Bennet, Lerone, 90
Benton, Thomas Hart, 211, 237
Berkeley, William, 42
Bible, 221; on blacks, 89; Calvinism, 106; on community, 309; Deists, 116; and evolution, 255; and Indians, 87; influence on government, 141; and Jews, 114; on marriage, 123; on nature, 159; Protestants,

111, 112, 286; Puritanism, 107; on slavery, 289, 296; on wealth, 194; on women, 124, 129, 301
Bickerdyke, "Mother," 304
Biddle, Nicholas, 222
Bingham, William, 326
Birkbeck, Morris, 329
Bishop's War, 115
Blacks, 10, 55, 80, 101; early arrival, 7; attitudes toward, 89; culture, 95–96, 97; education, 92; equality, 179, 181; family, 128, 134, 178; free, 39, 43, 92, 94, 95, 128, 179, 213, 244, 263–264, 267–268, 316; land, 31; oppression, 250; organizations, 263; population, 90, 91, 316; religion, 112, 263, 264; status, 89; suffrage, 263, 267, 305; trades, 263, 264, 267. *See also* Labor, and blacks; Slavery; Slaves; Women, black
Black Hawk War, 175, 258
Blackwell, Elizabeth, 304
Blackwell, Henry, 303
Bloomer, Amelia, 302–303
Bolivia, 146
Boone, Daniel, 104, 161, 332
Booth, Edwin, 319
Booth, John Wilkes, 181
Braddock, Edward, 68
Bradford, William, 141, 331
Bradstreet, Anne, 123, 129
Brant, Chief Joseph, 85
Brazil, 62, 92, 93–94, 113
Brent, Margaret, 130
Brook Farm, 177, 312–313
Brown, Clara, 264
Brown, John, 213, 264, 268
Bryant, William Cullen, 178, 332
Buchanan, James, 181, 202, 216, 225
Building industry, 326
Bureau of Indian Affairs (BIA), 175–176, 258
Burgoyne, John, 13, 71, 85
Burke, Edmund, 49
Burr, Aaron, 222, 286
Bush, George, 264
Business, *see* Commerce; Corporations; Economy
Byrd, William, 23, 87, 123, 129, 145

Cabot, John 4
Cabral, Pedro, 4

Calhoun, John C., 175, 212, 214, 222, 239, 258, 271
Calvert, Lord, 130, 139
Calvin, John, 7–8, 106–107, 121–122; Calvinism, 25, 106–109, 110, 116, 285
Canada: American Revolution, 71, 76, 95; French in, 4, 6, 10, 69, 139; government, 48; and Indians, 64; Oregon Territory, 177, 237–238; religion, 12, 47; salvery, 213, 268; wilderness, 157, 161
Capitalism: colonial, 21–25; laws favoring, 184, 185; and religion, 25; and war, 206
Carey, Eli, 191
Carson, Kit, 327
Cartier, Jacques, 4
Catholics: arrival, 6, 112–113, 139; discrimination, 113; ethnic schism, 288; immigrants, 283, 288; and Indians, 86–87; population, 101, 288; and politics, 113, 225, 282, 288; Protestant hatred, 6, 12, 42, 47, 55, 64, 86–87, 102, 103, 112–113, 240, 283, 288; slavery, 290; urban, 319. See also Education, religious; Prejudice, religious
Catlin, George, 333–334
Cayuga Indians, 85
Central America, 2–3, 4. See also individual countries
Channing, William Ellery, 286, 320
Cherokee Indians, 3, 63, 81, 175, 209, 256–257, 258, 260–262, 272
Chesnut, Mary Boykin, 296
Chicanos: history, 254, 270–273; militant, 241
Chickasaw Indians, 3, 81, 175, 257, 258
Children: adolescent, 128, 134, 297; custody, 131, 299, 303; education, 313; male, 297; organizations, 195; pioneer, 295; poor, 195; rearing, 120, 127–128, 134, 296–297, 310. See also Labor, child
China, 15, 61, 140; Communist, 71; emigrants, 254, 273–274, 275; trade with, 3, 237, 273
Chinese Americans, see Asian Americans; China, emigrants
Chivington, John, 262
Choctaw Indians, 3, 81, 175, 257, 258, 261
Cities: bias against, 153; bosses, 223–224; Catholics in, 319; colonial, 146–150; crime, 138, 195, 318–319; definition, 140, 146; disease in, 318, 319–320; environment, 163, 164–165; free blacks in, 263; government, 149–150, 319,

320; growth, 121, 139, 142–143, 146–152, 164–165, 174, 176, 296, 308, 314, 315, 316–318; immigrants in, 25–26, 279, 280–281, 283; labor, 199; planning, 94, 142–143, 148, 151, 335; port, 22, 188, 193, 237; pre-Colombian, 146; and railroads, 187, 192; riots in, 25, 26, 43, 44–45, 243–244, 283, 318–319; slums, 195–196, 203, 281, 283, 318; utilities, 164–165; wealth, 194–195, 210, 319
Civil War: battles and generals, 245, 247–248, 251, 290; beginning, 181; causes, 97, 206–207, 212–213, 226, 242–243, 268, 289–290; effect on economy, 184; and Indians, 262; nation prior to, 100, 170, 174, 176, 177, 179, 187, 192, 202; power struggles before, 206–217; and religion, 289–290; and women, 304–305. See also Confederacy; Union
Clark, William, 172, 210, 235, 325, 327
Clay, Henry, 175, 180, 211, 215, 221, 222, 224, 232, 264
Clemens, Samuel L., see Twain, Mark
Clinton, De Witt, 308, 320–321
Clinton, George, 54
Cole, Thomas, 332
Colles, Christopher, 20–21
Colt, Samuel, 191
Columbus, Christopher, 3–4, 61–62, 113
Commerce: and banking, 210; farmers, 200; fur trade, 85, 97, 147, 159, 160–161, 194, 210, 237, 264, 270, 310, 316, 317, 324, 327; interstate, 173, 203; maritime trade, 65, 75, 89, 147, 148, 150–151, 159, 161–162, 172–173, 178, 184, 187–188, 203, 231, 280, 314, 327–329; regional differences, 176, 179, 193, 210–218, 226; restrictions, 172–173, 185; shipbuilding, 19, 20, 22; wartime, 173; whaling, 19, 22, 161–162, 178, 327–329. See also Corporations; Economy; Factories; Industries; Labor, and management; and individual commodities
Committees of Correspondence, 45, 56
Commoner, Barry, 164–165
Communication: frontier, 329; telegraph, 186, 248. See also Hollywood; Press
Communities: colonial, 139–153; definition, 138; experimental, 177, 298; frontier, 202; government, 141–143, 145; immigrant, 310–311; plantation, 144–145; Puritan,

141–143; religious, 139–142, 298, 309–311; utopian, 308–309, 311–313
Confederacy: amnesty, 250; blockaded, 244, 245, 247; constitution, 217; defeat, 247–248, 250, 251, 316; draft law, 244; and Indians, 262; and Lee, 246; and Lincoln, 217, 242; military, 245, 247–248, 250; resources, 181, 242, 247; slaves, 270
Congress: under Articles of Confederation, 14; conservation, 334, 335; Democrats, 239, 240; farmers, 200–202; immigration, 280, 282; implied powers, 186, 209–210; Indians, 258, 260, 261; land laws, 200–202; manipulated by president, 236, 238–239; Mexican War, 238–239; new states, 234; political parties in, 172, 218, 221–222; relations with presidents, 170, 209; slavery, 212, 216, 244, 263, 264, 268, 301; and South, 215, 216–217; southerners in, 179; Supreme Court, 173, 209; tax powers, 185; War of 1812, 172, 173, 232; war powers, 60, 173, 232; westerners in, 216–217. See also Continental Congress; House of Representatives; Senate
Conservation: movement, 157–158, 165, 333, 334–335; soil, 163–164, 165
Constitution: antipopulism of, 57, 173, 218, 282; Bill of Rights, 14–15, 54–55, 76, 115, 117, 170; and capitalism, 185, 202; implied powers, 173, 186, 209–210; Indian influence on, 88; political parties, 57; presidency, 172; ratification, 14–15, 54–55, 170, 172; religion, 115–116, 117; separation of powers, 53–54; slavery, 14, 53, 80, 95, 97, 180, 213–214; strict constructionism, 171, 186, 235; Supreme Court, 173, 209–210; war-making powers, 73, 76
   Amendments: First, 115, 117; Thirteenth, 226, 268, 270, 305
Constitutional Convention, 14, 38, 51–53, 152–153, 213, 226
Continental Congresses, 12–14, 47–50, 57, 73–74, 94, 95, 133
Cooper, James Fenimore, 178, 332
Cooper, Peter, 191–192
Cornish, Samuel, 268
Cornplanter, Chief, 158
Cornwallis, Charles, 13, 72
Coronado, Francisco de, 4
Corporations: growth, 187. See also

Commerce; Industries; *and individual commodities*
Cortina, Juan M., 272
Cotton, 188, 190, 234; technology, 179, 190–191, 203, 263. *See also* South, cotton; Textile industry
Cotton, John, 39, 130
Cuffe, Paul, 264
Crandall, Prudence, 300
Crawford, William H., 221
Creek Indians, 3, 81, 175, 257, 258, 259, 260–262
Crèvecoeur, J. Hector St. John de, 32, 34, 101, 103, 104, 106
Crittenden, John J., 217
Crockett, Davy, 332
Cuba, 4
Currency, 171, 185, 209, 217

Darwin, Charles, 255
Davenport, John, 139
Davis, Jefferson, 217, 244, 245, 247
Dawes, Tom, 56
Declaration of Independence, 10, 12–13, 30, 49–50, 53, 57, 86, 88, 94, 104, 115, 121, 171, 217, 257, 294
Deere, John, 192
Deism, 115–116, 117
de la Guerra, Pablo, 272
Delaware Indians, 68, 87
Democracy: v. aristocracy, 207–208, 222; in clothing, 208; colonial, 55–57; and Indians, 88; Jacksonian, 294, 313; law and order, 55, 185; participatory, 142; and religion, 284, 288; Revolutionary War, 72–74; and Romantic movement, 331; and Wealth, 50, 52, 173, 184, 194–195, 203, 207, 243–244
Democratic party: in Congress, 239, 240; and ethnics, 281; origins, 171, 172, 222, 223–225, 227; slavery, 180–181, 212, 225, 226; in South, 222, 225, 226, 227
Democratic-Republican party, 171, 172–173, 186, 207, 218–219, 221–222, 227
Dickson, Anna, 305
Dix, Dorothea, 304
Douglas, Stephen A., 180, 215, 226
Douglass, Frederick, 266, 268, 301
Draft: Civil War, 243–244; resistance, 319
Dred Scott decision, *see* Scott, Dred
Dudley, Thomas, 124
Dunmore, Lord, 94–95

Ecology, *see* United States, ecology
Economy: and bankers, 210; and corporations, 187; colonial, 21–25;

depressions, 175, 176, 184, 187, 190, 191, 195, 198, 199, 214, 231, 232, 237, 317; government controls, 185; growth, 186–188, 202; Jacksonian, 209; postwar, 250; potential, 184; and technology, 190–193. *See also* Gross National Product; Hamilton, Alexander, economic policy; Slavery, economic importance
Education: federal aid to, 100, 217; and labor, 199; progressive, 313; public, 177, 193, 199, 296, 297; religious, 100, 112, 193, 283, 288, 289; rural, 295; vocational, 192–193; of young, 120, 127–128, 192–193, 297, 313. *See also* Immigrants, education; Women, education; *and individual ethnic and racial groups*
Edwards, Jonathan, 111, 159
Egypt, 3
Eliot, John, 87
Emancipation Proclamation, 213, 245, 270, 290
Emanuel, David, 114
Emerson, Ralph Waldo, 178, 237, 273, 286, 302, 313, 320, 332
England: and Civil War, 213, 242–243, 247; American colonies, 6–7, 10–13, 19, 22–24, 44, 51, 57, 163; emigrants, 28, 107, 279, 283, 329; and France, 171, 188, 218, 231, 232; and Indians, 85, 86–87, 255, 256, 257, 260; in New World, 62–63; relations with U.S., 177, 185, 188, 190, 214, 230, 231–234, 236, 237–238, 251; religion, 114; Revolutionary War, 10–13, 71–75; slavery in, 89–90; War of 1812, 173, 188, 251
Environment, *see* Conservation, movement; Pollution, environmental; United States, forests, wilderness, wildlife
Equiano, Olaudah, 90
Ericson, Leif, 3
Eskimo Indians, 81

Factories: technology, 330–331; wartime, 248; women in, 295. *See also* Labor, conditions; *and individual commodities*
Family: black, 128, 134, 178; decline of, 308; extended, 296, 309; function, 120–121, 134; and industrialism, 295; nuclear, 121, 124, 134, 294, 298; patriarchal, 294, 295–296; permissive, 297; Puritan, 120–124, 127–128, 134; slave, 128; structure, 124–125, 134; Victorian, 294; working-class, 295

Farmers/farming: attitudes toward, 197, 199–200, 210, 236; history, 2, 3; colonial, 13, 26, 30–35, 142, 143, 165; commercial, 26, 32–35, 54, 211; and environment, 163–164, 165; European, 279; family, 31, 33, 295, 297; Indian, 83, 97, 146; labor, 28–29, 30; markets, 188, 200, 234, 235, 237; pioneer, 31–32, 48, 86, 159–161, 211, 304, 324; political power, 171, 172, 175, 200; produce, 202, 314; production, 19, 31–34; rebellions, 14, 35, 43, 51, 200; Revolutionary War, 48, 51, 66, 73, 152; roads, 211; subsistence, 211; and slavery, 211, 216–217, 225; southern, 48, 200; technology, 20–21, 31, 33, 35, 158, 192, 202; tenant, 202; tobacco, 19, 22, 34–35, 39, 43, 48, 62, 89, 92, 121, 144, 147, 158, 163, 242; wartime, 232; western, 211; wheat, 330. *See also* Women, farm
Federal government: beginnings, 7, 8, 12–15; and business, 186–187, 191, 202–203; bureaucracy, 207; checks and balances, 209; and economy, 186–187; national debt, 171, 184–186, 200; patronage, 175, 207, 222, 224; power, 175, 226; spending, 172; taxes, 185
Federalist party, 15, 171, 207, 209, 218, 221–222, 227; aristocracy of, 282; power, 172, 173, 199, 219; War of 1812, 231–233, 234
Fillmore, Millard, 284
Filson, John, 332
Fitzhugh, George, 296
Five Civilized Tribes, *see* Chickasaw; Cherokee; Choctaw; Creek; Seminole
Ford, Henry, 191
Forten, James, 263
Foster, Stephen, 178
Fourier, Charles, 312–313
Fox, George, 108–109
Fox Indians, 175, 258–259
France, 106, 111; in American Revolution, 13, 71–72, 75, 113; and Civil War, 242; explorers, 4, 6; and England, 10, 11, 19, 62–66, 68–69, 71, 76, 85, 112, 172, 188, 218, 231, 232; French Revolution, 15, 44, 71, 171, 207, 218, 219, 231, 279, 282; and Indians, 64, 85, 87; sells Louisiana, 172, 186; under Napoleon, 171, 172, 173, 231–232; relations with U.S., 185, 231, 251
Franklin, Benjamin: in Congress, 49–50; Constitution, 51–52; Declaration of Independence, 12; on

environment, 164; on immigrants, 105; on Indians, 69, 86, 88; maxims, 194; peace treaty, 75; on cities, 148, 150; religion, 111, 116; on slavery, 95; wealth, 25, 29, 35; on women, 125, 132

Free-Soil party, 225

Frémont, John C., 181, 225

French and Indian War, 10, 20, 23, 44, 61, 64, 65, 66, 68–69, 71, 75, 76–77, 85, 94, 104, 105, 113, 123

Freud, Sigmund, 60, 86, 123

Fugitive slave laws, 180, 213, 215, 263, 269, 301

Fuller, Margaret, 302, 313

Fulton, Robert, 176, 191

Gadsden, Christopher, 48

Gadsden Purchase, 234, 241

Gage, Thomas, 12, 49

Galloway, Joseph, 47, 48

Gandhi, Mahatma, 239

Gannett, Deborah, 132, 134

Garrison, William Lloyd, 179, 213

Gates, Horatio, 71, 75

George III, 12, 44, 47, 71, 94

Gerard, Stephan, 194

Germany, 103, 111

Gilpin, William, 320

Gold: California, 170, 184, 262, 264, 271–272, 289, 318, 330

GOP, see Republican party

Government, see Congress; House of Representatives; Federal government; Senate; Presidency

Grant, Ulysses S., 181, 226; administration, 290; Civil War, 245, 247, 251, 289

Great Britain, see England

Greeley, Horace, 334

Greene, Nathanael, 72

Greenhow, Rose O'Neal, 304

Grenville, George, 11, 44

Grimké, Angelina and Sarah, 301

Gross National Product (GNP), 18, 193

Haiti, 6, 235, 262–263

Hall, G. Stanley, 192

Hamilton, Alexander, 15, 51, 54, 57, 152, 231, 286; economic policy, 170–171, 172, 185–186, 200, 202, 218–219, 221; biography, 220

Hammond, Samuel H., 334

Hancock, John, 22, 45, 49

Handlin, Oscar, 281

Harmony Society, 311, 312

Harrison, William Henry, 224

Hawthorne, Nathaniel, 130, 178, 313, 320

Henry, Patrick, 44, 48, 49, 103, 115

Herskovits, Melville J., 96

Hickel, Walter J., 38

Holland, 19, 24, 62, 103, 106, 107, 111, 113, 185, 234, 279

Hollywood, 255

Holmes, Oliver Wendell, 178

Homestead Act, 202, 203, 217

Hopewell Indians, 81

Hopi Indians, 3, 81

House of Representatives: electoral college, 175, 181, 222, 225, 227; on Indians, 258; Mexican War, 238–239; and South, 212; southerners in, 179

Hovland, Gjert, 280

Howe, Richard, 13

Howe, William, 13, 71

Hudson's Bay Company, 85, 161, 264, 327

Huguenots, 55, 101, 104, 149

Hunt, Thomas P., 194

Huron Indians, 68

Hutchinson, Anne, 129–130

Immigrants: aid societies, 281; Asian, 273–274, 275; attitudes toward, 225; Catholic, 283, 288; colonial, 25–26, 28, 31; communities, 310–311; Dutch, 63, 103–104, 113, 144, 148; education, 281; European, 100, 101–106, 113–114, 195, 210, 212, 243, 279–284; Jewish, 288–290; poverty, 195. See also Labor, immigrant; Women, immigrant

Inca Indians, 2, 4

Indians, 2, 55, 61, 101, 102, 146, 230, 239; alliances between, 257; attacks of, 34, 42, 43, 64, 65, 81, 84–85, 106, 130, 257, 258, 272; and blacks, 264; civilizations, 2–3, 6, 146; colonial period, 20, 63, 64, 68–69, 81–88, 97; culture, 81, 86, 87–88, 97, 139; genocide of, 68, 84–85, 87, 105, 145, 202, 255, 261–262, 327; hunting, 158, 160, 236; lands, 31, 33, 81–84, 86, 87, 88, 97, 157–158, 165, 255–259; of Mexico, 270, 273; and Quakers, 65, 68; religion, 112; forced removal, 174, 175–176, 258–262; Revolutionary War, 73; and slavery, 93, 94; Stone Age, 157–158; trade with, 23, 27; treaties, 176, 255, 256, 258, 260, 262; white view, 84–87, 97, 110. See also French and Indian War; War, Indian; and individual tribes

Industries/industrialism: environment, 330–331; European, 279; and families, 295; and poverty, 184; and social change, 207, 210, 308; technology, 190

Inspirationalists, 103

Iroquois Indians, 3, 63, 64, 81, 85, 88, 158

Irving, Washington, 177, 332

Italy, 61

Jackson, Andrew, 173, 221, 224; administration, 175–176, 207–208, 209, 210, 214–215, 222–223, 244, 258, 267, 299, 320; election, 222, 227; and Indians, 258, 260; at New Orleans, 232–233, 234, 251, 263. See also Democracy, Jacksonian

Jackson, Thomas J. ("Stonewall"), 245

Japan, 3

Japanese Americans, see Asian Americans

Jay, John, 15, 47, 54, 75, 171, 231

Jefferson, Thomas, 12, 30, 42, 49–50, 170, 212, 233, 260, 325; administration, 172, 186, 188, 200, 203, 219, 221, 222; on cities, 319–320; on democracy, 207; on farmers, 153, 171, 199–200, 221, 320; foreign policy, 231, 251; on Indians, 88, 256–257; buys Louisiana, 234–235; on political parties, 218–219, 227; on religion, 115, 116; on slavery, 94, 263

Jerome, Chauncey, 191

Jews, 101, 112, 288–290, 331; arrival, 113–114

Johnson, Andrew, 250

Jones, Absalom, 263

Judiciary: review powers, 53, 173, 180, 209, 216; on women, 299

Juveniles, see Children, adolescent

Kalm, Peter, 163–164

Kansas-Nebraska Act, 180, 181, 212, 213, 215–216, 225, 226

Kendrick, Francis P., 290

Kennedy, John Pendleton, 178

Key, Francis Scott, 234

King, Martin Luther, Jr., 239

King George's War, 64, 65, 68, 77

King Philip's War, 84–85, 87

King William's War, 64, 65, 76, 112

Know-Nothing party, 225, 283–284

Knox, Henry, 255

Labor: apprentices, 29–30, 35, 40, 127, 134, 193, 297; and blacks, 89–90, 267; child, 197–198, 296–297, 311; colonial, 26–30, 35, 149; conditions, 196–199, 203, 302, 311–312; convict, 199; diseases of, 331;

exploited, 195–196; farm, 28–29, 30, 202; free black, 263, 264; immigrant, 195, 197, 203, 217, 225, 281, 283, 295, 318; industrial, 210; organizing, 177, 313; politics, 175; rights, 198; skilled, 29–30; and slavery, 95, 216–217; strikes, 30, 199, 302; and technology, 190–193, 198, 203; unions, 197, 199, 203; and women, 121, 131, 295, 299–300, 302. *See also* Unemployment

Land: grants, 186; greed, 236–237, 255–257; laws, 200–202; ownership, 19, 25, 26, 30–31, 33, 34, 35, 52, 55, 83, 142, 173, 207, 299; public, 50, 152–153, 163, 174, 200–202, 203, 210, 217, 324; reform, 201–202, 203; soil conservation, 163–164, 165; speculation, 190, 200–202, 210, 315, 316, 317–318, 324; use, 33, 143–144, 156, 163, 324; and voting, 39, 50, 55. *See also* Indians, land; Property

Land Ordinance of 1785, 152
Langston, John Mercer, 268
Latin America, 176–177, 236, 314. *See also individual countries*
Lee, Mother Ann, 309
Lee, Richard Henry, 54
Lee, Robert E., 181, 226, 245, 247, 251, 268; biography, 246
Lee, Thomas, 68
Leisler, Jacob, 42–43
L'Enfant, Pierre, 315
Levi, Asser, 113, 172, 210, 235, 325, 327
Liberty party, 225
Lincoln, Abraham, 211, 216, 242, 325; administration, 217, 226; commander-in-chief, 242, 244–245, 251, 289; death, 170, 181, 227, 250; election, 181, 225–226, 227, 281; Gettysburg Address, 181, 250, 290; on immigrants, 283–284; on Mexican War, 239; and Lee, 246; on slavery, 211, 213, 217, 225, 242, 245, 268, 270, 290
Livingston, Robert, 235
Locke, John, 12, 47, 50
Logan, James, 104–105
Long, Stephen H., 329
Longfellow, Henry Wadsworth, 178
Longstreet, Augustus B., 178
Lopez, Aaron, 113
Louisiana Territory, 172, 179, 180, 186, 214, 215, 221, 234–235, 256, 263, 325
L'Ouverture, Toussaint, 262
Lowell, Francis Cabot, 210
Lowell, James Russell, 178
Lowell, Robert, 290

Lumber industry, 325–327, 334
Lyon, Mary, 300

Madison, James: administration, 173, 186, 221, 236; break with Federalists, 218–219; on compromise, 213; Constitution, 51–52; *Federalist*, 15; foreign policy, 231–232, 233; on military, 76; on presidency, 53–54; on religion, 115; on republics, 234
Malthus, Thomas, 325
Mann, Horace, 193
Marriage: communal, 303; customs, 120–124, 126, 134, 179, 303; and feminists, 303; group, 298, 310; and slavery, 128. *See also* Family; Women
Marsh, George Perkins, 334
Marshall, John, 173, 208, 209–210, 212, 226, 260
Martin, Luther, 52
Marx, Karl, 195, 312
Mason, George, 95
Massachusetts Bay Colony, 6–7, 39, 107, 127, 130, 141, 142, 270
Mather, Cotton, 122, 126, 142, 194
Maya Indians, 2
Mayflower Compact, 107, 141
McClellan, George B., 245
McCormick, Cyrus, 192
McGillivray, Alexander, 260
Meier, August, 96
Melville, Herman, 178, 320, 328, 332
Mercantilism, 8, 10, 23–24, 35, 64, 159, 185; defined, 19–20
Metz, Christian, 310
Mexican Americans, *see* Chicanos
Mexican Cession, 234, 240–241, 251, 254, 271
Mexican War, 177, 180, 226, 238–241, 270–271
Mexico, 2–3, 4, 80, 146, 157, 177, 215, 230; emigrants, 254; relations with U.S., 270–273; and Spain, 270; and Texas, 238. *See also* Chicanos; Mexican Cession; Mexican War
Middle East, 100
Military: civilian control, 60, 65; colonial, 65, 114, 132; draft, 73, 243–244; -industrial complex, 184; Revolutionary War, 73–75; War of 1812, 232. *See also* Army; Confederacy, military; Navy; Union, military
Miller, William, 286
Minutemen, 12, 49, 66
Missouri Compromise, 179, 180, 214
Mitchell, Maria, 304
Mohawk Indians, 85
Monk, Maria, 283

Monroe, James, 233, 235, 312; administration, 186, 221, 258; Doctrine, 176–177, 236, 251
Moravians, 103, 309
Mormons, 287, 298, 330
Morris, Gouverneur, 51, 75, 152
Morris, Robert, 25, 51
Mott, Lucretia and James, 301
Movies, *see* Hollywood
Murietta, Joaquín, 272

Napoleon, 172, 230, 231, 235, 262, 263
Nash, Roderick, 333
Navajo Indians, 87, 158, 262
Navigation Acts, 8, 19, 20, 24–25
Navy: blacks in, 263; Civil War, 245, 247; War of 1812, 232, 234
Netherlands, *see* Holland
Nevins, Allen, 206
New England: blacks, 90, 92, 95, 97, 263, 267–268; cities, 140–143, 146–150, 152, 164, 172; colonial governments, 39, 40, 45, 46; education, 193; Indians, 84–85, 87; industry, 188, 191, 197, 302; marriage, 121, 122–123, 124, 126; politics, 55, 210, 219; rebellion, 11–12, 14, 75; religion, 110, 112–117, 139, 284, 285, 309; resources, 31, 32; wealth, 210; whaling, 161–162, 178, 327–329; War of 1812, 173, 232, 233–234
New Harmony, 177, 311–312
Nez Percé Indians, 87
Nicholson, Francis, 151
Nisbet, Robert, 138
Nisei, *see* Asian Americans
Nixon, Richard M., 38
Northwest Ordinance, 88, 97, 234
Northwest Territory, 152, 234, 255, 256, 257, 258
Noyes, John Humphrey, 298, 308, 310
Nye, Russell, 300

Oglethorp, James, 139
Oil industry, 328–329
Oliver, Robert, 22
Olmec Indians, 2, 146
Olmsted, Frederick Law, 335
Oneida Colony, 298, 310
Oneida Indians, 85
Onondaga Indians, 85
Oregon Territory, 177, 237–238
Osceola, 259–260
O'Sullivan, John L., 236
Otis, James, 44
Ottawa Indians, 85
Owen, Robert, 177, 311–312

Pacifists/-ism, 61, 65, 103, 177
Paine, Thomas, 12, 49, 63, 132
Panama, 4
People's Republic of China, *see* China
Penn, William, 65, 68, 103, 109, 114, 139, 148, 163
Pequot War, 84
Peru, 2, 4
Philip, Chief, 84–85, 87
Philippine Islands, 80
Phips, William, 64, 126
Pietists, 103, 111, 309
Pike, Zebulon M., 329
Pilgrims, *see* Puritans
Pinckney, Eliza Lucas, 132
Pioneers, 20, 53, 86, 161, 176, 255, 329
Pitcher, Molly, 134
Pitt, William, 69
Pleasant, Mary Ellen, 264
Plymouth Colony, 141, 142, 163, 270, 331
Pocahontas, 27, 83
Poe, Edgar Allan, 178, 320
Police: colonial, 148, 149; urban, 319
Political parties: growth, 218–227; and immigrants, 281, 283; loyal opposition, 218–219, 221–222, 227; machinery of, 223–225; third, 224–225. *See also individual parties*
Polk, James K., 237–239, 251
Pollution: environmental, 156; industrial, 330–331
Pontiac, Chief, 85
Poor, Salem, 94
Population, *see* United States, population; *and individual ethnic, racial, and religious groups*
Poverty: and children, 297; colonial, 25–26, 35, 48; and industrialism, 184, 190, 195–196, 203; "poor laws," 26; southern, 145; urban, 25–26, 149, 179, 195–196, 318, 320; and welfare, 25–26, 145, 149, 283. *See also* Democracy, and wealth; *and individual ethnic and racial groups*
Power: balance of, 52–54, 230; distribution of, 38; regional, 210–218; and wealth, 52
Powhatan, Chief, 27; Confederacy, 83–84
Prejudice: ethnic, 100, 243–244; racial, 243–244, 254–255, 263, 267, 273–274, 275; religious, 55, 100, 109, 112–115, 117, 240, 282, 283. *See also* Racism; Women, sexism
Presidency: cabinet, 170, 175, 218; checks on, 76; election, 57; power of, 53–54, 172, 208–210, 221, 226, 282; veto power, 209; war powers

of, 244–245, 251
Press: abolitionist, 179, 213, 267–268; and political parties, 218, 219, 223; propaganda, 177, 236–237; religious, 286, 288; southern, 316; urban, 319; and women, 302
Price, Glenn S., 230
Prisons, 177, 179, 248, 304
Proclamation of 1763, 11, 44, 47–48, 88
Progressive era/party/movement, 157
Property: communal, 309–310, 311, 312; and democracy, 207; rights of, 173, 185; slaves as, 217, 263–264. *See also* Land; Women, property rights; Voting, requirements
Protestants: and capitalism, 25; and Catholics, 6, 12, 42, 47, 55, 64, 86–87, 102, 103, 112–113, 240, 283, 288; dissention among, 287–290; dominance, 50, 101–104, 106–117; Ethic, 8, 25, 27, 35, 108, 116, 194–195, 202, 203, 258; evangelical, 284–288; Fundamentalist, 116; Second Awakening, 273, 278, 284–286, 297, 309; and slavery, 289–290; and women, 124, 302
Pueblo Indians, 3, 81
Puerto Rico, 4
Puritan Ethic, *see* Protestants, Ethic
Puritans: beliefs, 6, 7–8, 64, 106, 107–108, 110, 116, 194; family, 120–124, 127–128, 134; government, 141–143; and Indians, 84–85, 87; on liquor, 150; on nature, 159; on slavery, 92; on women, 129

Quakers, 25–26, 55–56, 65–68, 95, 103, 107, 108–109, 112, 115, 123, 139, 148, 300–301
Quartering Acts, 11, 12, 44, 47
Quebec Act, 12, 47
Queen Anne's War, 64, 65, 76–77
Quincy, Josiah, 127

Racism: ethnic, 241; history of, 80, 89; northern, 213; WASP, 254–255, 270–275
Railroads, 184, 190, 237; builders, 210; and cities, 187, 192; corporations, 191–192, 202; and environment, 330; federal aid to, 210, 212, 217; growth, 176, 193, 314; and immigrants, 274, 281; southern, 316; steam-driven, 176, 191–192, 203, 248; transcontinental, 180, 217, 318
Raleigh, Sir Walter, 6, 139–140, 159
Rapp, George, 311, 312

Reed, Rebecca, 283
Reich, Charles A., 25
Republican party: and ethnics, 281; origins, 181, 225, 227; Reconstruction, 250
Revere, Paul, 29, 104
Revolutionary War, 64, 65, 66, 112, 232; alliance with France, 113; background and beginning, 10–11; battles and generals, 13, 71–75, 95; blacks in, 94–95; citizens in, 56, 72–74; effect on cities, 21, 151, 152–153; and Indians, 85; and women, 132, 134, 135
Ridge, John Rollin, 272
Ripley, George, 313
Rolfe, John, 27, 83, 89
Roman Catholics, *see* Catholics
Rosecrans, William S., 290
Ross, John, 262
Rudwick, Elliott, 96
Rush, Benjamin, 331
Russia, 62–63, 176, 236; Revolution, 44, 71
Russwurm, John B., 268

Sac Indians, 175, 258–259
St. Clair, Arthur, 256
Saint-Méry, Moreau de, 132
Salem, Peter, 94
Santo Domingo, *see* Haiti
Schlesinger, Arthur M., Sr., 120
Schools, *see* Education
Schurz, Carl, 279
Scott, Dred, 180, 216
Scott, Winfield, 239–240, 246
Seligman, Joseph, 290
Seminole Indians, 3, 81, 175, 257, 258, 259, 261, 262, 264
Senate: Mexican War, 238–239; and South, 212; treaty powers, 170, 235
Seneca Indians, 85
Sequoya, 260
Seven Years' War, *see* French and Indian War
Seward, William H., 180, 225
Sewell, Samuel, 159
Shakers, 309
Shaw, Anna Howard, 304
Shaw, Samuel, 273
Shawnee Indians, 68, 255, 257
Shays, Daniel, 14, 51, 56, 153, 185
Sherman, William Tecumseh, 247, 248
Silver, 318, 330. *See also* Currency
Simms, William G., 178
Sioux Indians, 87
Slater, Samuel, 190, 203
Slavery: and Civil War, 206; colonial, 7, 14, 91–95; Constitution, 53; debate over, 179–181; economic im-

portance, 21, 23, 28, 29, 35, 39, 62, 80, 89, 97, 144–145, 179, 191, 211, 213, 217, 263, 264, 266; literature of, 178, 179; morality, 206, 213, 242, 264, 289–290; politics of, 213–216, 225–226, 238–239; and religion, 287, 289–290, 295–296; resistance to, 266–270. *See also* Abolition movement; Slaves

Slaves: during Civil War, 245; education, 300; emancipation, 181, 242, 245, 250, 262–263, 267, 270; arrival, 80, 89, 97; Indian, 85–86, 262; population, 263, 264; as property, 217, 263–264; revolt, 92, 94, 95, 179, 213, 235, 262–263, 266, 267, 268; in Revolutionary War, 75; runaway, 11, 45, 46, 49, 53, 90, 94, 180, 185, 213, 215, 263, 264, 266, 268; trade in, 22, 53, 86, 89, 90–92, 94, 95, 148, 180, 215, 246, 264, 290; treatment, 91–94, 197, 212, 265–266; urban, 316. *See also* Blacks, free; Families, slave; Women, slave; Underground Railroad

Smith, Jedediah, 327
Smith, Capt. John, 26, 28, 39; biography, 27
Smith, Joseph, 287
Smith, William, 133
Socialism, 195, 312
Sons of Liberty, 11, 30, 45, 46, 114, 132
South: and abolitionists, 179, 213, 267, 268; cities, 148–149, 151, 152, 164–165, 172, 193, 316; cotton, 179, 191, 193, 201, 212–215, 239, 242, 247, 250, 263, 266, 314, 316; devastation, 184; economy, 264, 266; education, 193; governments, 39–42, 44; Indians of, 63, 81, 83–84, 86, 174, 256–257, 258, 260–262; plantations, 140, 144–145, 178, 197, 212–213, 246, 267, 295; political power, 212–213; population, 217; Reconstruction, 226, 250–251; religion, 112–115, 139, 141, 149, 285–286; resources, 22, 316; Revolutionary War, 42, 43, 72, 75; secedes, 181, 217, 225, 226, 242, 246, 290; slavery, 28, 29, 53, 80, 90, 91–92, 94–96, 179–181, 213, 242*n*, 263, 264, 266–267, 289, 295–296, 300, 316; society, 175, 211–212, 244, 246, 316; tariffs, 210, 212, 214–215, 217; War of 1812, 173, 232, 234. *See also* Confederacy; Democratic party, in South; Farmers, southern; Women, southern

South America, 2, 4, 63. *See also* individual countries
Soviet Union, *see* Russia

Spain: in California, 270; and England, 10, 19, 62–63, 64–65, 69, 112; explorers, 2, 4, 61–63, 146, 270; in Florida, 176, 235–236, 270; and France, 171; and Indians, 64, 87; in Latin America, 176; in Louisiana, 235; in New Mexico, 270; in Texas, 230, 238, 270–271; War of 1812, 232.
Spotswood, Alexander, 31
Stamp Act, 11, 44–45, 47, 115
Stanton, Elizabeth Cady, 301, 302, 305
"Star-Spangled Banner," 234
States: acquisition, 177, 221, 234–235; admission to Union, 53, 170, 174, 177, 180, 207, 214, 215, 233, 234, 236–238, 242*n*, 245, 251, 256; constitutions, 50, 52, 56, 57, 115, 117, 207; and federal government, 172, 173, 175, 200, 214, 217, 219, 226, 280; and immigrants, 31, 33, 102–105, 280; rights, 50, 209, 222, 226, 244, 260; and slavery, 91, 92, 95, 180, 214–216, 242, 263
Stevenson, Adlai E., 156
Stiles, Ezra, 278
Stokes, Darius, 264
Stone, Lucy, 301, 303
Stowe, Harriet Beecher, 178
Stuyvesant, Peter, 113
Suffrage, *see* Blacks, suffrage; Vote/Voters/Voting; Women, suffrage
Sugar Act, 11, 44
Sullivan, John, 85
Supreme Court, 53, 212; abortion, 299; on business, 187, 203; Indians, 175, 209, 255, 260; labor, 199; under Marshall, 173, 208, 209–210, 226, 260; organization of, 170; religion, 115; slavery, 180, 216

Tariffs, 171, 210; laws, 175; protective, 210, 212, 214–215, 217; rates, 185, 186, 201; and the South, 210, 212, 214–215, 217
Taylor, John, 207
Taylor, Zachary, 238, 239–240
Tea Act, 46
Technology: colonial, 20–21; cotton, 179, 190–191, 203, 263; effect on economy, 190–193; and environment, 156–158, 159, 165; farm, 31, 33, 35; gun, 20, 66, 104, 186, 191; industrial, 26, 29, 330–331; promises of, 278; steam, 170, 176, 184, 190–192, 193, 198, 203; war, 248, 251
Tecumseh, 255, 257, 258
Temperance movement, 177, 302, 313

Tenskwatawa, 257
Textile industry, 191, 210, 213; conditions in, 311–312; growth, 196–198; and women, 295
Theater, 149–150, 319
Thoreau, Henry David, 178, 239, 287, 320, 332, 334
Tocqueville, Alexis de, 178–179, 194, 208, 258, 267, 284, 298, 324
Tolles, F. B., 139
Torres, Luis de, 113
Tory party, 49, 57, 74, 75–76, 77, 95, 114, 152
Towns, *see* Cities
Townshend, Charles, 11, 44, 45
Transcendentalism, 177, 178, 286–287, 302, 313
Transportation: canals, 176, 186, 187, 190, 193, 210, 212, 216, 237, 314, 316, 320, 330; farm, 211; federal aid to, 210, 212, 217; growth, 186, 187, 191–192, 193. *See also* Railroads; Travel
Travel: colonial, 15, 33, 110; Conestoga wagon, 20, 104; road system, 176, 186, 187, 200, 219, 212, 316; steamboat, 170, 176, 184, 190, 191, 192, 193, 203, 248. *See also* Transportation
Trollope, Anthony, 297
Truth, Sojourner, 303
Tubman, Harriet, 268, 304; biography, 269
Tuckerman, Joseph, 320
Turner, Nat, 179, 267
Twain, Mark, 26

Udall, Stewart, 163
Underground Railroad, 201, 213, 268–269
Unemployment, 190, 195, 198
Union: military, 243–244, 245, 247–248, 250, 304; resources, 181, 242, 247; and slaves, 268, 270
United States: American Dream, 35, 176, 208, 279–280; Anglo dominance, 101–104, 106, 116; anticommunism of, 71; boundaries, 237–238, 240, 272; British influence, 6–8, 10, 12, 19, 26, 47, 49, 50, 56–57, 63, 101–103, 121, 143; character of people, 184, 194, 234, 313; chauvinism of, 176–177, 282–284; class structure, 39–40, 41, 47–48, 54–55, 57, 174, 208, 210, 218; culture, 313, 319, 332–334; desert, 329–330; ecology, 157, 164–165, 329, 330–331; ethnic groups, 10, 20, 26, 29, 32, 68, 80, 100–101, 116, 195, 197, 240, 241, 270–275, 279–284, 288; expansion, 176–177, 234–

236, 251, 308; explorations, 3–4, 6, 61–63; folk heroines and heroes, 134, 332; forests, 159–160, 186, 325, 330, 331–332, 334; Founding Fathers, 52, 54, 56, 57, 60, 76, 115–116, 117, 121, 133, 213, 218, 227, 234, 294; frontier, 26, 31, 53, 68, 80, 86, 144, 147, 160, 163, 176, 202, 207, 231, 264, 289, 295, 316–318, 325, 329–330; Indian contributions, 88, 97; imperialism, 236, 238–240, 251; intellectuals, 320; literature, 129, 177–179, 313, 332; Manifest Destiny, 177, 236–237, 238, 251, 313; melting-pot theory, 100–101, 104–106; merchant class, 21–25, 39, 45, 51, 54, 57, 110, 149, 151, 199, 200, 210, 219; middle class, 106, 121, 132, 227, 310; natural resources, 21–25, 156, 157–158, 186, 190, 230, 325–331; patriotism, 290, 311; planter class, 21, 22–23, 29, 33–35, 39, 41–42, 51, 54, 57, 75, 144–145, 149, 152, 163, 175, 200, 206, 212–213, 219, 226, 263, 264, 266, 314; population, 3, 10, 19, 90, 101–104, 126, 143, 146, 152, 174, 212, 217, 242, 263, 271, 273–274, 279, 317, 325; prehistoric, 2–3; racial types, 254; early rebellions in, 41–49; regionalism, 176, 210–218, 226; religious influences on, 7–8, 25, 42, 43, 47, 55, 100, 101, 106–117, 139–142, 159, 165, 179, 194, 195, 219, 221, 258, 284–291, 309, 331; social movements, 170, 175, 177, 199, 203, 286, 309–313; Spanish influence, 272–273; treaties, 13, 62, 63, 69, 75–76, 77, 171, 231, 236, 237–238, 240–241, 255, 256, 258, 260, 262, 271, 272; urbanization, 138–139, 308, 314–321; wilderness, 331–335; wildlife, 157, 161–163, 165, 327, 329–330, 332, 333–334; working class, 295

U.S.S.R., *See* Russia

Van Buren, Martin, 222, 224, 261
Vane, Henry, 130
Verrazano, Giovanni de, 4
Vesey, Denmark, 179, 267
Vespucci, Amerigo, 4
Veterans, 185
Villa, Francisco (Pancho), 272
Vote/Voters/Voting: immigrant, 224, 225, 281, 282, 283; labor, 199; requirements, 26, 39, 40, 50, 55, 142, 143, 223, 299; rights, 207, 218, 227, 294; taxes, 239; universal, 114. *See also* Black, suffrage; Women, suffrage

Walker, Amasa, 320
Walker, David, 179
Wampanoag Indians, 84
War: amnesty, 250; atrocities, 239–240; attitudes toward, 230; and civilians, 239–240; and defeat, 248, 250; gang, 318–319; guerrilla, 73, 77; Indian, 175, 255–256, 257, 258, 260, 262, 264, 272; opposition to, 233, 239, 243; and population, 325; pre-Revolutionary, 64–65, 76–77; race, 241; technology, 248, 251. *See also* Battles; *and individual wars*
War of 1812, 65, 186, 326, 410; aftermath, 174, 179, 255, 327; and blacks, 263; campaign, 232–234; causes, 231–232; effect, 173, 188, 320; and Indians, 257–258
Warren, Josiah, 313
Warren, Mercy Otis, 134
Washington, George, 7, 35, 49, 51, 68, 158, 175, 260, 288, 332; administration, 170–171, 172, 185–186, 200, 208–209, 218–219, 226, 227, 255, 256, 273; election, 15, 57, 218; foreign policy, 231, 251; as husband, 131; landowner, 145; character, 152; on religion, 113, 116; in Revolutionary War, 12, 71–75, 77; and slavery, 94–95
Washington, Martha Custis, 131
Watergate, 38
Wayne, Anthony, 256
Wealth: distribution, 26, 30, 39, 51, 184, 186, 194–195, 203; and social class, 208, 211, 218
Webster, Daniel, 180, 210, 215, 222
Webster, Noah, 51
Welfare, *see* Poverty, welfare
Welter, Barbara, 299
Wesley, John, 285
West: cities, 237, 316–318, 320; Indians, 262; migration to, 170, 174, 195, 201–202, 203, 207, 210–211, 227, 264, 316, 324; religion, 283, 285–286, 287, 289; slavery, 179, 180, 212, 215–216, 225, 226. *See also* Farmers, western
Wheatley, Phyllis and Susannah, 92
Whig party, 48, 49, 51, 57, 94, 114, 152, 181, 222, 224, 225, 227, 239, 240, 281
White, Ellen G., 286
White, Lynn, Jr., 159
Whitefield, George, 111
Whitman, Walt, 178, 332
Whitney, Eli, 191, 263
Whittier, John Greenleaf, 178
Wigglesworth, Michael, 123
Willard, Emma, 300
Williams, Roger, 87, 114, 130, 139

Wilmot, David, 241, 267
Winthrop, John, 39, 127, 129, 139, 141
Wise, Isaac Mayer, 289, 290
Witches, 110, 142
Wolfe, James, 69
Wollstonecraft, Mary, 300, 302
Women: abortion, 130, 294, 299; adultery, 122, 130; attitudes toward, 124, 129–130; black, 93, 296, 300, 301, 303; careers, 131–132, 134; child custody, 131, 299, 303; colonial, 120–135; conventions, 294, 301, 303; divorce, 124, 131, 299; dress, 299, 302–303, 328; education, 132, 133, 192–193, 297, 300, 304; farm, 32, 120; feminists/-ism, 120, 130, 294, 299–305; immigrant, 125, 130, 134; Indian, 327; legal rights, 120, 121, 130–131, 134, 299–300; lifespan, 127; movement, 170, 177, 294, 300–301, 302, 313; myths about, 296, 299; organizations, 132, 302, 304, 305; pioneer, 129, 132, 191, 295, 300, 304; in politics, 305; power, 30, 299; professional, 300, 303–304; and prostitution, 43, 125, 195, 295, 296; property rights, 131, 299, 303; and religion, 286, 288, 289, 299, 301, 302; roles, 120, 121, 129, 132, 134, 297, 299, 304; and sex, 124–125; sexism, 55–56, 120, 132, 294, 300, 302; slave, 97, 124, 128, 134, 303; southern, 132, 296, 304; status, 294; suffrage, 39, 121, 299, 301, 303, 305; white servant, 124–125; widows, 131, 195; working, 197–198, 295, 299–300, 302, 311. *See also* Children; Family; Labor, and women; Marriage
Woolman, John, 68, 109
Work ethic, *see* Protestants, Ethic
World War I, 65, 71, 100, 230
World War II, 65, 71
Wright, Frances, 313

XYZ Affair, 171

Yamasee Indians, 63
Young, Brigham, 287, 298

Zuñi Indians, 3, 81

Index prepared by Dennis Williams